Spoke

Also by Charles C. Alexander

Crusade for Conformity: The Ku Klux Klan in Texas, 1920–1930

The Ku Klux Klan in the Southwest

This New Ocean: A History of Project Mercury

Nationalism in American Thought, 1930–1945

Holding the Line: The Eisenhower Era, 1952–1961

Here the Country Lies: Nationalism and the Arts in Twentieth-Century America

Ty Cobb

John McGraw

Our Game: An American Baseball History

Rogers Hornsby: A Biography

Breaking the Slump: Baseball in the Depression Era

Spoke

A Biography
of Tris Speaker

Charles C. Alexander

Sport in American Life
C. Paul Rogers III, series editor

SOUTHERN METHODIST UNIVERSITY PRESS
Dallas

Frontispiece: Cleveland player-manager Tris Speaker and Brooklyn manager
Wilbert Robinson before the first game of the 1920 World Series, Ebbets Field, Brooklyn.
(Courtesy of Roy Anderson, Dallas, Texas)

Requests for permission to reproduce material from this work should be sent to:
Rights and Permissions
Southern Methodist University Press
PO Box 750415
Dallas, Texas 75275-0415

Cover image: "Tris Speaker, 1918." Painting by Arthur K. Miller, artofthegame.com.
Courtesy of C. Paul Rogers III

Jacket and text design: Tom Dawson

Library of Congress Cataloging-in-Publication Data
Alexander, Charles C.
    Spoke : a biography of Tris Speaker / Charles C. Alexander. — 1st ed.
      p. cm. — (Sport in American life)
    Includes bibliographical references and index.
    ISBN 978-0-87074-517-1 (alk. paper)
   1. Speaker, Tris. 2. Baseball players—United States—Biography. I.
Title.

GV865.S72A44 2007
796.357092—dc22
[B]

                                                        2007018219

Printed in the United States of America on acid-free paper

10   9   8   7   6   5   4   3   2   1

For the Breakfast ROMEOs of Athens, Ohio:

Nick Dinos
Lon Hamby
Bill Kaldis

Acknowledgments

Once again, my thanks go to the staff of the Giamatti Research Center and other offices of the National Baseball Hall of Fame Museum and Library, Cooperstown, New York. I'm also appreciative of the assistance provided by the archives and photo staffs of the Public Library, Cleveland, Ohio. In my thirty-seven years of using the resources of Ohio University's Alden Library, I have found the staff to be invariably helpful. On my visit to Hubbard, Texas, Tris Speaker's hometown, William McDonald, then Hubbard's city manager, took time out from his busy schedule to show me around Speaker-related sites; and Laura Walton provided useful information on the Speaker family. William Burgess of Mountain View, California, introduced me to the resources of www.ancestry.com and helped me in a variety of other ways. JoAnn Erwin Alexander, my loving companion for close to half a century, and my daughter Rachel C. Alexander, D.V.M., have continued to make my life a happy experience.

Finally, I would be remiss if I didn't acknowledge Timothy Gay's biography of Tris Speaker, published by the University of Nebraska Press in the spring of 2005—by which time my own Speaker biography project was well underway. I encourage anyone interested in comparing this book to Timothy Gay's to do so.

Charles C. Alexander
Athens, Ohio
February 2007

Contents

Foreword: "No Place for Me"   xv

1. "I Played Baseball and Drove the Cows to Pasture"   1

2. "By No Means a Finished Outfielder"   17

3. "Well, There Goes Your World Series"   39

4. "For God's Sake, Men, Take the Money Away"   59

5. "Baseball Is a Business"   83

6. "New Life into a Half-Dead, Despondent City"   105

7. "The Inspiration of Speaker's Leadership"   135

8. "I Knew My Team"   153

9. "I Will Never be a Bench Manager"   177

10. "We'll Finish in the League Anyway"   205

11. "A Veritable Judas"   233

12. "A Sort of Twilight to His Career"   253

13. "My Name Is Tris Speaker"   277

Afterword: "Let Your Voices Soften to a Mere Whisper"   305

Notes   311

Bibliography   327

Index   337

Spoke

"No Place for Me"

In March 1908 the New York Giants were in the midst of preseason conditioning and practice at Marlin, Texas. It was the first of eleven consecutive
springtime stays at the little town in the central part of the state, known mainly
(at least until the Giants began their annual assemblies there) for its supposedly
health-restoring mineral springs. Though still a few weeks shy of his thirty-fifth
birthday, manager John McGraw was already hailed as the "Little Napoleon" for
his wizardry in taking over a downtrodden Giants team in 1901 and producing
back-to-back pennant-winners in 1904 and 1905 and a World Series victory in
the latter year—in the process making the New York National League franchise
the richest in baseball.[1] Now, busy trying to put together still another winning
combination, McGraw had little time for several young ballplayers who showed
up at Marlin, uninvited but hoping for a tryout.

One of those youngsters was Tris Speaker, whose home at Hubbard City was
only about thirty-five miles away. Following two seasons of professional baseball
in Texas and a brief American League trial the previous September with the Boston American Leaguers, Speaker had assumed that he remained Boston's property, until February came and went and he received no contract. Under baseball
"law," that made him a free agent, so he went to Marlin to beseech McGraw to
take him on for 1908. He got to talk with McGraw twice, but, as Speaker related
the story many years later, "He said he had no place for me. I did everything I
could, but I couldn't get him to change his mind."[2]

Over the next two decades, John McGraw had many occasions to rue the
day he dismissed Tris Speaker—most of all, perhaps, a late October afternoon in
1912. In the deciding game of that year's World Series, Speaker's base hit brought

home the tying run and put a runner on thirdbase, from which he scored on a sacrifice fly to win the Series for the Boston Red Sox and send McGraw's Giants to the second of three straight Series defeats. By that time Speaker had established himself as one of baseball's reigning stars, although throughout his long career—twenty full major-league seasons and parts of two others—he was overshadowed by the unmatched brilliance of Ty Cobb.

Speaker always acknowledged that Cobb was his superior and, for all-around ability and competitive drive, superior to everybody else of their time, including Babe Ruth. "When we were both young and good," Speaker said toward the end of his life, "the writers were kind enough to say of me that I was the closest thing to [Cobb]. Now, let's not be immodest about this. I was good and I knew it. . . . But good as I was, I never was close to Cobb and neither was Ruth or anybody else."[3]

If, by his own estimation, nobody was the equal of Cobb, Speaker was plenty good himself—good enough to become one of the original inductees into the National Baseball Hall of Fame when it opened in 1939. Speaker hit (and threw) from the left side, usually held his thirty-eight-ounce bat at the end, swung it back and forth, an onlooker commented, "like the lazy switching of a cat's tail" as he awaited the pitch, and then brought the bat level with his left shoulder. He always tried (as he insisted every batter should do) to take a level swing. Speaker's lifetime major-league batting average of .345 places him fifth on the all-time list. He made 3,514 base hits, scored 1,881 runs, drove in 1,529, and hit 792 doubles—more two-base hits than anybody ever has or probably ever will. In 10,196 official times at bat (to which can be added 1,381 bases on balls and an undetermined number of sacrifice flys and bunts), he struck out just 220 times. And he stole 432 bases.[4]

But for all his offensive prowess, it was Speaker's superb play as a centerfielder that gained him the greatest accolades from contemporaries and in the reminiscences of aging ballplayers, fans, and sportswriters. In 1915 Damon Runyon of the *New York American* proclaimed that "For years and years to come we will be contemplating the possibilities of a human being who could field and throw like Speaker." That same year Hugh Fullerton of the *Chicago Herald and Examiner* estimated that Speaker saved his pitchers about a run and a half per game. Eleven years later, when it seemed (prematurely) that Speaker's playing days were over, his friend Joe Williams of the *Cleveland Press* wrote, "Inevitably all outfield stars will be compared to Speaker and inevitably all will suffer." One of his old Boston Red Sox teammates remembered that on balls hit over his head, "He'd turn and run—and you'd think he had a radar or magnet or something because just at the proper time he'd turn his head and catch the ball over his shoulder." Joe Sewell, who played with and for player-manager Speaker for seven years, beginning in 1920, remarked that he had watched outstanding later centerfielders such as Joe DiMaggio, Willie Mays, and Mickey Mantle, but "Nobody could play centerfield like Speaker." Sam Crawford, Speaker's American League outfielding adversary for nearly a decade, simply said, "I guess the best centerfielder of them all was Tris Speaker."[5]

Speaker spent most of his playing career in the so-called "dead-ball era"—the years prior to 1920 when balls were kept in play inning after inning, scarred, scuffed, stained, and softened. Pitchers freely and legally threw spitballs and an assortment of other "doctored" pitches; most hitters choked up on their bats and chopped, slapped, and poked to put the ball in play instead of taking full swings. (Opponents of the spitball, which was delivered with applications of anything from saliva to licorice to slippery elm, might condemn the pitch on various grounds, including sanitation—"a dirty habit" that compelled batters to face "a ball covered with microbes," as Cleveland's public health officer protested in 1907—but pitchers were free to "load up" until 1920.)[6]

Although outfielders generally played closer to the infield than they did in the post-1920 era of the "lively ball," Speaker played closest of all, in his oft-stated conviction that most balls hit beyond the infield would be in front of outfielders, and that he could judge accurately and run down nearly anything hit over his head. How closely he played has sometimes been exaggerated. One source, insisting that Speaker "revolutionized the position" of centerfield, puts him typically only thirty or forty feet behind secondbase.[7] Actually, in the pre-1920 years, he positioned himself about seventy-five to one hundred feet behind second, although he became renowned for sneaking in behind runners to take pickoff throws, participate in rundowns, and even execute unassisted double plays—once in the minor leagues and six times in the majors (including one in World

Series play). He was also part of 133 other double plays. Speaker possessed one of the most powerful throwing arms in the game's history. Besides his 6,941 put-outs, his record of 462 assists, like his career doubles total, is not likely ever to be equaled.

By the 1930s at least one in ten major-league players was a native Texan. But when Speaker came into the major leagues to stay in 1909, only a few undistinguished Texans had made it to the top; the prime sources of players were still New York state, Pennsylvania, and Ohio. As was the case with Ty Cobb from Georgia, Speaker was the first ballplayer from his state to achieve stardom. (Rogers Hornsby, who arrived in 1915, was the second Texan to do so.)

In Speaker's day (and until 1956), all of the big-league cities were in the northeastern quadrant of the United States. With the exception of St. Louis, on the western bank of the Mississippi, all were east of that river. Most baseball writers in those cities knew little of the rest of the country, apart from what they experienced at spring-training sites from Florida across the southern U.S. to California. Often they wrote patronizingly of the food and lodging in such places as Marlin or Waxahachie, Texas, Hot Springs, Arkansas, or Gulfport, Mississippi; of the rutted roads and rattling railways teams had to travel for exhibition games; and maybe most of all, of the Sunday boredom where local and state laws prohibited commercial amusements.

Speaker was what used to be called a "man's man." Preferring the company of other men who shared his interests and values, he didn't marry until he was in his mid-thirties. He was a skilled horseback rider, calf roper, marksman, and all-around outdoorsman who loved to hunt and fish in remote areas of the United States and Canada, sleeping on the ground and preparing his own sparse meals.

Yet for all his rugged masculinity, Speaker had a softer side. He was youngest—the "baby"—in a large family. His father died when he was a child. As is often true of people who grow up fatherless, Speaker maintained a close relationship to his mother, sharing much of his adult life with her and, once established as a big-leaguer, supporting her in fine style out of his salaries. And although Speaker and his wife were childless, once his playing days were over, he spent much of his time working with boys in baseball clinics and in fund-raising activities for amateur baseball organizations and for the Society for Crippled Children.

Speaker never got far from his Texas roots. Sportswriters often characterized him as a product of the arid and barely tamed West, as did William A. "Bill" Phelon of the *Chicago Inter-Ocean,* who called Speaker "the bounding cowboy of the Texas plains, the bad man of the lariat and revolver."[8] The fact that Hubbard was a well-settled little town of about 1,600 residents—with stores, schools, and even a bank, in an area where rainfall was generally adequate for the cotton cultivation that dominated the eastern half of Texas—usually escaped people from the East who wrote about Speaker.

Considered more western than southern geographically, Texas was more southern than western culturally. When Speaker was growing up in Texas and for long afterward, white supremacy prevailed across the southern United States, from the Atlantic seaboard to El Paso. The segregation of black from white people—from schools, churches, and public transportation to hospitals, cemeteries, and seating arrangements at public events—governed the social order. Although his hometown had a good-sized African American population, Speaker's world was totally white-dominated, a fact he simply accepted as the way things always had been and presumably always would be.

Like its neighboring counties in central Texas, Hill County had a history of bloody Indian conflict, slave ownership (albeit relatively small-scale), and acts of violence toward Unionist elements during and after the Civil War. Beginning in the late nineteenth century, the area attracted regional and even national publicity for a succession of lynchings, with mobs of white people hanging and sometimes burning and mutilating black men accused or convicted of crimes against whites, usually rape or murder. The first such atrocity in Hill County occurred only a few years before Speaker's birth, when Zeke Handley was taken from his cell in the county courthouse in Hillsboro and hanged from a nearby tree.

When Speaker became a professional in what was called Organized Baseball (meaning the two major leagues and the officially recognized lesser, or "minor," leagues), everything was all white, a circumstance that persisted until 1946 under baseball's unwritten but universally accepted "gentleman's agreement" to exclude black professionals. It's become almost obligatory to point out that as talented as Speaker, Cobb, and the other great white players of their time undoubtedly were, in the circumstances of segregated, or "Jim Crow," baseball, they didn't have to face such top-flight black pitchers as Smoky Joe Williams, Frank Wickware, or the Cuban José Mendez, and that such dominating white pitchers as Christy Mathewson, Walter Johnson, and Grover Cleveland Alexander didn't have to pitch to outstanding hitters such as John Henry Lloyd, Grant "Home Run" Johnson, and Oscar Charleston on the other side of the color line. True enough, but then one can also reverse that: Williams, Wickware, and Mendez didn't have to pitch to Speaker or Cobb (or Joe Jackson or Babe Ruth); Lloyd, Home Run Johnson, and Charleston didn't have to hit against Mathewson, Walter Johnson, or Alexander.[9] Such speculations don't seem to profit one a great deal. Things were as they were; all-white baseball was the only baseball that mattered to the great majority of baseball-followers, who were white people. Black baseball remained a world apart, little known or cared about by white fans or sportswriters.

However one looks at his time and the racial environment in which he performed, Tris Speaker must be regarded as one of the greatest players ever to step onto a baseball field. If he wasn't universally liked (and he wasn't), most people seem to have thought well of him, unlike the widespread ill-feelings (which *didn't* include Speaker's feelings) toward the volatile and often mean-spirited Cobb. Speaker had plenty of run-ins with umpires and received his share of ejections from games, and near the end of his and Cobb's careers, they, as well as Speaker's close friend and former teammate Joe Wood, were implicated in a sensational scandal over the alleged fixing of a game years earlier. But the opinion of Branch Rickey, as Rickey closed out his sixty years in the game as a player, manager, and visionary executive, was generally shared inside and outside baseball: "[Speaker] came from Texas, but he made many friends everywhere. He really did, and I mean friends. He was a beloved player."[10]

As a Cleveland Indians player and player-manager for eleven seasons and the man who led the Indians to Cleveland's first pennant and then a World Series victory, Speaker became probably the most memorable figure in the city's baseball history—at least for a long time. An old saying goes, "How soon they forget," to which one might add, "How little they ever knew." Speaker entered professional baseball a century ago, played his last major-league game nearly eighty years ago, and has been dead nearly half a century. Almost anybody still living today who might have seen him play would have been a child at the time.

Tris Speaker's name is no longer the household word it was when he was slashing line drives, running down balls hit to the far reaches of outfields, and building the career that made him a charter electee to the National Baseball Hall of Fame. But if younger baseball fans typically have little knowledge of the heroes of the past—if, as is often the case, their sense of history dates from their own birth—we should still try to understand the significance in the game's history of someone such as Tris Speaker. What follows is an effort to show why he's significant and to sustain—even to awaken—an awareness of why we ought to remember him.

Chapter 1

"I Played Baseball and Drove the Cows to Pasture"

Tris Speaker's records in professional baseball are exact; we know precisely what he did as a player and when and where he did it. But we can't say with certainty what his name was or the exact year of his birth. We *can* be certain he was born on April 4, but whereas Speaker always gave his birth year as 1888, his mother (who should have known) reported it as 1889 in the decennial manuscript census returns. (It's likely that when Speaker, still a minor, signed his first professional contract in 1906, he said he was born in 1888 so he wouldn't have to obtain parental consent.) To complicate the matter, an entry in an early baseball guide gave his birth year as 1883; that, and the fact that his hair began to gray when he was still in his mid-twenties, caused some sportswriters to assume he was several years older than what he told them.

Then there's the business of Speaker's given name. For the census-takers, his mother variously listed it as "Tristram," "Tristram E.," "Tris E.," and simply "Tris." In a 1914 interview with F. C. Lane, editor of the monthly *Baseball Magazine,* Speaker was adamant that his name wasn't Tristram. "My real name," he said, "is Tris, just Tris for whatever it's worth." The next year, in another magazine interview, he explained that his name was an abbreviation of "the old English Tristram." Yet in May 1917, when he registered for the military draft, he put down "Tristram."[1] After his first season in professional baseball, he was put on a reserve list as "T. E. Speaker," and in his early years in the major leagues he had "T. E. S." monogrammed on his automobile doors and his luggage. Eventually he acknowledged that when he was a youngster he started adding the "E." to his name, simply because he thought he ought to have a middle initial. In any case, in baseball circles he was always "just Tris," and his birth year was always given as 1888, although he may actually have been a year younger.

We know for sure that he was born at Hubbard, Texas, and that he was the son of Archery O. Speaker, who farmed and practiced carpentry, and the former Nancy Jane Poer. "Hubbard City," as it was ambitiously named and called well into the twentieth century, was in the extreme southeastern corner of Hill County in central Texas, about sixty miles south and thirty miles northeast, respectively, of the rapidly growing cities of Dallas and Waco. Founded in 1881 as a supply point for freight traffic on the St. Louis and Southwestern Railroad, the town was named for Richard B. Hubbard, a native of the area who had been a colonel in the Confederacy's Twenty-second Texas Infantry and the state's governor from 1876 to 1879. (Later Hubbard served as U.S. minister to Japan during the first administration of President Grover Cleveland.) The railroad and cotton were the main stimuli for Hubbard's economy, although like Marlin and a number of other places in Texas, the town boasted of its healing mineral springs. By the early twentieth century "Hubbard City" had a population of about 1,600.

Archery O. Speaker (or A. O., as he was locally known) was born in 1852 in Ohio. A few years later his father moved his family to Texas, just in time to be caught up in the cataclysmic war that followed the secession of Texas and ten other states in 1860–1861. A. O. Speaker's father and two uncles enlisted on the side of the Confederacy; one uncle was captured and spent time in a federal prison at Chicago (presumably Camp Douglass). The Speakers were supposedly of English ancestry, although it's possible the name was a derivation of the German "Speicher," which shows up frequently in mid-nineteenth-century census returns from Maryland across the middle states.

Seven years older than her husband, Nancy Jane Poer (who was called "Jenny") was born in Georgia. When her family moved to Texas is not known, but at some point they settled in Hill County and she met and married A. O. Speaker. They wasted no time building a family; beginning in 1872, children came with remarkable regularity—eight in all, six girls, two boys. The last of the Speaker offspring, born in 1888 (or 1889), was Tris (or Tristram) Speaker. The Speakers were Methodists, and although family members subsequently changed over to the Episcopal Church, young Tris Speaker was raised in evangelical

Methodism. (A boyhood photo shows him in top hat, suit, and big white bow tie in a church recital group of boys and girls.) Speaker remained generically Protestant, although later in his life, as the late-nineteenth-century sociologist and social philosopher William Graham Sumner said of himself, he seemed to have put his religious beliefs in a drawer and left them there.

When Speaker was nine years old, with two of his sisters already married and living elsewhere, his father died in his mid-forties. Jenny Speaker did what women commonly did in those days when left in such circumstances: she took in boarders and depended on her teenage son Murry Lloyd and, within a few years, young Tris to earn an income from the farm and whatever other sources they could manage.

"I played baseball and drove the cows to pasture," was the terse way Speaker described to F. C. Lane his growing-up years at Hubbard. Of course he did a lot more than that. In the fall he played on the high school football team (although Texas wasn't as football-crazy as it became later on), and he worked as a janitor for $4.50 per week at the local cottonseed-oil plant. He also engaged in more than his share of foolhardy stunts, including one occasion when, on a bet with one of his pals, he threw a discarded bedpost roller 180 feet through the "dog run," or open hallway, of a black family's shack. "Tris admits this episode," F. C. Lane wrote, "but was noncommittal on the results of the episode, which precipitated the wrath of the somber denizens of the community on his head." Young Speaker was "never bad, you understand," recalled an elderly local resident, "but wild. When he wasn't much more than 12 years old, he packed a six-shooter as big as he was. Used to worry the life out of the town marshal, but I never heard of him getting into any real scrapes."[2]

As for his baseball-playing, that was, of course, the principal pastime for boys (and many girls) everywhere across the United States. Baseball was played in rural communities, villages, towns, and cities; on cow pastures and vacant lots; in city streets and alleys; in every kind of competition from loosely organized kids' play and local "town teams" to well-organized "semipro" leagues in which mostly adult males competed, backed by such sponsors as textile mills, factories, retail stores, insurance and oil companies, even urban churches.

Tris Speaker started playing baseball about as soon as he could hold a bat and throw a ball, but as his sister Pearl related many years later, "Baseball just seemed to me to be too tame to hold him long. Not enough excitement, you know. Why, that young one used to ride high-spirited horses without a saddle or bridle when he wasn't much more than a baby." The boy was naturally right-handed, but when he was ten years old, he was thrown from one of those unruly horses and suffered fractures of his right shoulder and arm. Fortunately, the accident happened before his protracted growth spurt and the full formation of his muscle and bone structures. Determined to keep playing baseball, he worked to master throwing and batting lefthanded. By the time he entered the local high school, he said in 1915, "Everything was easy, and I have worked left-handed ever since."[3]

He became so proficient as a lefty that he was the star pitcher for the high school team and for the local team of boys and men who played against nearby communities in the summer. One time, as he related the story to F. C. Lane, he skipped Methodist Sunday school to play a game. Upon reporting to his mother that his team had won and he had made two home runs and a single, he found himself in for a severe scolding, maybe worse. "I never played Sunday baseball again," said Speaker, "until I was a semi-pro."[4]

In the summer of 1905 Speaker worked as a telegraph repair lineman, then, with his mother's encouragement, decided he needed to prepare for something better. Having finished the eleven years of schooling available in Hubbard, he enrolled in the Polytechnic Institute at Fort Worth, some seventy-five miles to the northwest, to study bookkeeping and banking. Once Speaker became an established major-leaguer, sportswriters—in their effort to counter a persistent image of professional ballplayers as crude and semiliterate, given to beer-drinking and wenching—sometimes referred to Speaker as a "college man." Although most so-called "college men" in baseball had attended colleges or universities but hadn't actually earned degrees, in Speaker's case it was a complete misnomer. Fort Worth Polytechnic was a business school, offering a two-year program that presumably qualified one for a white-collar, quasi-professional occupation.

At Polytechnic, Speaker played a little football in the fall and starred for the baseball team in the spring, but he couldn't work up much enthusiasm for what he was studying. Early in the summer of 1905 he was earning a few dollars per game pitching for the Nicholson and Watson Grocery team at Corsicana. Doak Roberts, who was both president of the professional North Texas League and owner of the Cleburne Railroaders in that league, watched Speaker in action.[5] Dode Criss, Cleburne's star pitcher and hard-hitting outfielder, had a sore shoulder and couldn't pitch, so Roberts gave Speaker train fare to join the Railroaders at Waco, where they were playing a series against the local Navigators. (One unlikely account has Speaker pocketing the $1.00 train fare and instead hopping aboard a freight train.)

The North Texas League (often called simply the Texas League) was a shaky little operation at the bottom of the minor leagues, classified as Class D in the four-tier system set up in Organized Baseball under the National Agreement of 1903. Consisting of Cleburne, Waco, Fort Worth, Dallas, Greenville, and Temple, the league had an aggregate population considerably below the Class C South Texas League (made up of San Antonio, Houston, Beaumont, Galveston, Austin, and Lake Charles, Louisiana). But it was professional baseball, and as Speaker told Lane, he knew that a ballplayer "drew good money, rode around the country, was a local celebrity and had always the opportunity to make entry into the big leagues."[6]

After an all-night ride from Corsicana, Speaker woke up Benny Shelton, Cleburne's player-manager, at 6:30 A.M. to announce that he was the new pitcher, only to be told to get out and wait in the lobby. Three hours later Shelton came down to inform the youngster that he was pitching that afternoon. In the case of Tris Speaker, as with other players of that era, yarn-spinning about his early career has often superseded factual accounts. According to what became a widely told story, Speaker was bombarded for twenty-two runs that afternoon, after which Shelton told him he'd be better off in the outfield.

What happened was that on May 20 Speaker made a respectable professional debut. He allowed Waco only five hits, but he also walked five, his teammates made four errors, he yielded four runs in the sixth inning, and he lost the game, 4-1. Shelton offered him a contract, which he signed for a salary of $50 per month. Speaker also lost his next five games, but in each he allowed four or fewer hits. Then came the 22-4 debacle and his shift to the outfield, where he played seventy-seven games. In a pitching-dominated league, Speaker batted

.268 with 77 hits in 287 at bats—hardly a sensational showing. His most impressive statistic was 43 assists, some when he was pitching but most on throws from the outfield. Dode Criss recovered from his sore shoulder to win nineteen games and, as an outfielder-firstbaseman, batted .396 in fifty-two games, although the certified league leader was Cleburne outfielder George Whiteman at .281.

As was the practice in various other minor circuits, the North Texas League played a split season. Fort Worth won the first half, but with Greenville and Temple dropping out, Cleburne finished on top of the remaining four teams in the second half, with a record of 39 wins, 27 losses. Dallas edged Fort Worth for second place by half a game and claimed the pennant by virtue of having the best overall record for the season. Fort Worth's owner and manager announced that they couldn't keep their players together for a championship series with Cleburne, then voted with Cleburne and Waco to award the pennant to Cleburne. Brice Haskins, a Dallas sportswriter, called it a "gigantic fizzle."[7]

Speaker returned to Hubbard and the cottonseed-oil plant, his job now upgraded to night superintendent. Bobby Gilks, who had managed Shreveport in the Southern League that year, wanted to buy another one of the Cleburne players. As Gilks told the story many years later, Doak Roberts wanted $1,000 for the player; when Gilks balked at that price, Roberts offered to throw in Speaker, but the Shreveport club owner turned down the deal. "And here they were," reminisced Gilks, "trying to throw in one of baseball's greatest hitters as an inducement that I buy a player who never was heard of outside his own league."[8]

Doak Roberts kept "T. E. Speaker," Dode Criss, and George Whiteman under reserve. According to a practice dating back to 1879 that had become codified as a standard clause in players' contracts throughout Organized Baseball, that meant Roberts "reserved" the exclusive right to re-sign those players for the 1907 season, or sell them whenever he wished. That was precisely what irked Jenny Speaker, who supposedly announced that she wouldn't stand for her son's being bought and sold "like a longhorn steer."[9] But that was the way things were for young Speaker and everybody else who signed a contract within Organized Baseball.

In November, in San Antonio, the "All-State League" was formed with franchises in that city, Houston, Austin, Galveston, Dallas, and Fort Worth. The next month Cleburne and Waco were also given franchises in the new amalgamated league. Subsequently Roberts and Houston's owners merged their two franchises; shortly thereafter Temple joined to fill out an eight-team league, called simply the Texas League and classified by the minor-league-governing National Association as Class C. With William R. Robbie, owner of the San Antonio club, serving as league president, the franchise presidents agreed on a 140-game schedule and a roster limit of fourteen per club.

That season with Houston, performing in a faster league, Tris Speaker came into his own as a professional baseball player. It wasn't a memorable season for his team, which finished in fourth place with a 79-60 record, eight and a half games behind pennant-winner Austin. At the beginning, Speaker was supposed to be "one of the regular pitchers and tried as an emergency batter," according to the *Sporting News*'s Texas correspondent.[10] But his hitting was so impressive in the spring that he quickly became manager Wade Moore's regular centerfielder. In 118 games (of the 139 Houston played), in a league that, like the North Texas League of 1906, featured superb pitching, Speaker outbatted everybody else, finishing at .314 on 147 hits in 468 times at bat. He hit only 3 home runs (all inside-the-park blows) but made 32 doubles and 12 triples, both records tops in the league. He also stole 32 bases, although Fort Worth's Harry Short stole 78.

At a time long before major-league franchises controlled strings of minor-league teams in "farm systems" and operated highly organized development camps, young prospects were often identified rather offhandedly. It might happen as the result of personal acquaintance or perhaps the chance visit of a "bird dog," a man paid to do part-time scouting for one or more of the big-league teams. Back in the spring, the American League's St. Louis Browns, training in Texas, had played an exhibition series with Houston. Browns manager Jimmy McAleer expressed an interest in Speaker and told Doak Roberts to let him know when he thought the youngster might be ready for purchase. At some point during the season Roberts wired McAleer that the Browns could have Speaker for $1,500, adding that if Speaker didn't stick with the Browns, he would deed McAleer two hundred acres of Texas land he owned. When no reply was forthcoming from McAleer, Roberts turned to George M. Huff, athletic director and baseball coach at the University of Illinois, who scouted for the Boston American League club during the summer. As authorized by Boston president John I. Taylor, Huff offered $400 each for Speaker and George Whiteman (even though Whiteman had batted only .232 that season). About to sell his interest in the Houston franchise, Roberts took what he could get, and, at the age of nineteen (or eighteen), Tris Speaker became the property of a big-league franchise.[11]

Jenny Speaker wasn't happy with the turn of events. Roberts, Huff, and John Callicutt, an attorney and family friend from Corsicana, all had to join Speaker at Hubbard in persuading her to give her consent to her son's departure for faraway Boston. "She made me promise," Speaker told a banquet audience many years later, "that if I failed to make the grade that I would come back home and go to work."[12]

When the Texas League season closed on September 3, Speaker left the state for the first time in his life. Involving several train changes and delays, it was a long, tiring trip Speaker made all the way in day coaches, unable to afford sleeping-car accommodations. His destination was Philadelphia, where the Boston team was to play a series with the Philadelphia Athletics, who were in a tight pennant race with Ty Cobb's Detroit Tigers. When he finally arrived, he introduced himself to Boston manager Jim "Deacon" McGuire, who greeted him brusquely and told him to get into a uniform. The Boston regulars paid little attention to him or to Whiteman, who had also arrived from Texas, except that when the newcomers tried to take their swings in batting practice, they were ordered to get away from the plate—common treatment for rookies in that day.

It was also common for rookies to play in the first major-league game they ever saw. That was the case with Speaker, who made his debut on Thursday, September 12, 1907, before 9,056 people at Columbia Park, when he entered the game in the sixth inning, taking the place of Bill Congalton in rightfield. In the remainder of what ended as a 7-1 Athletics victory, Speaker batted unsuccessfully twice against Jimmy Dygert, the Athletics' little righthander. Two days later, before a huge Saturday crowd of 26,505 that overflowed the playing field of the Philadelphia ballpark, Boston dropped a doubleheader to the Athletics. In the eighth inning of the nightcap, Speaker pinch-hit for pitcher Harry "Cy" Morgan; again Dygert got him out. He started for the first time two days later, in Washington, playing rightfield and going hitless in five times at bat in still another Boston loss. He finally managed a base hit the next day—a single off Washington righthander Tom Hughes.

When the team returned to Boston for a home stand that closed the season, Jacob C. Morse, the Boston correspondent for *Sporting Life,* wrote, "The return of the Americans gave us a chance to behold one of the new outfielders in action—Chris [*sic*] Speaker of Texas—it being necessary for Congalton to lay off owing to a bad side. Speaker showed himself to be a fast fielder and did very good work and made a favorable impression." (As when Rogers Hornsby came into the majors eight years later, it would take a while for everybody to get Speaker's first name right.) Morse added that McGuire "thinks very well of him as well as Whiteman, the other new outfielder."[13]

Nice words, but they hardly fit what Speaker did in his trial with Boston that September. In seven games and twenty times at bat, he made only three hits, all singles, for a .150 average. He watched from the bench as the Detroit Tigers, sparked by twenty-year-old Ty Cobb, swept a three-game series on their way to that city's first American League pennant, and he didn't play at all in the last nine games of the season. Whiteman saw even less action, appearing in only three games and making two hits in eleven at bats. Neither seemed to have much of a future as big-leaguers, not even for a team that finished in seventh place with a 59-90 record.

After also sitting out a desultory seven-game postseason series between the Boston Americans and Boston's National League team (which also finished seventh, with an almost identical record), Speaker went home thinking that during the winter he would receive his Boston contract for next year. Whiteman was sold back to Houston. (Except for parts of two seasons, Whiteman spent the next twenty-two years in the minors as a player and player-manager.) At Hubbard, Speaker waited—and waited.

Since 1904 the Boston American League franchise had been owned by General Charles H. Taylor, a Civil War veteran and publisher and editor of the *Boston Globe.* The general made his son, who had a reputation as a playboy, president of the franchise and owner of half its stock. That was supposed to keep him occupied. Universally called "John I.," the son took to his new responsibilities with vigor, proving to be what a later generation would call a hands-on owner. Bill

Carrigan, a catcher for the Boston team beginning in 1906 and its manager from 1913 to 1916, described him as more fan than owner. The veteran baseball writer Irving I. Sanborn thought Taylor "was chiefly handicapped by the fact that he was too hard a loser and thought he knew more about baseball than he did." He showed up at spring training, attended every home game, and accompanied his team on road trips. On off days he sent his players on excursions to the mountains or the shore, and, Carrigan recalled, "He'd wine and dine us and foot all the bills." But John I. also stormed into the dressing room to berate the players after losses, fined and suspended them without consulting his manager, and snooped into what they did away from the ballpark.[14]

The Taylors acquired the franchise at the start of a second consecutive pennant-winning year, following a surprising victory over the three-time National League champion Pittsburgh Pirates in the first "modern" World Series. Like nearly everybody else, the Taylors were unhappy when John T. Brush and John McGraw refused to meet them in a second Series. After that season, though, age and infirmity started catching up with what had been a veteran ball club. Over the next three years the Boston American Leaguers finished in fourth, eighth, and seventh places. John I. had plenty of occasion to berate his men.

In the off-season of 1907–1908, John I. announced that his team, which had never had a nickname (though sometimes called "Puritans" or "Pilgrims"), would abandon the blue stockings and blue-trimmed uniforms they had worn since the inaugural American League season in 1901 in favor of red stockings and trim, and that the team would now be known as "Red Sox."[15] But if John I. gets credit for the enduring nickname and colors of the Boston American Leaguers, he and Hugh McBreen, his club secretary, were less meticulous in their paperwork, at least where Tris Speaker was concerned. The weeks and months passed, and still nothing from Boston arrived at the Hubbard post office.

Speaker was in limbo. When he hadn't received his 1908 contract by the official deadline and had gotten nowhere with John McGraw at the New York Giants' training site at Marlin, Speaker sent telegrams to various clubs stating that he was a free agent and offering his services. He received one encouraging reply, from Michael J. Finn, manager of the Little Rock Travelers in the Class A Southern League.

As it happened, John I. Taylor had arranged for his newly christened Boston Red Sox to do spring training at Little Rock. Mike Finn, a portly and full-mustached man who directed his team from the bench in street clothes, liked what he saw in the young Texan nobody else seemed to want. He put Speaker in centerfield for exhibition games versus the Red Sox, the St. Louis Cardinals (who now included Speaker's old Cleburne teammate Dode Criss), and the Detroit Tigers, whom Ty Cobb, chronically late in the spring, had just joined. On April 1, 1908, Speaker and Cobb competed against each other in the first of what would be hundreds of meetings, Cobb making two singles, Speaker singling and doubling off three Tigers pitchers. Little Rock's *Sporting News* correspondent, writing under the pseudonym "Coca-Cola," reported that "Speaker, our new center fielder, has already won a home with the fans by his all-around work."[16]

According to a frequently repeated story, John I. Taylor and Mike Finn agreed that, in payment for the use of the Little Rock ballpark for their spring training, the Red Sox would leave Speaker behind to play for the Travelers. The problem with the story is that, not having put Speaker under contract, the Red Sox had no hold on him. In fact, Speaker had already signed a contract with Finn before the Red Sox left. What Taylor did was get Finn to promise that he could buy Speaker's contract (again) before the season was over.

The Southern League had a 140-game schedule (although because of un-replayed rainouts, none of the eight teams played the full number) and specified a roster limit of fifteen players. Only two rungs below the majors, it was one of the five strongest of thirty-eight minor leagues operating in 1908. Its teams fielded such former big-leaguers as forty-nine-year-old Ted Breitenstein, Mobile's pitcher and manager, who had won 160 games in the National League; George Rohe, who, only two years earlier, had helped spark the Chicago White Sox's "Hitless Wonders" to a World Series upset of the Chicago Cubs; and Frank Delahanty, one of five brothers to play in the majors. Besides Speaker, other youngsters on their way to big-league stardom included Jake Daubert, firstbaseman with New Orleans; Zack Wheat, outfielder with Mobile; and Russell Ford, pitcher with Atlanta.

But in later decades, it would be Speaker whom fans in the Southern League cities would remember most vividly. Speaker accomplished what all young ballplayers strive for but most don't achieve—to improve their performance at each level of the minor leagues. The ball club he played on was pitching poor, and the 1908 Travelers ended up in seventh place with a 62-76 record. That put them sixteen and a half games behind Nashville, which won the pennant by beating runner-up New Orleans on the final day of the season. But after making two singles and stealing two bases in the season opener at Memphis, Speaker batted consistently week after week. And while he was still honing his outfield skills, he showed flashes of the brilliance that would later become commonplace. At Mobile on May 2, for example, he caught a soft liner a short distance behind secondbase and beat the runner back to the base, completing his first unassisted double play. In July of that season, in another first, he argued with such vehemence with the lone umpire (most games were worked by only one) that he was ordered out of the game.

With a month to go in the season, Speaker was leading the league in batting with a .333 average, despite having gone hitless in twelve at bats in a recent series at Memphis. In that and other Little Rock stays at Memphis's Red Elm Park, nineteen-year-old Joe Williams, soon to join the local *Commercial Appeal* and begin a long and distinguished career in sports journalism, watched Speaker and realized his potential. So did the *Nashville Tennessean*'s Grantland Rice, who later described him as "the smoothest minor leaguer I ever saw." A *Sporting Life* correspondent, in an anonymous "Southern Sayings" column, declared: "Triss [*sic*] Speaker of Little Rock is the outfield find of the season. Strong with the stick, covers a world of ground, and has a wonderful arm. He has, perhaps, thrown out as many men at the plate as any other two fielders." And from Memphis came another report declaring Speaker "the sensation of the Southern League this season."[17]

As word of Speaker's ability spread, Finn was contacted by several major-league teams with offers to buy him for sums reportedly ranging from $2,000 to $7,500; among the bidders was a regretful John McGraw. But in an act of extraordinary fidelity, Finn kept his word to John I. Taylor and, after what was reported as "a heated controversy" among the Little Rock stockholders, sold Speaker's contract for $500. That gave the Texan the distinction of having been sold to the same major-league organization twice within one year, for a total of

$900.[18] With nine games left in the season, Speaker appeared for the last time in the Southern League on Friday, September 4, at Little Rock, when he hit two singles and drove in two runs in still another loss, 4-3, to Atlanta.

Up to that point, Speaker had played in every game in the 1908 season. One of only four .300 hitters appearing in at least one hundred games, he gained his second straight minor-league batting title, with a mark of .350 on 165 hits in 471 times at bat. He also led the league in runs (81) as well as putouts (330), while committing 13 errors. (His 37 assists were long thought to tie a Southern League record, but a 1953 recheck revealed that William Lee of Nashville had thrown out 39 runners that year.) Oddly for the man who ended up hitting more major-league doubles than anybody else in history, Speaker had only 13 two-baggers to go with 10 triples.

This time Speaker traveled directly to Boston, less tortuously than a year earlier because his train connections out of Little Rock were more efficient. He got there in only two days, in time for a Labor Day doubleheader with the Phila-delphia Athletics, who this year were far out of the pennant race. He rented a room on Huntington Avenue in an apartment building called Putnam's Place, where most of the Red Sox lodged, across from the New England Conservatory of Music and a short walk north to the Huntington Avenue Grounds. Speaker reported to Fred Lake, who had recently succeeded Jim McGuire as Boston manager.

Bounded by Huntington Avenue on the east, Rogers Street on the north, and New Gravelly Point Road, which angled around from the west to the south, the Red Sox's home ballpark was a typical turn-of-the-century baseball facility. Hurriedly built eight years earlier on property leased from the Boston Elevated Railway Company, it was barely ready in time for the first American League sea-son. Huntington Avenue Grounds was constructed entirely of wood and could seat could only about 9,000 people in a covered grandstand and pavilion extend-ing from firstbase down the leftfield line and bleachers running across leftfield. As with the other "premodern" ballparks, the Red Sox playing field was oddly configured to fit into the dimensions of the privately owned property on which it was built. By 1908 its distances had been altered, so that when Speaker arrived for his second big-league trial, the leftfield corner was 350 feet from home plate, rightfield was 320 feet, and deepest centerfield was a staggering 635 feet from the batter. Big centerfields were also typical of the time, intended to provide over-flow space for customers paying twenty-five cents for standing-room admissions. The Red Sox's park had the biggest "pasture" of all. Sunday baseball was illegal in all four of the eastern major-league cities (as well as in Cleveland until 1911), so the overflows—if they happened—were nearly always on Saturdays, a half-workday for most fans.

The Red Sox had a dressing room at their ballpark, but visiting teams had to don their uniforms at their hotels and ride the elevated railway to the game site. That was also typical of the times; it was another four years before all the major-league ballparks had dressing facilities for visitors. The rail line to Huntington Avenue Grounds ran from the north alongside New Gravelly Point Road and ended at the New York, New Haven, and Hartford Railroad maintenance yards. The tracks ran along the leftfield side of South End Grounds, home of the usually hapless Boston National League entry. Thus both Boston big-league parks were in the same neighborhood.

Manager Lake penciled in Speaker in centerfield and seventh in the batting order for both games with the Athletics. The Red Sox swept the doubleheader, played morning and afternoon (for two separate admissions). Speaker faced Athletics manager Connie Mack's two aces: lefthander Eddie Plank and right-hander Charles "Chief" Bender, both future Hall of Famers. Off Plank he singled and stole a base; off Bender he singled, tripled, and scored twice.

Speaker was in the lineup for each of the thirty-one games the Red Sox played after he arrived from Little Rock. On September 21, 1908, at Detroit, with the Tigers in a tight battle for the pennant with Cleveland and Chicago, Speaker was on the field with Ty Cobb for the first time in a regular-season game. It wasn't a memorable occasion for either; they each went hitless in four times up. Twelve days later Boston split a doubleheader in Philadelphia, where the Shibe brothers, majority owners of the Athletics, were building a new and bigger ballpark. Those games, which attracted only 1,281 fans, were the last ever played at Columbia Park by American League teams.[19] In the nightcap, Howard Ellsworth "Joe" Wood, not yet nineteen, a righthander recently purchased from Kansas City of the American Association, shut out the Athletics for his first big-league victory.

Soon he became "Smokey Joe," so dubbed by the *Boston Post*'s Paul Shannon. Wood also became Speaker's roommate and closest friend.

The Red Sox ended their 1908 season back in Boston with still another doubleheader split with Philadelphia. Speaker had joined a better team than he had the previous year, one that improved to fifth place with a 75-79 record, but the Southern League's batting champion wasn't a great deal more impressive than he had been in his 1907 trial. In 116 times at bat, Speaker had 26 hits for a .224 batting average, although he hit a couple of doubles and triples and drove in 10 runs, played errorlessly in centerfield, and threw out 9 runners. His overall comportment prompted the *Sporting News*'s Boston correspondent to report that manager Lake "is looking at this boy Speaker carefully, as he has the potential of a good player." A week or so later, Jacob C. Morse wrote of Speaker in *Sporting Life* that he "has a regular 'Ty' Cobb future before him. . . . There seems to be no doubt that he will be in center field next season."[20]

The Cobb-Speaker comparisons had already begun. For the next twenty years, baseball fans would relish those comparisons.

"By No Means a Finished Outfielder"

Early in 1909, in *Sporting Life,* Jacob C. Morse wrote from Boston that, having recently purchased catcher Lou Criger from the Red Sox for $10,000, St. Louis Browns manager Jimmy McAleer also wanted Tris Speaker. Morse praised Speaker's "easy artistic way of playing the game. . . . He works very easily, without the spread-eagle grandstand style of some, and in a very modest, businesslike way." Yet thirty-five years later, Speaker acknowledged, "I was by no means a finished outfielder when I started in the American League." Then and on many other occasions, he gave credit to the great Denton True "Cy" Young for helping him develop into the player he became. "I learned to watch batters by watching Cy pitch. I didn't start with the crack of the bat, I started before the ball was hit." Young, said Speaker, "had great patience with me and believed in me and he would hit fungos to me for 30 minutes a day. A wonderful pitcher and a wonderful man."[1]

Those fungo sessions with Young had taken place during Speaker's stays with the Boston team the past two Septembers. But in February 1909 John I. Taylor completed disposing of the famous battery of Young and Criger by selling the forty-one-year-old pitcher to the Cleveland Naps for $12,500. Over the past nineteen seasons, the big righthander had accumulated 476 wins (283 in the National League, 193 in the American), more than any pitcher ever had or ever would. He had also pitched 3 no-hit games. (Young won 33 more before retiring to his eastern Ohio farm in 1912.) If Speaker had ever harbored any illusions about sentiment and loyalty in professional baseball, the cold-blooded jettisoning of the venerable Young should have disabused him of them.

In the spring of 1909 the Red Sox trained at Hot Springs, Arkansas, some forty-five miles southwest of Little Rock. Like Marlin and Mineral Wells in Texas and various other southwestern training sites of that time, Hot Springs was attractive partly because of its spring-fed mineral waters, which stayed at a constant 147 degrees and were supposed to ameliorate all kinds of ailments. A town of some 15,000 permanent residents, Hot Springs was a popular regional resort not only for its waters and generally mild climate but for the local race-track, which operated year-round. Many ballplayers, especially as they got older, liked to come to Hot Springs in the late winter to exercise and soak their muscles, try to shed excess poundage accumulated in an off-season of eating and drinking, and play the horses.

Lodged at the Majestic Hotel, the Red Sox practiced on property recently purchased by John I. Taylor that had a skinned diamond and little grass otherwise. The National League's Pittsburgh team stayed at another hotel and practiced at another and better facility. As usual, John I. arrived early and was on hand every morning to watch his players work out.

The most talked-about Boston rookie that spring (Speaker no longer qualified as such) was Harry Hooper, an engineering graduate of St. Mary's College in California. After two strong seasons in the "outlaw" California State League, Hooper, a free agent because he had played in a league outside Organized Baseball, had taken John I.'s offer of $2,800 to join the Red Sox. Manager Fred Lake must already have decided on his regular centerfielder, because, Hooper later said, "Tris Speaker was there ... and it looked like he had a stranglehold on the center-field job."[2] After several games with the crosstown Pirates and a week in Memphis for games with that city's Southern League team, the Red Sox headed for Philadelphia to open the 1909 season, playing at various sites along the way.

Meanwhile what happened that spring to the New York American Leaguers—now generally known as the Yankees—pointed up the occasional hazards of spring training, such as spring storms that washed out railroad tracks and bridges, as well as exposure to potentially lethal diseases. After the Yankees vacated their Macon, Georgia, training base, they stopped at Augusta, where they learned that Hal Chase, their star firstbaseman, had contracted smallpox—one of the dreaded contagions still common at that time—and would have to be left behind. Manager George Stallings and the rest of the Yankees were vaccinated at Augusta, but a couple of days later, six more players had to undergo a second painful injection after they were examined in Richmond. Chase wasn't able to rejoin the Yankees for six weeks.

Then there were the inherent dangers in playing the game itself, as it was played a century ago. At the start of the 1907 season, catcher Roger Bresnahan of the New York Giants had taken the field in a modified version of cricket leg guards—the first catcher's shin guards. Younger catchers soon added Bresnahan's innovation to the wire mask and thinly padded chest-crotch protector long in use, but veterans such as Lou Criger continued to disdain shin guards for the rest of their careers—and continued to endure spikings by sliding runners and the ever-present possibility of infection and blood poisoning.

After he was knocked unconscious by a pitch, Bresnahan developed a pneumatic "head protector" that covered one side of a batter's head and face and was secured by a strap around the cap, but the device proved so cumbersome that not even its inventor would wear it for games. More than forty years passed before some players began wearing plastic liners inside their caps, and it would be another fifteen years before baseball officialdom made hard-surface batting helmets mandatory.

Throughout Tris Speaker's playing career, the only protection batters wore on their heads was a cloth cap, styled more like the short-billed beanies imposed on college freshmen than the full-billed caps of a later time. Moreover, everybody from umpires to managers to fans to the players themselves accepted the prerogative of pitchers to "brush back" batters who crowded the plate. If sometimes batters were "skulled" or "beaned," that was simply accepted as a part of baseball. At some time, virtually every player who had a professional career was hit in the head by an errant (or intentional) high-and-inside pitch.

Lightweight uniforms of artificial fibers were far, far into the future; players of Speaker's time and for long thereafter wore woolen flannel pants and shirts (with full collars during the first years of his career) and woolen socks. Catchers used a big, heavily padded mitt, but fielders' gloves were literally that—pancake-like five-fingered gloves, little bigger than a man's hand, with sparse padding, although the firstbaseman's mitt had somewhat more padding and was rounded at the fingers. Yet fielding had improved significantly over the past few years,

partly because infields were better maintained, but largely because of the addition of a strap of leather between the thumb and forefinger of fielders' gloves.
Ballplayers' shoes, which only recently had become available in lighter-weight,
low-quarter style, had steel spikes attached to the soles.

Those steel spikes often served as weapons, especially as employed by the
eminently aggressive Ty Cobb, who insisted that the base paths belonged to the
runner. Cobb had little compunction about coming into a base with spikes flash-
ing and inflicting wounds on infielders. In general, baseball was a rougher game
than it would be a century later. The complaint of the *New York Morning Sun*'s
Joe Vila about "too much personal animosity in professional baseball" was a
common one. "Some players," Vila wrote in 1911, "seem to think that playing
the part of ruffians helps to win games. They seek to intimidate opponents with
threats of physical violence." (Vila probably had Cobb in mind, though by no
means Cobb alone.) As for verbal abuse of opposing players, Vila observed that
"calling them vile names appears to be the proper caper in many instances, for it
is believed that by insulting a player his anger can be aroused so that he can not
do his best work."[3]

But if professional baseball was a rough and often dangerous way to make
a living, the players' lifestyles were the envy of the great majority of their fellow
citizens. "The major league player," wrote Hugh S. Fullerton in 1911, "is the most
pampered, best cared for and conditioned live stock in the world. He rides in
special cars, or on special trains, stops at exclusive hotels, is hauled to and from
grounds, hotels and railway stations in automobiles or carriages. His transportation and sleeping-car accommodations all are arranged for him, his baggage is
hauled, checked and placed in his room, trainers wait upon him as valets. He has
the best of everything."[4]

The best of everything—by early-twentieth-century standards. Ballplayers
had to make long, boring road trips on un-air-conditioned trains or, on trips
from Boston to New York or Cleveland to Detroit, on coastwise and lake steamers that were often tossed in rough waters. They broke the tedium with card
games, reading, songfests, and frequent conversations with newspapermen from
the home-city dailies who traveled with teams. Fred Lieb, who worked for various New York City papers over the years, remembered that "It was easier for a

writer to talk to a player on the road than it was when the club was at home." Some writers, mostly for the afternoon papers, showed up during practice before home games and interviewed players and managers, but "There was practically no interviewing after games."[5]

Players, managers, and writers tended to be smokers. Although pipes and cigars had long served the image of manliness and maturity, younger American males (and some females) were turning to mass-produced, "ready-rolled" cigarettes for a quicker and supposedly less odoriferous smoke. As did Tris Speaker, who at some point in his youth began to light up and inhale what churchmen and other moralists already were calling "coffin nails." He remained a heavy cigarette-smoker for the rest of his life, although he never chewed tobacco, as did so many other players. Speaker expended his nervous energy in centerfield between pitches by plucking and chewing stems of grass.

Cigarette-smoking among ballplayers often came in for disapproval from club owners and managers. Pittsburgh owner Barney Dreyfus supposedly lost interest in buying Speaker in 1908 when he learned about his liking for cigarettes. In 1911, John I. Taylor gave out free cigars to Speaker and other Red Sox in an unsuccessful effort to get them to give up cigarettes. Outfielder Charlie Jamieson remembered that Connie Mack forbade cigarette-smoking by the Philadelphia Athletics, so that when Mack came into sight, his players would hide their cigarettes and wave around cigars. Once, Detroit manager Hugh Jennings offered a bonus of $600 to any of his players willing to quit the cigarette habit. Whether Jennings had any takers isn't known, but cigarette-smoking continued to be common among baseball players until they, like most other Americans, finally came to realize the multiple health hazards it entailed.

Almost all train and steamer trips involved an overnight ride. On trains, players slept in cramped Pullman berths with coal dust blowing through window screens; in hotels, they tossed and turned in stuffy rooms with street noises coming in through open windows. Every game was played in the daytime, on diamonds that were often muddy in the spring and sun-baked hard by midseason, and on outfields enclosed by unpadded walls and without dirt tracks to warn outfielders of their proximity.

But if ballplayers of Tris Speaker's time had to be rugged to play the game, they were also generally smaller men than they were later in the twentieth century. A 1921 survey published in the monthly *Baseball Magazine* put the average size of big-leaguers at 169.5 pounds and 5' 10½" tall, although pitchers were usually heavier and taller. In 1909, when Speaker reached the majors to stay, he had grown to his full height of 5' 11½", weighed 175–180 pounds, and was, Joe Wood said, "strong as a bull."[6]

Speaker was one of the 27 percent of players batting from the left side; a third of the pitchers were lefthanders. (The percentage of players doing anything lefthanded was well above that in the general population, as was still the case into the next century.) He hadn't yet acquired the nickname "Gray Eagle." His complexion was ruddy; his hair was still brown; his eyes, according to his 1917 draft registration card, were "dark blue." To Alfred H. Spink, publisher of the *Sporting News,* Speaker's voice was "like rolling thunder, and his softest words sound like the growl of a mastiff."[7]

The Red Sox's opening game of the 154-game season—the standard major-league schedule since 1904—was also the christening of the Philadelphia Athletics' new Shibe Park, the first baseball facility of its kind. With a double-decked grandstand constructed of steel and concrete thought to be fireproof, it marked the beginning of the era of modern ballpark construction that witnessed the building or rebuilding of thirteen more such steel-and-concrete "baseball palaces," culminating in 1923 with the opening of the vast Yankee Stadium. Forbes Field in Pittsburgh, opened on June 30, 1909, was the second of the new generation of ballparks.

In its original form, Shibe Park seated slightly more than 22,000; but on April 12, 1909, the paid attendance was 30,162, with another thousand or so distinguished guests admitted free. Thousands more were turned away when the gates were closed at 2 P.M., an hour before game time. The colorful Tim Hurst and the taciturn Tom Connolly did the umpiring; by the edict of Byron Bancroft "Ban" Johnson, the American League's imperious president, all games were now to be worked by two officials. In a game lasting 2:06, longer than average for that period, Eddie Plank threw a six-hitter and yielded a single run, while the Athletics punched Frank Arellanes and Jack Ryan for thirteen hits and eight runs. Yet the victory was clouded for the Philadelphia players and fans, because, late in the game, catcher Mike Powers began experiencing severe abdominal pains. He finished the game, collapsed, and died twelve days later, apparently from a twisted intestine.

Although Speaker, batting fifth, was hitless in five times up that day, it was the beginning of a season in which he left no doubt that he was in the majors to stay. On April 21, when the Red Sox opened at home on a typically cold, overcast day before an overflow crowd of 12,343, he singled three times and stole three bases, as Plank, victimized by seven Philadelphia errors, took the loss, 6-2. Jacob C. Morse said about Speaker, "If there are any youngsters lying around who can do better work than this young man, let them show up." A few weeks later Morse was even more enthusiastic, calling Speaker "the sensation of the day. He surprises everybody by his speed, his grace and ease, and by his wonderful throwing powers and his splendid accuracy."[8]

Speaker had a unique theory about his throwing. He was convinced no lefthander could throw in a straight line from centerfield to home plate, so he usually aimed his throws halfway between thirdbase and home, and, as a sportswriter who watched him in action for many years described the effect, "The natural out-shoot on the ball would zoom it into [the catcher's] hands." Or as Harry Hooper put it, with some exaggeration, "Speaker's side-arm left-handed throw went home by way of third base but it was always on target."[9]

The white-maned Tim Murnane of the *Boston Globe,* dean of the city's baseball writers and an old-time big-leaguer himself, dubbed the 1909 Red Sox the "Speed Boys." They were faster and more daring on the base paths than in recent years; led by thirdbaseman Harry Lord's 36 thefts and Speaker's 35, they stole 215 bases. That was exceeded in the American League only by Detroit's 280, of which Cobb stole 76. Although Harry Hooper got into only eighty-one games and didn't become the regular rightfielder until Harry "Doc" Gessler was traded to Washington, he and Speaker were already being described as a tandem—"two wonderful ball players," as an anonymous commentator wrote in the *Sporting News,* "and no amount of coin would tempt John I. Taylor to part with them."[10]

On June 1, in a 1-0 win pitched by Boston's Fred Burchell in the second game of a doubleheader at Philadelphia, Speaker made the first of the six unassisted double plays he recorded during his big-league career. That first one, like the three that followed, involved his taking a ball hit to very short centerfield and racing in to touch secondbase before the runner, who had strayed off the bag, could get back.

Although the 1909 American League pennant race eventually came down to a bitter battle between Detroit and a resurgent Philadelphia team (highlighted by Cobb's celebrated spiking of thirdbaseman Frank Baker), the "Speed Boys" remained in contention most of the way. Their season's peak came on August 18, a doubleheader sweep in New York that gave them eleven wins in a row, fifteen wins in seventeen games, and put them in second place, one game behind Philadelphia and a game and a half ahead of Detroit. The next day, however, the Yankees returned the favor by winning two games, with Frank Arellanes and Charley Hall (born Carlos Clolo and nicknamed "Sea Lion" for his booming voice) taking the losses. Both were from California and of Hispanic ancestry, which prompted a *New York Times* reporter to quip that manager Fred Lake started "a Mexican" in each game, and that Hall was "as thoroughly a greaser as Arellanes."[11]

That double defeat dropped the Red Sox to third, and from then on they managed to win only four more games than they lost. As the Tigers and Athletics pulled away, Boston stayed in third place, finishing with an 88-65 record, six games behind Philadelphia, nine and a half behind three-time champion Detroit. John I.'s team had made its best showing since the 1904 pennant-winners. Arellanes won sixteen games; Eddie Cicotte, a stocky knuckleball pitcher who had originally been Detroit property, won fourteen; and Speaker's pal, nineteen-year-old Joe Wood, won eleven. The Red Sox might have done even better if Taylor hadn't sold Cy Young. Enthusiastically greeted in June when he made his first start in Boston as a Cleveland Nap, Young pitched a neat three-hit victory, one of nineteen games he won for a sixth-place team.

A leg injury that month caused Speaker to miss eight games of the 152 the Red Sox played; he also sat out a meaningless game near the end of the season. For most of the summer his batting average stayed in the mid-.280s, but over the last six weeks, as the team faded, his bat warmed. Cobb won his third straight batting title with a .377 average, thirty points better than Eddie Collins, the Athletics' brilliant young secondbaseman. (Collins's run-in with Tim Hurst in August ended with Hurst spitting tobacco juice in the player's face, by Hurst's prompt firing by Ban Johnson.) In a year in which only seven A. can League regulars batted .300, Speaker finished at .309, with 7 home runs (all inside the park) and 77 runs batted in to go with his 35 steals. He led the league's outfielders with 319 putouts and 35 assists while committing 10 errors, a modest number for that period, given the gloves then in use and the frequently lumpy condition of outfields. It was an impressive first full season, one demonstrating conclusively that Speaker had become a finished big-league outfielder.

It had also been the most prosperous season up to that time for the Boston American League franchise. Boosted by a number of overflow crowds, especially during the torrid home stand in August, the season's attendance at Huntington Avenue Grounds reached nearly 670,000, more than anybody in either league drew besides the Athletics. Baseball was booming; total attendance for the sixteen big-league clubs was a record 7,236,990, a figure that wasn't exceeded for another eleven years.

That high level of interest didn't carry over into a postseason series the Red Sox played with the New York Giants, who also finished in third place in the National League. As yet the World Series—in 1909 matching Detroit against Pittsburgh and opening at the Pirates' new Forbes Field—hadn't assumed the dominating place in the consciousness of baseball fans that it would within a few years. Postseason matchups of other teams were a common occurrence, although none of them generated as much local excitement as the "city series" between the two Chicago teams.

The Red Sox–Giants series was a big disappointment all around. Played in unpleasant weather in both cities and producing total receipts of only $12,862, it ended after five games, of which New York won only the opener, with the great Christy Mathewson outpitching Joe Wood. The fifth game was witnessed by 789 people in New York's Polo Grounds, which seated about 30,000. Twenty Boston players, plus manager Lake, the team trainer, and secretary Hugh McBreen, divided up $4,006.73.

The five games did, though, showcase Speaker's talents for the large contingent of New York baseball writers. He batted .600 (twelve hits in twenty times at bat), including a home run off Mathewson in game one and another off Otis Crandall that decided game three. Besides scoring five runs and stealing six bases, he threw out four runners and, in game four, pulled down two long drives to save rookie Ray Collins's shutout win over Mathewson. After the series, John McGraw commented, "I've never seen a greater exhibition in my life. That Speaker is headed for the top. I think he's a better ballplayer right now than the American League's Ty Cobb."[12] Maybe McGraw was thinking back to that spring day a year and a half earlier at Marlin, Texas.

Unlike baseball owners later in the era of free agency, the owners of Speaker's time were characteristically secretive about their payrolls. We don't know what Speaker's salary was for his first full season as a major-leaguer, but a decent guess would be in the $1,500–$1,800 range for the six months of his contract. In all probability he sent some of that back home to Hubbard, where, in the 1910 federal census, Nancy Jane Speaker, at age sixty-five, listed herself as "keeper boarding house." Still living at home were her thirty-one-year-old daughter Elaine, who gave her occupation as "book keeper dry goods," and son Murry Lloyd, twenty-six, who gave his as "hack driver, livery stable." (Speaker's occupation was listed simply as "Centerfielder Baseball.")[13]

Speaker apparently didn't like what the Red Sox offered him for 1910, because his contract didn't arrive at Hugh McBreen's office until mid-January—the last one to come in. John I. undoubtedly gave him a healthy raise, probably to $3,000 or a little more. At a time when the average American family income was well under $1,000 per year, major-league players were comparatively very well paid. (And as impecunious sportswriters liked to point out, for their money, ballplayers had to work only a few hours a day for half the year.) Yet the attitude of ballplayers then—and for generations to follow—was that their peak earning years were short, that their careers could be ended at any time by injury or illness (so, of course, could anybody else's), and that they had to make as much as they could as quickly as they could.

Fred Lake, who figured he had done well with the 1909 Red Sox, also wanted to get as much as he could, and supposedly demanded a $2,000 raise over the $4,500 he had been paid the past season. John I. balked at that and, unable to come to terms with his manager, fired him in November. Lake quickly signed to manage the nearby Boston National Leaguers, a last-place team in 1909 (as it was again in 1910). John I. hired Joseph "Patsy" Donovan, a former big-league out-fielder who had managed with little success at Pittsburgh, St. Louis, and Brook-lyn in the National League and Washington in the American, and for the past two years had scouted for the Red Sox.

In 1910 the Red Sox and the World Series champion Pirates returned to Hot Springs. The Cincinnati Reds were also based there, sharing the diamond on Taylor's property with the Red Sox, while the Pirates again used a different field. Tim Murnane wasn't convinced about the efficacy of the famous local mineral waters. They were good "for a man with ailments," Murnane thought, "but a shade trying for the man in good health, with a clear mind."[14] After playing each other twelve times at Hot Springs, the Red Sox and Reds traveled northeastward by separate routes before meeting for the thirteenth time in Cincinnati at the all-wooden, ornately carpentered Palace of the Fans.

Although they were to open the season in New York, the Red Sox first stopped over at Huntington Avenue Grounds for an exhibition game with Harvard University, and Speaker and Joe Wood again occupied their rooms at Putnam's Place. By now, about to begin another season in which Boston would be his home for half the time, Speaker was fairly well acquainted with the big-league city that was geographically farthest from his native territory. With a 1910 population of about 670,000, plus another 350,000 or so living in Cambridge, Somerville, Brockton, Chelsea, and other satellite municipalities, Boston was not only the hub of New England but the fourth-largest metropolis in the country, surpassed only by New York, Chicago, and Philadelphia.[15]

Once a bastion of Calvinist Protestantism, Boston had become a predomi-nantly Catholic city, to which, over the past sixty years, huge numbers of Irish, Italian, and other non-Protestant Europeans had migrated. Speaker had to get used to hearing people who spoke in Irish brogues and a cacophony of foreign tongues, and who had about as much trouble understanding his Texan accent as he had understanding theirs. As yet Boston had only a small African American population; black people who came to games at Huntington Avenue Grounds could sit wherever they could afford to, whereas in the cities where Speaker had played in Texas and the Southern League, they were forced to sit in separate sections—in what were usually the least desirable seats. The same segregated practice prevailed in two major-league cities, Washington and St. Louis.

John I. Taylor later said, "I believe my 1910 season was my biggest disappointment. I thought our young Speed Boys had arrived . . . but we just couldn't get anywhere."[16] The pitching staff was unreliable; Arellanes, the top winner in 1909, had a 4-7 record in August, when he was sold back to the Pacific Coast League. Various manifestations of ill feeling surfaced on the club. Team captain Harry Lord suffered an injury, then quarreled with Donovan when the manager wouldn't put him back in the lineup; in August, Taylor traded him and second-baseman Ambrose McConnell to Chicago for a run-of-the-mill infielder and an over-the-hill pitcher.

Then there was the cocky rookie outfielder up from Oakland of the Coast League. George "Duffy" Lewis arrived at Hot Springs wearing a velvet vest with diamond buttons. "They almost chased me out of training camp," Lewis recalled long afterward.[17] The native Californian was always known for his flashy clothes, and he joined the Red Sox with a decidedly un-rookie-like attitude. Lewis insisted on taking his batting-practice swings with the regulars, whereas when Speaker first came up, he and other rookies had to go to the outfield and pitch and hit to each other. Lewis also irked his manager by frequenting the local saloons and spending too much time at the racetrack. Donovan fined him and kept him on the bench when the season opened.

As Harry Hooper's biographer puts it, "His attitude particularly put Lewis on a collision course with Speaker and initiated ill feeling between them that lasted throughout their careers."[18] Lewis soon became part of a clique on the team that included catcher Bill Carrigan and shortstop Henry "Heinie" Wagner, who, like Lewis, were Roman Catholics and liked to drink and go to burlesque shows. Even if only nominally Protestant, Speaker, Joe Wood, thirdbaseman Larry Gardner, and the team's other non-Catholics had inherited a long tradition of distrust if not outright hostility toward the Church of Rome and its communicants. Speaker, Wood, and Gardner either had already joined or soon would join the Masonic Order, and they didn't go in much for the nightlife. Neither did Harry Hooper. Although he had been raised a Catholic and was a graduate of a Catholic college, Hooper had also become Gardner's close friend. Eventually Hooper, Gardner, Wood, and Speaker became a tightly knit quartet.

In the midst of baseball's general prosperity, the major-league owners had steadily increased roster limits. By 1910 teams could keep as many as twenty-five players between May 1, the spring cut-down date, and September 1, when additional players could be brought up from the minors. Although bigger rosters now included eight or nine pitchers (as opposed to five or six at the beginning of the century), those designated as starters were still expected to complete as many games as possible. Thus, on April 14, 1910, when the Red Sox opened the season before an overflow crowd at Hilltop Park, next to the Hudson River on upper Manhattan Island, the Yankees' Jim "Hippo" Vaughn, a big lefthander, went all the way in a fourteen-inning 4-4 tie, called at 6:15 (after 2:45 minutes of play) because of darkness. Cicotte and Wood pitched for Boston; Speaker had two hits in six times up and, in the eighth inning, caught up with Hal Chase's long drive to keep the game tied. Nine days later—in an eleven-inning, 5-3 loss to Philadelphia, with Eddie Plank outlasting Cicotte—Speaker made an unassisted double play, his second since coming to the majors.

The Red Sox's home opener was the annual Patriots' Day doubleheader, a morning-afternoon sweep of Washington before a combined attendance of some 45,000. Despite John I.'s subsequent lament, they actually played good baseball for most of that season. Late in May, after Taylor sold Harry Niles to Cleveland, Donovan finally put Duffy Lewis in the lineup to stay, installing him in leftfield to complete one of baseball's most celebrated outfields. Speaker, Hooper (who batted left but threw righthanded), and Lewis (righthanded all the way) liked to show off their arms in pregame practice, competing to see who could hit a cap placed off to the side of home plate. (But Hooper, with eighteen, and Lewis, with seventeen, also led American League rightfielders and leftfielders in errors.) The threesome never became close off the field, but they soon became, in Tim Murnane's phrase, "one of the smoothest [outfields] ever seen in baseball."[19]

On July 18, Boston swept a doubleheader at Cleveland, where in the off-season League Park's grandstand had been rebuilt in steel and concrete and double-decked. Speaker made six hits, including two doubles and a triple, in nine times at bat, as the Red Sox improved their season's record to 59-38. They held a solid second place, five and a half games behind Philadelphia. But then they lost all four games in Chicago, with the White Sox's Ed Walsh shutting them out and striking out fifteen on August 11. They continued to stumble in St. Louis, and by the time they returned home, they were eleven games in back of the Athletics.

While Connie Mack's splendid team continued to win, the Red Sox continued to slump. At the end they were in fourth place at 81-72, sixteen games behind Philadelphia. New York finished second; Detroit (whose fans didn't see another pennant for twenty-four years) finished third. The Athletics won 102 games, a new American League record, and had a fourteen-and-a-half-game margin over New York. The Yankees ended up with Hal Chase as their manager, Chase's systematic undermining having gotten George Stallings fired with two weeks left in the season.

But if 1910 was an all-around disappointment for John I. Taylor and Red Sox fans—of whom about 80,000 fewer came to the ballpark—it was anything but disappointing for Speaker. Assorted minor injuries occasionally kept him out of the lineup, but in 141 games he batted .340, third-best in the league behind Cleveland's Napoleon Lajoie and Ty Cobb. (In an effort to deny the batting title to the generally unpopular Cobb, the Browns had conceded seven bunt hits to Lajoie in a season-ending doubleheader, so that the well-liked "Frenchman" ended the day with eight hits for nine times at bat and presumably with the title. Outraged by such shamming and possessing authority no National League president ever had, Ban Johnson ignored the numbers and certified Cobb's fourth straight title.) Speaker also hit 7 homers and batted in 67 runs, while recording a league's-best 337 putouts, although his assists dropped to 20 and he erred six more times than in 1909.

During the 1910 season Speaker made a friendship that lasted the rest of his life. A teenager named Max "Lefty" Weisman, who came from a big Jewish family with an invalid father, rattled around and broke an occasional milk bottle while he delivered newspapers to Putnam's Place, prompting an awakened Speaker first to berate, then to befriend, and finally to assist the boy financially. Thereby Speaker acquired an acolyte. Twelve years later, as manager at Cleveland, he hired Weisman as team trainer.

Speaker's baseball-playing didn't end with the close of the American League season. Because the 1910 National League schedule extended a week longer, Johnson's office arranged a practice series between the Athletics and a team of picked American Leaguers, including Speaker, Cobb, and Washington's Walter Johnson, managed by Jimmy McAleer. Nobody took the games seriously. After dropping four of five to the "All Stars," the Athletics went on to dispatch the Chicago Cubs, winners of four of the last five National League titles, in only five games.

After that, still more baseball was planned. George "Tex" Rickard, fresh from promoting the racially charged and roundly condemned Jack Johnson–Jim Jeffries heavyweight championship fight, reportedly had recruited Speaker, Cobb, Lajoie, Christy Mathewson, and various others for a National League–American League All-Star tour. Under protests from *Sporting Life* and other voices that Rickard's involvement would sully baseball, Daniel Fletcher, a Toledo promoter, took over the project. Baseball's ruling National Commission publicly opposed the tour, which fell apart when Fletcher's financial backers deserted him. While Fletcher fled from his creditors, the National Commission ordered players who had received advances to return the money to whoever had put it up. Supposedly, about $5,000 was never returned, including $1,000 each paid to Cobb and Mathewson and $500 each to Speaker and various others.[20]

Whether or not Speaker kept $500 he was supposed to give back, by the fall of 1910 he could indulge himself with purchases that were beyond the reach of nearly all of his fellow citizens. In August the *Sporting News* described him as "an auto maniac," adding, "Experts fear that he is spoiling his batting eye riding recklessly over the country roads and city paving blocks." Presumably he was doing his daredevil driving in a rented or borrowed vehicle, because it wasn't until after the All-Stars–Athletics series that the baseball weekly was able to report Speaker had bought his own automobile, which would be the only one in Hubbard City. Bostonians gathered on downtown streets to witness Speaker's departure for Texas in his Velie, an open-air, two-seat roadster (which, like other early American automobiles, had the steering column mounted on the right side). When Speaker drove up to the steps of Boston's city hall, he was greeted by Mayor John F. "Honey Fitz" Fitzgerald, who threw a baseball Speaker caught. The grandfather of a future president of the United States then bounded down the steps to shake the ballplayer's hand and wish him well on his journey. Also in the vehicle were Walter P. Brown, an East Boston friend, plus Speaker's Irish setter, a shotgun, and camping gear. "Way across the continent has the wonderful ball player gone in his machine," the *Sporting News* proclaimed.[21]

What Speaker undertook was so extraordinary Tim Murnane felt obliged to report his progress Texasward. Early in November, when Speaker reached Chicago, Murnane wrote that now he "will dash merrily through the mud of a wild and wierd [*sic*] country with his trusty rifle [*sic*] and jack knife." Speaker had put Hubbard City on the map, Murnane went on, just as earlier Cy Young had done for the village of Paoli, Ohio. Two weeks later, more than a month after he left Boston and after many stops and detours, a tired and dirty Speaker drove into his hometown.

Apparently happy with his 1911 contract, Speaker had signed and mailed it in by December. Joe Wood, who had posted a 12-13 record the previous season (though allowing only 1.68 earned runs per nine innings), wasn't at all happy with John I. Taylor's insistence that he take a pay cut. But having just moved his father, mother, and little sister from Ness City, Kansas, to a farm he had bought near Parker's Glen, Pennsylvania, the young pitcher eventually wrote John I. that he would take what had been offered.

What Joe Wood faced in dealing with Taylor was the common lot of all ballplayers in the long history of the inviolate reserve clause. Washington's Walter Johnson, coming off a season in which he had won twenty-five games for a seventh-place team, complained bitterly in *Baseball Magazine* about "baseball slavery"—in his case, owner Thomas Noyes's hold over him. Denied the $7,500 he thought he was worth, Johnson described his situation as "simply the direct application of the great intelligent American business principle of dog eat dog.... Our business philosophy is that of the wolf pack."[22]

John I. Taylor wintered at Redondo Beach, California, so he decided that in 1911 his ball club would hold its spring training there. The plan was for the Red Sox to put in a couple of weeks of conditioning and practice, then split into two squads, one starting east by way of Sacramento and a northern route, the other playing exhibitions in Oakland and Los Angeles before crossing the country by a southern route. Besides the fact that the Red Sox's stay in California was plagued by almost daily rains, the trip out and back involved about 8,500 miles of travel and cost John I. an estimated $20,000. Patsy Donovan acknowledged that the whole business was enjoyable for neither rookies nor regulars.

Garland "Jake" Stahl, a former University of Illinois star athlete and a veteran firstbaseman who had also managed Washington in 1905 and 1906, had been one of the Boston team's stalwarts for the past three years. In 1910 he had led the American League in home runs with ten, then announced his retirement to become a bank executive in a Chicago suburb. After a couple of others were tried at firstbase and found wanting, Clyde Engle, a portly utility player, had to take over the position.

Stahl's retirement was one reason the Cincinnati baseball pundit Bill Phelon, who made annual predictions for *Baseball Magazine,* picked the Red Sox to do no better than sixth place. They did better than that, but not by much. Winning three fewer games and losing three more than in 1910, they barely beat out Chicago and New York for fourth place and lost another 80,000 paying customers. After the first month or so they were never really in the pennant race, but it wasn't much of a race. Still getting superb pitching from Eddie Plank, Chief Bender, and Jack Coombs (who followed his thirty-one wins in 1910 with twenty-eight in 1911) and boasting the "$100,000 infield" of John "Stuffy" McInnis, Eddie Collins, Jack Barry, and Frank Baker, the Athletics pulled away from everybody early. They won 101 games and finished thirteen and a half in front of Detroit.

Joe Wood left in the sixth inning of the chilly season opener in Washington, after his teammates had made five errors in what ended as an 8-5 loss to the locals. William "Dolly" Gray, a slender lefthander who won only one more major-league game before dropping to the minors, pitched for Washington, because Walter Johnson, who had been a stubborn holdout, had just joined his team. (Unhappy as he may have been with his contract, Johnson still put together another twenty-five-win season for another seventh-place outfit.) President William Howard Taft, who on a whim had tossed out the first ball a year earlier, happily did it again, thereby establishing an opening-day tradition in the nation's capital. A record crowd of 16,340 was on hand at the Georgia Avenue ballpark, whose new steel-and-concrete grandstand wasn't yet completed.

Wood often got erratic support that season, but at the age of twenty-one, he came into his own as a big-league pitcher. Allowing slightly more than two runs per nine innings, he won twenty-three times while losing seventeen and struck out 231 batters, second only to Ed Walsh's 255. On July 27, aided by Speaker's home run, he pitched a 5-0 no-hit game against the St. Louis Browns. At 5' 11" and 180 pounds, Wood wasn't especially big for a pitcher, but he threw a fastball that won him comparisons to Walter Johnson, generally thought to be the fastest pitcher ever.

On May 12, Speaker suffered the worst injury in his career to date when he badly sprained his ankle sliding back into firstbase in a 13-11, ten-inning loss to Detroit. On crutches, he took a train to Texas to heal and missed eight games. Hobbling, he returned to the lineup after two weeks, then, at Cleveland, tried to stretch a triple into a home run, collided with the catcher, and had to be carried from the field. The next day he was back in the lineup, although he narrowly missed even worse injury on August 28, when, in a 5-0, no-hit loss to Ed Walsh at Chicago, he collided with substitute outfielder Olaf Henriksen and was momentarily stunned.

On July 24, Wood and Speaker were part of a group of American Leaguers selected to meet the Cleveland Naps in a benefit game for the wife and children of Adrian "Addie" Joss, who had died of meningitis at the start of the season. Joss, a tall, lean righthander, had been the ace of the Cleveland staff for nine years and a popular player with fans in all of the league's cities. Paying their own travel expenses to Cleveland, the players who met the Naps constituted what was regarded at the time as the finest collection of talent ever assembled on one team. Besides Wood and Speaker, it included Ty Cobb and Sam Crawford of Detroit; Walter Johnson and Clyde Milan of Washington; Hal Chase and Russell Ford of New York; Frank Baker and Eddie Collins of Philadelphia; Bobby Wallace of St. Louis; and, to fill out the roster, lesser lights Herman "Germany" Schaefer and Charles "Gabby" Street of Washington and Philadelphia's Patrick "Paddy" Livingston. That the "All-Stars" won the game 5-3, with Wood, Johnson, and Ford dividing the pitching, was incidental to the fact that the crowd of 15,270 at League Park produced a purse of $12,914 for Joss's family.

A month earlier, Speaker had been part of another unique situation, although in that case it was a matter of confusion and embarrassment. In an effort to speed up games in his league, Ban Johnson had decreed that pitchers would no longer be allowed a few warmup tosses when they retook the mound to start a new half-inning. On June 27, in a game with the Athletics at Huntington Avenue Grounds, Boston's Ed Karger decided he would throw a couple anyhow. With Speaker pausing to exchange greetings with Eddie Collins before resuming his position, Stuffy McInnis jumped into the batter's box and whacked Karger's intended warmup throw into the untended centerfield, where it rolled all the way to the far-distant fence. Speaker could do nothing but watch as McInnis circled the bases for what the umpires, after considerable wrangling by Patsy Donovan and other Red Sox, ruled a home run.

McInnis's freak homer was one of 515 homers hit in the major leagues in 1911, which represented an increase of more than 40 percent over 1910. Although the aggregate batting average in the National League increased by only four points (.256 to .260), American Leaguers batted thirty points higher (.243 to .273) and scored some 800 more runs. The Athletics had five .300-plus regulars, headed by Eddie Collins at .365, and batted .296 as a team, the highest mark so far in the American League and the highest since the 1899 National League season. Cleveland's Joe Jackson, in his first full season, batted .408 but couldn't match Ty Cobb, who registered a career high .420, as well as career highs in hits, runs, doubles, triples, and runs batted in.

A month into the season, much was being made of the upsurge in hitting. On May 11, in the eight big-league games, 126 runs were scored on 177 hits. That day the Chicago White Sox ran up twenty runs on Washington; in the National League, the Philadelphia Phillies scored nineteen versus Cincinnati. More runs made for more pitching changes, which irked umpire Francis "Silk" O'Loughlin. "Too many pitchers kill the game," protested O'Loughlin. "Make every pitcher stand on his own record and finish when physically able."[23]

Baseball Magazine editorialized, "Undoubtedly the ball is more active."[24] Indeed it seemed to be. From the time baseballs were mass-produced in the 1870s, the design hadn't changed: a hard rubber center, wrapped in two layers of woolen yarn, which in turn were enclosed in a stitched horsehide cover. Over the previous eight years or so, the trend had been for pitching to get stronger, batting weaker. Then, late in the 1910 season, A. G. Spalding and Brothers, manufacturers of baseballs for both major leagues (though under different labels), had introduced a new design with a cork center inside the hard rubber, resulting in an offensive spike in 1911 that would carry over into the next season.

(Yet balls still remained in play inning after inning, even if scuffed, discolored, and softened, and pitchers continued to be able to doctor balls in various ways. Over time pitchers would regain the advantage and keep it until an even bigger batting boom got underway at the beginning of the 1920s.)

More hitting during the 1911 season and the next meant more scoring and longer game times. Frank Navin, president of the Detroit franchise, voiced a common complaint about that. "There can be no doubt," Navin said after the season, "of the desirability of doing something to shorten the games played in American League parks. Last summer the average playing period in Detroit was close to two hours for an ordinary nine-inning game, which is altogether too long for the comfort and convenience of the fans."[25]

In 141 games, Speaker batted only .334—six points below what he had done in 1910—although he batted in eighty runs, his most so far. Meanwhile, Cobb, Jackson, Collins, Sam Crawford, and Frank Baker (who led the league with eleven homers), as well as lesser figures such as Jim Delahanty of Detroit, Matty McIntyre of Chicago, and William "Birdie" Cree of New York, either had their best years up to then or their best ever.

For most of the season, John I. Taylor was as involved and often as intrusive in team affairs as ever, suspending Eddie Cicotte in June for not running out ground balls and spatting with his manager over various matters. But as the Red Sox continued to lose almost as often as they won, he increasingly gave his attention to planning for a new ballpark in an area called The Fens, about a mile from Huntington Avenue Grounds. Though wealthier than most of his baseball peers, John I. needed additional money for the project; so in mid-September, for $148,000, he sold his father's half-interest in the franchise to Jimmy McAleer, Washington's manager, and Robert McRoy, secretary to Ban Johnson in the American League office in Chicago.

Although McAleer was to be released from the remaining year of his two-year contract, Johnson had no qualms about having him continue in his position at Washington for the rest of the season. In fact Johnson was the central figure in the deal. McAleer and McRoy could raise only $60,000 and $20,000, respectively, so Johnson arranged loans for the remainder of the purchase price on notes covered by two other American League owners, Charles Comiskey of Chicago and Charles Somers of Cleveland. Things could be done that way in Ban Johnson's league.

Speaker again made the long automobile trip back to Hubbard City, passing up another tune-up series with the Athletics while the National League finished its schedule, with McGraw's Giants as the pennant-winners (and World Series losers to Philadelphia in six games). After he got home, Speaker went to San Antonio to attend the annual convention of the National Association, the governing body for the minor leagues, and play in a charity game. Meanwhile the baseball talk in Boston was about the new ballpark under construction; the dismissal of Patsy Donovan by McAleer, who had assumed the presidency of the franchise; and McAleer's successful wooing of Jake Stahl out of retirement to become the Red Sox's player-manager. Stahl also acquired 10 percent of franchise stock.

If the 1911 season had been another disappointment, things were definitely looking up for Boston's American League fandom. The Red Sox would start the next season with a new ballpark, a new manager, and a franchise president who was a "real" baseball man. A onetime star centerfielder (whom some rated the best before Speaker), McAleer had already managed three American League teams. Ahead was a season that turned out to be one of the most memorable in the history of Boston baseball.

"Well, There Goes Your World Series"

I n the off-season of 1911–1912, it seemed matters might even be improving for the Red Sox's National League counterparts, downtrodden since 1901, when most of their top players deserted to the upstart American Leaguers. Over the winter James Gaffney, a prominent figure in New York City politics, and John Montgomery Ward, once a star ballplayer and now a successful attorney, purchased the Boston National League franchise from the heirs of the recently deceased William Russell. They chose the nickname Braves for the team once known, in its glory days in the 1890s, as Beaneaters and in recent years as Doves and then Rustlers. It was more than three years, however, before the Braves could move out of their rickety little South End Grounds and into a modern structure of their own.

Meanwhile, despite the bitter cold and heavy snows of the New England winter, work went forward on the ballpark envisioned by John I. Taylor. Having been relegated to the vice presidency of the Red Sox franchise, John I. was never to be the powerful presence in Boston baseball affairs he had been for the past seven years. But he would leave a legacy for the city and all big-league baseball in the form of what he (or somebody) decided to call Fenway Park.

The site for the new ballpark was already owned by the Fenway Realty Company, in which John I. and his father held a majority interest. It was an undeveloped ten-block section, with a residential area to the south and a second-class hotel district to the north. Erected at a cost of about $350,000, Fenway Park was still under construction as the Red Sox went to spring training. Bounded by Lansdowne, Jersey, Van Ness, and Ipswich Streets, it could seat about 27,000 people in its original configuration. Fans were accommodated in a single-deck grandstand extending from firstbase around to third, covered pavilions down the foul lines, and a large bleacher section in rightfield. As with the other new ballparks, only Fenway's grandstand was constructed in concrete and steel. That turned out to be advantageous; under subsequent improvement projects, the wooden stands could be easily dismantled and rebuilt in the durable materials of the grandstand.

With the exception of symmetrical Comiskey Park in Chicago, opened two years earlier, Fenway Park was like the other ballparks of the day (old and new), in that its dimensions had to be fitted into the asymmetrical shape of a particular building lot. The original outfield distances were 324 feet down the leftfield line, 388 feet to the flagpole in deep left-center, 488 feet to a corner just to the right of dead center, and 313.5 feet to the rightfield corner, where the fence angled out sharply to 405 feet in right-centerfield. The leftfield fence wasn't the "Green Monster" of later renown. Originally 25 feet high, it was extended by 13 feet in 1934, and it wasn't until 1947 that its advertisements were painted over in green. Running along the bottom of the fence was a slope intended as a vantage point for overflow standees. Duffy Lewis became so adept at dashing up the slope to catch fly balls that Boston fans named it "Duffy's cliff."

Fenway Park's plain-brick exterior was undistinguished in contrast to the ornate façades of Shibe Park, Forbes Field, Comiskey Park, and Brooklyn's Ebbets Field (which opened in 1913). But it had features designed to enhance customer convenience and comfort. Its eighteen turnstiles were second in number only to those at the new Polo Grounds in New York. In place of the steep stairways of older parks, Fenway had winding ramps, and in place of the one entrance at Huntington Avenue Grounds, it had separate entrances for the grandstand, bleachers, and pavilions.

Work on Fenway Park continued as the Red Sox assembled for spring training. After the costly and wearying experiment of training in California the previous year, Jimmy McAleer decided that the team would return to Hot Springs. Although earlier Tim Murnane had been skeptical about Hot Springs's mineral waters, now he hailed the town as "the best place in the country to train ball players."[1] But for much of the time at Hot Springs, it rained so often that the Red Sox and the Philadelphia Phillies, also training at Hot Springs, could do little but hike over the hills and take the waters. Twenty-nine Boston players were on hand, plus five Boston writers and a dozen or so representatives of the "Royal Rooters," an organization of several hundred do-or-die fans, mostly Irish-Americans. Originally followers of the Boston National Leaguers, the Royal Rooters had shifted allegiance when the new American League outfit won back-to-back pennants.

Speaker wasn't present with the others at the beginning of practice at Hot Springs, didn't show up for another couple of weeks, and, when he did arrive, hung around the ball field for several days more before signing his contract. Obviously he wasn't happy with what McAleer had offered him. Baseball executives then were fully as attuned to a player's statistical performance as they became in later times. The difference was that they had fewer statistics to look at. Runs batted in, for example, of which Speaker had more in 1911 than in 1910, didn't become an official statistical category until the 1920s. His batting average, the most commonly cited measure of an everyday player's performance, had dropped a few points, and his stolen bases and assists had dropped even more. *Baseball Magazine* commented that "Speaker's record for the past season was not so conspicuously brilliant as usual, his achievements being fully equaled by those of his capable associate in the outfield, Harry Hooper."[2] Less inclined toward generosity than John I. Taylor, McAleer probably offered Speaker a few hundred dollars' increase over 1911. Speaker may have coaxed a little more from the new club president, but his 1912 contract, which he finally signed on March 19, left him a long way from Ty Cobb's $9,000, the top salary in the American League.

The Red Sox managed to get in a few games with the Phillies, which gave Speaker his first look at Grover Cleveland Alexander, a twenty-four-year-old righthander who was coming off a remarkable twenty-eight victories in his rookie season. Following stopovers for games in Nashville and Dayton, the Red Sox played a two-game series in Cincinnati, where the Reds inaugurated their new ballpark, Redland Field. Back in Boston, Speaker and Joe Wood settled into a house they had rented in the little town of Winthrop (Winthrop Center, the railroad stop was called), located on a peninsula extending into Boston Harbor north of Boston. They could either take the rail line into the city or drive their automobiles directly to Fenway Park.

After the Red Sox showed off their own new ballpark to a few thousand chilled fans in an exhibition game with Harvard, they opened the season in New York, whose American League team—under new manager Harry Wolverton but with Hal Chase still a troublesome presence—was about to lose 102 games and finish dead last. The first of those 102 losses, witnessed by about 12,000 at Hilltop Park, was a 5-3 win for Wood, who was the beneficiary of Boston's four-run ninth-inning rally. Speaker was hitless in that game, but the next day he cracked an inside-the-park homer with Hooper on base, and Jake Stahl went four for four in a 5-2 victory for rookie righthander and Brockton native Thomas "Buck" O'Brien. The Red Sox completed a series sweep the next day, knocking out Jim Vaughn and giving "Sea Lion" Hall the victory in relief, 8-4. A couple of weeks earlier, McAleer had said he expected the Red Sox's "speed and slugging" to produce a pennant; so far it looked as if they just might.[3]

By now Speaker's teammates had taken to calling him "Spoke." The origins of the nickname—apart from the play on his last name—are obscure. The story goes that once, when Speaker made a key hit, Bill Carrigan or somebody announced, "Speaker has spoke." However the nickname came about, it remained a familiar form of address for the rest of Speaker's life.

Early in the morning of Monday, April 15, with the Red Sox back in Boston, the reputedly unsinkable ocean liner *Titanic* went down in the North Atlantic after hitting an iceberg, taking more than 1,500 passengers and crew to their deaths. Unlike some other executives, McAleer and associates didn't have to fret over whether they should cancel the next day's game out of respect for those lost on the great ship, because two off days and three days of rainouts followed. Tim Murnane estimated that the rainouts, including two games on Patriots' Day, cost the club $90,000 in admissions. Finally, on Saturday, April 20, 1912, the new ballpark was opened with a satisfying eleven-inning, 7-6 win over the increasingly inept Yankees. Speaker's over-the-shoulder catch saved a tie; his single brought in the winning run. The Red Sox took the field in new uniforms that, following the trend in baseball attire, dispensed with full collars in favor of short, military-like borders at the neck.

The bigger structure still couldn't hold everybody who wanted to attend; a couple of thousand people overflowed the outfield and stood behind restraining ropes. Soon thereafter, A. C. Mitchell, now *Sporting Life's* Boston correspondent, reported grumbling from local fans that the 25-cent rightfield bleachers and the 50-cent pavilions were too far away from the action. Bill Phelon saw that as a drawback for all the new ballparks. "With the building of the gigantic stands," complained Phelon, "has passed much of the fun, the comedy, the neighborly diversion of the long ago."[4]

Amid much ceremony and with Ban Johnson and a host of other dignitaries on hand, the formal dedication of Fenway Park took place on May 16. That was one day after Johnson had watched Ty Cobb leap into the stands in New York and beat up a hectoring spectator, thereby precipitating a national sensation and short-lived strike by Cobb's teammates to protest his suspension (which also turned out to be short-lived). Things were calmer at Fenway, where Chicago's Ed Walsh, who usually handled the Red Sox, beat them again, 5-2. At that point Boston's record was 16-10, well behind Jimmy Callahan's surprising White Sox, who had won twenty-three of their first twenty-nine games.

Within a month, though, the Red Sox had taken over first place. The White Sox were fading, the Athletics were struggling, and Washington had won seventeen consecutive games to climb into second place. The Red Sox began their first western swing by losing three of four games in Cleveland, the finale of which was a commemoration of Napoleon Lajoie's tenth anniversary with the Naps. Lajoie received a floral horseshoe studded with 1,609 silver dollars donated by local fans and $125 in gold from his teammates, then doubled and tripled in a 5-1 win. But Boston won two of three games from Detroit, swept four in St. Louis, and took three of four in Chicago, defeating Ed Walsh twice. By July 10, having recently run off eleven straight wins themselves, the Red Sox had a 52-24 record and led Washington by six and a half games. After they swept five games in New York and took four of six before huge crowds in Philadelphia, the pennant race was virtually over, although Walter Johnson continued to pitch heroically for a Washington team that was the year's biggest surprise.

Speaker was playing his best baseball so far. If he hadn't been a full participant in the offensive upsurge of the previous year, he was a big part of its continuation in 1912. For about the first third of the season he was the league's top hitter. By mid-July he was still batting .401, although by then the indefatigable Cobb had built his average to .415. Nonetheless, Billy Murray, former National League manager and now a scout for Pittsburgh, was ready to pronounce Speaker "the best player on the diamond today. As a hitter, fielder, thrower and base-runner he has Cobb and the others beaten. I've seen all the stars of 25 years and the Bean-eater is the king."[5]

About that time the *Boston Globe's* Robert Ripley (later the originator of the "Believe It or Not" syndicated newspaper feature) asked Speaker the secret of his batting ability. Although he came to be regarded as an authority on hitting, at that point he could only say, "I always could hit. Really, I couldn't tell you how I hit. I just hit 'em. That's all I know." Later that year Hugh S. Fullerton described Speaker's technique: ". . . jockeying back and forth in the batter's box, front and back and close to the plate and far away, and he can bunt besides all that."[6]

During August, Speaker batted at a two-hits-per-game pace and continued to excite spectators around the league with his exploits in the field. On August 4, for example, in an 8-4 victory in Cleveland, he singled, doubled, caught up with a line drive and threw to secondbase to double up the runner, and threw out another runner at home plate. Three weeks later, at Fenway Park, he tripled and homered off Eddie Cicotte, who had been claimed by the White Sox on waivers earlier in the summer. By that time the Red Sox, with an 82-37 record, held an eight-game lead over Washington.

The Boston team's roster was unusual in that it included four catchers, although Bill Carrigan and Forrest "Hick" Cady caught nearly all the time. Car-rigan, so hard-nosed his teammates called him simply "Rough," had finished two years at Holy Cross College and was considered a "college man," although manager Stahl (Illinois), Harry Hooper (St. Mary's), and Ray Collins and Larry Gardner (Vermont) were all degree-holders. Carrigan caught lefthander Col-lins and first-year righthanders Buck O'Brien and Hugh Bedient; Cady was Joe Wood's favorite catcher. The pairings worked: O'Brien and Bedient each won twenty games; Collins won thirteen; Charley Hall won fifteen, often as a reliever; and Wood enjoyed a spectacular season.

At the end of July, Wood already had twenty wins. Walter Johnson matched him win for win and on August 23 defeated Detroit, 8-1, for his sixteenth vic-tory in a row. Johnson's streak ended three days later in Washington, when he took a controversial 3-2 loss to St. Louis. Johnson relieved Tom Hughes in the seventh inning with one out and runners on first and second. After his wild pitch moved the runners up, he struck out Burt Shotton, but Pete Compton's single drove in both runners. When Washington remained runless the rest of the way, the official scorer, according to the rule then in place, recorded Johnson as the losing pitcher. Manager Clark Griffith wired the league office in protest, but Ban Johnson upheld the scorer's verdict. District of Columbia fans, Joe R. Jackson reported in the *Sporting News,* "frothed at the mouth."[7] (Coincidentally, the previous month, the streak of Giants lefthander Richard "Rube" Marquard, who had won his first nineteen games and twenty-six straight going back to 1911, was broken as a result of the same scoring rule.)

At New York on September 2, cheered on by some 250 Royal Rooters, the Red Sox swept a doubleheader, 2-1 and 1-0, behind Bedient and Wood. Wood's victory, won when Hooper scored on Speaker's sacrifice fly, was his thirtieth of the season and his fifteenth in a row. With a thirteen-game lead over Washington and Philadelphia, Boston had the pennant safely tucked away, but the most dramatic game of the regular season was just ahead.

The Red Sox returned home to host Washington and won the first two games of a four-game series. Looking for the biggest return possible from the visitors' share of the gate receipts, Washington manager Clark Griffith instructed the press, "Tell Wood that we'll consider him a coward if he doesn't pitch against Johnson." In turn McAleer, also eager for a big money-maker, instructed Stahl to move up Wood's pitching turn by one day, so that he could be matched with Johnson. "The newspapers publicized us like prizefighters," reminisced Wood a half-century later, "giving statistics comparing our height, weight, biceps, triceps, arm span, and whatnot. The Champion, Walter Johnson, versus the Challenger, Joe Wood."[8]

On Friday, September 6, the grandstand, pavilions, and bleachers filled up well before the 3:00 starting time; for 25 cents, thousands were allowed to stand not only on the leftfield incline and around the rest of the outfield, but from either side of home plate all the way down each foul line. Warming up in front of the Red Sox's firstbase dugout (as pitchers did back then), Wood was surrounded by well-dressed standees. People also crowded into both teams' dugouts, so that the players had to sit in chairs close to the foul lines.

Despite its bizarre environment, the game was the classic everybody had anticipated. Both pitchers held the opposition scoreless until the bottom of the sixth inning. Then, with two out, Johnson got two strikes on Speaker and tried to make him bite on a ball that was low and outside. Speaker reached out and sliced the ball down the leftfield line and into the crowd for a double. Duffy Lewis followed with a blooper down the rightfield line; Danny Moeller managed to get to it, but the ball ticked off his glove and rolled among the standing spectators as Speaker scored. That was the lone run of the afternoon. Wood allowed five hits and struck out eight; Johnson gave up six hits and fanned five.

The Red Sox won eighteen of twenty-two games on that home stand, then traveled west and clinched the pennant in Detroit, although the Tigers broke Wood's winning streak on September 20. Wood regained form five days later with a shutout of New York, the Red Sox's one hundredth win of the season. His final record was 34-5; Johnson's, 33-12. Wood pitched 35 complete games to Johnson's 33 and Ed Walsh's 32; he worked 344 innings to Johnson's 369 and the redoubtable Walsh's 393; he struck out 258 batters to Johnson's 303 and Walsh's 254; and, although earned run averages weren't yet officially recorded, Wood allowed 1.91 runs per nine innings to Johnson's 1.39 and Walsh's 2.15.

Boston ended up with 105 wins, a new American League record, and finished fourteen games ahead of Washington, which made the best showing up to then in the city's history. Philadelphia, heavily favored in the spring to take a third consecutive pennant, finished fifteen games out. Speaker, Larry Gardner, and Stahl (who played only about two-thirds of the time), were the team's only .300 hitters, but Lewis, usually batting fourth behind Speaker, batted in 109 runs with a .284 average. Speaker played in every one of his team's games, including one tie. After batting around .400 for most of the season, he tailed off over the final six weeks, finishing with a .383 average, third behind Cobb's .410 and Joe Jackson's .395. He scored 136 runs, one less than league-leader Eddie Collins; he made 222 hits to Cobb's 227 and Jackson's 226; he tied with Frank Baker for the home-run lead with 10; and he drove in 90 runs. The 1912 season also saw Speaker make two-base hits his particular specialty. His 53 doubles were nine more than Jackson's total and twelve more than what the Chicago Cubs' Henry "Heinie" Zimmerman hit in the other league.

Speaker also stole 52 bases, his career high. Yet he was caught stealing 28 times, including a game with the Yankees on June 22 in which he was thrown out 3 times. Cobb was caught 34 times; Washington's Clyde Milan, whose 88 steals led the majors, was unsuccessful on 31 tries. Besides the fact that base runners tried to steal more often in the pre-1920 period than they did later on, it may also be that because catchers assumed a shallower crouch and kept both hands in front of them, they could get off throws more quickly than catchers using the deep crouch and one-handed style in vogue much later in the century.

Speaker went after everything he thought he could reach, from balls hit right behind secondbase to those that soared to the far reaches of the arc from right-center to left-center. Sometimes he got his hands on balls that, with his little glove, he couldn't manage to hold. And despite his later reputation for inerrant throwing, sometimes he hurried his throws and missed his mark. In 1912, scorers assigned him 18 errors, but he also topped the league with 35 assists and 372 putouts.

Even though it had been Speaker's greatest season in any league, and he was making more money than he could have made in any other legitimate line of work, his mother remained unconvinced that he had made the right career choice. Interviewed in Boston in mid-August when she came up to visit her now-famous son, Jenny Speaker told reporters that since his father's death, "My boy has taken care of me. . . . He always was a smart boy." Again giving Speaker's age as "only 23," she said, "I want him—my boy and my man—to come home. He should have been a mechanic."[9]

Jenny Speaker was back in Texas by the time the Red Sox clinched the pennant. The Giants were repeat winners in the National League, their 103 victories outdistancing Pittsburgh by ten games. Although John McGraw had no everyday player of Speaker's stature, he had a well-balanced lineup and received superb pitching from the illustrious Christy Mathewson; from Charles "Jeff" Tesreau, a burly young righthander from the Missouri Ozarks; and from Rube Marquard, who led his league with twenty-six wins but had only a 7-10 record after his nineteen-game victory streak was broken in July.

In his annual syndicated column comparing World Series opponents position-by-position, Hugh S. Fullerton put Speaker "in the near-Cobb class as a player." Fullerton also described Speaker as "one of the most likeable of players, a steady grinner and cheery soul who cannot stay grouchy ten minutes under any circumstances," although "he came near it last season [1911]," when he sometimes "played careless and indifferent ball." But with Jake Stahl back and in charge of the team, "Speaker revived interest and went at it in earnest." To Bill Phelon, Speaker was "a whirlwind of power and well-directed fury," while Browns manager George Stovall thought that "Speaker does more work for the Boston Club than Cobb does for Detroit. Speaker plays for the good of the club, while Cobb plays for himself to a great extent."[10]

As had been the case since 1905, the format for the World Series was best four out of seven games. The teams were to alternate games in New York and Boston, with no break in the sequence except for Sunday, when baseball could be played in neither city. A passenger train made good time if it traveled between the two cities in six hours, but after one game, the teams and a car full of writers, delayed by a wreck on the track ahead, didn't get into Boston until two A.M., amid sleepy grumbling all around. Still, it would be one of the most memorable of all World Series.

It was also to be one of the most written-about by ballplayers, if one were naive enough to believe that they actually wrote the syndicated columns appearing under their names. Speaker, who was probably paid $500–$750, relied on Tim Murnane to produce his game-by-game rundowns. Other sportswriters did the job for other players: Jack O'Leary wrote for Wood, John E. Wheeler for Mathewson, and Stoney McLinn for Ty Cobb. All told, thirteen players as well as John McGraw were paid for the use of their names on columns purporting to give their close analyses of the Series.

The Boston team arrived in New York on Monday night, October 7, and put up at the Bretton Hall Hotel, Broadway and Eighty-sixth Street. About three hundred Royal Rooters with their band were already in town. With red ribbons on their top hats and derbies and red sashes across their chests, the Rooters paraded up and down midtown Manhattan streets singing "Tessie," their theme song. The next day the Red Sox players took taxis north to the Polo Grounds at Eighth Avenue and 157th Street for the Series opener.

Built on the same site as the wooden structure that had burned a year and a half earlier, the new Polo Grounds was the largest baseball facility in the world, seating some 36,000 in an ornately faced, double-decked grandstand of steel and concrete wedged against a rock formation called Coogan's Bluff, and in big wooden bleachers curving around the outfield. Shaped like a horseshoe (or bathtub), the Polo Grounds had particularly odd outfield dimensions. Down the lines it was only 257 feet in right and 277 in left, but the walls quickly veered out to more than 400 feet. As of 1912, dead-centerfield was 433 feet from home plate. The foul territory off first and third bases was huge.

On Tuesday, October 8, 1912, a paying crowd of 35,730 and several hundred dignitaries with passes filled the Polo Grounds, as the Giants took the field in new violet-trimmed, pin-striped uniforms. Among the nonpaying spectators was Albert G. Spalding—retired sporting goods tycoon, onetime star pitcher, and former National League club owner—who came all the way from his estate in southern California. Before that game and the others played in New York, Giants president John T. Brush, suffering from a degenerative disease that killed him within a month, was driven in his automobile through the centerfield gate to a place just outside the rightfield foul line. There he watched the action with a board positioned across the lower front of the auto to keep baseballs from rolling underneath. Across the field, in seats reserved for them behind the thirdbase visitors' dugout, the Royal Rooters kept singing "Tessie," to the increasing annoyance of the New Yorkers.

What Brush, the Rooters, and the capacity crowd watched was a tough, taut ball game. Wood, of course, was Stahl's choice to start the Series; McGraw held back Mathewson and Marquard and sent first-year man Tesreau to the mound. With New York ahead 2-1 in the fifth inning, Speaker tripled to deep left-center and scored on Lewis's groundout to tie it. Shortstop Heinie Wagner singled in two more runs in the seventh, and although the Giants got another run in the ninth, Wood ended the game with his tenth and eleventh strikeouts.

The next day, at Fenway Park, with 30,148 fans filling the regular stands and temporary bleachers erected in front of the leftfield wall, Mathewson and Ray Collins started the game. Neither had his best stuff that day. Boston scored three runs in the first inning when Speaker beat out a bunt to load the bases, second-baseman Steve Yerkes scored on a fielder's choice, and Stahl's single brought in

Speaker and Duffy Lewis. In the sixth inning, with the score 3-2, Hooper singled, gained secondbase when Giants shortstop Art Fletcher dropped the catcher's throw, and scored on Yerkes's triple to deep centerfield. But the Giants came back with three runs in the eighth, initiated by Lewis's muff of centerfielder Fred Snodgrass's fly. After secondbaseman Larry Doyle singled, Snodgrass scored on leftfielder Jack "Red" Murray's ground-rule double into the temporary bleachers in leftfield. At that point Stahl replaced Collins with Charley Hall, who gave up another ground-rule double to thirdbaseman Charles "Buck" Herzog, making the score 5-3.

In the eighth inning, Lewis drove in a run when he sent Murray back to the fence in front of the leftfield seats; Murray fell in among the spectators, was momentarily stunned, lost his cap to a spectator, but couldn't catch Lewis's drive, which went for another ground-rule double. Larry Gardner hit a ball that went through Fletcher's legs, Lewis came home, and the score was 5-5. The Giants went ahead again in the ninth on firstbaseman Fred Merkle's triple and a sacrifice fly, but in the bottom of the inning, Speaker tripled to deep centerfield, hesitated when the relay throw was fumbled, struggled to get around Herzog, who was trying to block him at thirdbase, and scored to tie the game when the ball got away from catcher Art Wilson. Speaker twisted his ankle on the slide, but that didn't keep him from going after Herzog. "A wild cat when started," in Tim Murnane's description, he intended to commit mayhem on the Giants' thirdbaseman, but Doyle and Heinie Wagner got between them.[11] Hugh Bedient retired the Giants in order in the top of the tenth. Mathewson needed only three pitches to do the same to the Red Sox. At that point the umpires decided it was too dark to continue.

As might have been expected, the tie created confusion. The National Commission—which consisted of Ban Johnson; Thomas Lynch, his National League counterpart; and August "Garry" Herrmann, president of the Cincinnati club and Commission chairman—announced that the teams would remain in Boston for the third game and, over the protests of a delegation of Red Sox and Giants, ruled that the tie would count for purposes of figuring the players' share, based on receipts from the first four games. Thousands of fans showed up on Thursday assuming that because they had paid to see the tie, they ought to be admitted free. When told otherwise, many of them became unruly, whereupon nightstick-wielding police moved in to restore order.

Somehow, 34,624 people jammed into Fenway Park for the third game of the Series. In pregame ceremonies, Hugh Chalmers, president of the automobile company that bore his name, presented Speaker with a big Chalmers "30" automobile for being the most valuable player in the American League. Speaker drove his new vehicle onto the field, with the Giants' Larry Doyle, who had also been honored with a Chalmers at the Polo Grounds, as his passenger.

Then Rube Marquard took the mound and pitched a gem, holding the Red Sox scoreless for eight innings. Buck O'Brien started for Boston and pitched well, although he yielded two runs before Bedient relieved him to start the ninth. The Red Sox finally made a run in their last chance at bat. After Speaker, playing with a sore ankle, popped out to Fletcher, Lewis reached on an infield hit. Gardner lined the ball inside the firstbase line, and although Stahl had Wagner coaching at thirdbase, a fired-up Speaker dashed out of the dugout to help him. Wagner gave Lewis the hold-up sign, but as Merkle fumbled the relay from rightfield, Speaker waved Lewis home to make the score 2-1, New York. Gardner was forced at second when Stahl hit back to Marquard; Stahl then made it all the way to third when Fletcher threw wide to first on Wagner's grounder. Wagner stole second without drawing a throw, putting the tying and winning runs in scoring position. Hick Cady then hit a long drive into right-centerfield that 5'6" Josh Devore barely reached, ending the game.

A fog had moved in from Boston Harbor, so that many of those in the grandstand and pavilions couldn't make out Devore; what they saw was Stahl and Wagner crossing the plate. A short while later, at the Copley Square Hotel, Fred Lieb encountered a joyous Boston fan who was convinced the Red Sox had won. At first incredulous, he became downright belligerent when Lieb repeated that Devore had caught the ball.

The fourth game, in New York, was another Wood-Tesreau matchup. Smokey Joe gave up nine hits but struck out eight and allowed only one run. The Red Sox got to Tesreau for single runs in the second and fourth innings and to Leon "Red" Ames for another run in the ninth, driven in by Wood himself. The Giants' run came in the seventh inning on the troublesome Herzog's single and Fletcher's double. When Fletcher tried to score on a hit off Yerkes's glove by pinch hitter Harry "Moose" McCormick, he banged into Cady at home plate. While those two squared off, Speaker ran in from centerfield to wrangle with McGraw. Various players joined Charles "Cy" Rigler, the three-hundred-pound home-plate umpire, in calming things down.

Another capacity-plus throng was at Fenway Park on Columbus Day, Saturday, October 12. Hugh Bedient pitched the finest game of his big-league career, holding the Giants to three hits and one run and defeating Mathewson, 2-1. The rookie pitcher got all the runs he needed in the third inning on back-to-back triples by Hooper and Yerkes and Doyle's error on Speaker's hot grounder. New York's run came in the seventh when Merkle hit into the temporary leftfield seats for a double and later scored when Gardner let McCormick's grounder go through his legs.

On the obligatory Sunday off day, the ebullient Red Sox, confident the Series was all but won, followed the Giants back to New York. If John I. Taylor no longer had much to do with club affairs, Jimmy McAleer was just as likely to interfere with his manager's judgment as Taylor had been. On Sunday night, McAleer went to Stahl's room at the Bretton Hall and told him that instead of starting Wood the next day, as Stahl intended to do, he should hold back his ace and pitch Buck O'Brien. Stahl finally gave in to the demands of the franchise president, although the news didn't please most of the Red Sox, especially Wood and his pal Speaker.

The Polo Grounds crowd was about 6,000 smaller than for the previous two games in New York. As they arrived, many people buzzed with the news that earlier that day, in Milwaukee, Theodore Roosevelt, seeking to regain the presidency as the candidate of the Progressive Party, had been shot by a would-be assassin, although the wound hadn't been bad enough to keep the gutsy "T. R." from going ahead with his scheduled speech.

Having pitched superbly in one outing, Buck O'Brien couldn't do it again. The Giants jumped on him in the first inning, beginning with his balk that brought Doyle in from thirdbase. Doubles by Herzog and Merkle and a triple by catcher John "Chief" Meyers scored four more runs before Stahl waved in Ray Collins. The Giants' Marquard allowed two runs in the second inning on pinch hitter Clyde Engle's double that scored Gardner and Stahl, then shut down the Red Sox the rest of the way.

Paul Wood, Smokey Joe's brother, had come from Kansas City for the Series and had been traveling back and forth with the Boston team. Expecting to pitch that day, Joe Wood had advised his brother to put some money on the Red Sox. In the Polo Grounds visitors' clubhouse following the loss, the Boston players groused about McAleer's interference; Joe Wood personally berated O'Brien, especially for his first-inning balk. On the train back to Boston, O'Brien and Paul Wood, who had lost $100 on the game, exchanged punches, with the pitcher's brother supposedly getting the worst of it.

There was no question that Joe Wood would pitch the next day in Boston. But before he could face leadoff batter Josh Devore, he had to wait on the mound, "chilled and miserable," as Bill Phelon put it, as a near riot by the Royal Rooters went on.[12] It all resulted from a mistake in the handling of ticket sales by club secretary Robert McRoy, who put the section in the leftfield stands reserved for the Rooters on sale to the general public the day of the game. The Rooters, led by their band, marched onto the field as usual and headed for their usual seats, only to find the section already filled. Cursing and shaking fists, they refused to leave the field, but instead paraded back and forth for close to half an hour. Mounted police finally rode in and pushed the Rooters into the leftfield corner and, in many cases, completely out of the park.

Wood didn't retire a batter. He threw only thirteen pitches before yielding the mound to Charley Hall with the Giants ahead by six runs. Hall pitched until the ninth inning, when he was relieved by Bedient, having given up five more runs, including a two-run homer by Doyle on a hit that bounced into the right-field bleachers. (Balls that bounced into regular outfield stands—such as those in rightfield at Fenway Park—had always been home runs and continued to be until 1931. Balls bouncing into temporary stands—such as those installed in front of the leftfield fence at Fenway for the Series—were ground-rule doubles.) Tesreau allowed nine hits but coasted to an 11-4 win that tied the Series. The only pleasant memory Red Sox fans took from that drearily cold afternoon was Speaker's unassisted double play in the ninth inning, the third of his career. Art Wilson singled and proceeded to secondbase when Speaker threw wildly behind him as he rounded first. Then Speaker ran in to grab Fletcher's short fly and kept running to beat the slow-footed Wilson back to the base.

New York's victory created a unique situation that was resolved by a coin toss in Garry Herrmann's hotel room. McAleer called it right, so the Series remained in Boston for the eighth game on Wednesday, October 16. The four previous games at Fenway Park had been sellouts, but only 17,034, occupying a little more than half the available seats, showed up for the decisive contest. The Royal Rooters, furious with McAleer and McRoy, boycotted the event, while thousands of others, dismayed by Wood's debacle, pessimistically stayed away. Yet if fewer people were there to see it, the game was to be the one Speaker remembered as "my greatest day in baseball."[13]

As McGraw had done so many times before in critical games, he gave the ball to Mathewson. Although Wood had hardly pitched at all the day before, Stahl named Bedient to start. The rookie acquitted himself well for seven innings, giving up only a single run in the third inning on Murray's double that sent Devore home. In the sixth inning, Harry Hooper kept the Giants from scoring again when he made a leaping, twisting, one-handed catch at the low fence enclosing the rightfield bleachers and fell in among the spectators. The umpires signaled Doyle out, despite McGraw's protests that Hooper hadn't been on the playing field when he made the catch.

The Red Sox tied the game in the seventh inning. With one out, Stahl's soft fly fell between Fletcher and all three New York outfielders. Mathewson walked Wagner, and after Cady had popped out to Fletcher, Stahl sent up Olaf Henriksen to bat for Bedient. Batting lefthanded, the little-used outfielder took two strikes, then hit Mathewson's next pitch off the thirdbase bag for a double that scored Stahl. Centerfielder Fred Snodgrass caught Hooper's fly to end the inning.

Joe Wood came on to try to keep it tied, which he did until the top of the tenth inning, when, with one out, Murray lifted a ball into the temporary seats in front of the leftfield fence for a ground-rule double, followed by Merkle's single to center. Speaker, his ankle still bothering him, let the ball get away for his second error of the game, as Merkle ran to secondbase. But Wood struck out Herzog, then knocked down Meyers's hot smash with his bare hand, and tossed to first to retire the side. Wood's hand quickly began to swell; if the game had continued beyond the tenth inning, he couldn't have gone back out to pitch.

But it didn't continue, because the Giants made two of the most infamous miscues in the history of the World Series—one of commission, the other of omission. Stahl sent up Engle to pinch-hit for Wood, and the utility man lifted a lazy fly ball to left-centerfield. In his late seventies, Fred Snodgrass recalled the moment: "I yelled that I'd take it and waved Murray off, and—well—I dropped the darn thing." Hustling all the way, Engle was standing at secondbase before Snodgrass's throw got there. Then Hooper drove the ball far over Snodgrass's head for what seemed a sure game-tying triple. "I made one of the greatest catches of my life on it," Snodgrass said, "catching the ball over my shoulder while on the dead run out in deep left center. They always forget about that play when they write about that inning. In fact, I almost doubled up Engle at second base." Speaker never forgot Snodgrass's catch, saying a few years later that it was "one of the most sensational plays I ever saw."[14]

Mathewson, known for his fine control, inexplicably walked the light-hitting Yerkes, bringing up Speaker. The Giants' second miscue of the inning followed. Speaker swung at Mathewson's first pitch and sent a high foul off the firstbase line that seemed a sure second out, an easy play for Merkle at firstbase. Speaker was about to try to confuse things by yelling for catcher Meyers to take it, when he heard Mathewson doing just that. Meyers made a futile lunge as the ball fell several feet in front of him.

Many years later, Hugh Fullerton, who was sitting at field level in the press section behind home plate, described what Speaker did: "Tris was really excited then. Returning to the plate, he leaped into the air, shook both fists at Matty, telling him what he intended to do with the next pitch." Fullerton may have exaggerated what he saw, but Speaker did say something to Mathewson as he stopped halfway down the base line. Over the years what he said varied in the telling, including what Speaker himself recalled. The version he gave in a 1938 interview is probably as reliable as any: "Well, there goes your World Series." Ty Cobb, sitting in the press section with Stoney McLinn, remarked to his ghost writer, "Tris will get one now sure and break up the game."[15]

"You just feel your luck when you have a break like that," Speaker said in that same 1938 interview. "I went back and plastered the next ball for a single."[16] Actually, Speaker swung and missed on the next pitch, hit another foul ball that was unreachable, and then lined Mathewson's 0-2 pitch over firstbase. Engle scored from secondbase to tie the game; Yerkes raced around to third. McGraw signaled for Mathewson to give Duffy Lewis an intentional walk to set up a double-play possibility, but Gardner, after fouling off one pitch and taking two balls, hit a high, inside pitch far into rightfield. Devore caught it too deep to make a play, and Yerkes scored easily to end the game and give Boston the Series championship. Fred Lieb remembered that the *New York Globe*'s Sid Mercer, dictating his account of the inning to a telegraph operator, had tears streaming down his face.

As Speaker ran for the clubhouse behind the centerfield fence, several women jumped onto the field and planted kisses on him, Yerkes, and Engle. Meanwhile McGraw tussled with a local partisan as the Giants' manager made his way to the Red Sox's dugout to congratulate Jake Stahl. McGraw, who believed physical errors were just part of the game, refused to blame Snodgrass for the loss. "It could happen to anyone," he said a little later. "If it hadn't been for a lot that Snodgrass did, we wouldn't have been playing in that game at all."[17]

Speaker agreed. Whenever he talked about the game, he blamed Mathewson, not Snodgrass and not even Merkle, for what happened in that fateful tenth inning. But poor Snodgrass would go to his grave known as the man who lost the Series with his "$30,000 muff" (which was roughly the difference between the teams' shares of Series receipts). "I did drop that fly ball," said Snodgrass, "and that did put what turned out to be the tying run on base, but that's a long way from 'losing a World Series.'"[18]

Actually, it was a loosely played eight games on both sides. Together, the teams committed 31 errors, 14 by Boston (two by Speaker) and 17 by New York, including four each by Fletcher and Doyle. The Giants, who had stolen 296 bases during the regular season, stole 12 times on Cady (who caught all but two games) and Carrigan.

But it had also been the richest World Series up to then, with receipts totaling $490,833. The five games in Boston, bringing in $252,037 in ticket sales, supposedly gave the franchise a $147,000 profit, even though the team had drawn about

71,000 fewer people into Fenway Park than had come to Huntington Avenue Grounds back in 1909. Divided twenty-two ways, the Boston players' share came out to $4,024.66 apiece. The Giants, splitting their shares twenty-three ways, each went home with $2,566.40. Both McAleer and John T. Brush added an extra day's pay for the eighth game. The National Commission paid umpires Billy Evans, Silk O'Loughlin, Bill Klem, and Cy Rigler $1,000 each.

The Red Sox didn't win the Series on hitting prowess; as a team the Giants outhit them by fifty points and outscored them 31 to 25. Speaker was the only Boston regular to bat as high as .300, but for New York, Herzog batted .400; Meyers, .357; and Murray, .323. Bill Phelon attributed New York's defeat to a "wholesale output of atrocious fumbles or muffs." But McGraw, in remarks at a reception during a November appearance in Boston on his vaudeville tour, pointed to several critical stops by shortstop Heinie Wagner as the main reason the Red Sox won. He added that Speaker had been "a tower of strength," and that Hooper's catch in the last game was the greatest he'd ever seen.[19]

If in defeat McGraw was prepared to be generous, in victory Boston mayor Fitzgerald—"that comic opera burgomaster [sic]," as the *Sporting News* sneered editorially from faraway St. Louis—was initially indignant.[20] The most regal of Royal Rooters, "Honey Fitz" demanded an apology from McAleer for the seventh-game ticket fiasco and the ouster of Robert McRoy, whom he denounced for, among other sins, being a Chicago man. Following a big parade of auto-borne players and marching Royal Rooters (playing and singing "Tessie," of course) from Fenway Park to venerable Faneuil Hall, speeches by the mayor and various others in praise of the Boston champions, and McAleer's formal apology to the Rooters for the seventh-game ticket fiasco, the mayor was reasonably mollified, even though McAleer kept McRoy on as franchise secretary.

Speaker cashed his Series check and arranged for his new Chalmers to be shipped to Hubbard City. After he and Wood had reportedly turned down an offer of $1,000 apiece for a vaudeville stint, they made a rendezvous in Chicago with Jake Stahl and Frank Laporte, a veteran infielder-outfielder now with Washington. The foursome spent three weeks hunting and fishing on Reelfoot Lake, Tennessee, after which "Woody," as Speaker called him, went with his close friend to spend a month in and around Hubbard, meeting the Texan's relatives and acquaintances. According to Tim Murnane, Wood "could not say enough nice things about the people who live in that sun-kissed country."[21] They then returned to the two-hundred-acre chicken farm in Pennsylvania where Wood lived in the off-season with his parents and little sister.

With much talk in the air about the prospect of a third major league that might try to siphon off established American and National Leaguers, McAleer signed Larry Gardner to a three-year contract. He offered Wood a one-year deal for $7,000; early in February, they settled for $7,500. Speaker expected a big raise and got one, signing for one year at $9,000 after a meeting with McAleer in Chicago. (Cobb eventually signed for $12,500 after an acrimonious holdout.)

As they looked ahead to 1913, both Wood and Speaker must have seen years of fame and money. Wood had just put in one of the greatest seasons any pitcher ever had or ever would have, and Speaker had become one of the game's brightest stars. Speaker went on to future glories and lots more money, but Smokey Joe Wood, who turned twenty-three on October 25 and was about to marry, had ahead years of frustration and uncertainty about his future in professional baseball.

"For God's Sake, Men, Take the Money Away"

Tris Speaker and Joe Wood may have been satisfied with their 1913 contracts, but others weren't. Duffy Lewis, Bill Carrigan, and Harry Hooper (who married Esther Henchy, his California sweetheart, in the off-season) were all unhappy with the money they were offered. Officially holdouts after February, the three didn't sign their contracts until they showed up for spring training at Hot Springs. They may have wondered why Jimmy McAleer hadn't also taken out $25,000 life insurance policies on them, as he had on Speaker, Wood, Larry Gardner, and Buck O'Brien. In any case, Lewis and Hooper reportedly signed for $5,000 each, Carrigan for $4,500. That pushed the Red Sox's payroll to an estimated $80,000.

If the Red Sox's drop from a good third place in 1909 to fourth the next season had been a disappointment, in 1913 the dreary fourth-place showing of the defending World Series champions must have been downright disheartening. Many things went wrong, starting with a bad foot injury incurred by player-manager Jake Stahl at Hot Springs, where the Red Sox and Pittsburgh again held their spring training. It was a cold, rainy spring there and over most of the eastern half of the United States. The two teams managed to get in only five exhibition games, during one of which Joe Wood almost killed Bobby Byrne, the Pirates' little thirdbaseman, when his fast ball struck Byrne in the head. Another ill omen was a loss to the University of Illinois on a muddy ballfield in Champaign, where the Red Sox arrived after various rainouts and train delays on their way north and east.

Wood exited from the season opener, with Philadelphia at Fenway Park, after giving up seven runs in five innings in a game Boston eventually lost, 10-

9. A few days later he came back to pitch a four-hit, 2-1 victory over New York and Ray Caldwell. After the Red Sox lost three out of four games in Philadelphia, Hubert "Dutch" Leonard, a stocky, baby-faced lefthander purchased from Denver, started in the opener of a series in Washington and struggled to his first major-league victory, 8-5. Newly inaugurated President Woodrow Wilson (who proved to be a real baseball fan) was among those present for that game, as he was for the remaining three games of the series, which the teams split.

Leonard won his second start in New York, where the Yankees had become tenants of the Giants at the Polo Grounds. Frank Chance, who as player-manager had led the Chicago Cubs to four National League pennants and two World Series victories, had ill-advisedly left his California farm to take over the woeful Yankees. Like George Stallings (now managing the Boston Braves) and Harry Wolverton before him, Chance had to put up with Hal Chase—or at least he did until June 1, when he persuaded the team's owners to trade the gifted but fractious player to the White Sox. With Chase gone, the Yankees' morale may have improved, but they still finished in seventh place, a half-game from the bottom. With a month to go in the next season and the Yankees again mired in seventh place, Chance quit and returned to his farm.

For the first third or so of the 1913 season, the Red Sox weren't much better than Chance's team, although Speaker was batting nearly .400 at the end of May. But Joe Wood slipped on wet grass trying to make a play during the first visit to Detroit and broke the thumb on his pitching hand. After the cast was removed, he may have tried to pitch too soon, or perhaps he had also hurt his shoulder. In any case, as he related long afterward, "I never pitched again without a terrific amount of pain in my right shoulder. Never again."[1]

With the Red Sox in fifth place with a 16-21 record—already ten and a half games behind the Athletics—the rest of the American League, wrote Bill Phelon (blithely mixing his metaphors), "lit on J. Garland Stahl like buzzards on an over-ripe steak, and when the smoke blew away the world's champions were way back yonder somewhere."[2] His bad foot unhealed, Stahl pinch-hit twice but otherwise kept himself out of the lineup in favor of Clyde Engle, as Jimmy McAleer became increasingly impatient with Stahl's refusal to try to play. It was rumored that

Stahl, a minority stockholder along with his father-in-law, was working behind the scenes to displace McAleer as franchise president.

Not that the Red Sox lacked combativeness. Stahl remained in Boston to have surgery on his foot as the team began its first western trip, so he missed the melee that followed a rowdy series opener in Cleveland, won by the Naps, 3-2. In the course of that game, Carrigan blocked Naps outfielder Jack Graney off the plate and rendered him briefly unconscious, then roughed up Joe Jackson when he slid in with spikes high; Naps thirdbaseman Ivan "Ivy" Olson collided with rookie pitcher George Foster at firstbase and tore Foster's pants; and Cleveland catcher Fred Carish knocked over Harold Janvrin, another Boston rookie, at secondbase. In the runway from the home dugout both teams used to get to their dressing rooms, Olson and Boston reserve catcher Les Nunamaker exchanged insults, precipitating a ten-minute fight. The combatants included, among others, Speaker, Carrigan, Graney, Duffy Lewis, Charley Hall, and Nap Lajoie.

Afterward *Sporting Life*'s Cleveland correspondent mentioned "several bloody shirts, buttonless sweaters and torn trousers in the club houses," adding that Nunamaker had a closed eye and Speaker had to be treated for three spike wounds.[3] Both teams were to be guests that evening at a local theater, but the Naps refused to join their adversaries. After reviewing the umpires' reports, league president Ban Johnson punished only Nunamaker and Olson, fining them $25 each.

Boston lost three of four games at League Park, although in the final game, Speaker hit the first home run (inside the park) of only three he had all season. The bad feeling between the Boston and Cleveland teams was still alive by the time the Naps came to Fenway Park in June. In the fifteenth inning of the finale of that series, Ivy Olson stole home on Dutch Leonard, and the Naps scored three more times to win the game, 9-5. But before the game ended, Lajoie had accused Wood of throwing at his head; shortstop Ray Chapman had been badly spiked by Carrigan; and Olson had been knocked off balance by Engle as Olson rounded firstbase.

On June 25 the Red Sox raised their World Series flag at Fenway Park, then lost to the Chase-less Yankees, 5-2, Russell Ford gaining the victory over Wood, who walked five batters and hit three. Wood was pitching with difficulty and irregularly, but also by then the team's overall play had greatly improved. The Red Sox had climbed to third place with a 31-26 record, although they still trailed Philadelphia by eleven games. Washington, again relying on Walter Johnson's valiant work, was in second place, five and a half back.

It was an open secret—shared by Boston's baseball writers and many local fans—that things weren't right on the Red Sox team. The gossip around town was that more than ever the players were divided into Catholic and Protestant cliques—the Knights of Columbus, or "K.C.'s," versus the "Masons," "Carrigan men" versus "Stahl men." Presumably the "Carrigan men" would also be "McAleer men" in the increasingly bad relationship between club president and manager.

In particular, Speaker, loyal to Stahl, and Duffy Lewis, who supposedly wanted Carrigan to succeed Stahl, were on the outs. Speaker was something of a practical joker; though usually harmless, his pranks sometimes suggested a cruel streak. Starting to go bald, Lewis took somebody's advice that if he had his head shaved, his hair would likely grow back. So during a mid-season series in St. Louis, played in typically oppressive heat, the Californian did just that. Whereupon Speaker took to sneaking up behind Lewis, snatching his cap, and laughing and gesturing for the nearby spectators to take notice of his teammate's hairless pate. Several times Lewis warned Speaker to stop it; before a game at Fenway Park, when Speaker repeated his prank, Lewis slung his bat and hit Speaker in the shins. In pain, Speaker had to be helped to the dressing room, and he limped through that day's game. The two outfielders didn't speak—for the rest of the season, by some accounts, from then on, according to others—except to call out who would take fly balls. Speaker's friendship with Harry Hooper, on the other hand, remained unshaken. Hooper and his wife Esther, who also rented a place at Winthrop, often dined with Speaker and Wood.

To what extent the ill feeling among various Boston players hampered their play in 1913 can't be determined. Baseball history is full of teams that were clique-ridden but successful. It seems a safe assumption, however, that for a team that got off to a slow start, the lack of camaraderie didn't help its chances of winning.

Some elements of that frustrating season were almost comical. On two different occasions—one at the start of a series in St. Louis, the other in Philadelphia—the Red Sox had to borrow uniforms, bats, and gloves from their hosts because their equipment had been lost in transit.

Joe Wood's predicament, though, was anything but comical. On July 13, sore arm and all, Wood shut out Chicago in the nightcap of a doubleheader split at Comiskey Park for his eleventh win, his last in 1913. Five days later, in Detroit, where he had broken his thumb earlier in the season, Wood took a hard-hit ball from Bobby Veach's bat on his pitching hand and had to leave a scoreless game, subsequently lost by rookie righthander Earl Moseley. Smokey Joe, who had pitched in forty-three games the past season and won thirty-four, ended up working only twenty-three games in 1913. He made one more mound appearance, pitching the ninth inning of a 2-0 loss to Cleveland on September 17.

Two months earlier Jimmy McAleer had run out of patience with his non-playing manager and given him an ultimatum: If Stahl didn't start playing, he would be fired at the end of the season. Following three losses in a row in Chicago that left the Red Sox in fifth place, two games under .500, Stahl decided to save McAleer the trouble. When he quit, he gave up a $10,000 salary, although as a college graduate and the son-in-law of a wealthy Chicagoan who had set him up in banking, he was hardly destitute. Moreover, his combined 1912 income from his salary, his dividend from Red Sox profits, and his World Series share had been about $25,000. Stahl, with his wife and son, left Boston and baseball worries behind to spend the rest of the summer at a cabin in rural Massachusetts.

One might have assumed that the removal of a manager by a club president would be strictly an internal matter, but not so in Ban Johnson's league. Johnson, a friend of both Stahl and McAleer, had helped talk Stahl out of retirement and had effectively engineered the purchase of half of the Boston franchise by McAleer, Robert McRoy, and associates, including Stahl and his father-in-law. The American League president was much put out by the goings-on in Boston, especially by the ouster of Stahl. McAleer didn't know it, but his days in Boston were also numbered.

Bill Carrigan, at age twenty-nine, became acting Red Sox manager, although McAleer didn't make it official for another month. Carrigan barred McAleer from the dressing room and started holding daily pregame meetings (which Stahl hadn't done), but the Red Sox continued to win some, lose some, and go nowhere. They had the satisfaction of killing off the pennant chances of the Cleveland Naps, toward whom they still held hard feelings, by sweeping three games at League Park in mid-August and dropping the Naps eight and a half games behind Philadelphia. Cleveland was never in the race after that.

A week or so later, Speaker and his teammates gained mixed satisfaction from ending Walter Johnson's fourteen-game winning streak. The "Big Train," as the baseball press had dubbed Johnson, or "Barney," as he was known to his peers, had such an amiable and unaffected disposition that he had become roundly popular in the American League. In the eleventh inning at Fenway Park, Carrigan singled in Heinie Wagner for the only run of the game, giving the win to Ray Collins. Up to that point Johnson had allowed only two hits and struck out ten. Speaker hurried to the visitors' dressing room to shake Johnson's hand and say, "It was the greatest exhibition of pitching that I have ever seen in my life, and you deserved to win."[4]

Maybe it wasn't Johnson's greatest game; he pitched many other masterpieces, a number of which he also lost with weak-hitting teams behind him. But 1913 was Johnson's finest single season: 36 wins, 7 defeats, a 1.09 earned run average, 11 shutouts, 243 strikeouts, 346 innings pitched. No pitcher in either league matched him in any of those categories. Johnson's brilliant work was the main reason Washington, with a late-season spurt, beat out Cleveland for another second-place finish. The Nationals' 90-64 record left them seven and a half games behind the pennant-winning Athletics.

The Red Sox, with an encouraging 40-20 record under "Rough" Carrigan, managed to slip past Chicago to finish in fourth place. Their final record was 79 wins, 71 losses. In addition to Wood's woes, Buck O'Brien, a twenty-game winner in 1912, was a complete flop; with a 4-9 record in July and gossip about his being "out of shape" (a euphemism for a player who drank and caroused too much), he was sold to the White Sox. Hugh Bedient, another twenty-game winner the previous season, won fifteen games and improved his earned run average, but he also lost fourteen. Dutch Leonard, like Bedient, often getting sparse run support, finished at 14-16; Ray Collins, with nineteen wins, led the staff.

After eighty-nine games, Speaker was batting .389, but he tailed off in August and September to finish with a .366 average, again third-best in the league, behind Joe Jackson's .373 and Ty Cobb's .390. (Because he staged a protracted holdout, Cobb missed the first two weeks of the season; that and injuries limited him to 122 games.) Speaker missed the Red Sox's last nine games of the season, spending several days in a Boston hospital having a nonmalignant tumor removed from one of his ears. Statistically, his performance fell below that of 1912 in nearly every category: 91 runs, 71 runs batted in, only 3 home runs, 35 doubles. He belted 22 triples, his career's best, although he still trailed Detroit's Sam Crawford, who continued to accumulate more three-base hits than anybody has ever equaled. Speaker's 42 stolen bases were unimpressive, given that he was also caught 29 times.

He had 30 assists, but his 24 errors—the most of his career, including 3 in three days in April—suggested that sometimes he may not have had his mind completely on his work. Or it may have been that he simply took more chances. In August, Paul Eaton reported that Speaker "has no regard for imaginary boundaries between outfield and infield," and that when he came pounding in for pop flies back of secondbase, he scared young Harold Janvrin so much that "he is playing the dickens with Janvrin's chances of ever making good." Speaker, Eaton wrote, "is so full of life and energy that he wants to play every position on the team at one and the same time."[5]

Despite the Red Sox's turnaround under Carrigan, it had been an unsatisfactory season, with attendance at Fenway Park plunging by 160,000, to just above 437,000. It had also been an unsettling season, especially for the club owners. There was the growing threat of a new league that promised to operate as a third major circuit in 1914 and go after as many players in Organized Baseball as it could sign who weren't already under contracts. In 1913 the Federal League, as it was called, left big-league rosters alone and operated in eight cities with a mix of semipro players, former minor-leaguers, and a few ex-big-leaguers. (Cy Young came out of retirement to manage the Cleveland entry for what turned out to be a one-year engagement, for both himself and that city.) But the league's financial backers were well-heeled, ambitious, and determined; they also promised to offer contracts without the reserve clause. Back in 1901, Ban Johnson and his comrades had proclaimed their American League to be a second major circuit and lured dozens of players away from the National League. Now Johnson and everybody else within Organized Baseball insisted there was room for no more than two major leagues. A new "baseball war" was looming.

Then there was the Baseball Players' Fraternity, which had been organized a few years earlier by David Fultz, a former National League player and a Brown University graduate and New York attorney. Unlike the Major League Baseball Players' Association formed later in the century, the Fraternity sought to represent the interests of minor-leaguers as well as those at the top of Organized Baseball. Initially, Fultz put forward modest goals, such as ensuring that contracts were honored and protecting players from the kind of abusive fan behavior that had provoked Ty Cobb to beat up a spectator in New York. With the Federal League threat, however, Fultz had the opportunity to pressure owners into bigger concessions, such as the abrogation of the clause whereby a player could be released with only ten days' notice and the payment of players' travel expenses to spring-training sites.

Early in the season, in New York, Fultz met with both Red Sox and Yankees players; afterward he claimed that the Fraternity already had three hundred members, including all of the Red Sox. Speaker was an early supporter of the movement, lending his name to its board of directors, as did Ty Cobb, Sam Crawford, Christy Mathewson, and other luminaries. Brooklyn firstbaseman Jake Daubert served as Fultz's vice president. Speaker called the Fraternity "a great organization, and I propose to do what I can to make it a success."[6] By the fall of 1914, it appeared that the Players' Fraternity had become the strongest counterforce to the owners' power since the Brotherhood of Professional Baseball Players, which had climaxed with the one-season Players League in 1890. The Fraternity, owners feared, might even threaten the sacrosanct reserve clause.

Within five weeks after the season ended, Tris Speaker had put all that behind him, both literally and figuratively. Along with a party of sixty-six others, he had embarked upon a globe-circling baseball journey that would be the grandest adventure any of them would ever know.

The project was conceived in December 1912 by John McGraw and Charles Comiskey during McGraw's stopover in Chicago on his vaudeville tour. In the course of a convivial evening at Smiley Corbett's bar, the Giants' manager and the White Sox owner began talking about the globe-circling trip on which Albert

G. Spalding had led two baseball teams in the 1888–1889 off-season. Joe Farrell, a White Sox devotee and privileged member of Comiskey's Woodland Bards social club, suggested that the two celebrated baseball figures might undertake the same kind of venture. Right then and there, McGraw and Comiskey decided to emulate what Spalding had done—organize two teams and take them on a postseason around-the-world trip to showcase baseball in faraway places, where people who hadn't seen the game were presumably eager to do so.

During the next half year or so, McGraw and Comiskey put their plan into effect. Jimmy Callahan, Comiskey's manager, headed up one team, made up mostly of White Sox but enlisting a few other American Leaguers; McGraw put together a team from his New York Giants and other National Leaguers. Each player was to post a $300 guarantee that he would make the trip. As soon as the 1914 World Series was completed, the players would form their teams and start playing their way across the country to the Pacific Coast. The receipts they earned were expected to be sufficient to cover the costs of their overseas travels.

The tour began in Cincinnati on October 18, a week after McGraw's Giants lost the World Series in five games to the Athletics—New York's third Series defeat in a row. Speaker didn't join Callahan's "White Sox"—which also included Detroit's Sam Crawford and Washington's Germany Schaefer, Browns pitcher Walter Leverenz, and three National Leaguers—until the team reached St. Joseph, Missouri. Except for a quick trip from Dallas to Hubbard to see his mother, he was with the group from then on. Christy Mathewson traveled as far as San Francisco before leaving the tour, as did Jeff Tesreau and Fred Snodgrass of the Giants and Hal Chase and two other White Sox. Rube Marquard had also declined to make the trip, so McGraw had to borrow Urban "Red" Faber, a pitcher just purchased by the White Sox from Des Moines. McGraw had with him Chief Meyers, Fred Merkle, Larry Doyle, and other Giants regulars. He also had Jim Thorpe, whom the Giants had signed earlier in the year following the great Indian athlete's triumphs at the 1912 Olympic Games in Stockholm and an outstanding football season at Carlisle Institute.[7]

The American phase of the expedition followed a zigzag route, with the "White Sox" and "Giants" exhibiting their skills from Chicago, Kansas City, and Tulsa to Houston, El Paso, Los Angeles, Sacramento, Oakland, San Francisco,

Portland, and Seattle. They also stopped in such places as Blue Rapids, Kansas; Marlin, Texas; Douglas and Bisbee, Arizona; Oxnard, California (where the Phillies' John "Hans" Lobert lost a race around the bases to a horse); and Medford, Oregon, where, on November 18, the teams played in a driving rain. Admiring the dedication of the 2,500 Medford citizens who sat through the miserable afternoon, Speaker remarked that "a man would be willing to go out and court rheumatism just to gratify them."[8]

The baseball tourists had played thirty-one games by the time they sailed from Seattle on the coastal steamer *Prince Ruppert* for Vancouver, their transoceanic debarkation port. Speaker had intended to say goodbye to everybody and head home to Hubbard and his mother; but only a couple of hours before the departure for Vancouver, Jimmy McAleer, who was himself about to leave the tour, talked him into going along on the global jaunt. So like the others, he submitted to a smallpox vaccination, which left him feverish and feeling wretched.

The *Empress of China,* an elegant ocean liner operated by the Canadian Pacific Railroad, moved out of Vancouver harbor shortly before midnight on November 19, 1913, bound for Japan. Besides twenty-three ballplayers, the group included John and Blanche McGraw; Charles and Nancy Comiskey; Comiskey's son Louis and his wife Grace; twelve other wives (of whom Thorpe's and Doyle's were new brides); umpires Bill Klem and Jack Sheridan; McGraw's physician; a number of reporters, publicists, and White Sox fans; and Frank McGlynn, a West Coast motion-picture cameraman, who put together a full-length film on the trip.

Once the ocean liner cleared the Straits of San Juan de Fuca, the voyage became exceedingly unpleasant. Late in the year, the northern Pacific crossing, more than seven thousand miles, is notorious for its rough seas and frequent storms. Thorpe was experienced at ocean travel, having sailed to Stockholm and back, but nearly all the rest of the baseball tourists suffered some degree of seasickness. Not until the fifteenth day out of Vancouver did they all make it to the dining room.

Speaker was among the most miserable, his only significant water travel having been on the coastal steamers between Boston and New York and the lake steamers between Cleveland and Detroit. Unable to keep food down for six days, he must have cursed Jimmy McAleer for talking him out of going home to Texas.

Once he gained his sea legs, though, Speaker was in fine form, engaging in some literal horseplay organized by the puckish Germany Schaefer and Louis "Steve" Evans of the St. Louis Cardinals. The players performed "horse races" down the ship's corridors, with Speaker and Thorpe, on all fours, carrying the lighter men.

The crossing was also cold and lonely; during the twenty-three days it took to reach Japan, the *Empress of China*'s crew and passengers saw only three other ships. But if bored and tired by the time they reached Yokohama harbor, they were reinvigorated by the large and enthusiastic crowds that greeted them there and for the three games they played in a country that had already embraced baseball as a national pastime. The Japanese were fascinated by Thorpe, who was the most internationally known of the whole party. The combined American teams won two lopsided games against Japanese university teams and played one against each other, with the "White Sox" winning, 12-9. That game ended when Speaker threw out Mike Donlin at home plate. Although the throw must have been a long one, the distance given in the report of the game cabled back to the States, 483 feet, had to be a mighty exaggeration.

From Japan the baseball tourists boarded the *St. Alban,* a smaller Australian steamer, for Shanghai. Waiting at the junction of the mouth of the Yangtze River for medical inspections before boarding a tender for the trip upriver to the city, the tourists gazed down at boats full of beggars surrounding the ship. One boat nearly capsized in the scramble when Speaker tossed down a silver dollar.

At Shanghai, nominally a part of the three-year-old Republic of China but largely controlled by British and other foreign interests, torrential rains made baseball impossible. To kill the time, Speaker, Fred Merkle, and Joe Farrell ventured into the walled-off area of Shanghai westerners called "Chinatown," notorious for its brothels and opium dens. In his history of the global tour, James Elfers wonders whether they might have been seeking prostitutes or an experiment with opium, although the *New York Times* writer along on the trip reported only that the three got lost in the maze of Chinatown's streets.

Speculation about Speaker's sexual experiences—up to that point in his life or at any time until he married more than a decade later—leads us nowhere. He was a healthy, reasonably attractive bachelor who traveled extensively and had more money to spend than most young men, but he would also have feared both venereal disease and the possibility of impregnating someone. In any case, the private lives of ballplayers in his day generally remained private. (An exception was Rube Marquard's scandalous affair with the vaudeville star Blossom Seeley. Seeley's estranged husband first threatened her life, then filed a civil action against Marquard, and finally divorced her, after which she and the pitcher married—and became parents within five months.)

Whatever Speaker, Merkle, and Farrell were doing in Chinatown, they barely made it back to the Astor House Hotel before the party left to board the smaller vessel that would take them back down the Yangtze to where their ship had docked. The next stop was Hong Kong for a game that did nothing to persuade the British colonials there that baseball had anything over cricket. Then the *St. Alban* steamed to Manila, where the local Americans were delighted to welcome them, especially Arlie Pond, an army surgeon who had been McGraw's teammate at Baltimore in the 1890s.

From Manila the *St. Alban* transported the party to Sydney, where Australian health officials decreed another round of vaccinations. The shots again made Speaker and several others so ill that they stayed in their cabins for a day or two. As had been the case at Hong Kong, the spectators at Sydney and then at Melbourne were politely underwhelmed by the exhibition of the American game. It was the same at Colombo, the capital of the British colony of Ceylon, to which the *St. Alban* took them across the placid Indian Ocean. After a long stretch at sea, the ship steamed through the Suez Canal to Cairo. Because Spalding's party had done it in 1889, the two teams felt they had to play a game at Giza, in the shadow of the Sphinx, before an audience that included a number of puzzled Egyptians.

By February the tourists had reached Rome, where rains again kept them from showing the local populace how baseball was played. For the Roman Catholics in the party, an audience with Pope Pius X was arranged for the morning of February 11, 1914. The men donned formal evening attire; the women dressed in black. Speaker and Sam Crawford, both Protestants, also attended the event. "As the Pope entered the room," recorded Frank McGlynn, "all knelt," whereupon the Pope gave them his blessing and had medals distributed to the supplicants. If the occasion was inspirational for the Catholics, it must have been a strange one indeed for Speaker and Crawford, Protestants from small-town Texas and Nebraska. Yet whatever Speaker's feelings about Catholics and Catholicism, he was impressed. In an interview after his return to the States, he remarked, "To my mind the most interesting thing was the audience granted us by the Pope at Rome. I am not a Catholic myself, but I shall always remember the scene."[9]

While Speaker was away, things were happening that significantly affected his life, both personally and professionally. He and Joe Wood remained fast friends and roommates on road trips, but on December 20, 1913, at Milford, Pennsylvania, Smokey Joe ended their bachelor friendship by marrying Laura Teresa O'Shea, a young woman Wood had known since his stay with the Kansas City team in 1908.

A couple of weeks before that, the presidency of the Red Sox had changed hands again, when forty-seven-year-old Joseph J. Lannin bought the stock of Jimmy McAleer, Robert McRoy, Jake Stahl and his father-in-law, and two other minor Chicago investors. John I. Taylor continued to hold half of the franchise's stock, but Lannin quickly fired McRoy, whose foul-up with seventh-game Series tickets in 1912 still rankled the Royal Rooters.

The Canadian-born Lannin was the proverbial self-made man, having risen from doorman to bellhop to clerk to ownership of a New York City hotel; he now owned two other New York hotels, as well as a high-rise apartment complex in Boston. The deal had been made again with the active involvement of Ban Johnson, who was still disgusted by the Stahl-McAleer troubles. Without McAleer's knowledge, Johnson worked out the particulars of Lannin's buyout of McAleer and the others. McAleer was in Hawaii when he heard the news that he was out of the picture. Upon his return to the States, Johnson gave him his part of the sale money.

While all that was going on, the Federal League promoters had undertaken an aggressive campaign to sign players from the two older leagues. Lannin personally grabbed Clyde Engle off a train as he was about to leave for Chicago to meet with Federal representatives, and Bill Carrigan hurried up to Burlington, Vermont, to sign Ray Collins. In Rome, Speaker and Crawford received telegrams urging them to wait until they got home and talked with Federal Leaguers before they signed their 1914 contracts. In Paris (after the party's stopover at

Nice), it was more rain and no baseball, but while the tourists enjoyed themselves in the City of Light, Jimmy Callahan received a wire from Lannin's office authorizing him to offer Speaker whatever was necessary to get him to agree to stay with the Red Sox. Callahan did his best, but all he got from Speaker was his word of honor that he wouldn't sign with the Federals without giving Lannin a chance to match their offer.

The last stop on the global journey was London. In most places the ballplayers had performed before large if often uncomprehending crowds, but in England they enjoyed the *succes d'estime* of the whole trip. On February 26, 1914, drawn at least in part by the news that King George V would be in attendance, some thirty thousand people—the biggest turnout since Japan—came to the Chelsea Football Grounds at Stamford, and saw probably the best exhibition of baseball the teams had put on. It ended in dramatic fashion when diminutive Tom Daly, who had appeared in only one game for Chicago in 1913 after arriving from the minors, lined Red Faber's pitch into the close rightfield seats for a 5-4 "White Sox" victory. "It may have been glorified rounders as some of the English papers thought," Speaker later said, "but it was the best game I ever saw."[10] Afterward the players had the thrill of shaking hands with his Royal Majesty. That was the final contest of the tour. The "White Sox" had won twenty-four times, the "Giants" twenty.

Two days later, the party took the boat train to Liverpool and boarded the Cunard liner *Lusitania* for the voyage home. On March 6, 1914, nearly four months after their departure from Vancouver, the globe-circlers arrived at New York harbor. As they waited for a snowstorm to abate so the *Lusitania* could clear quarantine, a cutter carrying Ban Johnson, Joseph Lannin, Frank Farrell of the Yankees, and Charles Ebbets and William Baker of the Brooklyn and Philadelphia National League clubs, respectively, pulled alongside the ship. Meanwhile James Gaffney, principal owner of the Boston Braves, used his local political clout to keep vessels carrying Federal League agents from leaving the docks. Aboard the *Lusitania,* Johnson and associates pleaded with the bewildered players not to sign anything with the Federals.

When the big ship finally docked, thousands of people were there to welcome them. James Gilmore, president of the Federal League; Mordecai "Three

Finger" Brown, a great pitcher for the Chicago Cubs a few years earlier and now manager of the St. Louis Federals; Walter Fritsch, junior partner in the St. Louis Federals franchise; and other Federal League representatives met the players at the gangplank and invited them to come to the Hotel Knickerbocker for contract talks. Two hours later, Speaker, together with the Cardinals' Steve Evans and Lee Magee (born Leopold Hoernschemeyer) and the Phillies' Mickey Doolan, arrived at the Knickerbocker.

What happened then has been told in various forms. Shortly before his death, Speaker gave a garbled version, claiming that what the Federal Leaguers offered was "mostly promises": $100,000 over three years to be player-manager of the Brooklyn team. They wouldn't give him more than $25,000 as a binder, "and when they wanted to put the balance in escrow, I took a walk." He went on to say that he and the other players "doubted the league would last. The fear of being blacklisted by Organized Ball was another deterrent." In 1926 Richard Carroll, a Cleveland businessman who in 1914 was business manager of the Brooklyn Federals, put the money offered Speaker at $55,000 for three years, plus a $10,000 signing bonus. Carroll quoted Speaker as saying, "I cannot sign that contract. I've always been an organized baseball man and will continue to be so."[11] John I. Taylor understood that fifteen $1,000 bills were put on the table in front of Speaker, with the condition that he sign a Brooklyn contract right then.

Probably the most reliable account is what Walter Fritsch told *Sporting Life* at the time: Federal League president Gilmore and Robert B. Ward, co-owner of the Brooklyn franchise, handed Speaker a certified check for $18,000, which would be his 1914 salary, plus two $500 bills as a bonus. Looking at more money than he had ever seen at one time, Speaker nonetheless handed the check and bills back to Ward, saying, "For God's sake, men, take the money away or I'll fall. I promised on my word of honor I would give Lannin a chance before I signed up."[12]

Magee, Evans, and Doolan, three ordinary players, signed with the Federals for substantial increases over what they had been making, but Speaker kept his promise to Lannin. As related by John I. Taylor, who had accompanied Lannin to New York, he and Lannin dined with Speaker that evening and proposed a one-year contract matching the $18,000 the Federals had offered. Speaker wanted a three-year deal; Lannin and Taylor finally compromised with their star player on a two-year contract at $18,000 per season. "It did not take long," said Taylor, "for us to find some ink and get a contract ready—and then the transaction was closed." Later that night, Taylor met with Gilmore and Ward to tell them Speaker was signed. They had been ready, they told Taylor, to add ten more $1,000 bills to get their man. The next day Lannin announced that Speaker would continue with the Red Sox at a salary "larger than any heretofore paid a player."[13] For the first (and only) time, Speaker was paid more than Ty Cobb, who signed for 1914 with Detroit for the $15,000 he had unsuccessfully sought a year earlier.

After a huge banquet thrown for the world travelers at the Biltmore Hotel in New York, John McGraw and his players left for spring training at Marlin, Texas. Speaker went with Comiskey and the remainder of the party to Chicago for another feast, where Speaker joined Faber, Evans, and others in rendering various popular songs. Four years earlier Comiskey had proclaimed Cobb the greatest player ever. Now he said of Speaker, "There is no man in the American League I would rather see with my own team—and I do not except Ty Cobb. . . . I liked his disposition as it was shown to me on this trip." Speaker and Jim Thorpe, Comiskey added, were "the men in whom all nationalities took the greatest interest."[14]

From Chicago, Speaker traveled to Hubbard for a short visit with his mother, then, on March 26, joined the Red Sox at Hot Springs. Joseph Lannin had been there for a couple of weeks, golfing and bathing in the mineral waters, "with some peace of mind after two strenuous months of player-signing labors," *Sporting Life* reported. In fact, Lannin spent much of his time at Hot Springs worrying about various still-unsigned players. As Bill Carrigan recalled, "You'd find them in little groups in . . . the clubhouse discussing the situation. I couldn't get their minds on baseball."[15] With Lannin's consent, Carrigan called a meeting and gave the holdouts twenty-four hours to decide whether they wanted to stay with the Red Sox or go with the Federal League. Within another couple of days, according to Carrigan, all the recalcitrants had signed Boston contracts.

Within another six weeks, Lannin alone would be responsible for funding Speaker's semimonthly $1,500 paychecks. On May 11, Ban Johnson was in Boston to announce personally that Lannin had bought the half-interest in the Red

Sox held by John I. Taylor and was now the sole owner of the franchise. Lannin's total investment was about $450,000.

As if Joe Wood's arm troubles weren't enough worry, late in February the new husband underwent an emergency appendectomy, which was a very serious operation then and for many years afterward. Apart from the sizable wound inflicted by the surgical methods of the time, there was always the danger of postoperative infection. Carrigan told Wood he wouldn't pitch before June 1 and advised Wood's wife to make sure he didn't do anything strenuous. So Wood sat on the bench and idled around Lannin's apartment complex, into which he, his wife, Speaker, Carrigan, and Heinie Wagner had moved.

With their former ace able only to watch, the Red Sox played their 1914 season opener on April 14 at Fenway Park, in all-too-familiar bone-chilling weather. It also ended in all-too-familiar fashion: a 3-0 blanking by Walter Johnson, Ray Collins taking the loss. The next day it was so cold that Washington manager Clark Griffith coached in a topcoat, Speaker played centerfield wearing a mackinaw, and the Boston players remained in their clubhouse until they were due to bat. George Foster pitched a 2-1 win over Yancy "Doc" Ayers.

The Federal League was also underway, with franchises directly competing with National and American League teams in Brooklyn, St. Louis, Chicago, and Pittsburgh and also offering "big-league baseball" to customers in the strong minor-league cities of Baltimore, Buffalo, Indianapolis, and Kansas City. The Federal promoters threw around enough money to attract eighty-one present or former major-leaguers, as well as 115 minor-leaguers who jumped reserve lists—despite the American and National League owners' loudly proclaimed intention to blacklist any player deserting Organized Baseball for the Federal League. And for all his formal erudition, Players' Fraternity president David Fultz had already demonstrated his lack of leadership savvy. Without consulting his board of directors, he agreed to the blacklist, thereby tacitly affirming the reserve clause and ruining his chance to effect some major changes in owner-player relations.

Hal Chase jumped from the White Sox in mid-season to become player-manager of the Buffalo Federals, but other big-name players signing with the new league for that season or the next had already seen their best days. Such standouts as Speaker, Cobb, Eddie Collins, Joe Jackson, Christy Mathewson, and Grover Cleveland Alexander had all signed for big pay increases, often for two or more years, and remained with the two established leagues. Lannin already had Larry Gardner tied up for two more years; besides Speaker, he also had Dutch Leonard and Duffy Lewis under two-year contracts and would do the same for Harry Hooper the next fall.

Competition from the Federal League had the effect of dramatically driving up overall salaries. By one careful calculation, the average major-leaguer's pay increased from $3,800 in 1913 to $7,500 by 1915, at the same time that the majors' aggregate attendance—hurt by head-to-head competition from the Federals in the four majors cities and perhaps by the widely shared perception (probably accurate) that the overall caliber of play had diminished—fell by about 1.2 million in the National League, 800,000 in the American.

Attendance woes were worse for the four top minor-league teams competing with the Fedcrals. In Baltimore, where the Federal League's Terrapins played right across the street from the International League's Orioles, Jack Dunn, Orioles owner, was in such financial straits that he had to start selling off players. In mid-season, for a total of $8,000, Dunn sold the Red Sox two big young pitchers—righthander Ernie Shore, a 6′ 4″, 220-pound North Carolinian out of Guilford College, and nineteen-year-old George Herman Ruth, 6′ 2″, 190 pounds. A native Baltimorean, Ruth had been signed the previous spring out of St. Mary's Industrial School, a combination orphanage and trade school for wayward boys. Dubbed "Jack Dunn's baby" in the local press, he had quickly become "Babe" to his teammates.

By then the Red Sox were in fifth place but only a few games from the lead, which, as usual, was held by Connie Mack's Philadelphia team. Speaker had gotten off to a slow start at the plate, although in the fifth game of the season, a 1-0 win over the Athletics at Fenway Park pitched by Hugh Bedient, he again showed his unique outfielding skills. First he threw out Frank Baker at home plate, then, after Gardner had tagged out Eddie Murphy in a rundown, took Clyde Engle's throw to tag Eddie Collins and complete a triple play. Three days after that, in a thirteen-inning, 1-1 tie, with Dutch Leonard and the Athletics' Bob Shawkey both going all the way, he recorded his fourth career unassisted double play, again grabbing a ball on the fly and tagging second before the runner could get back.

But Speaker's subpar work at bat, and the fact that he was making the most money a player ever had, let him in for a lot of derision from fans and sportswriters around the league and even from fans at Fenway Park. Early in May, after the Red Sox were shut out in New York by Ray Caldwell, a *New York Times* scribe wrote: "In the seventh inning Tris Speaker, although heavily endowed with salary, made the first hit of the game off the towering Yankee. That one hit cost the Boston club about $95."[16] In June, when he went hitless in a doubleheader with Philadelphia at Fenway Park, he gestured and grimaced at his hecklers, who taunted him throughout the five-game series, of which the Athletics won four.

In fifth place on June 8 with a 22-22 record, the whole Boston team was making its fans restless, according to Paul Eaton's report in the *Sporting News*. Customers at Fenway Park "nod sagely" and blamed "slow-thinking and inattentive playing" on too much running around in "the shining and polished engines of luxury which the players seem to prize rather more highly than they do their batting averages." Later on, Tim Murnane agreed that part of the Red Sox's disappointing showing had to do with "the player speed-merchants [who] can be seen flying over the Greater Boston speedways, night and day, a sure handicap to a ball player's effectiveness." Murnane had heard that, at Connie Mack's request, the Athletics had "put up their autos to the close of the season."[17]

Joe Wood, who was still being paid $7,500, pitched earlier than Carrigan had expected, working the ninth inning of a May 15 game that was already lost to St. Louis. Two weeks later he threw a complete-game win over Cleveland. That would be the pattern of his pitching for the remainder of the season: carefully spaced starts that gave his arm the rest it needed. Most of the time he was effective. His best outing came on August 31, when he struck out fourteen Browns in a game at Fenway Park called after eleven innings because of darkness. A year later Bill Carrigan attributed Wood's effectiveness in 1914 to the "emery ball," which involved rubbing the ball on a piece of emery paper tucked into a slit in the glove. Carrigan said Wood had become one of the "master hands at the business."[18] All told, Wood appeared in eighteen games, starting fourteen, completing eleven, and ending with a 9-3 record.

Wood's mound work, as good as it was in spots, didn't have much to do with the Red Sox's much-improved play in August and September. Although Hugh Bedient won only eight times, Ray Collins posted twenty wins, Dutch Leonard won nineteen with a 1.01 earned run average (the lowest in major-league history for a starting pitcher), and George Foster won fourteen and had a stretch of forty-two consecutive scoreless innings. Ernie Shore debuted with a two-hit, 2-1 victory over Cleveland and added nine more wins over the rest of the season.

Babe Ruth pitched his first big-league game on July 11, 1914, at Fenway Park versus Cleveland. He got credit for the 4-3 win, although Leonard relieved him to start the eighth inning, after Speaker's single scored Lewis with the go-ahead run. (Lewis had pinch-hit for Ruth and always enjoyed the distinction of being the only man who ever did.) The Babe won another and lost one before he was optioned back to the International League, this time joining the Providence team, which Lannin had also purchased. Largely because of Ruth's pitching and that of Carl Mays, a righthander who threw a three-quarter-underhanded, or "submarine," ball, Providence won its first minor-league pennant.[19] With that league's season over, Ruth rejoined the Red Sox for the remaining week of the schedule.

In the first part of August, Carrigan's team won ten games in a row, gained a firm hold on second place, and pulled within six and a half games of the Athletics. Speaker, after being knocked out briefly in a bad collision with Hooper that disabled Boston's rightfielder for nearly two weeks, went on a hot streak and finally pushed his batting average above .300. But then Connie Mack's team won twelve games in a row and virtually put the pennant out of reach—at which point Tim Murnane, ignoring the Red Sox's resurgence, blasted them as "a team with little apparent ambition, and a disposition to be satisfied while drawing princely salaries. . . . The money some of the Boston Red Sox players are drawing down for ordinary work is positively outrageous."[20]

In a bevy of doubleheaders from the end of August through September 22, the Red Sox won nine games, lost two, and tied one. That included a sweep of the Athletics at Fenway Park and Ray Collins's feat of pitching and winning both games on September 22 at Detroit. By that point Boston had drawn within five and a half games of the Athletics. Four days later, though, hope was lost when they dropped another doubleheader in St. Louis. That left them eight and a half back with only eleven games to play.

The Red Sox ended the season with three games in Washington and another with the Nationals at Fenway Park. The season-closer was an 11-6 loss to Clark Griffith's team, whose third-place finish was again due mainly to the workhorse pitching of Walter Johnson. As was common in such meaningless games, players engaged in various hijinks. Red Sox players shifted from position to position, with Speaker moving from centerfield to firstbase, even taking the mound for the ninth inning and giving up two hits and a run. To make the fun complete, forty-four-year-old Griffith pitched a scoreless bottom of the inning, which put Boston's season record at 91-62 to Philadelphia's 99-53. The Red Sox's fans—more numerous by about 44,000 than they had been in 1913—must have wondered if the Athletics' domination, now four pennants in five years, would ever come to an end.

But in the other league, the New York Giants' three-year pennant run had been stopped by the long-suffering Boston Beaneaters/Doves/Rustlers/Braves, of all teams. In last place following the traditional July 4th doubleheaders, the Braves then won sixty-eight of their last eighty-seven games, blew past everybody, finished ten and a half games ahead of McGraw's team, and won Boston's first National League pennant since 1898. George Stallings's "Miracle Braves," as they quickly came to be called, featured outstanding pitching and a cast of mostly nondescript regulars whom Stallings alternated—or "platooned"—against lefthanded and righthanded pitchers more than any manager before him had done. The crowd of 383,000 the Braves drew to little South End Grounds was by far the best attendance in the thirty-eight-year history of the franchise. In an act of civic generosity, Joseph Lannin loaned Fenway Park, with its much bigger seating capacity, for the Braves' home games in the World Series. Only two games were played there, because Stallings's team capped its astonishing season with perhaps the greatest upset in Series history, dispatching the lordly Athletics in four games.

Braves pitchers held the Athletics to twenty-two hits and a .172 team batting average. Pitching overall had improved steadily following the 1911–1912 upsurge in offense that accompanied the introduction of the cork-centered baseball.

Brooklyn's Jake Daubert led the National League with a .329 average, the lowest in the league's history up to that time. Ty Cobb, disabled for nearly three weeks when George Foster's pitch broke one of his ribs, and then out for six weeks more after he broke his thumb in a fight with a butcher's assistant, appeared in only ninety-seven games and had only 345 official at bats. Under later requirements, Cobb wouldn't have qualified for his eighth straight batting title, but Ban Johnson certified him anyway. His .368 average was his lowest since 1908.

By making nine hits in the last four games of the season, Speaker finished at .338, which tied him with Joe Jackson for third place in batting average behind Cobb and Eddie Collins. He hit 4 home runs, drove in 86 runs, scored an even 100, and led the majors with 46 doubles. On 71 attempts, he stole 42 bases. Playing in all 158 of the Red Sox's games (which included five ties), he had 30 assists, cut his errors to 15, and set a new major-league record with 425 putouts.

Babe Ruth looked like a promising young pitcher and nothing else; with only a double and a single in ten times at bat with the Red Sox, he hadn't given any indication of the slugging prowess that, within another six years, began to revolutionize the way baseball was played. But he had impressed teammates in various other ways—mostly negative.

Ruth came out of St. Mary's school with an unappeasable appetite for all things of the flesh. If he was, as Ernie Shore remembered him, generous to a fault, "the best-hearted fellow who ever lived," he was also boorish, gluttonous, and careless of personal hygiene, which was partly why Joe Wood and Speaker quickly took a dislike to him.[21] Then there was what should have been an inconsequential episode during a pregame practice, when Wood let a ball get away and, instead of stopping the ball, Ruth just let it roll through his legs. Wood was furious at such parvenu behavior, and Speaker joined his friend in upbraiding the rookie. Moreover, because Ruth had been born into a German Catholic family and raised (and ruled) by priests at St. Mary's school, Speaker and Wood identified him with the "K.C." element on the club.

According to the respected Boston journalist Ed Linn, "The Speaker-Wood faction ... ridiculed and abused Ruth from the beginning. ... They called him the Big Pig as well as the Big Baboon. They called him Nigger Lips."[22] At one point Ruth offered to fight his tormentors in the clubhouse—there were no takers. In the years ahead, Speaker and Ruth would come to admire each other's talents, but they never really became friends.

That fall, while Speaker went on his usual postseason hunting trips, Hugh Bedient refused to be sent down to Providence and instead joined the Buffalo Federal Leaguers. Clyde Engle and Steve Yerkes, released outright during the season, had signed with the "Buffeds" and Pittsburgh Federals, respectively. The Red Sox champions of 1912 were breaking up, but Bill Carrigan, who had received a new two-year contract, was mixing in newer players who, in combination with such veterans as Speaker, Lewis, Gardner, and Hooper, could build on the solid finish of 1914. Having won the season's series with Philadelphia, they seemed to have a good shot in 1915 at unseating the recently embarrassed Athletics.

"Baseball Is a Business"

It wouldn't be the Philadelphia Athletics the Red Sox had to overcome for the 1915 pennant. In the wake of the World Series debacle, Connie Mack, who was field manager, business manager, and minority stock owner, began to dismantle one of the finest teams in baseball history. Despite a fourth pennant in five years and no local competition from the Federal League, the Athletics' 1914 home attendance was only fifth-best in the American League, and some 230,000 below 1913. All season Mack had heard his players grumble about the big money they could get if they went over to the Federal League. So Mack asked waivers on aging Chief Bender and Eddie Plank and sore-armed Jack Coombs and, when nobody in either league claimed them, released them outright. Bender and Plank signed with the Baltimore Federals and St. Louis Federals, respectively; Coombs, who had won seventy games for Mack from 1910 through 1912, caught on with the Brooklyn National Leaguers. Eddie Collins, one of the greatest players ever at secondbase, went to Charles Comiskey's White Sox for a record price of $50,000. Frank Baker wouldn't take a pay cut, sat out the whole season, and was sold to the Yankees for $37,500.

Nonetheless, Mack started the 1915 season with some talented players, including Bob Shawkey, Herb Pennock, and Leslie "Joe" Bush, three good young pitchers, plus veterans Jack Barry and Stuffy McInnis from the famed "$100,000 infield." By mid-season, however, Shawkey, Pennock, and Barry had gone elsewhere in the American League. Over the next couple of years, Bush, McInnis, and various others would follow. From a 99-55 record and a pennant, the 1915 Athletics plummeted to 43-105 and dead last, fourteen games behind seventh-place Cleveland. To replace Collins, Mack claimed thirty-nine-year-old Napoleon Lajoie for $2,500 after Cleveland put the fading "Frenchman" on waivers. Sadly, Lajoie spent his last two big-league seasons with the miserable aggregation Mack's team had become—and would remain.[1] The Athletics didn't emerge from the American League cellar until 1922.

While Connie Mack began his dismembering process, the New York Yankees underwent a fateful change in ownership. Late in 1914, Ban Johnson arranged for Frank Farrell and associates to sell the franchise for $460,000 to Jacob Ruppert, a New York brewery operator and real-estate magnate, and T. L. (for Tillinghast L'hommedieu) Huston, a former army engineer who had made a fortune on construction projects in Cuba. The new owners hired Bill Donovan, who had directed Providence the past season, to manage the team that Frank Chance gave up on. In what would seem a startling irony a few years later, Ruppert and Huston appealed to the other American League owners to help them strengthen their team. They got a little help from Detroit president Frank Navin, who for waiver prices gave them Wally Pipp, a young firstbaseman, and Hugh High, a diminutive outfielder.

Meanwhile, as reported by Tim Murnane, Tris Speaker "spent a delightful winter in Texas, hunting some of the time, promoting an athletic club at his home city, and not only having a royal good time, but also making things pleasant for his old friends around Hubbard City."[2] With his $18,000 per year salary guaranteed for 1915, Speaker made things comfortable for his mother, who, if she chose, could stop taking in boarders.[3]

If Speaker was content with his current financial situation, Walter Johnson wasn't. For years the Big Train had resented the salaries he had drawn from what was, admittedly, one of the majors' less-prosperous operations. In 1914, Johnson had been paid $9,500, and although he won "only" twenty-eight games, he had been the main reason Washington fielded a respectable team. But that winter the money offered by Charles Weeghman, owner of the Federal League's Chicago Whales, proved too much to resist—at least at first. Johnson signed with the Whales for a reported $18,000 and accepted a $10,000 signing bonus, at which point Washington manager Clark Griffith and principal owner Thomas Minor woke up and counteroffered a three-year contract at $12,500 per year, enough to persuade Johnson to stay with the Nationals. As a result of some complicated maneuvering involving Charles Comiskey, who didn't want Johnson pitching for the competition in his city, he ended up being allowed to keep Weeghman's $10,000.

Besides the Red Sox players, Joe Lannin, six sportswriters, several Royal Rooters, and the Lannin-owned Providence team were present in the "Valley of Vapors," as Murnane called Hot Springs, where the Pirates again shared the training site. Murnane reported that Joe Wood's arm was still lame; that Heinie Wagner's arm, which had troubled him all the past season, was sound; and that Lannin liked to play catch with his players and personally warmed up Babe Ruth.

In 1915, as their National League counterparts had done a year earlier, Lannin and the rest of the American League club owners voted to economize on their payrolls by limiting their rosters to twenty-one. Although the Federal League employed some players who would otherwise have been in the major leagues, sixty-four fewer roster positions were available in the two older leagues than before the arrival of the "invaders," as most of the baseball press termed the Federals.

On April 14, 1915, only about 9,000 Philadelphians showed up for the Athletics' opener with the Red Sox. Besides lacking four future Hall of Famers (Collins, Baker, Bender, and Plank), the Athletics began the season without Louis Van Zeldt, their mascot the past few seasons. The deformed little man, whose humpback the Philadelphia players liked to touch for luck before they batted, had died the previous month. But the fans in half-empty Shibe Park cheered Herb Pennock as the nineteen-year-old lefthander gave up one hit, a questionable two-out scratch single by Harry Hooper, in besting Ernie Shore, 2-0. That was Pennock's biggest moment of the season; in June, having won only two more games, he was claimed on waivers by the Red Sox and then optioned to Providence.

But the Pennock-Shore opening-day gem was indicative of the kind of pitching fans saw in both leagues that season. National Leaguers scored nearly 1,000 fewer runs than they had four years earlier; American Leaguers scored 737 fewer. The National League's collective earned run average fell from 3.29 to 2.74, the American's from 3.34 to 2.95. Ban Johnson might urge shorter games so that fans could get home in time for a warm supper, but for F. C. Lane of *Baseball Magazine,* the trouble wasn't the length of games but the lack of action. "No pitcher," editorialized Lane, "should . . . dominate the game. No contest ought to . . . lie in the hollow of one man's hand." A livelier baseball, Lane believed, would make for "a better rounded, more balanced institution and . . . a new and powerful appeal to ten million prospective buyers of bleacher and grandstand seats."[4]

Despite bad weather, the Red Sox managed to get in their home opener, won 7-6 from Philadelphia when thirdbaseman Eddie Murphy dropped a pop fly and let in two runs—one of the Athletics' six errors, of which Lajoie made the rest. It was wetter than usual in the east that spring; by early May the western teams had played as many as ten games more than those in the east. Makeup doubleheaders loomed as the season went along. After Babe Ruth lost 5-1 to league-leading Detroit at the start of their first western swing, the Red Sox had only a 9-9 record. Yet Bill Phelon thought this year the Boston players gave "evidence of a fierce desire to win, by hook or crook. Complaints were heard, loud and long, about the way the Red Sox blocked runners and how Bill Carrigan deliberately bounced them off his shin guards."[5]

On the afternoon of May 7, 1915, a German submarine torpedoed the *Lusitania* off the southern coast of Ireland, sending 1,959 persons to their deaths, of whom 128 were American citizens traveling on what was supposed to be a nonmilitary vessel. Those who perished included crew members who had transported the globe-traveling baseball party from Liverpool to New York fourteen months earlier. The sinking of the *Lusitania* caused widespread indignation in the United States and brought home, as had nothing else up to then, an awareness of the enormity of the conflict among European nations that had been going on since the previous August, one that had already killed hundreds of thousands on the Continent. Although the United States remained out of the war for another two years, the *Lusitania* incident marked the beginning of a steady deterioration in relations between the administration of President Woodrow Wilson and the government of Imperial Germany.

Yet in 1915 the Great War, as it came to be called, was still far away. For Tris Speaker and his peers, the day-to-day routine of the baseball season remained the business at hand. After taking three of four games in Detroit, the Red Sox won a fourteen-inning game at Cleveland, where, with the departure of the revered Lajoie, the local team's nickname had been changed to "Indians." Joe Wood, making his first start of 1915, lasted eleven innings before giving way to rookie Carl Mays, who benefited from a three-run rally that gave him the win.

At the beginning of June, the Red Sox's record was 17-13, which put them in fourth place behind Chicago, Detroit, and New York. They were no more a happy family than they had been in past seasons, with cliquism still entrenched. Speaker, batting well below .300, and Wood, able to pitch only about every ten days, were still at odds with their manager and his "K.C." friends. "The trouble," reported *Sporting Life,* "is said to be a factional fight between Carrigan and the [two] stars."[6] For those who had been close to the team over the past few years, that was hardly news.

Dutch Leonard was also a problem for Carrigan and Lannin. Complaining of a sore arm since Hot Springs, Leonard had pitched little so far in the season. Lannin, who went with the team on its first trip west, ran out of patience with Leonard in Chicago and ordered him home, under suspension and without pay. When he got back to Boston, Leonard claimed that he had had to borrow train fare from Carrigan, then castigated Lannin for interfering in team affairs, Wood for not earning his salary, and Speaker and others for poor run support. (The Red Sox were batting only .220 as a team.) Leonard added that Lannin petted his players when they won, but if they lost they were afraid to be around him. Lannin retorted that the lefthander was "a spoiled, sore-headed kid" who, with the Federal League on his trail in 1914, had demanded and received a two-year contract raising his salary from $3,000 to $5,000.[7] Lannin insisted that he had been generous with all his players, paying their medical expenses and keeping them on full salary when they were unable to play, as in the case of Larry Gardner, who had appeared in only three games in the current season. Tim Murnane suggested that the Red Sox owner, with about $800,000 invested in the franchise, appeared to be getting discouraged with his baseball venture.

Then there was Babe Ruth, whose marriage the previous October to a teenage Boston waitress had done nothing to quell his lust for "broads," as he called women, not to mention his gargantuan and indiscriminate intake of food. Although Carrigan couldn't do much to police Ruth's nighttime carousals in Boston, he tried to keep a close watch on him on road trips, with limited success. The kid was a natural on the ballfield, though. On June 1 he pitched Boston to a 5-1 win in New York and hit his first big-league home run, a two-run clout in the second inning off veteran righthander Jack Warhop. Ruth went on to post eighteen wins against eight losses and become one of the mainstays on an extraordinarily deep and balanced pitching staff, although he frequently needed relief in the late innings. Fans around the league also began talking about his proficiency at bat. On June 25, at Fenway Park, he hit a pitch from the Yankees' Ray Caldwell into the distant bleachers in straight rightfield, only the third player to do so. He hit two more homers that season and, in ninety-two times at the plate, batted .315.

On June 4, a pitch from Chicago's Jim Scott hit Speaker on the right side of his face and knocked him unconscious. With the consent of Clarence "Pants" Rowland, the White Sox's manager, Carrigan used a pinch runner while Speaker regained his senses. Although he returned to centerfield, he left the game after two more innings and didn't play again for five days. In the meantime, Lannin lifted Leonard's suspension and refunded the salary he had lost. Denying that he was a "drinker and a loafer" and still complaining of a sore arm, Leonard allowed that he would do the best he could.[8]

Leonard kept his word, going on to win fifteen games. His return to the pitching rotation was one reason the Red Sox began to play up to expectations and became a factor in the pennant race. Another was the acquisition early in July of Jack Barry, for whom Lannin paid the Athletics $8,000. Barry took over secondbase from Heinie Wagner, and rookie Everett Scott replaced Harold Janvrin at shortstop. With Larry Gardner's return to thirdbase and competent play at firstbase from Dick Hoblitzell and Del Gainer, the infield was as good as any in the league.

By the time Barry arrived, Speaker had finally started to round into form. Batting only .268 in mid-June, he changed his batting style, shortening his swing, which now became, as described by A. C. Mitchell in *Sporting Life,* "more like a tap than a swing."[9] On June 29 his tenth-inning single, his fifth hit, won Ruth's game in the finale of a series with New York. He made six hits in two games with the Athletics, and in a messy 15-12, eleven-error, ten-inning victory that closed a split series in Detroit, he lashed two singles and a double and pushed his average comfortably above .300.

After winning three out of five games in Cleveland, the Red Sox had improved their record to 48-28 and moved into second place, a game and a half ahead of Detroit, two behind Chicago. At Comiskey Park, they took advantage of the home team's shoddy defense to win four out of five games and displace the White Sox at the top. The western trip ended in St. Louis, where the Red Sox won five of six games, in one of which Ruth doubled twice and hit the longest home run ever seen at Sportsman's Park—a drive over the rightfield bleachers and onto the sidewalk across Grand Avenue. (Boston lost the last game of the series on a home run off Wood by George Sisler, the Browns' young firstbaseman.) The Boston club returned east in first place with a 57-30 record, leading Chicago by two games, Detroit by three and one-half.

The White Sox stayed close for a while longer, but despite acquiring Joe Jackson from Cleveland on August 20—for $31,500 and two players—their stay in first place had ended for good. The pennant race became an often-rancorous battle between Boston and a Detroit team that was seriously contending for the first time in six years. Red Sox loyalists might acclaim their outfield as the best in baseball, but the Tigers also had quite an impressive outfield trio in Sam Crawford, Ty Cobb, and Bobby Veach (all lefthanded batters). Again the highest-paid player in baseball with a three-year contract at $20,000 per season, Cobb played in every game, including two ties. Slapping and pushing balls past infielders, driving them past outfielders, beating out bunts, he enjoyed what may have been all around the best season of his career. Besides leaving everybody behind in the batting race, he scored 144 runs and, running the bases more aggressively than ever, stole 96 times to establish a record that stood for forty-seven years.

On August 23, Walter Johnson stopped the Tigers' nine-game winning streak in a doubleheader split at Navin Field, while George Foster and Dutch Leonard pitched a doubleheader sweep at St. Louis, with Speaker going four-for-eight. The Red Sox arrived in Detroit with a two-game lead. Boston won the first of the series, defeating lefthander Harry Coveleski behind Ernie Shore, 3-1, despite Cobb's repeated accusations that the big righthander was throwing an emery ball (which was supposed to be illegal). At one point the fiery Georgian even went into the visitors' dugout to go chin-to-chin with Carrigan and almost came to blows with the Boston manager. The next day Everett Scott doubled to drive in the go-ahead run in the thirteenth inning, and Speaker chased Crawford's drive "nearly into the next county" before hauling it down, ending the game and making Leonard the winner in relief of Ruth.[10] On Thursday the 26th, Detroit took the series finale in twelve innings, 7-6, when Cobb singled, Crawford sacrificed him to secondbase, and Veach hit a pitch from Leonard, working in relief of Foster, against the leftfield fence.

From Detroit, the Red Sox took the lake steamer to Cleveland and won three of four from the seventh-place Indians, ending the western trip with a record of 79-39 to the Tigers' 79-43. Chicago's loss at Detroit on September 2 while Boston trounced the Athletics in Philadelphia shoved the White Sox eight and a half games back and effectively put them out of the race. But on Labor Day, before a combined morning-afternoon attendance of some 39,000 at Fenway Park, the Red Sox dropped both games to the Yankees to fall into a virtual tie with Detroit.

The Red Sox were still tied with the Tigers on Thursday, September 16, when the two teams began a four-game set in Boston that everybody assumed would settle the pennant race. By that time, the opposing players had managed to work up plenty of ill feeling. The Red Sox thought Cobb and others had used rough stuff in Detroit, and Cobb was convinced Carrigan was telling his pitchers to throw at him. Cobb's hometown fans might be taken aback by some of his off-the-field escapades, but they admired and cheered him for his sustained brilliance. Around the American League, though, he had faced crowd hostility for years and seemed to thrive on it. What he encountered on this trip into Fenway Park was about as bad as he had experienced.

Hearing jeers and insults all afternoon from the crowd of 22,000, Cobb scored three times as Detroit took the series opener, 6-1. Righthander George "Hooks" Dauss threw a five-hitter; Hooper and Gardner made critical errors behind Foster, who was relieved by Ray Collins, followed by Carl Mays. Mays worked in thirty-eight games in 1914, nearly all in relief, and at the age of twenty-one was already becoming known for throwing high and tight. After two such close ones in the eighth inning, Cobb slung his bat at Mays, who proceeded to nick him on the arm with the next pitch. (Umpires George Hildebrand and Silk O'Loughlin, following the permissive practices of the time, took no action.) As Cobb took his base, soda pop bottles landed between the grandstand and the firstbase line. When the Red Sox were retired in the ninth, thousands of angry, cursing locals surrounded him in centerfield. Several teammates armed with bats came to his aid as he walked deliberately toward the home-team dugout and the passageway to the dressing rooms.

The next day Leonard mastered the Tigers, Detroit's only two runs coming on Cobb's homer into the rightfield bleachers after Boston had built a seven-run lead. In the third game of the series, an overflow turnout of 37,528, the biggest in American League history, saw another taut Shore-Coveleski matchup, which again lasted twelve innings and again went to Shore, 1-0. Detroit's best chance to score came in the top of the ninth inning, when Cobb led off with a double but, with the bases loaded, was forced at the plate, after which a mixup on the bases led to the third out. In the twelfth inning the Red Sox loaded the bases with one out. Carrigan, batting for Shore, hit a potential double-play grounder to short-stop Owen "Donie" Bush, but secondbaseman Ralph Young dropped Bush's toss as Duffy Lewis scored.

After the obligatory off day on Sunday, the series ended on Monday with Boston's third win, this one 3-2 before a crowd of 27,000 that brought the total attendance for the four games to 107,400. Duffy Lewis's triple in the sixth inning keyed a two-run rally to put Boston in the lead, which Ruth held until giving way to Foster with two out in the eighth. Foster saved it for Ruth; Dauss took the complete-game loss for the Tigers.

That concluded the Boston-Detroit season's play, in which the Red Sox had won fourteen of twenty-two games. The Tigers left town with a 91-51 record to the Red Sox's 93-45, and the Tigers' pennant chances were all but dead. Neither Speaker nor Cobb had excelled in the four games. Each man had batted officially fourteen times; Cobb registered a double, home run, and two singles, Speaker a double and two singles.

The Red Sox then won back-to-back doubleheaders from Cleveland, with Speaker making seven hits in the four games, and Joe Wood, in his final appearance of the year, getting credit for the third-game win, with help from Mays. After the Tigers won three games in Philadelphia, they swept a doubleheader in Washington, while the Red Sox were beating the Browns in a single game at Fenway. On the morning of September 26, the teams stood at 98-46 and 96-52. Detroit had only six games left to play; Boston had ten. Four days later, with Boston idle, Carl Weilman, St. Louis's tall lefthander, held the Tigers to two runs as George Sisler homered and the Browns pounded Dauss for eight runs. Weilman's eighth victory of the season over Detroit clinched it for the Red Sox, who learned of the outcome as they boarded a train for Washington.

On October 3 the Tigers closed their season by beating Cleveland for their one hundredth victory, which made them the first team in the American League's fifteen-year history to win that many games without winning a pennant. Ty Cobb would never get that close to another World Series. Five days later the Red Sox finished with a loss in New York, leaving their record at 101-50 to Detroit's 100-54. The White Sox were third at 93-61, their best showing in seven years.

In the end, it was the Red Sox's deep and mostly young pitching staff that made the biggest difference. Although nobody won twenty games, Shore and Foster had identical 19-8 records; Ruth was 18-8; Leonard, 15-7; and, whether he was using the emery ball or not, Joe Wood made a considerable comeback, pitching in twenty-five games, winning 15, losing only 5, and recording the league's lowest earned run average at 1.49. Boston's pitchers allowed the second-fewest runs in the league and showed the second-best staff earned run average, behind Washington in both instances. The acquisition of Jack Barry made a difference, too. When Barry joined the Red Sox, their record was 36-34; from then on it was 65-26 (54-23 with Barry in the lineup).

In 1912 the Red Sox had a collective batting average of .277 and scored 799 times; the 1915 team batted .260 and scored 131 fewer runs. No Boston player besides Speaker (and Ruth in his ninety-two at bats) managed to hit .300. Quantitatively, Speaker's performance was down in nearly every category, although he scored 8 more runs than in 1914. But he didn't hit a single home run, drove in only 69 runs, and a half-dozen or so players bettered his 22 doubles. Although he stole 25 bases, he was thrown out nearly half the time. Speaker's .322 batting average, his lowest since his first full season in 1909, tied him for third-best in the league with firstbaseman Jacques Fournier of Chicago; Eddie Collins batted ten points higher. Cobb's .369, which won him his ninth consecutive batting title, was a majestic mark in a year in which the .320 of the Giants' Larry Doyle led the National League.

Boston's "Miracle Braves" couldn't repeat the miracle in 1915, although they made a good run for the pennant until September. George Stallings's team had broken the New York–Chicago–Pittsburgh axis that had dominated the National League for fourteen seasons. Now, with Chicago and Pittsburgh fielding mediocre outfits and the Giants falling to last place, the Philadelphia Phillies, under rookie manager Pat Moran, with 90 wins and 62 losses, gained the first pennant in the franchise's history.

Grover Cleveland Alexander, the Phillies' twenty-eight-year-old righthander, led both leagues with 31 wins, as well as innings pitched (376), complete games (36), strikeouts (241), earned run average (1.22), and shutouts (12). Although the Phillies batted only .247 as a team, their pitchers allowed the fewest runs (463) in the majors. Righthanders Erskine Mayer and Al Demaree won 21 and 14 times, respectively, and Eppa Rixey, a tall lefthander, added 11. Otherwise, the Phillies were a collection of ordinary players, with a few the notable exceptions: firstbaseman Fred Luderus, their only .300 batter; Dave Bancroft, a far-ranging shortstop; and rightfielder Clifford "Gavvy" Cravath, who had played briefly for the Red Sox in 1908.

Baker Bowl, the Phillies' home grounds, dated from 1896. It was oddly configured even for its time. Located at Huntingdon Avenue and Broad Street, a short distance from the Athletics' Shibe Park, it seated only 18,800 in a double-decked grandstand and bleachers in leftfield. The distance down the line in left was a respectable 341 feet; to dead centerfield it was 408. But the rightfield fence was only 280 feet from home plate at the line; unlike rightfield at the Polo Grounds or Fenway Park, the fence didn't veer out sharply from the line but ran straight across, so that right-center was no more than 320 feet away. But the fence was 60 feet high—40 feet of tin over brick, topped by a 20-foot screen. Gavvy Cravath, who batted from the right side, had become remarkably adept at slicing drives against and over that fence. In 1915 his 24 home runs were the most anybody had hit since 1899; he also led his league with 89 runs and the majors with 115 runs batted in. For the World Series, Phillies president William F. Baker narrowed the playing area still more by having temporary bleachers built in left- and centerfields.

The Red Sox needed no temporary seats for the 1915 Series, because they rented brand new Braves Field, inaugurated only six weeks earlier. Having made a considerable profit with his low-payroll 1914 champions, Braves president James Gaffney had put together enough money to build what was then the biggest baseball facility anywhere, with a capacity of some 42,000 in a single-decked grandstand, huge pavilions down the foul lines, and a small bleacher section, called the "jury box," in right-center. Gaffney had purchased the grounds of what had been a golf club on Commonwealth Avenue in the Allston district, sold the frontage, and had his ballpark built on the back of the property. Railroad tracks ran behind the leftfield fence; beyond that was the Charles River. Braves Field had not only the top seating capacity but the most spacious outfield in the majors. Ty Cobb took one look at its dimensions—402 feet down the foul lines, 550 feet to dead center—and predicted that no ball would ever be hit out of the park. (None was until 1920.)

The World Series began in Philadelphia on Friday, October 8. The Royal Rooters arrived in force and paraded around Baker Bowl singing "Tessie" and carrying a banner that read, "We Never Followed a Loser." Playing on a soggy field before a paying audience of 19,343, Boston lost to Alexander, 3-1, although Ernie Shore yielded only five hits to eight by the Phillies' ace. Philadelphia scored a run in the fourth inning when leftfielder George "Possum" Whitted beat out a slow bounder to second, scoring centerfielder George "Dode" Paskert. Boston tied the game in the eighth when Speaker walked, went to second on Hoblitzell's grounder to third, and beat Whitted's throw on Duffy Lewis's line single. But in the bottom of the inning, with the bases loaded, Cravath scored thirdbaseman Milton Stock on a groundout to shortstop Everett Scott, after which Shore fumbled Fred Luderus's tap, scoring Dave Bancroft. In the ninth, with one out, pinch hitter Forrest Cady reached first on Luderus's fumble, but Luderus then grabbed a line drive by pinch hitter Ruth and caught Hooper's pop fly to end it. At various points during the game, plate umpire Bill Klem admonished the Boston bench to stop what *Sporting Life*'s reporter termed a "running fire of abusive personalities," mostly directed at Alexander.[11]

Saturday's game drew a capacity crowd of 20,306, including President Wilson, the first chief executive to attend a World Series game, and his fiancée, Edith Galt. They saw the Red Sox even the Series in another pitching duel, George Foster throwing a three-hitter and besting Erskine Mayer, 2-1. Foster himself was Boston's batting star, with a double and two singles, the second of which drove in the winning run in the top of the ninth inning. The Red Sox scored in the first on Speaker's single that sent Hooper around to third, followed by a double-steal attempt. Speaker was thrown out at second, but Hooper scored when catcher Ed Burns dropped the return throw. Philadelphia's only run scored in the fifth on back-to-back doubles by Cravath and Luderus. In the ninth, with two down, Paskert lifted a long fly ball to centerfield. Caught by a high wind, it kept drifting. At the last moment Speaker lunged over the temporary fence and snatched the ball for the third out.

With no Sunday baseball in either city, the teams resumed play on Monday the 11th at Braves Field. Paying $5 for box seats, $3 for grandstand, $2 for pavilions, and 50 cents for bleachers, 42,360 people were present. They included a delegation from the Massachusetts Women's Suffrage Association, which gave Speaker a $10 gold piece for scoring the first Red Sox run of the Series. The largest crowd up to then for a professional baseball game saw Alexander take a heartbreaking loss, 2-1, with Dutch Leonard yielding only three hits.

One of the three hits was Stock's first-inning double on a lazy fly Speaker lost in the sun, although Leonard struck out Cravath to end the threat. The Phillies scored in the third on Bancroft's single that brought in Burns, but Boston tied it the next inning on Speaker's triple into the faraway rightfield corner and Hoblitzell's sacrifice fly. Alexander pitched almost flawlessly from then on until the bottom of the ninth. Hooper hit a leadoff single; Scott bunted him to secondbase; and Alexander gave Speaker an intentional pass, whereupon Speaker doffed his cap to the Phillies' bench as he trotted to first.[12] Hoblitzell advanced the runners on a groundout to second, and Lewis hit Alexander's first pitch into centerfield to score Hooper and set off the most thunderous demonstration in the short history of Braves Field.

Game four was another tightly pitched, suspenseful encounter. Babe Ruth kept nagging Bill Carrigan for a chance to pitch, but the Boston manager again called on Shore. Shore and Scots-born George Chalmers, a righthander who had only an 8-9 record that season, dueled before 41,096 fans. Hooper's scratch hit in the third inning scored Jack Barry; the Red Sox made it 2-0 in the sixth on Hoblitzell's single and Lewis's double to the fence in left-centerfield. Shore scattered seven hits but held the Phillies scoreless until the eighth inning, when Cravath's liner to center bounced over Speaker's head for a triple, and Luderus singled him in. In the ninth, Shore retired the side on four pitches.

The format of the Series was a 2-2-2-1 alternation, so the fifth game was played back at Baker Bowl. (Boston's three hundred or so Royal Rooters, who had traveled to Philadelphia for the first two games, were so confident that the Series would end with the fifth game—and unhappy with the seats Baker had set aside for them—that all but a few of them stayed home.) Pat Moran, in a desperate gamble, held Alexander back and sent Mayer to the mound. Ruth continued to pester Carrigan, but Foster was the choice to try to close it out. That he did, pitching a complete-game win, although he was reached for nine hits and five runs and was in trouble much of the way. Another capacity turnout saw the two teams finally generate some punch.

Philadelphia loaded the bases in the bottom of the first inning and, despite a double play on Cravath's attempted squeeze bunt, scored twice on Luderus's two-run single. The Red Sox came back with single runs in the next two innings on Larry Gardner's triple to deep centerfield and Barry's single, then on Hooper's one-bounce home run into the temporary seats in the same area. Speaker's single sent Mayer to the showers in favor of Eppa Rixey, who retired Boston without further scoring. Philadelphia went up by two runs in the fourth inning when Luderus clouted a high drive that cleared the towering rightfield fence, second-baseman Bert Niehoff singled, and Hooper fielded Burns's single and threw wildly over Gardner's head at third in an effort to beat the sliding Niehoff.

Rixey seemed to have things in hand, retiring the first batter in the eighth inning. But then Del Gainer, who had replaced Hoblitzell after the lefthanded Rixey entered the game, beat out an infield grounder, and Lewis tied the game with a drive over the temporary seats in leftfield and into the bleachers for a two-run home run. In the bottom of the inning, Carrigan and other Red Sox protested at length but in vain when plate umpire Bill Klem ruled that Foster's pitch had hit Luderus, negating the third out on a steal attempt. The protest amounted to nothing, because Whitted, who had only one hit the whole Series, bounced an easy chance back to Foster.

In the top of the ninth, Boston won the game and the Series. After Foster struck out to start the inning, Hooper drove Rixey's pitch into the centerfield bleachers, again on one bounce, for his second homer of the day. Rixey retired the side, but Foster quickly did the same in the bottom of the inning, striking out Niehoff and getting Burns and pinch hitter Bill Killefer on easy groundouts.

Over the five games, the two teams had combined for twenty-two runs. Boston's pitchers showed a collective 1.84 earned run average and held Philadelphia to an anemic .182 at bat. It was a well-played Series in which only seven errors were recorded. Boston's batting stars were Lewis with a .444 average, including a home run and five runs driven in, and Hooper, who batted .350 and bounced in those two homers in game five. Bill Phelon rhapsodized, "There never was such all round ball played in any [S]eries as Duffy Lewis played in these great games." Speaker was held to a .294 average on five hits—four singles and a triple—in seventeen at bats. Apart from his game-saving catch in the second game, he wasn't impressive in centerfield. He had no assists, lost one ball in the sun, and had another bounce over his head for a triple. Phelon thought that Dode Paskert's centerfield play "completely showed up Speaker, ranging deep[,] taking flies that seemed impossible, while Speaker stumbled and staggered in the sun and mishandled at least three hostile hits."[13] That was unfair, perhaps, but for Speaker it was a middling performance following what had been, at least for him, a middling season.

If Speaker felt any disappointment with his play, Babe Ruth felt even more at never being called upon to pitch. But then there was the payoff of $3,780.25 for each Red Sox, which more than doubled Ruth's salary. The Phillies received $2,520.17 per man. At Lannin's request, there would be neither a celebration banquet nor a victory parade, so the hometown fans, including mayor James Curley (as much a fan as John F. Fitzgerald, his predecessor, had been), were denied what they had enjoyed three years earlier. That might have been a hint of Lannin's intentions for the coming season.

Outwardly, though, everything seemed rosy enough in Red Sox affairs. Duffy Lewis capitalized on his Series acclaim by returning to California and doing a four-week vaudeville swing from San Francisco to San Diego for $1,000 per week. Speaker, with baseball earnings for the year of close to $22,000, went off on his annual hunting foray, first to Lake Squam, New Hampshire, in the company of Ernie Shore and Tim Murnane, among others, then to the province of New Brunswick with the Yankees' Les Nunamaker, a former teammate.

Actually, the owner of neither Boston team was happy with his baseball investment. Although total National League attendance had recovered, showing a 700,000 increase over 1915, James Gaffney decided it was time to get out altogether. For $260,000, he sold his interest in the Braves to a syndicate headed by Percy Haughton, Harvard University's famed football coach. (Bankers who had financed construction of Braves Field continued to control the ballpark.)

Overall American League attendance fell by another 300,000; the champion Red Sox drew only about 60,000 more than in 1914. Joseph Lannin spent much of the off-season complaining publicly about his big payroll, although he acknowledged that he had cleared a small profit, enough to cover this year's expenses and last year's deficit. But he couldn't have done that, he said, without receipts from the four games in September with Detroit and the two World Series dates. Lannin had moved the club's offices from downtown Boston to rooms at the street level of his apartment complex. His Providence team wouldn't train at Hot Springs, and he would no longer pay expenses for injured players on road trips. "Once this is understood," wrote A. C. Mitchell, "and certain players given to understand that they must pay for their own keep while their arms are lame, the sooner they will show a disposition to stop loafing."[14]

In the aftermath of the Federal League war, economy was the order of the day among baseball owners, and Lannin was in the vanguard of the cost-cutters. He made it known that some players would have to take sizable pay cuts, mentioning specifically Ray Collins, whose record had fallen to 4-7, and Joe Wood, who had pitched commendably and never without pain. (Wood hadn't seen action in the

World Series, but he had been a noisy bench-rider, so much so that the National Commission fined him $25 for excessive verbal abuse of Erskine Mayer in game two.) Wood's contract for 1915 provided for a one-third salary slash, to $5,000. When he wouldn't sign for that figure, he learned that, along with Collins, Forrest Cady, and reserve catcher Chet Thomas, he had been put on waivers. They all cleared waivers; nobody in either league thought any of the four was worth the $2,500 claiming price.[15] Angry and bitter, struggling to remedy his aching arm with visits to a New York chiropractor, Wood announced that he wouldn't report to the Red Sox and might retire from the game altogether.

As for Wood's pal Speaker, who was at the end of his two-year contract, Lannin was upbeat: "Speaker will be with us next season and for several seasons, too. I feel that there will not be the slightest trouble in coming to terms with him." Speaker was supposed to visit Boston after New Year's, and then he and Lannin would "quickly get together."[16] Yet when Speaker got back to Hubbard and looked at his 1916 contract, he was indignant. Lannin wanted to roll back his salary to $9,000, where it had been in 1913. The line between professional pride and personal ego is indistinct; what Lannin had done inflamed both in the proud Texan. So he sent the contract back to Boston unsigned and settled in to wait out the Red Sox owner.

By the end of the year the Federal League option was no longer available to Speaker or anybody else. That league's two seasons of operations as the putative third major circuit had produced successive down-to-the-wire pennant races, but the league as a whole had suffered significant losses in 1914 and staggering ones the past season. Oil tycoon Harry Sinclair's publicized plans to move the Newark franchise (which had relocated from Indianapolis after the 1914 season) into Manhattan was a bluff on the part of the Federal League investors, who knew their venture was doomed. So James Gilmore and associates were more than amenable to overtures from the two older leagues for peace discussions, which began shortly after the World Series. The dismissal of the Federal League's antitrust suit against Organized Baseball—on which federal judge Kenesaw Mountain Landis had delayed a decision for nearly a year in anticipation that the baseball moguls would work things out among themselves—removed the final obstacle to a peace settlement.

On December 22, 1915, representatives of the American, National, and Federal Leagues, as well as the International League and American Association, signed an agreement ending the "baseball war" and extinguishing the Federal League. Organized Baseball paid the Federals $600,000 to disband and consented to the purchase of the Chicago Cubs by Charles Weeghman, owner of the local Whales, and the St. Louis Browns by Philip de Catesby Ball, who had operated the local Terriers. Also, despite their loudly proclaimed intention to blacklist jumping players, the major-league owners recognized the legitimacy of Federal League contracts. Harry Sinclair assumed them all (except for those held by Weeghman and Ball) and brokered the sale of seventeen players for a total of $129,500. All pending lawsuits involving particular players were dropped.

Where did that leave Tris Speaker, who was being asked to accept the same salary he had been making before the advent of the baseball war? Bill Carrigan pointed out, correctly, that "This was considered a big salary then," but that was then.[17] The waiting game continued into 1916 as Carrigan, several players, and the usual six reporters left Boston in a blizzard en route to Hot Springs. When the *Boston Globe*'s Paul Shannon took it upon himself to travel to Hubbard to query Speaker in person, he found a resentful young man, grousing that various players who had jumped to the Federals had then returned to the majors for more money than they had made before jumping. On March 22, Speaker wrote Carrigan that he was about to leave for Hot Springs; he gave no mention of whether he was ready to sign.

At Hot Springs, according to some accounts, Speaker told Lannin that he would sign a five-year contract at $12,000 per year, although Joe Vila wrote that he had learned Speaker wanted $15,000 for the same term. Whatever Speaker wanted, Lannin turned him down, whereupon the stubborn ballplayer entered into an odd arrangement with his equally stubborn employer. Speaker would practice with the rest of the squad and play in games against Pittsburgh at Hot Springs and then, for a fixed fee per outing, appear in exhibition games as the team traveled north, the presumption being that Speaker's presence in the lineup would swell gate receipts. Speaker had already picked up a tidy sum by the time the Red Sox reached Brooklyn on April 6 for a two-game set. In the first game

Speaker doubled in a run in a 6-0 win; the next day he cut down a runner trying to score, singled twice, and won the game, 3-2, with an eighth-inning home run off Rube Marquard.[18]

After the game, Lannin congratulated Speaker, told him his terms were acceptable, and assured him that he could sign his contract in Boston tomorrow. But Lannin was at best being disingenuous, at worst duplicitous. He had already concluded a deal with Phil Ball of the Browns to buy Clarence "Tilly" Walker, a good center-fielder (but no Speaker), for $15,000. Speaker was in his New York hotel room, packing his things and preparing to leave on the midnight train for Boston, when Robert McRoy, now business manager for the Cleveland Indians, telephoned from the lobby to say he wanted to come up. As soon as he sat down, McRoy asked Speaker how he would like to play for Cleveland. Taken aback, Speaker replied, "You've not only got a bad ball club, but you've got a bad baseball town." "I wish you wouldn't feel that way," said McRoy. "We've made a deal for you."[19]

McRoy represented James C. Dunn, a Chicago railroad builder who headed up a group of nine investors that had bought the Cleveland franchise only six weeks earlier. For $300,000 in cash and the assumption of a $210,000 debt on League Park, Dunn and associates purchased the Indians from local bankers, who had foreclosed on Charles Somers, owner of the franchise from its inception. Somers had once been a young multimillionaire with extensive holdings in Great Lakes shipping, but a series of business setbacks had put him $1,750,000 in debt and, among other exigent moves, prompted his sale of Joe Jackson the previous August. Ban Johnson, who had originally put some of his own money into the Cleveland operation, persuaded Dunn to buy the franchise. Among the other investors was Robert McRoy, who bought $5,000 worth of stock and became the Indians' business manager.

About the time the Red Sox arrived in Brooklyn, Ed Bang, sports editor of the *Cleveland News*, read a wire-service story quoting Lannin as being fed up with Speaker's holdout. Bang called McRoy at League Park; McRoy called Dunn in Chicago; and, with Dunn's approval, McRoy caught the first train for Boston. There he kept in touch by telephone with Dunn, running up $50 in long-distance charges. At two P.M. on Saturday, April 8, Dunn and Lannin concluded the particulars of their deal. Meanwhile the Red Sox front office announced the acquisition of Tilly Walker.

Speaker became the property of the Cleveland ball club in return for a cash payment of $55,000, plus transfer to the Red Sox of the contracts of Sam Jones, a righthanded pitcher coming off a 4-9 record in his rookie season, and Roy Thomas, a minor-league infielder. Speaker refused to accompany McRoy to Cleveland; instead he went to Boston, where, visibly angry but apparently resigned to his fate, he told local sportswriters, "I suppose I must play in Cleveland. If you want to continue in the big show you must go where the club owners send you. . . . I hate to leave Boston, for I like the people here. [But] I'll go where the money is. Baseball is a business and you've got to be ready for any and everything."[20]

Yet Speaker wasn't about to go quietly—or empty-handedly. He called Lannin and demanded $10,000 of the sale price, then finally boarded a train for Cleveland, arriving on the afternoon of April 11. After he checked into the Colonial Hotel, he threatened to return to Texas unless he got his money. He didn't want it from Dunn, but personally from Lannin. A flustered Dunn called his friend Ban Johnson, who then called Lannin and asked him to mail a check for what Speaker wanted, but the Red Sox owner would have none of that. "Speaker has been well paid for his work and I will do absolutely nothing more for him," Lannin declared.[21] That night Speaker met with Dunn at the Hollenden Hotel and said he would settle for a $5,000 signing bonus, but the Indians' new owner wasn't willing to go that far. At noon the next day, at League Park, they finally agreed on a $2,500 bonus, and Speaker signed a two-year contract for what Ed Bang, who probably had it right, reported to be $15,000 per season. Speaker then jumped into a taxi, rushed back downtown to his hotel to retrieve his baseball equipment, and rushed back to the ballpark.

Despite overcast and chilly weather, a capacity crowd of 18,351—many wearing Indian headdresses handed out by the management—cheered Speaker as he emerged from the home dugout in his pin-striped home uniform, trimmed in blue, with the number 9 on the left sleeve. (The 1916 Indians were the first to display numbers anywhere on uniforms, although they discontinued the practice after one season.) It wasn't a glorious debut for Speaker or his new ball club. The St. Louis Browns' Bob Groom, who had jumped from Washington to join the St. Louis Federals, threw a three-hit shutout. Benefiting from four Cleveland errors, the Browns scored six times on lefthander Willie Mitchell and rookie righthander Jim Bagby. Speaker flied out to centerfield in his only official time at bat; Groom passed him three times.

Ed Bang described the Speaker deal as "the biggest in the history of the game" and estimated its total value—cash and the players sent to Boston—at $75,000. That was basically accurate, even if Bang exaggerated the value of Sam Jones and Roy Thomas (who didn't play in a big-league game until 1918). The whole business left the Boston faithful confused and dismayed. The local *Herald* believed that the Red Sox had lost their chance for another pennant, and the *Globe* reported, "There is no joy for the Red Sox in the prologue of their 1916 drama." Grantland Rice, now a syndicated columnist, estimated that Speaker's presence in the lineup had meant at least ten additional wins for the Red Sox, and Bozeman Bulger in the *New York Evening World* thought that without Speaker, the Boston team "may turn out to be like the well-known sailless ship." Quipped George Foster, "Half my stuff is going to Cleveland."[22]

Joseph Lannin, though, was eminently pleased with the deal he had made. Lannin had convinced himself that Speaker, at the age of twenty-eight (or twenty-seven), was on the downgrade, noting that Lewis and Hooper had outshone him in last fall's World Series, and that his batting averages and most other offensive statistics had declined steadily for the past three seasons. Every season from then on, Lannin feared, Speaker's market value would drop. Of course Lannin might also have observed the general falloff of batting and scoring since 1911–1912— that, for example, Ty Cobb's 1915 average was fifty-one points below that of 1911, Joe Jackson's exactly one hundred points. "I never dreamed that I could get so much money for [Speaker's] release," Lannin told the Boston press. "I do not believe that any ball player is worth the money I received for Speaker. I also wish to say that Speaker isn't worth the salary he demanded."[23]

Lannin was wrong on both counts, both about Speaker's decline as a player and his not being worth the money Dunn paid for him. As reluctant as he had been to come to Cleveland, Speaker discovered that the city's fandom had quickly taken him to its heart. Following the departures of first Napoleon Lajoie and then Joe Jackson, Speaker was welcomed as something of a baseball messiah. Some of his greatest seasons were still ahead of him, and as the key figure in the regeneration of Cleveland's baseball fortunes, he proved a far more valuable asset to James C. Dunn than Joseph J. Lannin could have imagined.

"New Life into a Half-Dead, Despondent City"

Baseball Magazine editor F. C. Lane observed (less than presciently) that when Speaker left Boston, "He said goodbye forever to the glamor and the money of a world's series." Meanwhile Joe Wood had decided to sit out the season, prompting the *Sporting News* to editorialize: "It is comforting to hear that the transfer of Speaker and the absence of Joe Wood have made for harmony on the Red Sox ball team." But for Bill Phelon, the important thing was that the Speaker deal had "brought new life into a half-dead, despondent city."[1]

Although Cleveland possessed flourishing amateur and semipro baseball programs, "half-dead" and "despondent" didn't seem too strong to describe the city's big-league situation before Speaker arrived. Cleveland had never had a pennant-winner—as a member of the major-league American Association in the 1880s, the National League in the 1890s, or the American League since 1901. The local contingent had come close in 1908, when player-manager Napoleon Lajoie led his Naps in a battle with Detroit and Chicago that ended with Cleveland losing to the Tigers by only half a game. After that, Cleveland's entries hadn't been a factor in league races except for third-place finishes in 1911 and 1913.

The past two seasons had been fairly miserable. In 1914, Lajoie's last year with Cleveland, the Naps won only fifty-one games and finished last; in 1915 the newly named Indians were better than the gutted Athletics but still worse than everybody else. With a population of about 750,000 (nearly a third of which was foreign-born), Cleveland boasted of being the nation's "sixth city." Yet home attendance in 1915 was only 160,000, down 70 percent from what it had been two years earlier. A month into the season, Cleveland president Charles Somers had fired manager Joe Birmingham and given the job to Lee Fohl, a stolid, forty-four-year-old native of nearby Akron and a career minor-league catcher except for four games in the National League. Fohl's prospects looked bleaker than ever when Somers sold Joe Jackson to Chicago. Now, though, Fohl worked for a new owner, and he had Speaker, to whose judgment he would usually be willing to defer—to such an extent that Speaker became his unofficial assistant manager.

Aside from Speaker, Fohl didn't have a lot to work with. Native Canadian Jack Graney was a capable leftfielder; hot-tempered little Bobby "Braggo" Roth, obtained in the Jackson deal, occupied rightfield; Ray Chapman and Bill Wamb-sganss were promising young infielders; and the veteran Arnold "Chick" Gandil, purchased from Washington in February, held down firstbase. Cleveland's top pitcher in 1915 had been rookie righthander Guy Morton, with a 16-15 record. The best-looking new hurlers were righthanders Jim Bagby, who wasn't fast but showed excellent control for a rookie, and Stanley Coveleski, the younger brother of Detroit's Harry Coveleski and already an adept spitballer.

Although Speaker wasn't considered a "hard hitter" on the order of Lajoie, Joe Jackson, or Sam Crawford, he was expected to gain an advantage by play-ing half his games in League Park. Located at East 66th Street and Lexington Avenue, the second-edition League Park was similar to Philadelphia's Baker Bowl. It seated about 18,500 in a double-decked grandstand and shallow bleach-ers extending across leftfield, and like Baker Bowl, it had a spacious playing area except for rightfield. The distance down the leftfield line was a formidable 385 feet. The deepest point, just left of dead centerfield, was 505 feet from home plate, but it was only 290 feet down the line in right. Fielders had to learn the tricks of playing balls off the rightfield wall—20 feet of concrete, topped by another 20 feet of chicken-wire fencing—because its protruding steel supports were not only hazards but often caused crazy caroms into right-center and centerfield.

In Cleveland, Speaker's new teammates and his growing number of local acquaintances continued to call him "Tris" or "Spoke," just as he had been called in Boston. But Joe Williams, who had moved from the *Memphis Commercial Appeal* to the *Cleveland Press* two years earlier, came up with a nickname that quickly worked its way into contemporary press coverage and stayed with him for the rest of his life: the "Gray Eagle."

Tris Speaker, Texas League batting champion with the Houston Buffaloes, 1907.
(National Baseball Hall of Fame Library, Cooperstown, N.Y.)

Left: Boston Red Sox, American League and World Series champions, 1912. *Left to right, front row:* Ray Collins, Harold Janvrin, Harry Hooper, Joe Wood, Tris Speaker; *middle row:* Steve Yerkes, Bill Carrigan, Buck O'Brien, Charlie Hall, Les Nunamaker, Jake Stahl, Forrest Cady, Larry Pape, Clyde Engel; *back row:* Duffy Lewis, Chet Thomas, Larry Gardner, Olaf Henriksen, Hugh Bedient, Marty Krug, Heinie Wagner, trainer Kirke. (National Baseball Hall of Fame Library, Cooperstown, N.Y.)

Below: Speaker in batting practice at Hot Springs, Arkansas, ca. 1913. The catcher is Chet Thomas. (National Baseball Hall of Fame Library, Cooperstown, N.Y.)

Walter Johnson warming up at the Polo Grounds, New York, while a teammate chats with spectators, ca. 1913. (National Baseball Hall of Fame Library, Cooperstown, N.Y.)

Joe Jackson, 1918. (National Baseball Hall of Fame Library, Cooperstown, N.Y.)

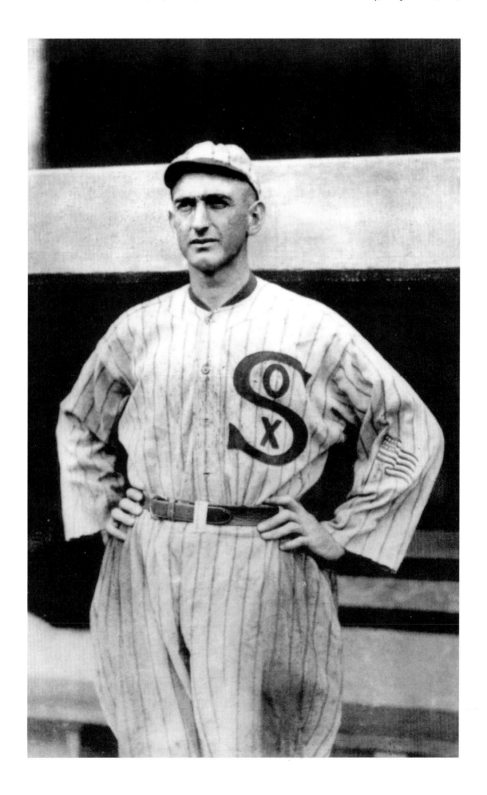

Left: Cleveland Indians, American League and World Series champions, 1920. *Left to right, front row:* Coach Jack McCallister, Joe Evans, Charlie Jamieson, Doc Johnston, club president Jim Dunn, player-manager Tris Speaker, club secretary Walter McNichol, Elmer Smith, Stanley Coveleski, Joe Sewell; *middle row:* Chet Thomas, Jack Graney, Guy Morton, Jim Bagby, Ray Caldwell, Les Nunamaker, George Burns, Bob Clark, Steve O'Neill, Larry Gardner, Ted Odenwald; *back row:* Duster Mails, Cykowski, Hamilton, George Uhle, Joe Wood, Bill Wambsganss, Harry Lunte, trainer Percy Smallwood. *Inset:* Ray Chapman. (National Baseball Hall of Fame Library, Cooperstown, N.Y.)

Below: Napoleon Lajoie, Speaker, and Cy Young before the fourth game of the 1920 World Series, the first played in Cleveland. (National Baseball Hall of Fame Library, Cooperstown, N.Y.)

Below: Speaker's leap into the League Park box seats to embrace his mother after the final out of the 1920 World Series. (National Baseball Hall of Fame Library, Cooperstown, N.Y.)

Right: Speaker with his wife Mary Frances in Washington, D.C., in 1925, a few months after their marriage. (National Baseball Hall of Fame Library, Cooperstown, N.Y.)

Below: Kenesaw Mountain Landis, 1923. (National Baseball Hall of Fame Library, Cooperstown, N.Y.)

Right: Speaker, Clark Griffith, and Bucky Harris at the Washington Senators' spring training, Tampa, Florida, 1927. (Cleveland Public Library)

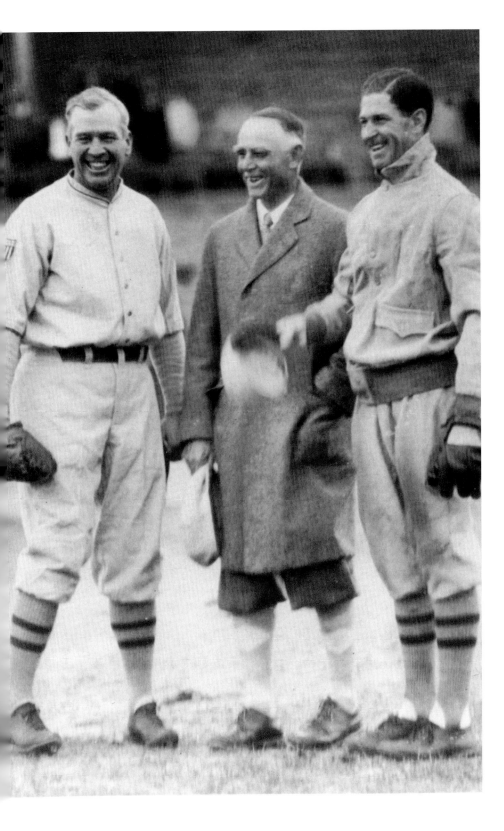

Speaker and Ty Cobb as teammates on the Philadelphia Athletics, 1928.
(Courtesy of C. Paul Rogers III, Dallas, Texas)

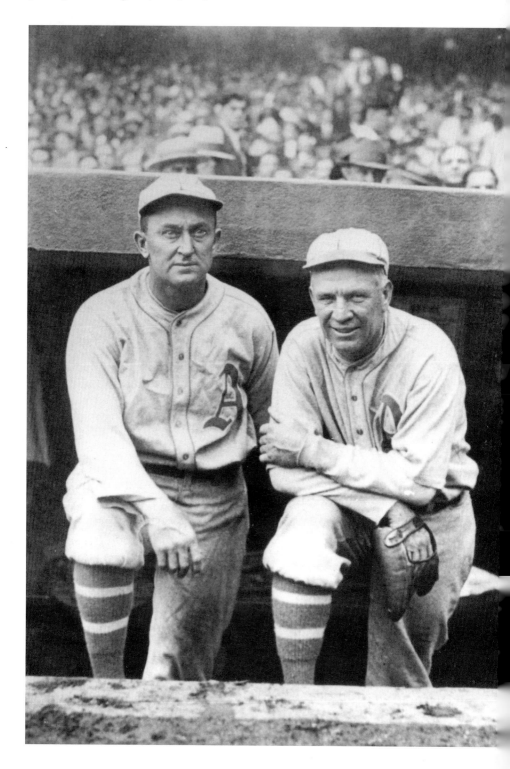

Speaker examining his liquor stock at his Cleveland distributorship in the 1930s.
(Cleveland Public Library)

Below: Ty Cobb, terminally ill Babe Ruth, and Speaker before ceremonies honoring Ruth at Yankee Stadium, September 1947. (Cleveland Public Library and © Bettmann/Corbis)

Right: Speaker convalescing at home in 1954 following his heart attack, in the company of his Irish setter. (Cleveland Public Library)

Speaker chatting with Sam Jones (to his immediate left) and others at Cy Young's funeral, November 1955. (Courtesy of Matthew Gladman, Tippecanoe, Ohio)

Speaker's hair had grayed prematurely; that and the weathered look he acquired spending most of his time outdoors made him appear older than he was. F. C. Lane cited "the persistent rumor that Tris is 32 years of age"; the *Sporting News* averred that "few fans will believe that Tris is as young as he would like to have people believe."[2] Of course, he had just turned twenty-eight (or twenty-seven) when he arrived in Cleveland. Speaker was quoted to the effect that he didn't mind fans riding him about how old he was when he was going well, but he didn't like it when he wasn't.

Speaker also acknowledged that if he had to give an interview, he wanted it to be short. Lane characterized him as "a silent man, moody, taciturn." That may have been the case at various times during Speaker's years in Boston, especially given his barely concealed dislike for Bill Carrigan and some of his teammates and his contract battle with Joe Lannin the past off-season. But he quickly developed a warm personal relationship with the rotund, sunny-dispositioned Jim Dunn, whose Irish Catholicism seemed not to matter at all to the Methodist-reared Texan. About a week after Speaker joined the Indians, Dunn later said, he told the club president, "When I came to Cleveland I came with a bad taste in my mouth," unhappy about leaving Boston to join a team "which seemed in pretty bad shape." But Dunn and everybody else had treated him so well that "I will guarantee to give my best work to you and do all I can toward making your proposition here a success." Dunn also mentioned that when Speaker's mother and his sister Elaine visited Cleveland during the 1916 season, Jenny Speaker told him, "You look fat and good natured. I guess you'll take good care of my boy."[3]

After losing two of three games in the opening series with the Browns, the Indians attracted a Sunday overflow crowd of 23,981 for a ten-inning, 4-3 victory over Detroit. Speaker, for whom St. Louis manager Fielder Jones had ordered five intentional walks in that series, singled twice, doubled, drove in one run, scored another, made a running one-handed catch in deep left-centerfield, and threw out the Tigers' Ralph Young at home plate in the top of the tenth to keep the game tied. On Monday, however, Speaker's close-in play in centerfield cost him, when three balls—two hit by Bobby Veach and one by Harry Heilmann—went over his head for triples in a 4-3 loss to the Tigers. He came back the next day with four singles, although Stanley Coveleski lost, 3-1. George Cunningham pitched for Detroit in place of Harry Coveleski, who had refused to be matched against his kid brother in Stanley's major-league debut.

Soon, though, Speaker's hitting, together with sturdy pitching by Coveleski, Jim Bagby, and, over the first half of the season, Carl Morton, made the Indians a hot ball club. After they swept four games in Chicago and three in Detroit, the Indians found themselves in first place with a 15-7 record. Henry P. Edwards of the *Cleveland Plain Dealer* effused that Speaker and Lee Fohl "make a great pair, working together like two parts of a perfectly oiled machine."[4] When the team was on the road, Edwards reported, they got together each night after dinner for strategy sessions. Sometimes Speaker would call time and run in from centerfield to advise pitchers on what to throw to particular batters, especially when the Indians played the Red Sox.

Speaker also felt free to offer batting tips to his new teammates. He asked Steve O'Neill, the team's regular catcher, if he ever guessed on pitches. When O'Neill replied that he didn't, Speaker told him, "Well, you'll never be a better hitter until you do."[5] (O'Neill took the advice, although it apparently did him little good, because he batted only .236 in 1916 and .184 the next year.)

Speaker, Edwards told his readers, had become a popular figure everywhere he went around the American League. In Chicago, for example, the musical comedy star Fred Stone, appearing in the hit revue *Chin Chin,* called Speaker, invited him to lunch, and gave him tickets for all his teammates to that night's show. Later, Jake Stahl, now a bank vice president in suburban Englewood, picked up Speaker and Robert McRoy to take them to dinner. When Speaker said he needed a shave, Stahl stopped off at a barbershop and persuaded the shop's owner, a black Chicagoan, to interrupt his own dinner and shave Speaker ahead of a dozen waiting customers. Star status brought special privileges.

Speaker's first appearance of the season in Boston, early in May, drew 14,353 to Fenway Park on a Tuesday. Ralph E. McMillen of the local press was carried away with the event, which he called "one of the most remarkable things that Boston or any other town ever saw."[6] In pregame ceremonies, Speaker received an emblem and a fez from a group of fellow Shriners and a silver loving cup from Joe Lannin. In the game that followed, he tripled off the flagpole in deep centerfield, although Cleveland lost to Dutch Leonard, 5-1. The Indians won the next day but lost on Thursday. Speaker made five hits in the three games but fumbled a ball that led to Boston's winning run in the series finale.

On their first trip into Washington, the "Tribe" (as the Cleveland writers had taken to calling the Indians) won the first two games from the Nationals and, in between, visited President Wilson at the White House. Having pushed their record to 21-9, they made a jump back to Cleveland with the Nats for a Sunday game, which they lost to Walter Johnson, 4-3, before an overflow crowd of 25,522—the biggest ever for a game at League Park. (Such jumps back west were a common practice in both leagues before Sunday baseball was legalized in the eastern cities.) At that point Cleveland held first place by two and a half games over Washington, although Clark Griffith's club soon fell back in the race.

The Indians' second western swing was a grueling journey lasting twenty-eight days, with the players spending twelve nights on Pullman cars. They came home in second place, trailing a New York team that was making its strongest showing in six years. But by beating Boston twice, with Speaker pounding a double and two triples in the first game, Cleveland dislodged the Yankees and, as of June 5, again led the league.

Like a growing number of other people in baseball—players, managers, club owners, and writers—Speaker had taken up golf and quickly become addicted to the game. His mornings in Cleveland or in other American League cities he frequently spent on the links at an area country club. Being naturally righthanded, Speaker swung his golf clubs that way. (He also signed his name righthanded.) Henry P. Edwards, who occasionally played with him, reported that Speaker wasn't an accurate driver and was still trying to break 90.

Speaker also took on a lot of public-relations activity for the Cleveland franchise, something he had done little of in Boston. With Washington in town, he and Clark Griffith spoke at an Ad Club luncheon at the Statler Hotel, where he "acquitted himself as creditably as a talker as he does in center field," or so it was reported.[7] That evening he gave a talk to members of the Lakewood Masonic Lodge. The next morning he and the city welfare director spoke to an assembly of male students at East High School.

With two rainouts, the Tribe got in only one game with Washington, a fourteen-inning tie, before battering Philadelphia four times and taking a four-game advantage over the second-place Yankees.[8] Yet the season was shaping up as an extraordinarily competitive one for everybody but Connie Mack's dismal outfit. On June 13, Cleveland led the Yankees by four games, but only a game and a half separated New York, Washington, Boston, and Detroit. By then Lee Fohl was trying to get along with a badly weakened pitching staff, because Carl Morton and Ed Klepfer, two of his starting pitchers, had developed sore arms. Morton had won eleven of thirteen decisions; he would win only one more the rest of the season.

On June 29 Speaker had a frightening experience when his foul ball hit a woman in the face. The first report was that she was dying in the League Park ladies' room. Apparently shaken, he dropped two fly balls that helped St. Louis win, 7-0, with Dave Davenport, a towering righthander, pitching the shutout. After the game, Speaker phoned the hospital where the woman had been taken and learned that she hadn't been seriously hurt after all.

In July the Tribe could do no better than a 9-9 record in the east and came home in third place. Although they trailed the Yankees by only two games, they didn't see first place again. Speaker had pushed his average to .391, and his manager couldn't praise him enough. "Tris Speaker is the best ball player in the world," raved Fohl, "and he's doing for Cleveland something that all the other stars couldn't do."[9]

But on July 30, in the first inning of a 2-1 loss to Washington at League Park, Speaker tried for a shoestring catch, caught his spikes in the turf, and had to be carried from the field with a badly sprained ankle. On crutches for a few days and disabled for a week, he limped noticeably when he returned to the lineup to hit two singles in a 12-3 pummeling of the Athletics. After sweeping four games from Connie Mack's abject club, the Indians, at 50-42, were tied with Chicago for third place, two games behind Boston, three and a half behind New York. From then on, though, the Yankees, plagued by injuries, fell back. By August 15 the champion Red Sox, again getting superlative pitching from Ruth, Leonard, Shore, Foster, and now Carl Mays in a starting role, had moved into the lead.

A couple of weeks later, Bobby Roth, who was hitting better than anybody on the Tribe besides Speaker, got himself ejected from a game in St. Louis. His behavior, the umpires reported to Ban Johnson's Chicago office, was such that he should be suspended. But because the next day was Sunday and Johnson's office was closed, Roth remained in the lineup. Fans in Sportsman's Park's rightfield bleachers showered him with bottles, whereupon Roth fired a baseball into the bleachers, received more bottles, threw one of them back, and made obscene gestures to the people in the bleachers as well as the firstbase grandstand. His eventful day climaxed with a home run that won the game for Jim Bagby, 4-3. The next morning, Roth received a wire from Chicago informing him that he was suspended for three days.

In mid-August, the Indians were still in hot pursuit of the pennant. Boston, Cleveland, and Chicago all had won 62 games; but their losses, respectively, were 45, 48, and 49. The Browns, sparked by George Sisler, their brilliant young firstbaseman, and Federal League returnee Eddie Plank, having his last strong season, had climbed to fourth at 60-52. Then the Indians traveled east, stopping off at Scranton, Pennsylvania, and losing an exhibition game to the local New York State League club. They proceeded to lose all eight games they played in New York and Boston before splitting the eight they played in Philadelphia and Washington. On August 24 Speaker and his teammates suffered the ignominy of being no-hit by the Athletics' Joe Bush. At the end, many among the Saturday turnout of three thousand poured onto the field to pound the back of the young pitcher, who endured a 15-24 record for the season.

That dreary journey left the Indians in sixth place with a 67-60 record, although they were still only eight games behind front-running Boston. Then came six more losses in a row in Detroit and Chicago. After falling to the Tigers, 10-2, at League Park on September 12, with Ty Cobb homering twice, the Indians were in seventh place. With the league's standings changing daily, Detroit was in a virtual tie with the Red Sox.

If his team's pennant hopes had faded, Speaker slammed the ball at such a pace that it seemed at last he might wrest the American League's batting title from Cobb. "And the beauty of Speaker's hits," wrote Henry P. Edwards, "is that nearly all of them have been convincing smashes to the outfield, infield scratches being very scarce articles with Tris." Later Edwards described Speaker as excelling at the "short, snappy jolt that sends the ball just beyond the reach of the infielders—sharp singles as a rule."[10] Contrary to what Cobb and John McGraw thought, Speaker believed that golf-playing helped his ball-playing. On an off day late in September, he golfed at the Shaker Lakes Country Club with Fred Stone, who was in Cleveland with his show.

A three-game Red Sox sweep in Detroit on the pitching of Mays, Leonard, and Ruth dropped the Tigers to third place, behind Chicago, and effectively squelched their chances for a pennant. On Sunday, October 1, in the opener of a season-closing doubleheader at League Park, Cleveland lefthander Fritz Coumbe shut out the White Sox on two hits to win his seventh game of 1916. That loss, combined with Dutch Leonard's 1-0 victory over New York the previous day, clinched Boston's third pennant in five years. In the inconsequential nightcap, which the Indians lost, 8-4, Speaker had a double and single in four times at bat.

On Tuesday, the Red Sox closed the season by nonchalantly losing twice to Philadelphia. At 91-63, the Speaker-less Red Sox finished two games in front of Chicago but ten games shy of their 1915 record. Edwards believed that with Speaker in the lineup, Boston would have run away from the rest of the league. With Speaker, Cleveland ended at 77-77, a twenty-game improvement over 1915 and a remarkable showing for a sixth-place team, especially a team with only one outstanding everyday player. What doomed the Tribe were a spotty corps of pitchers aside from Bagby (16-16) and Coveleski (15-13) and, except for Speaker, a team-wide batting slump over the season's final six weeks.

But for the first time since 1907, somebody besides Ty Cobb was the American League's batting champion. Speaker batted .386, his top average thus far, with a majors'-best 211 hits in 151 games, including a league's-best 41 doubles—many of which bounced off League Park's short rightfield wall. He also scored 102 runs, about 16 percent of the Tribe's total; and although he registered only 2 home runs (both inside the park), he led his club with 83 runs batted in. His 10 errors matched his fewest as a big-leaguer, and he was again among the leaders with 25 assists. Cobb batted .371, which improved on his 1915 average by two points, but he had gotten off to a slow start—too slow, it turned out, to catch Speaker. As for his other two perennial rivals, Joe Jackson led the White Sox at .341, but Eddie Collins struggled to bat .308. (That stellar tandem, however, had better things in store for Chicago.)

A few years later, with perhaps more than a hint of sarcasm, Speaker commented regarding his 1916 batting title, "Cobb had had his honors enough. He ought to give the rest of us a look in once in a while." He went on, "I claim no such magic power as Ty Cobb is supposed to possess. All I know is that I have made a study of placing hits and can frequently drive a ball pretty close to where I want it to go."[11]

Despite the disappointing last six weeks of the season, it had been a resoundingly successful one not only for Tris Speaker but for the Cleveland franchise. Attendance at League Park was close to a half million, more than had ever paid to see professional baseball in the city.

Speaker turned down a reported offer of $1,500 to have a ghost writer prepare his game-by-game comments on the World Series for a newspaper syndicate. Instead he joined a team that included Chick Gandil, Ray Chapman, and Detroit pitcher Jean Dubuc on a barnstorming tour into Ontario. Then he was off to New Brunswick for deer-hunting with former Red Sox teammates Les Nunamaker of the Yankees and Walter Rehg, who had played at Providence in 1916.

Afterward he stopped off in Cleveland to get his automobile serviced and to attend a dinner for local sportswriters and club officials, hosted by Jim Dunn at the Hollenden Hotel. Dunn extolled Speaker as having done more than anybody to put Cleveland back on the baseball map. "I found Tris to be not only a wonderful ball player," he said, "but a man of his word, and today I regard him as one of my very best friends, a player who has my interests at heart all the time." Speaker then praised Dunn and Lee Fohl, saying he never wanted to play for another manager. When one of the writers asked him how he could take the batting title while playing so much golf, he replied, "Golf is a great game for ball players," one that helps their batting eye.[12]

As for the World Series Speaker didn't attend, it was again a Boston triumph in five games, this time over the Brooklyn Robins, and it was again the Red Sox's masterful pitching that decided the outcome. Ernie Shore pitched two winning games; Dutch Leonard and Babe Ruth the other two. At the age of twenty-one, Ruth had become the best lefthander in baseball, with twenty-three wins for the season, a majors'-best 1.75 earned-run average, and a brilliant fourteen-inning, 2-1, victory in game two.

The two Series games in Boston, played again at Braves Field, took place before capacity crowds, but for the season, the Red Sox attracted about 44,000 fewer people into Fenway Park than in 1915. Joe Lannin had had enough of being a baseball "magnate." Early in December he sold the Red Sox franchise to Harry Frazee, a native of Peoria, Illinois, who financed New York theatrical productions and owned a couple of theaters. Frazee and Hugh F. Ward, his junior partner, supposedly paid Lannin $1 million for the franchise and Fenway Park, although Frazee went deeply into debt to make the deal. With Bill Carrigan intending to retire to Lewiston, Maine, to look after his business interests, Frazee made Jack Barry his manager.

Although the Red Sox had drawn fewer home fans in 1916, overall American League attendance, Ban Johnson reported at the league's annual meeting in Chicago, had increased by more than a million over the previous year. With the Federal League now history, the combined major league total had climbed to 6.5 million, although that was still well below the peak season of 1909.

Back in Texas, while Speaker put in a round of duck-hunting, people were keeping a close watch on the situation in Mexico, especially those living along the Rio Grande. Relations between the governments in Washington and Mexico City were in disarray as a consequence of President Wilson's decision the previous spring to send some 16,000 troops into northern Mexico. Commanded by General John J. Pershing, the expedition turned out to be a vain effort to find and apprehend Francisco "Pancho" Villa, leader of an outlaw force that had raided along the U.S.-Mexican border and killed U.S. citizens. By early 1917, however, Wilson faced a more critical situation with Imperial Germany and had ordered Pershing to start withdrawing his army from Mexico.

Meanwhile, David Fultz, president of the Players' Fraternity, made his most ambitious move so far to redress the imbalance of power between owners and players. Late in January 1917, frustrated in his efforts to get baseball's ruling National Commission and the National Association, the governing body for the minor leagues, to agree to a variety of reforms affecting minor-leaguers, Fultz held a series of meetings in New York City with the Fraternity's board of directors. He urged all players within Organized Baseball to refuse to sign their contracts for the coming season unless the Fraternity's demands were met. Six or seven hundred players—big-leaguers and minor-leaguers alike—pledged not to sign, which amounted to a threat to strike.

Speaker had been a Players' Fraternity member since its formation and had served a term on its board. Stopping in Cleveland on his way to Boston for surgery on his nasal passages (which had been bothering him since 1915 when Jim Scott's errant pitch hit him on the cheek), Speaker joked, "I'm on strike until March 1." But a few days later, from Boston, he wired Fultz and the twenty players meeting in New York, "I am sorry I cannot be with you tonight. I am with the boys. I feel sure we will win."[13] But of course he was already signed for 1917, under the contract he and Jim Dunn had agreed upon the previous April.

Although Fultz talked strike and the prospect of affiliating with the American Federation of Labor, baseball's officialdom and its club owners were adamant, so much so that they abrogated the so-called Cincinnati Agreement of 1914 and the modest concessions they had made at that time. As the late Harold Seymour has written, "The folly of the Fraternity's unrealistic expectation that major-leaguers would risk their necks in the interests of 'bushers' became increasingly plain."[14] With the players being threatened with suspension and replacement, Fultz canceled his strike plans and released Fraternity members from their pledges not to sign contracts. The Fraternity was virtually finished. The next year, with the United States at war, Fultz joined the Air Service and went to France. Subsequently he himself joined baseball's ruling elite, serving two years as president of the International League. As for Speaker, like his peers, he would put the Fraternity episode behind him and continue to pursue his professional career, expecting to be evaluated by his individual achievements and to be rewarded accordingly.

At the age of twenty-six, Joe Wood wasn't ready to give up his professional career. After sitting out the 1916 season with his family on his chicken farm in Pennsylvania, Wood got permission from the new Red Sox ownership to make whatever deal he could elsewhere. Once asked what kind of friend Speaker had been, Wood replied simply, "perfect."[15] Now that perfect friend, trading on the affection and respect Dunn had for him, convinced the Cleveland president to purchase Wood's contract for $15,000—a sum far above fair market value for the sore-armed pitcher. The deal happened only a week before Lee Fohl and his players began to assemble in New Orleans for spring training.

Wood came to the Indians with the expectation that he could still pitch, but in 1917 he worked only fifteen and two-thirds innings in five games and lost his only start. A good all-around athlete, he had hit a few home runs for the Red Sox (two in one game in 1911) and batted .290 during his magnificent 1912 season. In effect, Wood had to reinvent himself as a baseball player. As he told it much later, "I played in the infield during fielding practice. I shagged flies in the outfield. I was ready to pinch-run, pinch-hit. . . . The hell with my pride. I wasn't the invincible Joe Wood anymore. I was just another ballplayer who wanted a job and wanted it bad."[16] So he stayed on with the Indians, dressing at a locker next to Speaker's, rooming with him on the road, and filling in whenever he was needed.

As Wood joined the Indians, Chick Gandil was on his way to the White Sox after only one season with Cleveland. Gandil had driven in seventy-two runs for the Tribe, but he was a hard-bitten, surly man who hadn't cared much for Speaker or most of his teammates, and they hadn't cared much for him. Dunn wanted to cut his salary from $5,000 to $3,000. When Gandil balked at that, he was sold to Chicago for $3,500 cash. Rookie Louis Guisto, purchased from the Pacific Coast League, began the season at firstbase, although by June, Joe Harris, a veteran minor-leaguer finally getting his chance in the big show, had become Lee Fohl's regular at the position.

For the past year the government of Imperial Germany had restricted attacks in the North Atlantic against British and French vessels and avoided actions against neutral shipping, but on January 31 it announced the resumption of unrestricted submarine warfare. Inevitably, passenger ships would be attacked and U.S. lives lost. That move, and the revelation of the so-called Zimmerman Note proffering an alliance between Germany and Mexico, put the Wilson administration on an irreversible course toward war. On April 2, 1917, President Wilson addressed a joint session of Congress and asked for a declaration of war, which both Houses voted within four days.

Since the previous year, "preparedness" had been the call issuing from the Wilson administration and from pro-Allied elements in the U.S. population. With war impending, Ban Johnson arranged for army officers to be assigned to American League spring-training sites to drill the players in regular military order. Players were also to go through their drill routines before regular-season games, with a $500 prize to be awarded to the best-drilled team. Although president John Tener saw no need for such quasi-military displays in the National League, for players in Johnson's league, the drills became an almost-daily accompaniment to hitting, fielding, and throwing practice.

Speaker didn't show up at Heinemann Park in New Orleans until March 17, by which time the Cleveland players had drilled for two weeks under a lieutenant from the coast artillery. Speaker played that same day, tripling off a New Orleans pitcher, and he also took to the drills with enthusiasm. When the army lieutenant was reassigned, his assistant, a sergeant, took over the exercises; when the sergeant was also reassigned, Speaker assumed the role of drillmaster. After several games in New Orleans, the Indians headed north to open the season in Detroit, stopping in Birmingham, Memphis, Louisville, Cincinnati, Columbus, and Toledo. They won eighteen of twenty-one exhibition contests, only two of which, with Pittsburgh and Cincinnati, were played against big-league teams. On April 3, rained out in Memphis, they learned that the U. S. Senate had just voted 82-6 for a declaration of war.

For the first time in professional baseball history, the season began with the country at war. The ballpark ambience became decidedly patriotic, with bands playing martial airs at all the major-league openers. On April 11 an overflow crowd of 28,884 in Detroit, including about six hundred members of the Indians' Boosters Club, watched the Tigers and Indians, shouldering bats instead of rifles, go through their drill routines before marching to the flagpole in center-field for the raising of the flag.[17] Then the crowd rose and sang the "Star Spangled Banner" (which Congress didn't make the official national anthem for another fifteen years). Cleveland won the game, 6-4, with Stanley Coveleski going the route despite giving up two doubles to Ty Cobb and a home run to Bobby Veach. The Indians won again the next day, then lost on Saturday in snow flurries and temperatures that froze pipes in the visitors' dressing room and caused the base-line coaches to don overcoats and gloves and the outfielders to wear sweaters. Speaker tallied six hits over the three games in Detroit.

Despite intermittent rain, the home opener at League Park on April 19 also drew an overflow crowd. The Tigers and Indians combined for eleven doubles (two by Speaker), with most of the two-baggers landing among the roped-off standees across leftfield. Cleveland overcame a six-run deficit to win, 8-7, Louis Guisto driving in the winning run in the ninth inning. The Tribe's record was now 4-3.

Off to another strong start, Speaker was batting .435 after twelve games, although he served a three-day suspension for bumping umpire George Hildebrand in the course of protesting a strike call. Adulation for him among Cleveland fans was virtually unbounded. May 16 was Speaker Day, sponsored by the Boosters Club, the local Elks and Eagles lodges, and the Cleveland Athletic Club. Besides the traditional floral horseshoe, Speaker received various small gifts and some of the newly issued Liberty Bonds. As was often the case on such occasions, the honoree wasn't able to do much in the game. Boston's Carl Mays hit him with a pitch but held him hitless otherwise in beating the Indians, 5-1, on four hits.

If Speaker was hitting well most of the time, most players in both leagues weren't. It was a baseball adage that in the spring pitchers would be ahead of hitters, but it looked as if matters might be getting out of hand. During the first month of the 1917 season, American League pitchers threw four no-hit games, and in the other league, on May 2 in Chicago, Cincinnati's Fred Toney and the Cubs' Jim Vaughn both held the opposition hitless for nine innings. Vaughn finally yielded two hits and one run in the tenth, after which Toney retired the Cubs in order to close out one of the greatest pitching duels ever. Moreover, from various quarters came complaints about the frequency with which pitchers were throwing at batters. Fred Mitchell, manager of the Cubs, publicly ordered his pitchers to retaliate when an opposing moundsman threw at his players, whereupon the National Commission proclaimed its intention to expel any pitcher who deliberately tried to hit a batter. It was one thing to proclaim such an intention, another to enforce it. In fact, nothing came of the Commission's posturing, then or later.

On May 18 the Selective Service Act, passed by Congress a few weeks earlier, became law, requiring all men between the ages of twenty-one and thirty to register. Speaker registered early. On May 24, in Cleveland, he gave his birthplace and address as Hubbard, Texas, and signed his draft card "Tristram Speaker" (no "E" middle initial). The registrar, perhaps an acquaintance, generously filled in the color of his hair as "slightly gray."[18]

Two days later, at League Park, the Indians beat New York with a six-run rally in the ninth inning, climaxed by a triple steal executed by Speaker, Wambsganss, and Guisto. As Speaker slid home safely, the ball got past Les Nunamaker, and Wambsganss scored all the way from secondbase with the winning tally. The next day Joe Wood, in his only start of the season, gave up eleven hits and departed in the eighth inning, trailing 4-3, which is the way it ended. The next day, a Sunday, Speaker tagged the Yankees' Ray Caldwell for a three-run homer over the right-field wall and screen—the first one he had sent out of the park in Cleveland. The Indians won, 7-3, bringing their record to 21-18, good for fourth place.

On their first eastern swing the Tribe played to two ties and a loss in Washington—thirty-six innings in all—in abnormally hot weather, even for summertime in the nation's capital. Between the heat and construction work starting at seven A.M. on an addition to the team's hotel, reported Henry P. Edwards, the Cleveland players were getting little sleep. With the clerks in government offices working longer wartime hours, attendance for three games with the Nationals (before a rainout) had totaled slightly more than three thousand. Edwards thought that for the duration of the war, the Washington franchise ought to shift to Newark or Toronto.

Although Speaker received mostly accolades from the Cleveland sportswriters, he wasn't always above criticism. One example was an anonymous *Cleveland Press* reporter's account of a game in Boston on June 4, on that same eastern trip, in which Speaker made two futile attempts to throw out runners at home plate, one of which allowed a batter who had taken secondbase on the throw subsequently to score and hand Coveleski a 2-1 defeat.

Although draft call-ups and increasingly unsettled wartime conditions hurt the minor leagues, with ten of the twenty-one circuits unable to complete the season, major-league baseball was able to operate pretty much as usual. Teams experienced little trouble getting railroad transportation to meet their schedule commitments, even though, as of June, the government restricted passenger trains to one Pullman car each. Thereafter players had to occupy upper and lower berths in one sleeper, as opposed to the usual two-Pullman arrangement that enabled everybody to have a lower berth.

Jim Bagby, with twenty-three wins, and Stanley Coveleski, with nineteen, were again Lee Fohl's best pitchers. Ed Klepfer and Carl Morton avoided arm trouble to gain fourteen and ten decisions, respectively. Ray Chapman, batting a surprising .302, established himself as the Tribe's regular shortstop, while Joe Harris took over firstbase and hit .304 in 369 at bats. By the last part of June, Speaker had dropped to .348 and fallen behind Cobb, who was on his way to regaining his batting crown. A few weeks later, Henry P. Edwards wrote that Speaker was more concerned with finishing ahead of George Sisler than with catching Cobb, which seemed unlikely. Edwards also thought that the official scorers in St. Louis were giving Sisler base hits on what should have been ruled as errors.

Over the second half of the season, the Indians never got higher than third place, and the pennant race became a two-team battle between Boston and Chicago. Babe Ruth was a twenty-four-game winner and Carl Mays won twenty-two, but the Red Sox lacked the pitching consistency of the past two seasons and had only one .300 hitter (Duffy Lewis). Jack Barry's team stayed in contention until September, when the White Sox pulled away to a safe lead and won their first pennant in eleven years. Besides Eddie Collins and Joe Jackson, Chicago had a sparkling thirdbaseman in George "Buck" Weaver, a hard-hitting young centerfielder in Oscar "Happy" Felsch, and a dandy little catcher in Ray Schalk. Chick Gandil raised his batting average fourteen points over what he had done with Cleveland—and became the leader of one of the two increasingly hostile factions on the ball club.

With everybody struggling to score runs, the White Sox's pitching proved superior. Claude "Lefty" Williams, Urban "Red" Faber, and Ewell "Reb" Russell gained seventeen, sixteen, and fifteen decisions, respectively; but the ace of the staff was Eddie Cicotte. Now in his tenth full season in the big leagues, the stocky righthander had had a respectable if not noteworthy career, relying largely on his knuckleball. By 1917, though, Cicotte was using another highly deceptive pitch, variously called a "shine ball" or a "sailer," delivered after he had rubbed the ball on a spot of paraffin on his right pants leg. Dubiously legal even during that pitcher-permissive time, Cicotte's "mystery pitch," as some also called it, helped carry him to his finest year so far: a league's-best twenty-eight victories and majors'-best 1.53 earned run average.

Speaker believed that lefthander Dave Danforth, who often worked in relief for the 1917 White Sox, had taught the new pitch to Cicotte when he joined the team a year earlier. Whether or not that was true, it was Danforth who dealt Speaker his second frightening injury in three seasons. It happened in the second game of an August 14 doubleheader split at League Park. After Danforth relieved Faber in the eighth inning of the nightcap, which ended as a 4-2 Indians win, his first pitch struck Speaker above the right temple and knocked him flat. As players crowded around, he remained unconscious for nearly five minutes, until a physician called out of the grandstand managed to revive him. Speaker got to his feet and started for firstbase, but Fohl held him back and sent Bobby Roth in to run. With the right side of his face having purpled and with vision in his right eye blurred, Speaker went to a local hospital, where M. H. Castle, M.D., the Indians' team physician, judged that he had a slight concussion. Slight or not, he spent the night fighting nausea. "About an inch lower," Castle told reporters, "and it might have been all up with Spoke."[19] Speaker spent a couple of days in the hospital and missed seven games, of which the Tribe won four. In his absence, Bobby Roth moved over to centerfield, and Elmer Smith, traded to Washington the previous year and then reacquired for the waiver price in June, played in right.

Like Cobb, Collins, Sisler, and most of his contemporaries, Speaker often moved around in the batter's box, shifting his feet in anticipation of what he expected the next pitch would be. The St. Louis sportswriter John B. Sheridan thought that Speaker's practice of taking "two short, sneaking steps on the pitch" was "the finest and prettiest attack the game has known."[20] Once asked why he drew a line with his bat at the front of the batter's box, Speaker said that in the minors, where the box often wasn't well marked, he started drawing the line "so that I could tell how much room I had to move around in. It got be a habit with me and it followed me into the Big Leagues." Newspaper accounts made no mention of it, but it's possible that he was moving up in the box when Danforth's pitch hit him. In any case, he seemed less unhappy that he had been disabled than that Cicotte and other White Sox pitchers were dominating hitters with the "sailer." "I think it is time to call a halt," he said, "before batting becomes a lost art."[21]

Showing no ill effects from being "skulled," Speaker returned to the lineup on August 25 and singled and doubled in a loss to New York. Over the next two weeks, the Indians built a comfortable six-game lead over fourth-place Detroit.

On September 9, with the Danforth incident still fresh in their minds, they opened a long road trip in Chicago by being shut out by Cicotte. The next day's game, played on a Sunday in cold rain, went into the tenth inning, tied 3-3. The Indians had a good chance to go ahead until umpire Clarence "Brick" Owens ended their threat by calling out Jack Graney after he had stolen thirdbase. The Cleveland players surrounded Owens and argued at length that Chicago third-baseman Fred McMullin had held Graney down when he tried to start home after Ray Schalk's throw bounced away, but Owens ruled that Graney had actually interfered with McMullin. In disgust, several Indians threw their gloves into the air; a couple of players even rolled in the soggy infield dirt in feigned anguish. Finally they took their positions, but when Fritz Coumbe struck out Danforth to start the bottom of the inning, catcher Steve O'Neill deliberately threw the ball into centerfield. At that point Owens declared a forfeit, which, under National Commission rules, would automatically impose a $1,000 fine on the Cleveland franchise.[22]

Afterward, Lee Fohl revealed that Speaker had pledged $200 toward a fund to pay the fine; others had chipped in with lesser amounts. Jim Dunn, who had watched the whole thing from the grandstand, advised his players to continue the game, but whether out of anger or a desire to get out of the rain, they wouldn't retake the field. How much of the fine the players made up and how much Dunn was stuck with wasn't reported.

Four days later, with attendance sagging for the seventh-place Browns, owner Phil Ball tried to lure some people to Sportsman's Park by staging a day to commemorate the tenth anniversary of Speaker's first big-league appearance. Only about six hundred showed up, although it was a nice occasion for Speaker, who received a silver cigarette case from local acquaintances and an amethyst stickpin from members of the two teams. He later hit two singles and a double and scored three times for Coumbe in a 6-1 victory.

Chicago clinched the pennant on September 21 in Boston, Red Faber outdueling Dutch Leonard, 2-1. Six days later, in the midst of a Cleveland-Boston series at Fenway Park, Walter Johnson, Ty Cobb, Joe Jackson, Buck Weaver, and five other big-leaguers joined Speaker, Chapman, and O'Neill for an exhibition game with the Red Sox to benefit the family of the much-admired Tim Murnane, who had died suddenly the previous February at the age of sixty-five. Connie Mack served as manager of the "All-Stars," who lost, 2-0, Ruth and Leonard outpitching Johnson. About $14,000 was raised for Murnane's survivors.

The Indians won ten games in a row—three to end their western swing and another seven in New York and Philadelphia—before Ernie Shore shut them down in a series opener in Boston. They ended the season by splitting two games in Washington and then, on Sunday, September 30, won 2-1 from the Nationals at League Park. Jim Bagby's twenty-third victory made their record 88-66, which left them three games behind Boston, twelve behind Chicago. It was Cleveland's best record since 1908, although attendance at League Park was off by about 15,000 from 1916. (Attendance in both leagues sagged over the last month of the season, so that about 1,300,000 fewer people saw major-league games than in 1916. Fifth-place Washington drew only 89,682.)

Cobb won his tenth batting title in eleven years with an average of .383—a prodigious 137 points above the American League as a whole—and led in hits, total bases, and, as usual, in stolen bases. Friendly scoring at home or not, Sisler batted .353, one point better than Speaker. In 142 games, Speaker made 184 hits, including 42 doubles (to Cobb's 44). He hit a couple of home runs; his 65 runs batted in, 90 runs scored, and 30 steals left him well down in all of those categories.

Speaker played more baseball after the regular season ended. After a tuneup exhibition with the White Sox while the New York Giants, winners in the National League, concluded their schedule, the Indians began a series with the Cincinnati Reds. Apart from a well-established city series between the Chicago clubs, played when neither made it to the World Series, such postseason matchups generally hadn't been a good idea—the poorly attended Red Sox–Giants series in 1909 being a prime example. That was also the case with this series for the putative championship of Ohio, played in cold weather and drawing sparse crowds in both cities. On paper, the Indians were the superior team, but they didn't play that way except for Speaker, who made thirteen hits, including five triples, in the six games it took for the Reds to win. Two losses in Cincinnati were followed by another at League Park before Klepfer and Coveleski pitched back-to-back wins. Then the Reds ended it by driving out Bagby in the third inning and handing him his third loss of the series. Meanwhile the White Sox disposed of John McGraw's Giants in six games in the World Series.

The Reds and Indians also put on an exhibition for four thousand soldiers training at Camp Sherman outside Chillicothe, Ohio. Then a nearly intact Cleveland team, including Speaker, entertained National Guardsmen stationed at Camp Sheridan outside Montgomery, Alabama. By that time Joe Harris, Ed Klepfer, Elmer Smith, Louis Guisto, utilityman Joe Evans, and pitcher Chester "Red" Thorkelson had all received their draft notices.

Speaker may have registered early, but he was no more eager than the majority of the four hundred or so men on major-league rosters to follow the example of Hank Gowdy. The batting star in the Boston Braves' sweep of the Athletics in 1914, Gowdy had volunteered for army service early the previous summer and become something of a national hero. Others were content to play out the 1917 season, wait and see what happened with their draft situation, and hope to begin another season next spring.

So that winter, as more and more players got their draft notices, Speaker, Fohl, and Dunn got together in Cleveland to talk about how they might strengthen the team. Although they couldn't bring off any deals, others were being made by other clubs. The most notable was the sale by the Phillies to the Cubs of the illustrious battery of Grover Cleveland Alexander and Bill Killefer for $50,000. Connie Mack continued his open market for what was left of the talent on the Athletics, sending three players to Boston for a like number and subsequently also pedaling Stuffy McInnis to the Red Sox for cash, in exchange for Speaker's friend Larry Gardner, plus Tilly Walker and Forrest Cady. The Philadelphia writer Jimmy Isaminger, with pardonable exaggeration, commented that now all Mack had left was home plate and himself.

At the annual major-league winter meetings held in Cincinnati, the consensus among the owners was that more offense needed to be put into the game, although they couldn't agree on what to do. They did agree to dispense with the big trunks with which teams traveled with their equipment, given the baggage-handling difficulties on trains carrying troops. So for 1918, players not only had to continue to share upper and lower Pullman berths but had to lug bags with their own uniforms, gloves, and bats.

Early in February, Speaker returned to Cleveland, met with Dunn, and signed a new two-year contract for what was reported to be the same $15,000 per year he had drawn in 1916 and 1917. He kept considerably less of that, though. Since 1913, when Congress enacted a personal income tax (to compensate for revenue lost by tariff reduction), Speaker had been paying at a rate of 1 percent. Under wartime tax legislation passed in 1918, he now would pay at a base rate of 2 percent, plus a surtax of 12 percent.

Speaker arrived for spring training at New Orleans after a week at the annual livestock show in Fort Worth, where he bought a prize bull to upgrade the stock on a farm he had purchased on the outskirts of Hubbard. With Speaker on the scene and subsequently Jim Bagby, who had staged a mild holdout, Lee Fohl had a squad of only twenty-five. More dependent than ever on Speaker's abilities, Fohl remained as enthusiastic as ever about his centerfielder and right-hand man. In *Baseball Magazine,* he declared Speaker to have "more baseball brains than any other man I ever saw. He studies the opposing players and pitchers better than any other player I have known."[23]

That spring the Indians and Giants (training for the last time at Marlin) played an ambitious series of exhibitions at Houston; Dallas; New Orleans; Camp Shelby, Hattiesburg, Mississippi (in a sandstorm); Chattanooga; and Lexington, Kentucky, resulting in three wins apiece, plus a tie. After a stopover in Indianapolis to meet the local American Association team (now managed by Napoleon Lajoie), the Indians reached home to open the 1918 season, having spent eighteen nights aboard Pullman sleepers.

Two rainouts delayed the opening game of the 1918 season, with Detroit. When it was finally played on April 18, Ty Cobb was abed at the Hollenden Hotel with a cold, and Harry Heilmann was in San Francisco attending his mother's funeral. A chilled and wet crowd of only about eleven thousand watched not only a 6-2 Cleveland victory but the fifth unassisted double play of Speaker's career. In the top of the ninth inning, with Tigers on first and secondbase and nobody out, Speaker trapped Frank Walker's pop fly, ran in and touched Oscar Vitt before he could return to the bag, then tagged secondbase to force Herbert "Babe" Ellison. Bob Young ended the game by grounding to Ray Chapman, who tossed over to Bill Wambsganss to force Walker.

The next day it was too cold to play. A week later, with the Tribe in Detroit, so many Indians were sick with colds and flu that Fohl had to play substitutes in leftfield and at all the infield positions. Forty-one-year-old Germany Schaefer, recently hired as a player-coach, was at thirdbase for one game.

It was a faltering beginning to what was one of the strangest seasons in baseball history. Week by week, players answered draft call-ups, volunteered before they were drafted (mostly for the navy), or left their teams to work at steel mills, munitions plants, shipyards, and other employments deemed essential to the war effort. When Jack Barry joined the navy, the veteran manager and baseball executive Ed Barrow left the presidency of the International League to manage the Red Sox. Like his fellow-managers, Barrow had to fill in as best he could, holding onto older players and those with dependents, bringing up men from the rapidly contracting minor leagues, and in general struggling to keep a major-league team together.

Despite such difficulties, the season was no less competitive or lacking in memorable moments, especially for Speaker and Joe Wood. Eleven days after doubling up Detroit's Vitt and Ellison, Speaker did it again versus Chicago, in exactly the same manner. With one out in the seventh inning of an 8-4 loss at League Park, Speaker grabbed Happy Felsch's soft liner on one bounce, ran in and tagged Eddie Collins off secondbase, and stepped on the bag to force Joe Jackson, who had stopped between second and first. As Collins, who prided himself on heady base-running, protested loudly to the umpires that he had beaten Speaker to the bag, fans yelled "Page Heinie Zimmerman" (a reference to the sixth game of the 1917 World Series, when Collins scored while Giants thirdbaseman Zimmerman chased him across an uncovered home plate).

Jack Graney was ill for most of the season, so Lee Fohl made Wood an everyday player, using him mostly in leftfield but also in rightfield and at secondbase. The onetime Red Sox ace quickly demonstrated he had become a complete ballplayer. On May 3 he even replaced Speaker, who recovered sufficiently from an attack of ptomaine poisoning to enter in the late innings of a victory in St. Louis. In that game Wood hit a single and double, made two nice catches, and threw out a runner at home. For the season he batted .296 in 119 games, drove in sixty-six runs, and hit eight home runs, two of which came on May 24 in a nineteen-inning struggle in New York. The second blow, off Yankees lefthander George Mogridge (who had relieved Allan Russell), won the game for Stanley Coveleski, who pitched all the way. (That made forty-four innings Coveleski had pitched over ten days, including thirteen-inning and twelve-inning losses in Philadelphia and Washington, respectively.)

By mid-season the White Sox, favored to repeat at the start, had lost most of the 1917 championship team and were headed for a sixth-place finish. Eddie Cicotte lost his first seven starts and finished with a miserable 12-19 record. Some White Sox, such as Red Faber, entered military service. Others, such as Joe Jackson, Lefty Williams, and Happy Felsch, opted to sign on with shipbuilding and steel-producing companies and, like many other ballplayers, spend two or three work days per week, plus Sundays, performing for industrial-league teams. Of those who avoided conscription in such fashion, owner Charles Comiskey proclaimed, "Not one of them ever can come inside my ball park again."[24] By the next year Comiskey found it convenient to forget ever having said that.

With Chicago not a factor in the pennant race, it eventually became a three-team fight among Cleveland, Boston, and Washington, although New York and St. Louis acted like contenders over the first half of the season before fading to fourth and fifth, respectively. District of Columbia authorities finally legalized Sunday baseball to accommodate government workers, whose extended workdays kept them from attending weekday games, even at the traditional 4:30 local starting time. On May 19 the Indians and Nationals inaugurated Sunday play in the capital city with a fine pitching duel, won by Doc Ayers over Coveleski, 1-0. The game drew a near-capacity crowd of 15,352, including Ban Johnson, various government officials and foreign diplomats, and some two thousand soldiers seated in temporary stands along the base lines. Sunday baseball in the District obviously helped, because the 1918 Nats more than doubled their home attendance.

The next day, in the opener of a series in Boston, Carl Mays, known for his close pitches, again hit Speaker with one of his submarine deliveries. As Speaker shook off the blow and started for firstbase, Mays yelled that the pitch had been accidental, to which Speaker shot back, "I worked on the same team with you long enough to know different."[25]

The Tribe returned from that road trip in fourth place with a 19-17 record. Boston was leading New York by two and one-half games, St. Louis by three. By the end of June, however, the draft-depleted Clevelanders had climbed ten games above .500, before losing a doubleheader to Detroit at home. Cobb had one of his best days of the season, with seven hits in ten times up and two stolen bases. Speaker had one of his worst, getting only one hit in seven at bats and committing three errors in the first game. At that point Cobb was again well ahead in the batting race, while Speaker's average was down in the .290s.

By sweeping an Independence Day doubleheader from the Browns (winning the nightcap on Speaker's two-run triple), the Indians briefly moved into first place. Two days later, in Boston, they were defeated, 5-4, yielding the lead to the Red Sox. Babe Ruth, who had quarreled with manager Barrow and briefly deserted to join a team in the Delaware River Shipbuilding League, was back with the Red Sox and pinch-hit a two-run triple to tie the game, then ran home with the winning run when the throw to thirdbase from the outfield was wild. From then on, Ruth was in the lineup almost every day—on the mound, in left-field, or at firstbase.

Boston took four games of the five-game set. The Tribe left for New York two and a half games out of first place, which they would never reach again. Cleveland's only win in Boston was the nightcap of a Monday doubleheader split, but in the opener Sam Jones, who had come to the Red Sox in the deal for Speaker, threw a four-hit, 1-0 gem. In the twenty-four innings Jones had pitched against Cleveland up to that point in the season, "Sad Sam" (so-called because of his dour demeanor) had allowed a sole run.

Two weeks later, the War Department announced that all able-bodied males not in military service had to go to work in some essential wartime occupation. Theatrical and motion-picture people were exempted from the so-called "work or fight" order on the grounds that they provided necessary diversion for the troops, but on July 19, Secretary of War Newton D. Baker refused to exempt professional baseball. Whereupon Jim Dunn precipitously ordered League Park closed following a Sunday doubleheader with Philadelphia. The major-league owners appealed to Baker for a reprieve. At the end of the month he ruled that the baseball season could continue to September 1 (later changed to the 2nd). After that, the 237 players left on the sixteen rosters had to obtain war-essential jobs.

On August 3 the American League club owners met in Cleveland at the Hollenden to vote their agreement with their National League counterparts: the season would end with the traditional Labor Day doubleheaders; the World Series should be played quickly thereafter. Out at League Park, the Indians won their second straight from Boston, 5-1. Speaker doubled twice, singled, and drove in two runs, as Sam Jones finally lost to the team that traded him away. The next day Speaker was hitless in eight times up in a doubleheader split that moved the Indians to within two and a half games of the Red Sox. After beating Chicago on August 12 while Boston lost a third straight game to New York, the Tribe headed east only two games back. By then, with Bobby Roth suspended for the rest of the season for "not keeping in condition," Fohl had only seventeen men left.[26]

Cleveland won two of three games in New York (in the first of which Wood homered into the rightfield stands and made three difficult catches), then went to Boston, still within two games of the Red Sox. But in Fenway Park on Saturday, August 17, they played sloppily afield and lost, 4-2, with Ruth pitching and batting cleanup. On Monday they made only two hits and couldn't score on Sam Jones. The Tribe salvaged the finale by cuffing Ruth for twelve hits (including Speaker's single and double) and eight runs, Bagby getting the win with help from Coumbe.

The Indians left for Washington now trailing the Red Sox by three games. Having taken flying lessons in his spare time in the ungainly aircraft the navy operated on Lake Erie, Speaker had become a seaplane enthusiast. So in Washington he took the opportunity to apply for a commission in the naval air corps.

The Indians split four games with the Nationals, while Boston won three of four from the Browns to add another game to its lead. The bottom-dog Athletics should have been easy marks, but the Tribe could do no better than divide four games. In the third game in Philadelphia, which Cleveland won, 8-6, Ray Chapman scored from thirdbase on a drive by firstbaseman Wheeler "Doc" Johnston that got away from Athletics firstbaseman George Burns. When Speaker was tagged out also trying to score, he stormed at umpire Tom Connolly and bumped him. Dick Nallin, the other umpire, and players from both teams tried to restrain him, but Speaker broke loose and clipped Connolly on the chin, whereupon he was ejected from the game. That night he received Ban Johnson's wire levying an indefinite suspension. The Indians took a train for Detroit with only five pitchers. Carl Morton, called up by his draft board in Alabama, had pitched five innings of one of the Philadelphia games and then left to enlist in the army.

Despite the seriousness of a physical assault on an umpire, Johnson was remarkably lenient, lifting Speaker's suspension after the final game in Philadelphia and a day of travel. He was back in the lineup for a doubleheader sweep in Detroit, with the Tigers now playing without Cobb, who had left to take a captain's commission in the Chemical Warfare Service. But the Red Sox also took two from the Athletics, so that the standings were now Boston 72-49, Cleveland 71-54. Although the Indians won in Chicago two days later behind rookie Johnny Enzman, at Fenway Park the Red Sox clinched their fourth pennant of the decade when Ruth easily handled the Athletics in the opener of another doubleheader. The next day, Sunday, September 1, the Indians benefited from their opponents' eight errors and beat the White Sox, 8-5, thereby clinching second place over Washington.

After that messy victory, the Indians were supposed to go to St. Louis to end the season with a Labor Day doubleheader. Neither Fohl, Speaker, nor anybody else on the team saw the point of another train trip to play a couple of games in a mostly empty ballpark. Some of the players were about to change their uniforms to khaki or blue, while others were about to leave for work approved by the War Department. With Dunn's consent, the Indians didn't go to St. Louis and thereby forfeited the doubleheader, which prompted Boston president Harry Frazee to protest that Cleveland ought to be fined $1,000 for each of the two games not played. (Frazee had also vetoed Frank Navin's request that the August 30 Indians-Tigers doubleheader be moved from Detroit to Cleveland.) Dunn said that he and his players had only followed Secretary of War Baker's ruling. Ban Johnson declined to hold his friend Dunn to National Commission regulations, and Frazee did himself no good with the strong-willed league president.

In that disorderly fashion, the truncated 1918 major-league season came to its conclusion. Teams in the two major leagues ended up playing between 122 and 129 games. Of the ten minor leagues starting the season, only the International League lasted through a complete schedule. Cleveland's final record was 73-54 to Boston's 75-51; Washington finished at 72-56. The abbreviated schedule meant that the Indians played only fifty-eight home dates to Boston's seventy-one. And with the season ending a month earlier than usual, every big-leaguer missed his last two paychecks. In Speaker's case that came out to a hefty loss of $2,500, although his federal tax liability for the year remained at $2,100.

With a couple of hot streaks in August, Speaker managed to lift his average to .318, his lowest mark since 1909, his first full season. He went homerless and batted in 63 runs, although he topped both leagues with 33 doubles and struck out only 9 times in 427 official at bats. Cobb won his eleventh batting title with a .382 average over 111 games; Philadelphia's George Burns batted .352; George Sisler, .341. Babe Ruth played in 95 games, posted 13 wins against 7 losses, batted an even .300, and hit 11 home runs to tie Tilly Walker for the most in the majors.

The World Series began on September 5 in Comiskey Park, which had a bigger capacity than the Cubs' Weeghman Park (the former Federal League grounds). Ruth pitched two victories and extended his scoreless innings in Series play to twenty-nine and two-thirds, a record that stood for forty-three years. Carl Mays also threw two complete-game victories, as the Red Sox defeated the Cubs four games to two. In leftfield for Boston was thirty-five-year-old George Whiteman, Speaker's old teammate at Cleburne and Houston, brought up from the minors as a wartime fill-in. (Whiteman was back in the minors the following year.)

The six games of the Series drew 128,483 and yielded a players' share just under $70,000, half that of 1917. Only 15,238 attended the closeout game at Fenway Park. Before the season the club owners had ill-advisedly agreed that the players' portion of the receipts would be shared with the second-, third-, and fourth-place finishers in each league, on a prorated basis. Knowing that their individual shares would be much below normal, the Boston and Chicago players initially refused to take the field for the fifth game. They did so only after Harry Hooper persuaded them that they owed it to the fans and especially to the wounded servicemen in the stands at Fenway Park.

As a member of a second-place club, Speaker realized about $200 from the Series receipts, but that was of little consequence to him in the fall of 1918. While Cobb, Sisler, Christy Mathewson, and other baseball notables had received army commissions and sailed for France, Speaker had to hang around Cleveland, trying to get the local draft board to release him so he could join the naval aviation service. The release finally came through early in October, and Speaker was off to enroll in the navy's officer-training program at the Massachusetts Institute of Technology (M.I.T.), across the Charles River from Boston. By that time eighteen men on Cleveland's roster were in military service, more than on any other team, and Jim Dunn and the local press took pride in the fact that not a single Indian had "deserted" to wartime industry before September 2.

At M.I.T., Speaker was up at 5:45 A.M. to study aerodynamics and hydrodynamics, mathematics, seaplane design, engines, and signaling, then to spend much of the afternoon at close-order drill. He lived in a dormitory called the "receiving ship," where, among other duties, he mopped floors, picked up trash, and washed windows. After dinner he studied until lights out at 9:45. Also training at M.I.T. was Yankees firstbaseman Wally Pipp, who had already graduated from the "main ship" facility and was about to leave for flying school in Miami.

Although Speaker got his photo in the *Sporting News* in his navy training garb, by the time he was certified to progress to the "main ship," the war was over. The arrival of vast numbers of U.S. troops and their entry into combat on the western front had blunted a last, desperate German offensive and turned the advantage to the Allied forces. On November 11, with Kaiser Wilhelm II having fled to the neutral Netherlands, an armistice went into effect on the eleventh hour of that day. Within another month, Speaker had requested and received his discharge from naval service.

The Great War, as contemporaries called it, ended quicker than almost anyone had anticipated. When the World Series concluded on September 11, it seemed that the conflict would last well into the next year. Prospects for a 1919 baseball season were in doubt. The past season had been a bad one all-around. Major-league attendance had sagged to 3,080,126, the lowest so far in the century. With the possible exception of the Cubs, everybody lost money. The Indians' home attendance had fallen by 182,000, that of the White Sox by about 70 percent. Now peace was at hand, and ballplayers, owners, and fans, like the rest of the country, were eager to get back to what Warren G. Harding, the Republican Party's 1920 presidential candidate, called "normalcy."

Professional baseball at all levels and on both sides of the color line was about to enter the most prosperous times in the sport's history. Babe Ruth's prodigious hitting was about to make him a national phenomenon and an international celebrity. But also ahead was baseball's biggest scandal, without which the city of Cleveland might not have celebrated its first championship in any league.

"The Inspiration of Speaker's Leadership"

Once discharged from the navy, Speaker went on his usual off-season hunting expedition, heading to eastern Canada to shoot game with his favorite rifle, which had been mailed to Cleveland from Texas. In Boston, rumors caught up with him that he would succeed Lee Fohl as Cleveland manager, but that misunderstanding was cleared up a couple of weeks later when Jim Dunn rehired Fohl for 1919. On his way back to Texas, however, Speaker stopped off in Cleveland to give advice to Dunn and Fohl on possible trades.

On January 30, 1919, when Speaker was spending a few weeks with his mother at Hubbard, the last lynching in the history of Hill County took place. It was a notably grisly one. A mob used a telephone pole to batter down the doors to the county jail at Hillsboro, seized Bragg Williams, who had already been convicted of murdering a local white man, tied him to a nearby tree, doused him with kerosene, and burned him alive. Speaker undoubtedly read or heard about the atrocity, which happened only about twenty-five miles from Hubbard, but it's unlikely that it bothered him much, if at all. Such things had long been, if not routine, at least commonplace across the American South, although the war years and early postwar period also saw an upsurge of racial violence outside the former Confederacy—in East St. Louis, Chicago, and Tulsa, among other places.

Like Speaker, and like his former Boston teammates Ernie Shore, Jack Barry, and Duffy Lewis, who also joined the navy, most major-leaguers who entered military service had spent their time stateside. But some had seen hard fighting in the counteroffensive on the western front that forced the Germans to give up. Hank Gowdy and Ed Klepfer, for example, survived weeks of combat; Grover Cleveland Alexander served in a forward artillery unit and suffered damage to his hearing; Louis Guisto inhaled poison gas and was never again strong enough to be a full-time player; and Joe Harris, besides being under fire much of his time on the western front, had been severely injured in a truck accident that, despite several surgeries, left him with a deep scar on his face. Yet as far as Speaker was concerned, "the men who were fortunate enough to get across" shouldn't "look down on" those remaining stateside.[1]

Speaker also escaped the influenza pandemic that swept the globe beginning in the fall of 1918 and killed tens of millions, including as many as 700,000 Americans. Across the United States, schools, theaters, churches, and other public places closed for some part of the winter of 1918–1919. (In one game played in the California Winter League, at Pasadena, ballplayers wore surgical masks to guard against "flu germs.")

After their financial losses in 1918, and fearful of another bad year, the major-league club owners set a twenty-one-man roster limit, effective May 8, and voted for a 140-game season, thereby reducing players' salaries by two weeks. Spring training for 1919 wouldn't get underway until the middle of March. By then the influenza scourge hadn't completely abated, but the perils of venereal disease in New Orleans had been reduced—or so it was supposed. The previous year, as ordered by local navy authorities, the district of honky-tonks and bawdy houses called Storyville had been summarily shut down, never again to be the notorious vice center it had been.

Speaker reached New Orleans early in the morning on March 26, explaining that an unusual amount of rainfall in Texas had delayed his doing needed tasks on his farm. At the DeSoto Hotel, where the Indians were quartered, he went from room to room, rousting various teammates out of bed by pulling their feet, throwing cold water on them, and, in Steve O'Neill's case, holding a pillow over his head. He was, of course, especially glad to see Joe Wood. The *Sporting News* captioned a photo of Speaker and Wood: "They are inseparable in a baseball season, have their lockers together, sleep in the same bed and always order 'bring me the same' from the menu."[2] Not long after beginning practice, though, Wood had to return home to Pennsylvania to nurse his wife through a serious illness. Speaker was also gone for a few days, completing the purchase of a tract of land adjacent to his farm.

A few weeks earlier, Jim Dunn and Lee Fohl had taken Speaker's advice and concluded a deal Speaker always said was the best the Indians made while he was with them. The temperamental Bobby Roth went to Philadelphia for Larry Gardner, pitcher Elmer Myers, and Charlie Jamieson, a smallish lefthanded pitcher-outfielder who had done little to distinguish himself with Washington and the Athletics. Jamieson later described Speaker as "My best friend. He was the one who helped get me traded to Cleveland."[3] Connie Mack had cut Jamieson's salary to $2,250; Dunn restored it to $2,550.

Besides reuniting with Larry Gardner, who had been one of the "Masons" faction on the Red Sox, Speaker also greeted his hunting companion Les Nunamaker, acquired in a trade with the Browns. Still another new face at Heinemann Park that spring was that of George Uhle, a broad-shouldered, twenty-year-old righthanded pitcher signed directly out of Cleveland semipro ball. Throwing a fastball and a big side-arm curve, Uhle quickly showed enough ability to make the ball club. In a game with the Tulane University team, the youngster called in his outfielders and infielders, who gathered around the mound as he proceeded to strike out three batters in a row.[4] Joe Harris, however, wouldn't sign the contract offered him and left New Orleans to work at a hotel and play for a semipro team at Franklin, Pennsylvania. Doc Johnston was again the regular firstbaseman.

Wartime restrictions on railroad travel had been lifted, so that when the Indians left New Orleans, they again occupied two Pullman cars, each player having a lower berth to himself. The Tribe kept an exhibition date in Milwaukee (where Pants Rowland, fired by Charles Comiskey following the White Sox's sixth-place finish, had become manager), then moved on to Detroit to start the season. The April 23 opener was rained out, and snow and cold the next day again kept the Indians idling around the Fort Shelby Hotel. The season finally got underway on Friday, the 25th. With temperatures in the mid-thirties, only about 8,000 fans showed up at Navin Field to watch Howard Ehmke outpitch Stanley Coveleski, 4-2. In better weather on Saturday, an overflow attendance of more than 24,000 went home disappointed when Jim Bagby bested Bernie Boland, 3-1. Speaker had two of the six doubles that landed among the roped-off outfield standees.

George Uhle gained his first big-league decision in St. Louis, in one of the two games the Indians won there before opening at home on May 1. Among the people of prominence in the 16,000 or so on hand at League Park was William Gibbs McAdoo, director general of the railroads, former secretary of the treasury, and a Democratic Party presidential hopeful. An army band played as McAdoo sold Victory Loan bonds to Speaker and Ty Cobb. Then Cobb and the Tigers knocked Coveleski out of the game en route to an 8-1 victory for Boland.

Coveleski lost again a week later to the White Sox and Eddie Cicotte, 4-1. Charles Comiskey's vow not to rehire players who took jobs in war industry had proved so much bombast. The reconstituted Chicago team was virtually the same that had won it all in 1917. Cicotte's "sailer," or "shine ball," continued to generate controversy. Lee Fohl said other pitchers ought to start using the pitch "and spread the evil until real action will be taken against it."[5]

While they were in Cleveland, umpires George Moriarty and George Hildebrand were quoted as saying that the baseballs were of better quality than those used in 1918, which accounted for the fact that this season, balls Speaker would have caught in the past were sometimes landing beyond his reach. As the season progressed, Speaker began to play a deeper centerfield, especially when Babe Ruth, Joe Jackson, and other free-swingers were at bat.

After seventeen games, Speaker was batting .224 in what turned out to be, by his standards, a season-long slump. Yet even without his usual offensive output, the Indians won at a steady pace and stayed within reach of the White Sox. Meanwhile the Red Sox, winners of four World Series in seven years, had suddenly become a second-division outfit. The previous December, Harry Frazee had first shown that he was interested less in baseball than in generating money for his theatrical promotions by trading Ernie Shore, Dutch Leonard, and Duffy Lewis to the Yankees for four players and $15,000 cash. So began Frazee's deal-after-deal dismantling process, which came to be called the "rape of the Red Sox" and earned him undying enmity in Boston.

If Speaker's hitting wasn't up to par, his competitive spirit was as strong as ever. On Friday, May 30, in Chicago, Cicotte again defeated the Tribe, holding Speaker hitless in four at bats. In the eighth inning, Chick Gandil fielded Speaker's sharp grounder and tagged the base for the out. Gandil evidently thought Speaker had tried to spike him. They jawed at each other as Speaker went to the nearby visitors' dugout. Before Elmer Smith flied out to end the inning, Gandil, according to a naval officer sitting in back of the dugout, "made a megaphone of his hands and let loose with a torrent of vile abuse" at Speaker.[6]

As the sides changed, Gandil lingered off the base line, challenged Speaker, and struck him in the face with his left fist. Enraged, Speaker leaped at Gandil and knocked him down, shoved umpire Tom Connolly aside "as though he were a child," in Henry Edwards words, decked Gandil again, and began pounding him on the ground. Plate umpire Dick Nallin finally got between the combatants and ordered both from the game. Speaker left the field escorted by a policeman, several Cleveland players, and Chicago manager William "Kid" Gleason.[7] When play resumed, spectators in the leftfield bleachers threw bottles at Jack Graney, who had repeatedly complained to Nallin about Cicotte's doctoring the ball. Cicotte kept the Indians from scoring in the top of the ninth to end the raucous contest.

Most baseball fights haven't amounted to much, with players usually content to grab each other, dance around, maybe roll in the dirt, and wait to be pulled apart. The Speaker-Gandil encounter, though, was a genuine one-on-one brawl between men who hadn't liked each other for years, which is presumably why players from both teams gathered around and did nothing to interfere. Speaker came out of the fisticuffs with a bleeding mouth, a bruised cheek, and scratches on his ankle and arm. Gandil had cuts on his lips and forehead, lumps on his face, and one of his eyes was practically closed.

In the dressing room, an agitated Speaker gave his side of the fray. He had never before had a fight in baseball, but Gandil, he said, "called me names that no man could stand for." Intending to challenge Gandil to meet him under the stands after the game, Speaker had assumed Gandil "had too much sense to start anything on the ball field. . . . I wanted to keep on until I had him out but Nallin finally dragged me off. I'm sorry there was a fight in public, but I had to defend myself and once I got started I couldn't stop."[8]

Ban Johnson suspended both players for five days, which in Speaker's case amounted to four games plus a rainout. Johnson also wrote Speaker a personal letter regarding the affair. "You have always been the ideal clean player," scolded the league president, "and a great credit to the game. Being such a player and also a man of more than usual intelligence, I am astonished that you would do anything to bring the game into discredit."[9]

Four days after returning to the lineup, Speaker was a witness to but not a participant in another ugly scene, in Washington. At the conclusion of Cleveland's 3-2 win behind Bagby, during which umpire Nallin ejected Washington manager Clark Griffith, fans threw seat cushions and bottles and stormed onto the field. One spectator tried to attack Nallin, who was shielded by Steve O'Neill. (The would-be attacker turned out to be a Secret Service agent, released when he showed his identification.) Hundreds of Washingtonians harassed Nallin when he left the ballpark until police intervened and drove him to his hotel.

By the end of June it had become a three-way pennant race, with the Yankees fielding their first contending team since 1906. Despite the departure of Dutch Leonard, who was sold to Detroit in May, and Ernie Shore's ineffectiveness, the Yankees' pitching staff, led by Athletics alumnus Bob Shawkey and ex–Federal Leaguer Jack Quinn, was solid. Moreover, New York's everyday lineup—with Wally Pipp at first, Derrill Pratt at second, Roger Peckinpaugh at shortstop, Frank Baker at third, and Duffy Lewis and Ping Bodie (born Francesco Pezzolo) in the outfield—was its strongest up to then.

On July 17 and 18, Cleveland took the first two games of a series with Boston at League Park and held second place by a small margin over New York, while Chicago had moved out to a three-and-one-half-game lead. By that time Joe Harris had finally decided to sign his contract and had begun alternating with Doc Johnston at firstbase. In the last game of the Boston series, on Friday, July 19, Harris pinch-hit a three-run triple in a big eighth-inning rally that gave the Tribe a 7-3 lead. But in the top of the ninth, Elmer Myers, pitching in relief of Henry "Hi" Jasper, gave up one run on a double, then walked the next two men to load the bases. The next batter was Babe Ruth, who had already homered over the rightfield wall off Jasper. Ruth still pitched occasionally, but now, as manager Ed Barrow's full-time leftfielder, he was hitting home runs at such a rate that he had already become the biggest single gate attraction around the American League.

Lee Fohl signaled the bullpen in the rightfield corner for lefthander Fritz Coumbe, who hadn't pitched in two months. Out in centerfield, Speaker waved his right arm and jumped around in an effort to get Fohl's attention and let him know he was doing the wrong thing. But by the time Coumbe reached the mound, the home-plate umpire had grabbed his megaphone by the grandstand railing and bellowed the pitching change.

Ruth watched Coumbe's first pitch, a called strike; then Coumbe tried to fool the Red Sox slugger with a changeup. Ruth connected, and the ball went soaring over the rightfield barrier and into in the backyard of a house on the other side of Lexington Avenue, putting the Yankees in front, 8-7. Coumbe got the next batter to ground out, but the game was all but lost. In the bottom of the ninth, with one out, Speaker singled, and Sam Jones replaced Ray Caldwell. "Sad Sam" retired Larry Gardner and Bill Wambsganss to end it.

Afterward, Fohl went directly to Jim Dunn and offered his resignation. Dunn accepted it, although he assured Fohl that he could stay on with the Indians as a scout. Dunn then summoned Speaker and asked him to take the job, which Speaker refused to do unless Fohl okayed it. After Dunn and business manager Ernest S. Barnard reached Fohl on the telephone, Speaker heard what he wanted from the ex-manager and agreed to become the new manager. The next day Speaker walked into the Indians' dressing room and told the players he was now their boss. For his coach, Speaker brought in Jack McCallister, who had been scouting for the Indians.

That day, ten thousand people came to League Park for Speaker's managerial debut. He obliged them by rapping three singles and a triple and driving in two runs, as the Indians beat the Red Sox for the ninth time in ten meetings, 7-4. Fittingly, Coveleski struck out Ruth with two on base to close out the game.

In that game and from then on, Speaker had his right- and leftfielders do as he did when he caught a fly ball: with nobody on base, fire it to home plate or to the nearest base instead of lobbing it in. "We found," he said many years later, "that it kept the outfielders' arms in good shape and they were able to throw out plenty of base runners just from forming the habit of throwing that ball as soon as they caught it." Speaker acknowledged that players of a later generation might "fear the fans would think they were showing off. We never felt that way."[10]

In a home game six days later, Speaker's team was already behind five runs in the eighth inning when he made a diving catch of Cobb's drive, cut his knee and bruised his hip, and had to leave the game, which ended 11-5 in favor of Detroit.

Asked afterward why he risked injury with the game apparently out of reach, he replied, "I never call a game until the last man is retired and it has always been my system to get any ball I think I can reach. I never learned any other way." Back in action the next day, he stole home on Doc Ayers in a losing effort. The Tigers won three of four games in that series and moved past New York into third place.

The Yankees, already a potent outfit, became even more so at the end of July when they acquired Carl Mays. Disgusted with what he thought was poor defense by his Red Sox teammates (who actually topped the league in fielding that year), Mays simply walked off the mound in the second inning of a game in Chicago and deserted the team. Ten days later Harry Frazee obligingly dealt the irascible pitcher to the Yankees for $40,000 and two players. Furious both with Frazee and with Jacob Ruppert and T. L. Huston, Ban Johnson put Mays under suspension, whereupon the New York owners defiantly activated him, at the same time that they accused Johnson of owning stock in the Cleveland franchise and favoring the Indians in the pennant race.

On August 10, Mays won his first game as a Yankee, an 11-4 trouncing of the Indians at the Polo Grounds that put the teams in a tie, six games behind Chicago and one and a half behind Detroit, which had gone on a hot streak and made it a four-way race. But the next day, despite home runs by Pipp, Bodie, and Lewis, the Tribe scored nine times in the last three innings to win a 15-9 slugfest; and in the series finale, Coveleski outpitched George Mogridge, 2-1. Cleveland returned to League Park holding third place by a game and a half.

Having struggled to a 5-11 record with Boston, Mays won nine of twelve decisions for New York. Johnson went into court in an effort to keep Mays from pitching for the Yankees, but the season was well over before the case was decided in Supreme (district) Court in New York City. (Under questioning from the Yankees' attorney, Johnson had to admit that he owned stock—$58,000 worth—in the Cleveland franchise, and had done so since the first season of the American League.) The Yankees gained a permanent injunction against Johnson, thus succeeding in an unprecedented act of defiance of the man who, up to then, had dominated American League affairs. From that point on, Johnson's power steadily eroded.

In mid-August the Indians gained some pitching help of their own when they signed veteran righthander Ray Caldwell. Although Caldwell had put in some good seasons with the Yankees, he had a history of heavy drinking and getting fined, and New York had peddled him to the Red Sox the past December as part of the Shore-Lewis-Leonard deal. Despite his 7-4 record with Boston, Caldwell's carousals had so tried manager Ed Barrow's patience that he had Harry Frazee release the veteran righthander outright. Speaker later said that he put a clause in Caldwell's contract requiring the pitcher to get drunk after every game he worked, stay away from the ballpark the next day, and run twelve laps around the field when he returned.

Whether or not that actually happened, Caldwell became a steady pitcher for the Indians, winning five games and losing only one in the six weeks left in the season. His first start with Cleveland, however, was literally shocking. On Sunday, August 24, at League Park, he had a 2-1 lead in the ninth inning and was one out from defeating Philadelphia, when a bolt of lightning knocked him flat. The players on the field also felt the electrical charge, as did many people in the stands. Shaken but determined to finish his game, Caldwell got up to retire the side.

At the end of that month and the beginning of September, the Indians won six times in nine meetings with Detroit, Chicago, and St. Louis; they took over second place and arrived in Chicago trailing the White Sox by six and a half games. Before breakfast, Speaker called his players together in his hotel room to say that he was proud of them, and that the three games they were to play in Chicago were critical. They were, although the series turned out to be a critical disappointment.

On Friday, September 5, the White Sox shelled Elmer Myers and won 9-1 behind Cicotte, who walked Speaker three times but held the Indians to six hits. Local rooters, remembering Speaker's fight with Chick Gandil, jeered him at every turn. The Tribe came back on Saturday to hammer Lefty Williams and successors, 11-2, with Joe Wood and Jim Bagby homering and Speaker getting two singles and a triple. But in the rubber game, on Sunday, the White Sox scored four runs in the second inning on Coveleski and subsequently added four more. Dickie Kerr, a 5′ 7″ rookie lefthander, held the Indians to three scores. With an overflow crowd roped off in the outfield, the teams combined for seven doubles, by Speaker. Cleveland left town seven and a half games behind the White Sox and, given the 140-game schedule, little to hope for except second place.

As the Indians traveled east to begin a twelve-game tour, Babe Ruth hit his twenty-sixth home run to break what was thought to be the major-league record, set in 1899 by John "Buck" Freeman with Washington, then in the National League. On September 10, following a rainout, Cleveland took a doubleheader from the Yankees. In the opener, Ray Caldwell pitched the best game of his career, a 3-0 no-hitter, Mays taking the loss. In Boston, the Indians won back-to-back 4-3 games with late-inning rallies and, after another rainout, departed for Philadelphia, having won fifteen of nineteen meetings with the also-ran defending champions.

Before Cleveland's arrival, Detroit lost two of three games in Philadelphia during a skid in which the Tigers dropped six of seven to the Browns, Athletics, and Washington. Despite little production on Speaker's part, the Indians bombarded the Athletics three times, with Connie Mack using mainly recruits brought up from Atlanta. Henry P. Edwards couldn't figure how "a good minor league team, that is all," could have won two out of three from the Tigers and maybe killed their chances for second place. The Indians' doubleheader sweep in Washington six days later clinched second place. Speaker's team came home having won twelve of thirteen times in the eastern cities to pull within four games of the White Sox, who ended their road trip by losing a single game and then a doubleheader in Boston. H. C. Walker of the *Detroit Times* wrote, "The work of the Indians under the inspiration of Speaker's leadership in the last two weeks has been truly wonderful and for this the credit is Speaker's."[11]

Detroit and New York were still competing for a share of the World Series receipts, which would include the second- and third-place finishers in each league but not, as in 1918, the fourth-place teams. On September 24, the Indians opened a series in Detroit with a loss to Dutch Leonard, who bested Jim Bagby, 4-1. Meanwhile, in Chicago, the White Sox clinched the pennant by beating St. Louis, 6-5, on Joe Jackson's ninth-inning single.

At that point, Detroit held third place by only a half game over New York. On the 25th, in a free-hitting game notably free of arguments with umpires Dick Nallin and Brick Owens, Detroit won, 9-5. The *Cleveland Press* headlined its box score, "This doesn't matter."[12] (Seven years later, what happened or didn't happen before and during that long-ago game did come to matter desperately to Cobb, Speaker, and Joe Wood.)

On Saturday the 27th, an off day for the Indians, Speaker won a skeet-shooting match—staged by the Northern Ohio Gun Club on its range at Kirtland—in competition with Les Nunamaker, Larry Gardner, and Jim Dunn. Speaker broke forty of fifty targets to Les Nunamaker's thirty-nine. On Sunday, Cleveland closed its season by losing to St. Louis, 8-5, and on Monday the Yankees won in Philadelphia to edge Detroit for third-place money. The season's final standings were Chicago, 88-52; Cleveland, 84-55; New York, 80-59; Detroit, 80-60. After Speaker took over, Cleveland had run up a 40-21 record.

Having improved his batting average by thirty points or so over the past six weeks, Speaker made two hits in five chances in the season-closer but fell four points short of .300 for the first time since becoming a regular in 1909. Playing in 134 games, he scored 83 runs, drove in 69, and hit 2 home runs and 38 doubles (seven fewer than Detroit's Bobby Veach). Again he was among the leaders in assists (25) and made only 7 errors.

Speaker's subpar hitting was especially puzzling, given that the American League as a whole batted .268, twenty points higher than in 1917 (the last full big-league season). Ty Cobb hit .384 to garner his twelfth (and last) batting title; Veach (.355), George Sisler (.352), and Joe Jackson (.351) all had strong years. Babe Ruth, besides pitching nine wins for a fifth-place team, batted .322, led the majors with 122 runs batted in, surpassed all his predecessors with 29 home runs, and became the most talked-about baseball player in the world.

Even before the season ended, Speaker's name was appearing on a column in the *Cleveland Plain Dealer,* in which he analyzed the respective strengths of the White Sox and the Cincinnati Reds, pennant-winners for the first time in National League history. The practice of paying managers and players to put their names on ghost-written pieces at World Series time had long been a sore point with many baseball writers. The Boston scribe Ernest J. Lanigan derided Speaker and others paid for ghosted Series columns as having "never possessed the vocabularies from which the printed words were taken."[13]

For the first time since 1903, the Series format was five out of nine games.

Like most other supposed experts, Speaker thought the White Sox were a stronger team than Cincinnati. Some (though not Speaker) were ready to acclaim Kid Gleason's outfit the best ever and wondered why they hadn't won the pennant by a bigger margin. Eddie Collins and Joe Jackson were great players; Buck Weaver, Ray Schalk, and Happy Felsch were very good ones. Yet with Red Faber ill for much of the season and unavailable for the World Series, the White Sox lacked the pitching depth of various previous Series entrants, including the 1915–1916 Red Sox. Cicotte (twenty-eight), Williams (twenty-two), and Kerr (thirteen) accounted for nearly three-fourths of Chicago's wins.

If the White Sox were overrated, the Cincinnati Reds, managed by Pat Moran, were underrated by nearly everybody except their fans. Yet Cincinnati had won eight more games than Chicago and had led the National League in fielding. The Reds went into the Series with a deeper pitching staff, one that had allowed the fewest runs in the majors. In retrospect, Moran's Reds matched up well with the team that had beaten John McGraw's Giants two years earlier.[14]

The day before the Series was to open in Cincinnati, Kid Gleason cut short his team's practice at Redland Field so he could make the first race at the horse track at Latonia, Kentucky, on the other side of the Ohio River. But betting on the Series itself, reported the Associated Press, "was noticeable for its absence."[15] That was wildly off-base; Cincinnati was awash in gamblers, especially in the lobby of the Hotel Sinton, where the White Sox were staying and the National Commission had its headquarters. On the morning before the first game, the odds mysteriously began to shift in the Reds' favor—a sure sign something was afoot.

That same morning Speaker graciously went to the dining room in the Sinton, sought out Chick Gandil, shook his hand, and said he hoped the White Sox would win the Series. Gandil thanked him, but Speaker's well wishes were lost on the Chicago firstbaseman. Always a tough customer looking for the main chance, Gandil was the ringleader in a plot developed weeks earlier, according to which he and six other Chicago players—Cicotte, Williams, Felsch, Jackson, shortstop Charles "Swede" Risberg, and utility infielder Fred McMullin—had agreed to take money from gamblers to lose the Series. Aware of the fix, Buck Weaver intended to play the games honestly, but he wouldn't inform on his crooked teammates.

The 1919 Series fix was an inordinately complex, tangled episode, much of which is hard to understand, much of which will never be known. What is known is that Cicotte, Gandil, and three other White Sox took the field beholden to gamblers. After the first game, a 9-1 debacle in which the Reds drove Cicotte from the mound with five runs in the fourth inning, Speaker's column (which accurately stated his views, even if he didn't write the words) expressed bewilderment at the White Sox's shoddy play. It wasn't only Cicotte's ineffectiveness but various instances in which Chicago fielders failed to execute cutoff plays. Speaker also noted that batters didn't swing when runners tried to steal, yet swung at first pitches from Cincinnati's Walter "Dutch" Ruether after Ruether had made hard runs on his two triples and would still be regaining his wind. To Speaker, the White Sox just didn't look like the same team that had beaten out his Indians.

At Redland Field the next day, Lefty Williams, who had averaged fewer than two walks per game during the season, passed six Reds and lost, 4-2. Dickie Kerr pitched a beautiful three-hit shutout in the third game, in Chicago; but in game four Cicotte, though pitching well otherwise, made two critical errors in the fifth inning that produced the only two runs of the game. Williams lost again in the fifth game, also in Chicago, on Horace "Hod" Eller's three-hit, nine-strikeout shutout. Two of Cincinnati's five runs scored because Felsch made a wild throw that led to one run and then lost Edd Roush's fly ball for a triple, with Roush subsequently coming home. The White Sox, Speaker thought, "looked today as if they are just trying to play out the schedule."[16]

One of the biggest imponderables in a World Series full of them occurred in game six, in Cincinnati. In the tenth inning, Gandil singled in Weaver with the go-ahead run for Kerr, who won for the second time, 5-4. Also hard to figure was Cicotte's fine performance in game seven, a 4-1 victory in which the Reds made four errors, and Jackson and Felsch made two hits apiece. But then, back at Comiskey Park on October 9, Williams became the first pitcher to lose three games in a Series, when he yielded two singles and two doubles in the first inning for four runs. Although the White Sox scored five times on Eller, including Jackson's home run (the only one of the Series), the Reds accumulated sixteen hits and scored five more runs on Williams's two successors. Speaker expressed his disgust to Henry P. Edwards, but he had nothing to say in print about game eight and left quickly on his annual postseason hunting excursion.

Speaker and Les Nunamaker, together with Martin Ackerman, a fish and game writer, and two Indian guides, spent a week on lakes in the vicinity of Peterborough, Ontario, fishing for muskellunge and shooting ducks. At the nearby Mississauga Indian reservation, Speaker donned a war bonnet for a ceremony making him an honorary chief of the tribe. After a quick visit with his mother at Hubbard, he returned to Cleveland to serve as best man for Ray Chapman.

Chapman's bride-to-be was Kathleen Daly, daughter of the president of the East Ohio Gas Company. Kentucky born, Chapman had grown up in the coal-mining region of southern Illinois and had been reared as a Protestant, whereas Kathleen Daly came from a locally prominent Roman Catholic family. "Chappie" was popular with his teammates, whom he entertained on train and subway rides with melodies rendered in a fine tenor. He was also given to practical jokes, such as the time in New Orleans the previous spring when he tricked Steve O'Neill, who claimed he could hit a golf ball from home plate over the centerfield fence, into whacking a hollow object that shattered in all directions. Though Chapman was frequently injured, his strong work ethic and aggressive base-running had made him a favorite of Speaker. The fact that Chapman would be married in a Catholic ceremony doesn't seem to have bothered Speaker. In fact, given Speaker's strong friendship with Jim Dunn, it seemed that, at least since his coming to Cleveland, his attitude toward communicants of the Church of Rome had moderated.

Two nights before the wedding, Speaker, Ed Klepfer, Jack Graney, featherweight boxing champion Johnny Kilbane (a Cleveland native), Mayor Harry W. Davis, and about twenty-five others hosted Chapman for a bachelor dinner at the Hotel Winton. On October 25, with Speaker at his appointed place alongside the groom, Chapman and Kathleen Daly were married in the home of the bride's parents on Euclid Avenue. Although the ceremony was performed by the Reverend Joseph Smith, pastor of the family's parish church, it's possible that the site was chosen out of consideration for Speaker, Graney, and the groom's relatives. A reception followed at the clubhouse of the Grand Council of the Knights of Columbus.

Meanwhile, in Chicago, Hugh Fullerton published a series of articles raising questions about the World Series and fueling suspicions that things hadn't been on the up and up. Charles Comiskey made a grand gesture of offering a $10,000 reward for any evidence that the Series hadn't been honestly played. Privately he hoped he wouldn't get any takers. Yet based on what Kid Gleason and Eddie Collins, among others, had already told him, the White Sox owner had his own suspicions, because he held up mailing out his players' Series checks.

Fullerton's efforts were the exception. Most of the baseball press scoffed at the notion that a World Series—or baseball games in general—could be fixed. "If a man really knows so little about baseball," editorialized *Baseball Magazine,* "that he believes the game is or can be fixed, he should keep his mouth shut when in the presence of intelligent people." In a notorious editorial, the *Sporting News* declared that rumors of a fix came from "a lot of dirty, long-nosed, thick-lipped and strong-smelling gamblers." Nobody would try for Comiskey's reward "because there is no evidence except in the mucky minds of the stinkers."[17]

At the beginning of the new year, talk about what did or didn't happen in the Series was pushed aside by the news that Harry Frazee had sold Babe Ruth to the New York Yankees, and that Jacob Ruppert had paid a staggering $125,000 for his contract. (That wasn't even half the deal; it wasn't revealed at the time that Ruppert had loaned Frazee an additional $300,000, secured by the transfer to Ruppert of the mortgage on Fenway Park.) Ruth's departure was the pivotal event in the ongoing process—initiated with the trades involving Larry Gardner, Duffy Lewis, Ernie Shore, and Dutch Leonard and continuing with the Carl Mays deal—by which Frazee turned what had been one of the most successful teams and franchises into one of the worst. The principal beneficiaries of the "rape of the Red Sox" were the Yankees, who in the decade ahead would come to dominate the American League and become the richest operation in baseball. In 1923, having sold or traded away his marketable talent, Frazee unburdened himself of the Red Sox franchise and turned his full attention to the musical theater, always his first love.[18]

By the time Frazee left baseball, it was in the midst of the biggest upsurge in batting averages and scoring since the first years after 1893, when the pitching distance was extended by ten feet. But unlike the 1890s, the 1920s saw the advent of an unprecedented power-oriented game. The increasing proclivity of hitters to emulate the home-run exploits of Ruth—whose salary with the Yankees soared from $20,000 in 1920 to $80,000 by 1930—partly accounts for what happened, along with the increasing popularity of new-style, thin-handled bats, which concentrated the weight in the barrel, or "fat" part. That kind of bat made for a "torque" effect that could propel the ball to the far reaches of ballparks when batters took full swings, as more and more of them would do in the '20s.[19]

As much as anything, though, the batting boom resulted from the banning of the spitball and other "trick deliveries," as decreed early in 1920 by the majors leagues' joint rules committee. Seventeen veteran spitballers already in the majors—no more than two per team—were exempted from the ban for the 1920 season. A year later, the exemption was extended to the duration of their careers. The exemptees included Ray Caldwell and Stanley Coveleski, a twenty-four-game winner in 1919. Yet Coveleski worried about the overall effect of the ban on his fellow moundsmen. "If they abolish the spit ball," he predicted, "they will turn pitching in both leagues bottom up."[20] That was largely what happened.

Pitchers were forbidden even to use a resin bag to dry their fingers in hot weather. At the beginning of the 1920 season, moreover, the umpires received instructions not only to watch closely and eject from a game anybody "loading up" besides the designated seventeen pitchers, but also to keep clean baseballs in play and throw out any that became scuffed or discolored. That practice—together with the increasing willingness of club owners to permit spectators to keep foul balls (as Charles Weeghman had started doing in the Chicago Federal League park in 1914)—meant that batters would be swinging at clean, hard baseballs that traveled faster and farther when a hitter made solid contact. By 1924, Dan Comerford, property manager for the Brooklyn club, could report that in that season the Robins had used five hundred dozen balls, whereas twenty years earlier, when Comerford took the job, about fifty dozen were used.

So a variety of factors combined to produce what came to be known as the "lively ball era" (as opposed to the preceding "dead-ball era"). Actually the balls manufactured after the war by A. G. Spalding and Brothers were exactly the same in design as those in use since the introduction of the cork-centered ball late in the 1910 season. Spalding acknowledged that with the end of the war, a higher-grade Australian wool had become available, which made possible a tighter wind of the yarn around the cork-rubber center. However that may have been, the oft-stated view of veteran managers, players, sportswriters, and umpires was that beginning in 1920 the ball was "livelier" than it had ever been.

Whether one talked about balls, bats, or Babe Ruth, the 1920 season wasn't very old before it became obvious that the game was undergoing a change from the way it had been played over the previous two decades. Ruth astonished the baseball world and much of the world outside baseball with his 54 home runs, plus a .376 batting average, 137 runs driven in, 158 runs scored, and a wondrous .847 slugging average. As compared to 1917, the last previous 154-game season, the American League's collective average at bat jumped by thirty-four points, runs scored by 21 percent. The league as a whole hit 369 home runs—63 percent more than in 1917 (although Ruth alone accounted for nearly 16 percent of the total.)

Lacking a Babe Ruth, the National League showed less of an offensive surge in 1920, although the league's batting average was twenty-two points higher than in 1917, while nearly 10 percent more runs were scored. National Leaguers hit 261 homers, 22 percent more than three years earlier. In his fifth full season with the St. Louis Cardinals, Rogers Hornsby won the first of his seven batting titles with a .370 average, the highest in his league in eight years.

So Tris Speaker began his first full year as Cleveland's player-manager with a new style of baseball about to emerge—one featuring more hitting and especially more power-hitting, with a corresponding decline in the "scientific" game of place-hitting, base-stealing, hit-and-run plays, and tight, durable pitching. That was the game in which Speaker had risen to stardom and Ty Cobb had dominated. Both as a player and a manager, Speaker successfully adapted to the new way of playing the game. Cobb continued to be one of the game's stellar performers, but as a player and then as a player-manager, he was never reconciled to the eclipse of "Cobbian" baseball by "Ruthian" baseball.

Chapter 8

"I Knew My Team"

As the Indians began their 1920 spring training, again in New Orleans, the *Sporting News* columnist J. R. Young euphemistically referred to Ray Caldwell's "taking care of himself this winter," because "his sensational comeback with the Indians at the end of the 1919 race has taught him a lesson."[1] During that spring training and throughout the coming season, Caldwell presumably found it harder *not* to "take care of himself." The Eighteenth Amendment to the federal Constitution, submitted to the states in the fervor of wartime and ratified by the beginning of 1919, made alcoholic beverages—statutorily defined the following October as anything containing more than .05 percent alcohol—illegal to manufacture and sell anywhere in the United States. If vice was supposed to have been curbed in New Orleans with the closing down of Storyville during the war, then as of January 16, 1920, the Crescent City and the whole country were supposed to have been freed from the incubus of liquor.

Although the traditional view of Prohibition has been that it was ineffective from the outset, more recent studies have concluded that by 1925 the consumption of alcoholic beverages in the United States had diminished by at least a third. Over most of the country, it did become harder to find safe-to-drink liquor. But in the cities on the Atlantic, Pacific, and Gulf Coasts and along the Great Lakes, liquor continued to enter the country from Canada, Mexico, and the Caribbean, especially from Cuba. In the big-league cities, in other words, ballplayers could still slake their thirst just about whenever they wanted to.

That spring, J. R. Young called Speaker "the most democratic of managers," one who continued to room with Joe Wood and always stayed on the same floor as his players. Henry P. Edwards was rhapsodic about the Tribe's manager: "He is a human dynamo. He simply radiates enthusiasm." Speaker's players "swear by him. They are for him because they know positively that he is for them, and he plays no favorites and asks them to do nothing he would not do himself."[2]

With the roster limits in both leagues restored to twenty-five, Speaker had thirty-four players on hand at Heinemann Park. They didn't include Joe Harris, who was again unhappy with the money offered him and had decided to return to "outlaw" ball in Pennsylvania (as he did again in 1921). That spring the Indians played no exhibitions with other big-league teams, instead meeting New Orleans several times, then stopping for one game in Memphis and two in Louisville (where a veteran minor-leaguer named Joe McCarthy again occupied second-base). Most sportswriters around the American League had made Cleveland the pennant favorite. Curiously, Speaker named St. Louis and Detroit, not Chicago and New York, as the teams the Indians would have to beat. Like many other people, Speaker knew the White Sox were faction-ridden, and although he never said anything publicly, he may also have suspected the honesty of some of them.

On Wednesday, April 15, the Indians opened the 1920 season at League Park with a 5-0 victory over St. Louis, Coveleski doing the honors. The losing pitcher was Allen Sothoron, a twenty-game winner who had forsaken the spit-ball so that teammates Urban Shocker and Bert Gallia could continue to throw it. An overflow gathering of 19,984 shivered through the cold afternoon; fans sitting on the outfield grass lit small fires in an effort to keep warm. Rain kept the teams from playing the next two days. Speaker and several of his players, along with Jim Dunn and local baseball writers, were guests at a luncheon given by the Ad and Kiwanis Clubs. Speaker told the group that Dunn had given him freedom to make whatever player deals he wanted, "so I'll have no alibis if I don't deliver."[3] When play resumed on Saturday, Urban Shocker disappointed another big crowd by besting George Uhle, 5-4.

Speaker may have thought Detroit would be a pennant threat, but the Tigers lost their first thirteen games and didn't yield last place to the perennially pitiable Athletics until June. Seventh place was the highest they reached in the standings. Ty Cobb missed a month of the season with a bad knee injury. He played in only 112 games and struggled to bring his average up to .334. Although Cobb continued to be one of baseball's stellar performers, he had won his last batting title.

The Indians began the season in fine form, winning twenty-one of their first thirty games. On April 18, for only the second time in his career, Speaker sent a ball over League Park's rightfield wall, and also doubled up Detroit's Donie Bush when the little shortstop tried to score on a fly ball. Ten days later the Indians stopped Chicago's nine-game season-opening win streak at League Park, 5-4. Speaker saved the game by running down Joe Jackson's ninth-inning drive to deep right-centerfield, making a one-handed catch, and then crashing into one of the concrete supporting posts. Umpire Billy Evans declared the catch to be the greatest he had ever seen. (A few weeks later, in Philadelphia, Speaker, along with several of his players, returned the favor by grabbing bats and holding off a mob menacing Evans and fellow-umpire George Hildebrand at the conclusion of a 4-1 Athletics loss to Elmer Myers.)

Indicative of the batting upsurge in the American League that season was a stretch of nine games Cleveland played with Chicago and Detroit, from May 29 to June 4. The Indians scored 66 runs on 116 hits. Henry P. Edwards was convinced that a livelier ball was being used, because "It is not reasonable to suspect that two-thirds of the American League hurlers should go wrong all at once." Speaker's troubles at bat the previous season were forgotten. As his team stayed at or near the top of the league week after week, he pounded pitchers at a .390 pace and consistently hit the ball harder than ever before. Grantland Rice, now a featured writer for the *New York Tribune,* observed that "Speaker has his machine working smoothly. . . . The recipe is simple—to know baseball and to know how to lead men. Speaker is well fixed both ways."[4]

Coveleski was away for a week because of his wife's death at Shamokin, Pennsylvania, but the Tribe kept on winning and Speaker kept up his torrid hitting. In three games in Washington in July, he made ten hits in ten official at bats to raise his average to .402, although he still trailed George Sisler by sixteen points. By then Speaker was alternating Doc Johnston and George Burns (purchased from Philadelphia for $10,000) at firstbase, Joe Wood and Elmer Smith in rightfield, and Charlie Jamieson and Joe Evans in leftfield.

By the time manager Miller Huggins, Babe Ruth, and the Yankees arrived in mid-June for a big three-game series, Jim Dunn had had the opening between the leftfield bleachers and the grandstand enclosed with an uncovered stand, thus enlarging League Park's capacity by about 4,000. The ballpark still wasn't big enough to accommodate the turnout on Sunday the 14th. A paying crowd of 29,266 suffered through the Yankees' 14-0 rout of Uhle and two relievers. Ten doubles landed in the outfield overflow. Ruth sent his seventeenth home run soaring over the rightfield wall. The Tribe came back to win on Monday and Tuesday behind Coveleski and Bagby, so that New York left town trailing Cleveland by two games.

Within another three weeks, by winning three times from the Indians at Comiskey Park, the White Sox had pulled to within three and a half games of both Cleveland and New York and made it a three-way pennant race. Stopping in Cleveland en route to Washington to begin an eastern tour, Speaker gave his thoughts on the competition: "I figured if the Sox had the harmony," he said, "they would be harder to beat than the Yanks."[5] In fact the White Sox continued to be bitterly divided, one group identifying with Eddie Collins and Ray Schalk, the other with Eddie Cicotte and Lefty Williams. (In the off-season, Chick Gandil had quit Organized Baseball.)

With or without "the harmony," the White Sox remained a formidable outfit, one that steadily gained on Cleveland and New York. Despite losing three of four games in New York at the end of a month-long road trip, the Indians came home still in the lead. Speaker was having the best year of his career, including another streak—this one of eleven consecutive hits—to push his average to .417 and surpass George Sisler. To a *Sporting News* contributor, Speaker had become "the Moses to lead Cleveland to its first pennant."[6] But then the Yankees, who had played poorly in the west up to then, came into League Park and swept four games, dropping the Tribe into a virtual tie with Chicago and New York.

After ending their home stand with two wins over fourth-place St. Louis, the Indians traveled to New York to open a series on Monday, August 16. On the subway ride from the Ansonia Hotel up to the Polo Grounds, Ray Chapman raised his teammates' spirits by leading them in song. His brother-in-law Daniel Daly had accompanied the Indians to New York and rode along with the team. Before the game, Charlie Jamieson was honored by policemen and firemen from his Paterson, New Jersey, hometown. His mother and sister had come over for the game, although after what happened that day, Jamieson recalled decades later, his mother "never went to another game" and urged him to quit baseball.[7]

The day was overcast and muggy, with a drizzle falling during the early innings, but the game still attracted an excellent weekday crowd of 23,000. At the end of four innings, Carl Mays had given up three runs. Coveleski had held the Yankees scoreless.

Chapman led off the top of the fifth and took his usual stance, crouching and crowding the plate. Mays's first pitch, delivered with his characteristic submarine motion, was a fastball that came in high and inside. Chapman didn't move. The ball slammed against his left temple and bounced back to Mays, who, thinking the ball had hit the bat, fielded it and threw over to Wally Pipp at firstbase.[8] Pipp cocked his arm to start the routine infield toss-around, then saw Chapman slowly sink to his knees and be eased to the ground by Speaker, who was to bat next. Several minutes passed as players from both teams milled around. Two physicians left the grandstand to minister to the stricken player, who was bleeding from his left ear. Finally helped to his feet, Chapman took a few steps before collapsing again. Teammates carried him to the visitors' clubhouse in centerfield, where an ambulance was called to transport him to nearby St. Lawrence Hospital.

Of course, the game continued. Substitute infielder Harry Lunte ran for Chapman; Speaker's infield grounder forced him at secondbase. After Elmer Smith struck out, Larry Gardner singled Speaker over to third, and on Steve O'Neill's single, he scored Cleveland's fourth run. Hank Thormahlen replaced Mays to start the ninth inning and retired the side in order. In the bottom of the inning, the Yankees finally got to Coveleski for three runs before he made pinch hitter Frank "Lefty" O'Doul hit into a forceout to end the game. At that point, Cleveland's record was 71-40, Chicago's 72-42, and New York's 72-44.

That night, as the Indians waited anxiously at the Ansonia for word on Chapman's condition, Mays was quoted as saying he had complained to plate umpire Tom Connolly that the ball had a dark spot on it and should have been discarded. Speaker tried to be upbeat, comparing the blow Chapman took to the one Dave Danforth dealt him in 1917 (which he mistakenly dated a year earlier). But such optimism was futile. Although surgery lasting an hour and a half seemed to bring some improvement, Chapman's injury—a triple fracture of the left temple, with pieces of bone having been driven into his brain—was too much to overcome. He died at 4:40 A.M., at the age of twenty-nine.

Kathleen Chapman, who had recently learned that she was pregnant, arrived later that day, accompanied by her father and Jane McMahon, her cousin and bridesmaid. She said later that she knew her husband was dead by the expressions on the faces of Speaker and others when she arrived at the Ansonia. Carl Mays didn't learn of Chapman's death until mid-morning. Yankees manager Miller Huggins, who had a law degree, drove Mays to the nearest police station, where, for the record, he gave his account of what happened. (Subsequently, the district attorney for Manhattan summoned Mays for an interrogation, after which the fatality was officially recorded as accidental.)

Over the years, a handful of minor-leaguers have died from errant pitches, but Chapman's death remains unique in major-league history. Speaker was distraught and disconsolate. "Ray Chapman was the best friend I ever had," he said in a statement given to reporters. "I would willingly abandon all hope for the championship not only this season but in all years to come, and retire from the game forever, if by doing so I could recall my teammate and my best friend back to life."[9] The Indians didn't want to take the field on Tuesday, and Yankees owners Huston and Ruppert agreed that it was appropriate for the teams to take the day off. As the rest of the ball club idled gloomily at the Ansonia, Speaker and Joe Wood accompanied Kathleen Chapman, Daniel Daly, Jane McMahon, and Chapman's body back to Cleveland.

Asked about reports that Boston, Detroit, St. Louis, and Washington players were drawing up petitions calling for Mays's banishment from baseball, Speaker said that he had told T. L. Huston he didn't hold Mays responsible for what happened, "and in respect to Chapman's memory, as well as for the good of baseball, I hope all talk of this kind will stop." Years later, Speaker told the veteran baseball writer Fred Lieb, "I don't think Mays deliberately threw at him. There was time for Chappie to duck when the ball was coming at him, but he never moved." And in 1941, when Joe Williams wrote to ask Speaker about the incident, he replied that Chapman "just seemed in a strange daze. He just stood at the plate as if in a trance and made no effort to pull away from the pitch."[10]

Whether deserved or not, Mays had acquired a reputation as a mean pitcher, a man who liked to throw at batters' heads. Somebody counted that in his six years in the American League, Mays had hit fifty-five batters, although a couple of other pitchers had hit even more. Mays himself was aware that he was unpopular with most of his ball-playing peers and many others around baseball. "I have always wondered," he said in an interview some time afterward, "why I have encountered this antipathy from so many people wherever I have been. And I have never been able to explain it, even to myself."[11]

On Wednesday, August 18, without their manager, the Indians lost the second game of the New York series, 4-3, when Bagby gave up two runs in the bottom of the ninth inning. That cut their lead over Chicago to a half game, with the Yankees only a game out of first place. The next day, though, Ray Caldwell threw his spitter with sufficient effectiveness to best Bob Shawkey, 3-2, despite Ruth's forty-third home run. Elmer Smith's sixth-inning homer—his second in two days—provided the winning run and increased Cleveland's lead over idle Chicago by half a game.

From New York, the Indians were to travel to Boston to begin a series on Friday, but the game was rescheduled for a Saturday doubleheader so the team could return to Cleveland for Chapman's funeral. On the morning of the 20th, Steve O'Neill and Jack Graney broke down at the Daly home. Graney was so overwrought that Napoleon Lajoie, who had also come to pay his respects, put the little outfielder in his automobile and drove him around the city during the services. Speaker, in seclusion in his rooms at the Hotel Winton, became ill with what was diagnosed as ptomaine poisoning, although it may have been an intestinal virus, helped along by stress and depression. Whatever it was, with chills and fever, he was ordered to bed by his physician.

Original plans were for Chapman's funeral to be held at St. Philomena's Church, where the Dalys worshiped, but to accommodate the great number who wanted to attend, it was moved to St. John's Cathedral in the heart of the city. With thirty-six priests participating, the requiem mass began at ten A.M. It was standing room only inside the cathedral. Hundreds more gathered on its steps and up and down East Ninth Street. Ban Johnson sat with Jim Dunn and various city officials. Ernie Shore, Duffy Lewis, and Wally Pipp attended as representatives of the Yankees. Steve O'Neill and Joe Wood were among the honorary pallbearers. The altar was blanketed with twenty thousand flowers, paid for by local fans who contributed ten cents apiece. When the service ended at noon, the Cleveland players didn't accompany the funeral cortege to the burial site in Lake View Cemetery, because they had to hustle to catch the train to Boston. Speaker stayed behind and remained in bed, losing fourteen pounds over a five-day period.[12]

After an all-night train ride, Speaker's players arrived in Boston early in the afternoon of August 21 and went directly to Fenway Park, where, tired and downcast, they were shut out, 12-0 and 4-0, by Waite Hoyt and Herb Pennock. To the syndicated Boston writer Burt Whitman, "The Indians seemed stunned."[13] The White Sox, having won twelve of their last fourteen games, now led Cleveland by a game and a half; the Yankees were three back.

Following the Sunday off day, Speaker rejoined the team in Boston on Monday the 23rd, with another doubleheader scheduled. Weakened from his illness, he pinch-hit for O'Neill in the ninth inning and flied out, although the Indians came out on top, 2-1, as Caldwell continued his sterling mound work. Speaker put himself in the lineup in the nightcap, going hitless in a dispiriting thirteen-inning, 4-3 defeat for Jim Bagby. Meanwhile, in New York, Carl Mays took the mound for the first time since Chapman's death and pitched a shutout versus Detroit, in the face of pronouncements by Ban Johnson and various writers that Mays's career was probably over. Ty Cobb, whom the New York press had accused of trying to have Mays banned (which he denied), left a hotel sickbed to take the field and listen to hoots and curses from the pro-Mays crowd.

Speaker again limited himself to pinch hitting in another loss that concluded the series in Boston. Two more losses, to the tail-end Athletics, made the Tribe's post-Chapman record 2-5. In the first game in Philadelphia, plate umpire George Hildebrand ruled fair a bunt by Elmer Smith, although Smith, who thought it was foul, remained at home plate. The Athletics' catcher pegged to second to force Speaker; the throw to first doubled up Smith. Instead of bawling out Smith, Speaker got up in Hildebrand's face and harangued him for ten minutes, until umpire George Moriarty persuaded him to give up. Burt Whitman wrote, "the wrinkles in [Speaker's] face seem deeper cut and his hair grayer . . . But Tris' flareup proved one thing. The old fight is still there."[14]

Speaker might not have blamed Mays for Chapman's death, but some of his players were still angry enough to want to do something. From Philadelphia, they sent a petition to the other American League clubs, asking them not to take the field when Mays was to pitch. Walter McNichol, Cleveland club secretary, said that Speaker had nothing to do with the petition and hadn't even known about the meeting when it was gotten up. When he heard about the petition, Ban Johnson traveled to Philadelphia to meet with Speaker. Johnson shared Speaker's view of the fatality. In the absence of any kind of action on the part of the league president, the Cleveland petition fizzled.

Coveleski's loss at Washington on August 29, the Indians' thirteenth defeat in their last eighteen games, dropped them to third place. But three days later, when Bagby throttled the Nats, 7-1, and the White Sox and Yankees lost in Boston and St. Louis, respectively, Cleveland moved to within a half game of Chicago and a game ahead of New York. The next day Walter "Duster" Mails, a cocky, free-spirited lefthander just purchased from Sacramento of the Pacific Coast League, made his first start as an Indian a winning one, although he had to be relieved by Guy Morton. Cleveland took three of four games in Washington, while Chicago played shoddy ball and lost three straight in Boston. Speaker's team came home in first place by half a game, with the Yankees still only one game from the lead.

Harry Lunte, Chapman's replacement, was batting only .197 when he was disabled with a pulled hamstring. While Joe Evans filled in, Speaker contacted the New Orleans club, with which the Cleveland franchise had a long-standing if unofficial connection. Xen Scott, University of Alabama football coach and sometime Cleveland sportswriter, told Speaker the player he ought to get was Joe Sewell, who had signed with New Orleans after starring in both baseball and football at Alabama. The New Orleans ownership wanted $6,000 for the 5′ 6½″ shortstop and forfeiture of rights to various players Cleveland had optioned to the Pelicans. It was a stiff bargain, but Speaker was close to desperate for somebody who could handle the position. Sewell himself, not at all sure he was ready for the big time, had to be talked into leaving by Pelicans centerfielder Larry Gilbert.

Sewell joined the team in Cleveland on Thursday, September 9, just as the Yankees arrived for a big three-game series. At that point the respective records of the Indians, White Sox, and Yankees were 81-49, 83-52, and 81-53. Sewell sat at the end of the dugout and watched his new teammates pound Jack Quinn and his successors, 10-4. Coveleski passed Ruth three times but gave up the big Yankee's forty-seventh home run. Music was provided by the boys band from St. Mary's Industrial School, which was traveling with the Yankees on the western trip at Ruth's expense. Carl Mays, though, wasn't with the team.

The next day, Sewell got into his first big-league game, replacing Joe Evans at shortstop during a 6-1 loss to Bob Shawkey, with Ruth homering again. Sewell went hitless in two times up and erred on a throw to firstbase, but Speaker penciled him in to start the rubber game of the New York series, for which a crowd of 30,805 filled every seat and stood ten rows deep around the outfield. The Yankees jumped on Bagby for six runs; Hank Thormahlen held the Indians to two. Cleveland now held first place by one percentage point over New York, four points over Chicago, in what had become the tightest American League race since 1908.

Sewell was in the Indians' lineup to stay, but as Speaker reminisced forty years later, the little Alabamian, a lefthanded batter, "was without a doubt the worst hitter against lefthanded pitchers I ever saw. He couldn't even come close to hitting a southpaw's curve."[15] So every morning, in the rightfield corner of League Park, Speaker had Sewell bat against Duster Mails (his only lefthander), until the youngster began to gain a little confidence and proficiency.

Carl Mays joined the Yankees in Detroit and, though driven out, was the winning pitcher in a 13-6 rout of Hugh Jennings's floundering ball club. Chicago lost at Washington, while in Cleveland, Speaker singled twice, doubled, and scored twice on Elmer Smith's doubles, as Mails won his second start, 5-2, over Philadelphia. The next day, though, knuckleballer Eddie Rommel shut down the Tribe, 8-0. Late in the game, Speaker went into the leftfield bleachers to call down a spectator who had been cursing him, then ordered a park attendant to refund the man's fifty-cent ticket price and escort him from the ballpark. Meanwhile, at Comiskey Park, the White Sox were shut out by José Acosta, Washington's diminutive Cuban find. By a second straight 13-6 score, New York won at Detroit and thereby gained first place. But that lasted only one day. On September 15, with the Yankees and White Sox idle, the Indians piled up twenty-two hits and fourteen runs, while Bagby held the Athletics scoreless. Speaker had four hits and drove in four runs. Joe Sewell lined out three singles.

On the 16th, Mails won again, beating Washington's Tom Zachary on a four-hitter, 1-0. The Indians went on to sweep the three-game series with the Senators, winning a sloppy finale, 7-5, despite committing five errors, including three by Sewell, who was hitting well but was still shaky afield. In Chicago, the White Sox swept three from the Yankees, who then dropped their fourth straight game in St. Louis and, for all practical purposes, fell out of the race. By the next day, September 23, when the White Sox arrived to begin a showdown series at League Park, they had won six games in a row. The Indians had a seven-game streak going and held first place by a game and a half.

Yet by that time, Chicago's whole season was in jeopardy, as well as the careers of seven White Sox players. In Chicago, Cook County district attorney Hartley Replogle had convened a special grand jury to investigate gambling in baseball. The investigation had been triggered by a report of an attempt to bribe Cubs pitcher Claude Hendrix to lose an August 31 game in Philadelphia.[16] As the White Sox were en route to Cleveland, the grand jury hearings began as an inquiry into that game as well as other suspicious matters in the National League, notably efforts the previous season by Hal Chase and Heinie Zimmerman to corrupt teammates on the New York Giants. On September 22, however, Replogle announced that seven members of the 1919 White Sox (whom he didn't name) had been bribed to lose the World Series.

Nobody seemed to see anything remiss about the White Sox's taking the field at League Park on Thursday the 23rd with allegations of dishonest play hanging over their heads. (The Cleveland papers didn't think the story worth page-one treatment; Replogle's statement was relegated to the sports pages.) The White Sox played as if nothing was remiss. On an unusually warm day for late September, some twenty-four thousand filled the stands, and a couple thousand more stood behind ropes in leftfield. Writers from Chicago, Boston, Pittsburgh, and New York crowded the local newspaper contingent in the press box. The White Sox slammed Bagby and Caldwell for ten runs on fifteen hits, including five doubles, while Dickie Kerr held Speaker hitless and limited the Tribe to three scores.

Speaker was also hitless the next day against Red Faber, but Duster Mails continued to pitch brilliantly, shutting out Chicago while his new teammates scored twice. That moved the Indians' lead back to a game and a half. But the White Sox won the rubber game, 5-1, behind Lefty Williams. Coveleski left after five innings, having yielded all five runs, including a home run and a double to Joe Jackson. Speaker failed to hit again and ended the three games 0 for 13. Another overflow crowd—30,625—pushed the total for the series to some 75,000.

The White Sox returned home, while the Indians took a train to St. Louis. Speaker's hitless streak continued, although George Uhle struggled to a 7-5 win, aided by Sewell's single and double that brought in four runs. Chicago kept within a game of Cleveland on Eddie Cicotte's easy win over Detroit, 8-1. On the 27th, Speaker finally hit two singles to break his slump, which had reached 0 for 19, as Mails won his fourth game without defeat, 8-4. George Sisler, now leading Speaker in the batting race by about twenty points, made three hits to equal Ty Cobb's 1911 major-league record of 248. But in Chicago, Dickie Kerr again pitched masterfully, shutting out Detroit, 2-0, in an hour and fifteen minutes.

On the 28th, with the White Sox beginning a three-day break in their schedule, Speaker doubled, singled, and stole home, as Bagby labored to a 9-5 victory, his thirtieth of the season. Sisler singled and homered to break Cobb's record. By then, the foreman of the Cook County grand jury had said there was "convincing evidence" that the 1919 Series had been crooked, and the *Philadelphia North American* had published Jimmy Isaminger's exposé—based on an interview with Bill Maharg, a former prizefighter and small-time gambler—that provided most of the particulars of the fix.[17] Whereupon Eddie Cicotte and Joe Jackson caved in, went to the Cook County courthouse, signed confessions that they had taken money to throw the Series, and named six teammates who had been in on the fix. Cicotte and Jackson were indicted that day. The next day, Lefty Williams signed a confession and was also indicted. Having long maintained that he was seeking the truth, Charles Comiskey finally had to do something decisive. He announced that the seven players still with the team (Chick Gandil, of course, wasn't) were suspended forthwith.

No event in the history of American baseball has come as a greater shock and caused more dismay. The *Sporting News,* which the previous winter had ridiculed rumors of a Series fix, now editorialized: "The prayer of fandom . . . is for Cleveland to win the American League pennant, for the honor of baseball and the integrity of the league."[18] Joe Vila argued that Comiskey should not only have suspended the implicated players but also pulled Chicago out of the pennant race, and that all White Sox wins in 1920 should be voided.

On the 29th, the Tribe made it a four-game sweep in St. Louis. Speaker made three hits in a 10-2 hammering of Carl Weilman. Coveleski held the Browns to two runs, despite two errors apiece by Sewell, Elmer Smith, and Larry Gardner. Gaining another half game on the idle White Sox, Cleveland now showed a 96-54 record to Chicago's 95-56 and 95-59 for New York, which swept a doubleheader at Philadelphia.

On the 30th the games in the western cities were canceled because of rain and cold. Returning to play the next day in St. Louis, the White Sox had substitutes playing leftfield, rightfield, shortstop, and thirdbase and were without two of their pitching mainstays. Red Faber's spitball was ineffective; Chicago lost, 8-6. At Detroit, the Indians split a doubleheader. Bagby took the loss in relief of Mails in the opener; Coveleski won his twenty-fourth game in the nightcap and thereby gave Cleveland another half-game advantage over Chicago. Now ahead by two games, the Indians had two more to play in Detroit. The White Sox also had two in St. Louis.

On a bone-chilling Saturday, October 2, some ten thousand Detroiters came to Navin Field, most of whom, disgusted by the revelations in Chicago, were ready to cheer for a Cleveland victory. Speaker called on Bagby for the forty-eighth time that season, and the veteran Georgian came through splendidly, holding the Tigers to a single run, while the Indians rapped lefthander John "Red" Oldham for ten runs on thirteen hits. Bagby rang up a three-run triple; Speaker hit three singles, scored three runs, and made five difficult catches in the swirling winds. Bagby's win, his thirty-first of the season, gave the city of Cleveland its first championship in forty-two years in professional baseball. The White Sox beat the Browns behind Dickie Kerr to clinch second place, but the race was over. The Tribe still led by two games, with only a single game remaining for both Cleveland and Chicago.

When Speaker grabbed Clyde Manion's fly ball for the final out, normally partisan Tigers fans poured onto the field to surround him and cheer and clap him on the back as he made his way to the tunnel that led to the dressing rooms behind the Detroit dugout. Henry P. Edwards pointed out the various difficulties Speaker's men had had to overcome: Joe Harris's desertion, Coveleski's absence for ten days because of his wife's death, Speaker's lack of an effective lefthander until Mails's arrival, and, most of all, Chapman's death and the team's ensuing slump.

So the prayers of the *Sporting News* and legions of baseball fans had been answered—the Indians had won. The "Black Sox," as the accused Chicago players were already being called, wouldn't get the chance to corrupt still another World Series. Virtue had triumphed over vice. As Joe Vila put it, "Had the White Sox finished in front the World Series would have been both unpopular and farcical, and the game would have fallen deeper in the slough of despond."[19]

Would the White Sox have won the pennant if the blowup had come a week or so later? Until Comiskey was obliged to gut the team, it was probably stronger than his 1919 pennant-winners. With Faber healthy and posting 23 wins, Lefty Williams winning 22, and Cicotte and Kerr winning 21 apiece, the 1920 White Sox showed much more pitching depth. And they participated fully in the American League's offensive upsurge. Joe Jackson batted .382 and registered career highs with 12 home runs and 121 runs batted in (which became an official American League statistic that season).[20] Happy Felsch batted .332, with 14 homers and 115 runs batted in; Eddie Collins and Buck Weaver hit .372 and .331, respectively. But the fact remains that for the White Sox to have won, Speaker's team would have had to collapse in the Detroit series. It didn't.

Moreover, apparently those who had played dishonestly in the 1919 World Series continued to do so in 1920. Harvey McClellan, Swede Risberg's substitute at shortstop for the St. Louis games, and backup catcher Byrd Lynn went public with charges that "certain players" among their teammates had watched the scoreboards to see what the opposition was doing, then played to influence the betting odds. Lynn said, "They always made errors which lost us the game when Cleveland and New York were losing. If Cleveland won, we won. If Cleveland lost, we lost. The idea was to keep up the betting odds, but not let us win the pennant."[21] McClellan said he was convinced the three games the White Sox lost in

Boston on August 31 and September 1–2 had been thrown. From Boston, James O'Leary wrote that in the third game, which Cicotte lost, 7-3, the Red Sox's Tim Hendryx doubled to leftfield, where Joe Jackson kicked the ball around while two runs scored to put Boston ahead for good.

On Sunday, the Indians and White Sox both lost their season-closers, which made the final standings Cleveland, 98-56; Chicago, 96-58; New York, 95-59. A big crowd greeted the Indians upon their arrival at Union Station shortly before midnight. When Jim Dunn asked Speaker how he felt, he replied simply, "Tired." Speaker told his men he would meet with them at League Park the next morning; they would leave Monday evening for Brooklyn to begin the World Series.

Brooklyn had won Wilbert Robinson's second National League pennant by a seven-game margin over John McGraw's Giants. The Robins weren't at the top of their league in any offensive category except triples, although they did have a trio of .300 hitters in firstbaseman Ed Konetchy, centerfielder Henry "Hy" Myers, and leftfielder Zack Wheat, whose .328 average was fourth-best in the league. The National League was still basically a pitcher's league, and Brooklyn's staff was its main strength. Robinson's pitchers were the stingiest in the majors in runs allowed (528) and registered the lowest earned run average (2.62). Six pitchers won at least eleven games, led by righthanded spitballer Burleigh Grimes with 23.

Speaker, on the other hand, had depended nearly all season on three pitchers, who had combined for 75 of the Indians' wins. Bagby won 31 times (the first American Leaguer in seven years to win that many and the last for another eleven years); Coveleski won 24; Caldwell won 20. Duster Mails was a godsend over the last six weeks of the season, with a 7-0 record in eight starts.

Despite League Park's short rightfield distance, the 1920 Indians weren't a power-hitting outfit. They combined for only 35 home runs, but they slashed the ball to all fields and, topped by Speaker's 50, totaled 301 doubles. They also led the majors in runs (857) and compiled a .301 team batting average (second to St. Louis's .308).

Speaker always believed that his illness following Chapman's death had cost him his chance to bat .400. As it was, he finished at .388 and drove in 107 runs, both career highs for him up to then, and hit 8 home runs. George Sisler's 257

Chapter 8

base hits not only broke Ty Cobb's record, but his .407 average was the highest in either league since Cobb's .410 eight years earlier. His 19 homers were the most any American Leaguer had hit besides Babe Ruth. Of course Ruth's total that year was thirty-five more than Sisler's.

It was again scheduled as a five-of-nine World Series, although in 1920 the games alternated on a three-four-two basis. The Series was supposed to start in Cleveland, but the first three games were transferred to Brooklyn so that Jim Dunn could have more time to build temporary bleachers at League Park in centerfield and in front of the rightfield wall and the regular bleachers in left. Field-level additions to the grandstand extended down both base lines (which meant that players would have to stand on the dugout steps and crane their necks to see balls hit into the corners). League Park's capacity grew to nearly 26,000, which just about equaled that of Brooklyn's Ebbets Field.

After an all-night train ride, the Indians checked in at the Hotel Pennsylvania. Accompanying them to Brooklyn were sportswriters for the three Cleveland daily newspapers and seventy-five members of the "Stick to the Finish" boosters club, organized that season. That afternoon, Tuesday, October 5—a cold, gray day that held the crowd a couple thousand below capacity—the Indians took the field wearing black armbands on their left sleeves in memory of Ray Chapman. Before the game, Doc Johnston posed for photographers with his brother Jimmy, Brooklyn's thirdbaseman; Speaker posed with C. C. Cunningham, a close Texas friend from Corsicana who had come up to be with the team in St. Louis; and a Brooklyn Shriner presented Speaker a good-luck floral wreath on behalf of the Hella Temple of the Mystic Shrine of Dallas.

For that and succeeding games, scores were radioed inning by inning to U.S. ships operating out of Atlantic ports and to those in the Pacific based at San Diego, via the new invention of long-distance wireless transmission. In Times Square in New York, in Public Square in Cleveland, and in the hubs of other major cities, crowds gathered to watch huge electric-scoreboard play-by-play displays of the action, as received by telegraph.

Speaker's opening-game choice was Stanley Coveleski. "Uncle Robbie" countered with Rube Marquard, who had pitched for him since 1915, when John McGraw gave up on the lefthander and sold him to Brooklyn for the waiver

168

price. Only 10-7 in 1920, Marquard presumably was Robinson's pick because the Brooklyn manager thought he might neutralize Speaker and Cleveland's other lefthand batters. Speaker, of course, arranged his lineup the way he had for most of the season, putting righthand batters Joe Evans in leftfield, Joe Wood in right-field, and George Burns at firstbase.

Coveleski threw his spitter with his usual skill, limiting the Robins to five hits and a single run. The Indians also made only five hits, but two of them were run-scoring doubles by Steve O'Neill. Final score: 3-1, Cleveland. Although Marquard and two others held Speaker hitless in four times up, the Tribe's manager made four difficult catches in the swirling winds, prompting Damon Runyon in his syndicated column to resort to similes from the animal kingdom: "He has the speed of a greyhound. He has eyes like an antelope, which can see very far. His judgment of a fly ball corresponds in keenness to the sense of smell of a deer."[22]

On Wednesday, in better weather, a full house of 25,559 paid to get into Ebbets Field, and hundreds more crowded a hill outside the ballpark beyond centerfield and the rooftops of houses across the street from the rightfield fence. After giving up single runs in the first, third, and sixth innings, Jim Bagby left in favor of George Uhle. With Burleigh Grimes pitching, Speaker played his left-batting lineup: Doc Johnston at first, Charlie Jamieson in leftfield, and Elmer Smith in right. The Indians reached Grimes for seven hits, including a single and double by Speaker, but they never managed to score.

On Thursday, Sherry Smith, another lefthander, pitched even better than Grimes, yielding only three hits and a single run and getting twenty of twenty-seven outs on ground balls. Brooklyn scored twice in the first inning, partly because Joe Sewell fumbled a grounder. Speaker paced and chewed grass in centerfield before removing Ray Caldwell and bringing in Duster Mails, who pitched scorelessly for the rest of the game. Cleveland's run came in the fourth inning, when Speaker lined a hit to the leftfield corner and circled the bases after Zack Wheat let the ball get through his legs.

Both teams quickly changed into street clothes, jumped into waiting taxis, and, with a police escort, hurried across the Brooklyn Bridge to the Pennsylvania terminal to catch separate trains for Cleveland. When the Indians' train pulled into Union Station at nine A.M. (the Robins' train was three hours late), they were serenaded by factory whistles and bells, as arranged by Mayor W. C. Fitzgerald. A mass of people met them there; thousands of others lined the route of the automobiles carrying the players to the Hollenden Hotel. A *New York Times* reporter commented, "Here is one place where no one is talking about the crooked work in last year's World Series."[23]

At the Hollenden, Speaker greeted his mother, who had arrived before daylight, having ridden day coaches all the way from Hubbard because, she explained, she couldn't sleep on trains. The *Cleveland Press* sent Kate Carter, its "women's reporter," to interview Jenny Speaker for a page-one feature. Described as "white haired, motherly looking, with glasses and a merry twinkle in her kindly eyes," Speaker's mother mentioned that her son had had a lake made on his farm and had stocked it with fish. Then she was willing to talk a little about Speaker's love life—or lack thereof. He liked both blondes and brunettes, she said. "But he likes all women. So I don't know when he will begin to specialize." Asked if her son had ever had a "real romance," Jenny Speaker recalled, "There was a girl. He thinks a lot of her yet, I guess, but they're just good friends. I'm not sure he'll ever get married."[24]

Down two games to one but with the next four games at home, the thirty-two- (or thirty-one)-year-old bachelor exuded confidence on Friday, an off day in the Series. On Saturday, 25,734 spectators filled League Park and maintained a cacophony of horns, auto sirens, and cowbells. In his second time out, Coveleski was as much in command as in game one. Brooklyn managed five hits and one run on "the stolid-faced Pole" (as depicted in the equally stolid-faced *New York Times*). Cleveland accumulated twelve hits, all singles (two by Speaker), and five runs on Leon Cadore, Marquard, and Ed "Jeff" Pfeffer.[25]

The game on Sunday, October 10, attended by a standing room only crowd of 26,684, was a one-sided affair; yet it was one of the most memorable in Series history. Cleveland scored seven runs on Burleigh Grimes and one on lefthander Clarence Mitchell, Brooklyn's other spitballer. Bagby gave up twelve hits but held the Robins scoreless until they pushed over a single run in their last time at bat. What made the game memorable were three plays that had never before happened in the World Series.

From the start, it was apparent that Grimes, who had pitched so ably in game two, was in for a rough time. In the bottom of the first inning, Jamieson and Wambsganss singled. When Speaker dropped a bunt toward thirdbase, Grimes slipped trying to field it and landed on his rear. Elmer Smith followed with a high fly that cleared the rightfield wall for the first bases-loaded home run in Series history. In the fourth inning, with two out and two on base, Bagby became the first pitcher to homer in the Series, sending a drive into the temporary seats in right-centerfield. At that point Uncle Robbie waved in Mitchell, on whom the Indians scored their final run in the fifth.

In the next inning Brooklyn seemed to have something going on Bagby. With nobody out, infielder Pete Kilduff was on secondbase, catcher Otto Miller on first. Mitchell, who was a better-than-average-hitting pitcher, slashed a line drive just to the right of secondbase. Wambsganss leaped to his right, speared the liner, stepped on the base before Kilduff could get back, and then ran toward first to tag Miller, who had stopped in his tracks halfway up the line. It all happened so suddenly that the crowd was momentarily noiseless before erupting in a bleachers-shaking cheer. Wambsganss's unassisted triple play remains a unique feat in the Series' long history. Yet because the Indians were already way ahead, Speaker always considered Smith's grand slam the game's biggest moment.

Some writers had questioned Speaker's judgment in starting Caldwell rather than Mails in game two. Now Speaker gave the ebullient California lefthander the ball. Mails held a grudge against Wilbert Robinson, who had used him a total of seventeen innings when he had been with Brooklyn in 1916 and then released him. Now, given his big chance before 27,194 Tribe partisans, he pitched the game of his life—a beautiful three-hit, six-strikeout shutout. The game's only run scored in the sixth inning, when Speaker singled off Sherry Smith, and George Burns followed with a double over centerfielder Hy Myers's head. Second-inning errors by Sewell and Gardner had loaded the bases, but Mails got Smith to fly to Speaker for the third out. Sewell's second error, in the ninth, made more trouble for Mails, but Myers hit into a forceout and Kilduff flied to Evans in leftfield for the final out. Before the game, Mails had said, "Brooklyn will be lucky to get a foul off me today. If Spoke and the boys will give me one run, we'll win."[26] He had been as good as his word.

Several years earlier, Rube Marquard's affair with the vaudeville star Blossom Seeley during their off-season tour, the messy breakup of Seeley's marriage, Seeley's subsequent marriage to Marquard, and the birth of a healthy baby within five months—all that had amounted to a mini-scandal. Now Marquard found himself in difficulty of a different kind, when he was arrested on Tuesday morning and charged with ticket-scalping. Although Marquard professed his innocence, insisting that he had only given a friend some tickets he had bought himself, he was hauled into police court and fined twenty-five dollars. Only then was he allowed to proceed to League Park, where, as it happened, he had nothing to do but watch.

Sensing that the Indians would close it out that afternoon, 27,523 people from all over northern Ohio—the Series' biggest crowd—packed League Park for the eighth game. Speaker again chose Coveleski. Also for the third time, Robinson sent Grimes to the mound. Coveleski was even better than he had been in his first two victories. A product of the Pennsylvania coal fields, Coveleski threw only ninety pitches to blank the Robins, 3-0, again allowing only five hits. Grimes pitched creditably for seven innings, giving up single runs in the fourth, fifth, and seventh innings before Al Mamaux replaced him to begin the eighth.

An error by Grimes scored Cleveland's first run. On a delayed steal attempt by Doc Johnston, Grimes intercepted catcher Otto Miller's throw, turned and threw wildly to second, and Larry Gardner trotted home. In the fifth inning, Charlie Jamieson scratched an infield hit, stole secondbase, and scored on Speaker's triple to the exit gate in deepest centerfield. Then, in the seventh, Coveleski ended up at secondbase when O'Neill was run down between second and third, and scored on Jamieson's ground-rule double into the rightfield bleachers.

When Ed Konetchy hit into a forceout, Sewell to Wambsganss, to end the game, Speaker grabbed the ball from "Wamby," dashed through the crowd spilling onto the field, and leaped the railing in front of Jim Dunn's box. Waiting for him, as described in the sentimental language of the time, "was his gray-haired mother, with arms outstretched. Into them the Cleveland hero was wrapped in fond embrace and the 'boy,' mingling his tears of joy with her tears of pride, kissed again and again the woman who gave him birth in the little home town in Texas years ago." It was Jenny Speaker's seventy-fifth birthday. The championship, the now totally gray Gray Eagle told her, was her birthday present. "I am the happiest woman in the world," she told reporters gathered in front of her. "I am happy as only a mother can be happy, happy because of my son."[27] Then she sat down and cried.

Speaker finally made it to the clubhouse in the rightfield corner, while Dunn stood outside, accepted the congratulations of Brooklyn president Charles Ebbets, and even signed some scorecards. Inside, amid the tumult of the Indians' dressing room, Speaker received a congratulatory telegram from President Wilson, emptied two fountain pens autographing balls and scorecards, and revealed that when the Indians returned from Brooklyn down two games to one, he had told Dunn they would win four straight at League Park. Why so confident? he was asked. "I knew my team," he replied.[28]

As had been true most of the time in Series play, pitching predominated. Although the Indians batted only .244 for the eight games, their pitchers held Brooklyn hitters to .208 and allowed an average of a single run per game. O'Neill and Jamieson led Cleveland with .333 averages; Speaker batted .320. Joe Sewell struggled both at bat and at shortstop, managing only four hits for a .174 average and committing six errors. Coveleski, Bagby, and Mails pitched well despite weak support in the field. The Indians made twelve errors, twice as many as the Robins.

The local press couldn't say enough in praise of Speaker. William Slavens McNutt declared that Speaker exemplified the best baseball could be. McNutt called Speaker "an innately great man, natural gentleman, good friend, courageous fighter and marvellous [sic] baseball player. The mud that has daubed over the game has never bespattered the Cleveland club. . . . It never will as long as Speaker is connected with Cleveland baseball."[29] Six years later, such sentiments would acquire an ironic note, but for now Speaker, his team, and the city by the lake were at the top of the baseball world. On the day the Series ended, a baby boy was born to Mr. and Mrs. E. E. Lisse of Cleveland. They named him Tristram Speaker Lisse.

The winning players' shares of the Series receipts (figured on five games) were $3,986.33 each. Besides Mails and Sewell, Kathleen Daly Chapman also received a full share. Each Brooklyn player came out with $2,250. Jim Dunn's profits from the four games in Cleveland provided a nice bonus on top of a record home attendance of 912,820—a total the franchise didn't surpass for another twenty-six years. Only the New York Giants (929,609) and their American League tenants drew more. Babe Ruth's exploits and the Yankees' strong run for the pennant put 1,289,422 paid admissions into the Polo Grounds—the first seven-figure total in baseball history. Aggregate big-league attendance soared to 9,120,875, some 4.5 million more than the previous season.

Speaker may have been anxious to leave for his annual outdoor vacation and put baseball behind him for a while, and his players may have wanted to scatter to their homes, but city officials and Clevelanders in general insisted upon a celebratory event. It took the form of a vast gathering at Wade Park the next night that nearly became a riot. It began innocently enough. On the platform, Speaker, Joe Wood, Doc Johnston, and a local woman harmonized on "Watching the World Go By," after which the players leaned over the platform railing to shake hands with those closest to them. Suddenly those in the back of the mass of people began to push toward the front. Men, women, and children were jammed up against the platform; chairs were broken; fights broke out; some people were trampled; others were pushed into a nearby lagoon and brook—whereupon the players took off. That ugly scene climaxed Cleveland's greatest baseball season.

Speaker and Les Nunamaker spent the next week or so hunting and fishing near Rockport on the Texas Gulf Coast. Other Indians did what baseball players with modest salaries usually did then and for a long time afterward: take up a variety of off-season employments. George Burns returned to Philadelphia to work as a floor walker in Wanamaker's Department Store; Larry Gardner returned to the auto repair shop he and a partner ran in Enosburg, Vermont; Charlie Jamieson worked at a grocery store in Paterson, New Jersey; Joe Evans continued working toward his M.D. at Washington University in St. Louis; Jim Bagby became a salesman at an auto dealership in Augusta, Georgia; Joe Wood returned to raising chickens and selling firewood at his farm in Pennsylvania; Joe Sewell reenrolled at the University of Alabama to finish his degree.

The annually published *Reach's Baseball Guide,* which a year earlier, like the *Sporting News,* had dismissed talk about a World Series fix, now expressed thanks for Cleveland's victory in the pennant race, because "it would have been embarrassing had even the emasculated or purged Chicago team won out after the Chicago grand jury's exposure of the eight Chicago players."[30] It would have been embarrassing—and maybe a mortal blow to the baseball public's confidence in the game's integrity. As it was, the "Black Sox scandal" sent reverberations throughout the tight little world of Organized Baseball, dealing a coup de grace to the moribund National Commission and prompting the overhaul of baseball's system of governance.

"I Will Never Be a Bench Manager"

Eddie Cicotte had admitted taking $10,000 to lose two games in the 1919 World Series. Now, in the fall of 1920, the U.S. Bureau of Internal Revenue notified him that he owed $2,200 in taxes on that unreported income, plus penalty and interest. That was the least of Cicotte's worries, because he and seven others stigmatized as the "Black Sox" were facing trial on criminal charges for throwing the Series. Then matters took a turn that was weird even for Chicago-style criminal justice.

Cicotte and about two dozen other players and gamblers under indictment weren't arraigned until February, by which time Cook County had a new district attorney, and three of his predecessor's assistants had become part of the players' defense team. Then the new prosecutor announced that Cicotte's and Joe Jackson's confessions were nowhere to be found, whereupon the presiding judge threw out the indictments. The whole legal process would have to begin anew. Largely because of Ban Johnson's efforts—including, in effect, bribing Bill Maharg and "Sleepy Bill" Burns, a former big-league pitcher who had also been part of the fix, to tell what they knew—a second set of indictments was secured, this time against Cicotte, Jackson, Lefty Williams, Happy Felsch, Chick Gandil, Swede Risberg, and Buck Weaver. (The prosecution dropped charges against Fred McMullin for insufficient evidence.)

Also indicted the second time around were ten professional gamblers plus Hal Chase, who had possessed intimate knowledge of the fix and had won perhaps $40,000 betting on Cincinnati. Arrested in California, Chase managed to win his release on a technicality. Official baseball's long toleration of Chase's villainies upset the veteran St. Louis sportswriter John B. Sheridan. "What sort of an example," asked Sheridan in rhetorical disgust, "did the players get from their employers, elders, kings, popes and potentates in the various instances of Hal Chase?"[1]

By the time the new indictments came down, Charles Comiskey had reluctantly released Cicotte, Jackson, and the other named players. He had no choice in the matter, inasmuch as the man at the top of baseball's newly formed governing structure had placed all of them on the ineligible list. The major-league club owners—officially recognizing that the National Commission was moribund and tacitly acknowledging their inability to manage their own affairs—had created the office of Commissioner of Baseball and given the job to Kenesaw Mountain Landis. Fifty-three years old, wizened and white-maned, Landis was the federal judge who had put the owners in his debt by sitting on the Federal League's suit back in 1915. Nearly everybody hailed the advent of the commissionership and the choice of Landis as exactly what was necessary to clean up baseball's mess. The foremost dissenter from that consensus was Ban Johnson, once the game's most powerful figure, now relegated to a subordinate status as American League president—nothing else.

While all that was happening, Tris Speaker and his defending-champion Indians prepared for the 1921 season. Speaker and Jim Dunn had decided to move their spring-training site from New Orleans to Dallas, because even if prostitution no longer flourished openly in New Orleans and liquor had become illegal (if still plentiful), horse-racing was as much a part of the city's life as ever. Several Cleveland players, the rumor went, had lost heavily on the races the previous spring and had begun the season broke. Speaker apparently thought it would benefit his players to get them away from the tracks, although, according to the Cleveland writer Wilbur Wood, "there isn't a man in baseball or out of it who likes to watch a horse race and lay a few dimes on the result any better than Tris Speaker."[2] Probably a bigger reason for moving from New Orleans to Dallas was that six other major-league teams would also be based in Texas, and that, with eight steam railroad lines and four interurban electric lines, Dallas was well situated for exhibition-game trips.

Speaker arrived weighing 190 pounds and saying he wanted to lose 10 (although he remained at 190 or above for the rest of his playing career). Gardner

Field, which the Indians shared with the local Texas League team, had only one dressing room, so Speaker and his players had to don uniforms at the Hotel Jefferson and take a trolley to the ballpark. The Elks Club had offered its clubhouse to the Indians for pool and billiards, such establishments having been piously outlawed a year earlier by the Texas legislature.

Henry P. Edwards reported from Dallas that Speaker and Steve O'Neill had performed "their annual wrestling match in front of the grandstand." Speaker had thrown O'Neill for three years running, but this time the stocky catcher, with "a crotch and a half nelson," threw the manager in eight minutes.[3] A few days later, Speaker hosted Jim Dunn, Indians players, and Cleveland writers at his farm outside Hubbard for a feast of barbecued goat, calf, and sheep. There little Joe Sewell fell victim to the first of many pranks, when Stanley Coveleski took him out onto Speaker's lake in a rowboat, asked him if he could swim, and when Sewell said he couldn't, threw him in and rowed back to shore. Sewell thrashed around in the water until other teammates pulled him out.

Speaker stayed busy apart from baseball during the Tribe's stay at Dallas. One day he gave a talk to students at Forest Park High School, put in an hour at the ballpark, and took a taxi over to Fort Worth to participate in the Fat Stock Show rodeo held annually at the stockyards arena. Heedless of the possibility of injury, he roped, took down, and tied a calf in thirty-five seconds, good enough for third place. He did more calf-roping the next two days, donning a western hat, boots, and chaps and posing horseback between two women professional stunt riders.

The Indians played a crowded exhibition schedule in Texas. The White Sox, based at Fort Worth, had recently traded for Speaker's old friend Harry Hooper, who had been the last remaining member of the 1912 Red Sox. Also based in Texas were the Reds at Cisco and the Giants at San Antonio, besides the Dallas, San Antonio, and Houston Texas League outfits.

In one of the games with Houston, Bill Wambsganss was hit on his throwing arm. The next day, in Mobile, Joe Evans, serving as team physician, discovered the arm was broken. Then Harry Lunte, Wambsganss's substitute, suffered a bad ankle sprain at Chattanooga. By the time the Indians got to Cincinnati (where they again faced Rube Marquard, traded by Brooklyn over the winter),

Speaker found himself again in critical need of an infielder. As he had done the previous August, he turned to the University of Alabama, appealing to its president to allow Riggs Stephenson, the Crimson Tide's senior secondbaseman, to complete the term by taking early exams so he could then play for the Indians until May 1.

Having won thirteen of sixteen exhibition games, Cleveland opened the 1921 season on Wednesday, April 13, in St. Louis, where Lee Fohl was the new manager. The Indians took the field in new uniforms with "World's Champions" in blue lettering across their shirt fronts, apparently unaware of an unhappy precedent for that bit of flaunting. (In 1906 John McGraw had done the same for his Giants, victors over the Philadelphia Athletics the previous October; the Giants finished a distant second behind Chicago.) Then spitballer Urban Shocker, the Browns' ace, outpitched Coveleski, 4-2, in an hour and thirty-seven minutes. Sewell contributed to the defeat with three errors, although Stephenson, manning secondbase, hit two singles and drove in a run.

After four games in St. Louis and two in Detroit, the Tribe's record was 3-3. The games in Detroit for the first time pitted Cobb and Speaker, longtime rivals as players, against each other as managers. The previous fall, after fourteen seasons as Tigers manager and a seventh-place finish, a worn-down Hugh Jennings had resigned. Reluctantly, Cobb had taken the job, in one of seven managerial turnovers following the 1920 season. So now fans in Detroit and across the country would have the opportunity to judge whether Cobb, conceded to be the brainiest player of them all, could translate his idiosyncratic genius into the successful direction of others.

Meanwhile Riggs Stephenson, batting around .500 and hailed as one of the greatest athletes ever to come out of the South, had become the new darling of the Cleveland dailies. (Stephenson had gained All–Southern Conference honors in football, basketball, track, and baseball, besides being president of his class each of his four years at Alabama. Speaker, though, was convinced that the broad-shouldered youngster was "muscle bound" from playing football and would never be a big-league-caliber secondbaseman.[4] Stephenson's drawbacks were twofold: he had injured his right shoulder in football and would always have a subpar throwing arm, and he couldn't master the double-play pivot.)

Before the home opener, the Cleveland front office publicly announced that League Park ushers would no longer bother people about giving up foul balls. Customers would be on the honor system to throw balls back, but the management "would not make a scene about it." Every Friday, moreover, would be Ladies' Day, with female fans charged only the ten-cent "war tax" (although that only got them bleacher seats).[5]

On April 22, despite threatening rain, 18,813 paying customers (Harry W. Davis, former Cleveland mayor and now Ohio governor, got in free) were at League Park for the home opener. Besides the usual floral horseshoe, Speaker received a shower of presents, paid for by fan donations: an Airedale puppy, a new automobile, an $800 silver-plated bridle and saddle, plus chaps, boots, and spurs. Donning his cowboy attire, Speaker leaped on a prancing white horse (loaned for the occasion) and galloped around the outfield. The Indians then beat the Browns and Shocker, 4-3, Jim Bagby getting the win. It was quite a day for the Gray Eagle, one that left no doubt that he was the most popular person in Cleveland. Topping it off was an evening at the Hanna Theatre, where the Tribe players were hosted by musical-comedy star Joe E. Brown, who was touring in his revue *Jim, Jam, Jems.*

The next day Speaker lifted his second home run of the season over the rightfield wall, then tripled and scored on Elmer Smith's homer, in an 8-7 win over the Browns. It was apparent that neither Wambsganss nor Lunte would be ready to play by May 1, so Stephenson decided to remain with the Indians for the season, then return to his studies next winter. Despite his manager's misgivings, he continued to hold down secondbase.

When Detroit came into town on April 25, Cobb tried to cross up Speaker by starting rookie righthander Harvey "Suds" Sutherland against Speaker's lefty-oriented lineup. After Charlie Jamieson popped out, Cobb brought in lefthander Red Oldham, whereupon Speaker inserted George Burns, Joe Wood, and Joe Evans. It was an early example of the kind of managing—or overmanaging—for which Cobb was increasingly criticized. It gained him nothing that day, because the Indians got to Oldham and then to Jim Middleton for five runs, while Bagby held the Tigers to three.

Besides continuing to platoon his men at three positions, Speaker also managed in other ways that sometimes had old-time fans shaking their heads. On Tuesday, April 26, Ban Johnson, Nap Lajoie, and other notables joined Cleveland and Detroit players in a procession to the centerfield flagpole for the raising of the 1920 pennant. In the game that followed, Speaker used twenty-three players in a 9-8 win, with Bagby, in relief, garnering his second decision in two days. That put the Tribe's record at 9-3, good enough for the league lead.

Washington showed well over the first half of the season, but by the time the Yankees arrived in mid-May, New York occupied second place. On Saturday the 14th, Babe Ruth hit his eleventh homer of the season, the first one ever to land in League Park's faraway centerfield bleachers. New York won that one, 6-4; took over first place on Sunday by battering Ray Caldwell and others, 8-2, behind Waite Hoyt (another recent Red Sox); and won Monday's game, 6-3, on Bob Meusel's inside-the-park homer that bounced past Speaker. Duster Mails was the loser; Carl Mays, pitching for the first time in Cleveland since Ray Chapman's death, was the winner.

That game proceeded without incident, but on Tuesday, Ruth was trapped off secondbase. Before he was tagged out, he ran over Joe Sewell and bloodied his nose. Although Ruth tried to apologize, Speaker would have none of it. The two squared off, at which point Miller Huggins and Steve O'Neill pulled Ruth away, while umpire Bill Dineen herded Speaker back to centerfield. In the ninth inning, Ruth hit a bases-empty homer to make the score 4-2, but George Uhle then retired the side to end the Tribe's five-game losing streak.

A week later Hank Thormahlen, now with Boston, hit Speaker on the left wrist. Although X-rays proved negative, the wrist was badly swollen. Team physician M. H. Castle immobilized the arm in a splint, and for the next few games Speaker sat in the dugout in street clothes. In his absence, Jack Graney went on a hitting tear, homering twice in the 11-9 finale of a four-game sweep in St. Louis. Despite giving up eighteen hits, including two homers to Ken Williams, Uhle lasted all the way.

Speaker put himself back in the lineup in Boston, where the Tribe split four games. In New York, following two losses, he hit one of his longest home runs into the Polo Grounds' rightfield upper deck in a 14-4 battering of Miller Huggins's staff. Larry Gardner's homer in the eleventh inning won the last game of the series, 8-6. In that game, Speaker rang up a single, double, and triple, while Ruth slammed his seventeenth homer. Preserving a two-and-a-half-game advantage over the Yankees, the Indians headed for Washington with Wambsganss back at secondbase in place of the slumping and error-prone Stephenson. They played poor baseball against the Senators (as they were now usually called) and continued to falter against the last-place Athletics, so that they ended the eastern tour with a 7-8 record. But the Yankees were also faltering, while Washington, having moved to within three and a half games of the Tribe, was acting like a serious contender.

Complaints persisted about the supposedly livelier ball and the batting boom. The *Cleveland Plain Dealer's* Stuart Bell was dismayed at the way hits were shooting past infielders, while outfielders (including Speaker) were playing so deep that fewer runners were being thrown out at the plate. Noting that Ruth had hit two balls more than five hundred feet into the centerfield bleachers at the Polo Grounds, Bell groused that whereas poor fielders hadn't been tolerated in the past, now "Anybody that has a big pair of shoulders and can lay a bat against a ball with vigor can hold his job."[6] Responding to the changing style of play, the *Plain Dealer* and other newspapers had started listing home runs and omitting sacrifice hits in the Sunday edition batting figures.

As of June 24, Speaker was batting .400, but Harry Heilmann, Detroit's husky outfielder, was at .422. Four days later, having scored thirty-one runs in three games and swept St. Louis, the Indians enjoyed a four-game lead over New York. Washington, with Walter Johnson having an off year, had faded to seven games back and ended up in fourth place, a half-game behind St. Louis. From late June on, Cleveland and New York were left to battle it out.

In mid-July, however, Wambsganss was disabled again, and by then Speaker could no longer count on Jim Bagby and Ray Caldwell, two of his mound stalwarts in 1920. Bagby developed a sore arm and was unavailable for several weeks; Caldwell was generally ineffective and was resuming old bad habits. Although Mails won fourteen games, he worked erratically in the second half of the season. Speaker claimed Allen Sothoron on waivers from St. Louis. The veterans Coveleski and Sothoron and twenty-two-year-old Uhle carried most of the pitching load down the stretch.

Often thought to be much older than he was (and looking it), Speaker claimed that he had wanted to quit baseball after winning last fall's World Series, but Jim Dunn talked him out of it. Questioned by Stuart Bell about whether he might retire as a player but continue as manager, he was adamant: "I will never be a bench manager." Dunn had made him a stockholder in his construction company, and he looked forward to going into business. No, he wouldn't say whether he would give up baseball after the present season. "But it can't go on much longer," he said. "If I'm to get anywhere in the construction business . . . I must start soon." Some people thought the strain of managing was turning Speaker into a "crab," Bell wrote, but he still joked around with his players "and will sit up all night and listen to stories about horses." Recently, when a game was rained out in Philadelphia, Speaker spent the day having fun at an amusement park in Atlantic City. "Speaker . . . is as far from being a crab as a grammar school boy."[7]

After splitting four games with the Yankees before big crowds at League Park, the Indians headed east on July 25 with their lead shaved to one game. On the 28th, in Boston, Speaker pulled a muscle in his right leg making a shoestring catch and sat out a game in which Guy Morton finally pitched well, holding the Red Sox runless on two hits. Then, in New York, Speaker limped in to score twice as Coveleski coasted to a 16-1 walkover. But the Yankees did their own bombarding the next day, 12-2, with Ruth hitting his thirty-seventh home run. Waite Hoyt bested Bagby in the third game, and after the last game was rained out, the Indians left for Washington with their lead cut to five percentage points. There they lost a doubleheader, and although New York lost a single game to Detroit, the Yankees slipped into first place.

For the next two weeks, the two teams swapped places. Back at League Park on August 16, the first anniversary of Ray Chapman's fatal beaning, something ominously reminiscent happened. In the first inning of a series-opener with Philadelphia, Charlie Jamieson led off with a wicked drive that bounced up and hit firstbaseman Johnny Walker on the right side of his head, knocking him unconscious. After being attended by Joe Evans, Walker was taken to Lakeside Hospital, where X-rays showed no fracture, only a severe concussion. In the fifth inning—with Walker's condition still unknown—the crowd of 6,000 stood for a moment of silence in memory of Chapman. The Indians went on to win a 15-8 slugfest, but in Chicago, the Yankees also won, as Ruth drove his forty-fifth home run over the back wall of the bleachers in right-centerfield. Both teams lost the next day. Another Yankees loss on the 19th while the Indians were idle put Cleveland back in first place by a couple of percentage points.

On August 21, while Allen Sothoron was shutting out Boston and the Yankees were dropping a doubleheader in St. Louis, the jury in the trial of the seven accused Chicago White Sox players returned a not-guilty verdict, prompting a courtroom celebration. That evening, the ballplayers dined in one room of a locally popular Italian restaurant; the jurors dined in an adjoining room. Presumably they all thought that the acquitted players would be able to resume their careers in professional baseball, but Commissioner Landis had other ideas. Even as the players celebrated, Landis released his wholly extralegal but roundly praised ruling, banning forever from professional baseball the seven cleared players, as well as the unindicted Fred McMullin.

Speaker and some of the other Indians may have felt sorry for the banished players, especially the effervescent, popular Buck Weaver, whose sin had been simply keeping his mouth shut about the fix. But if professional baseball often indulges in sentimentalism, it has little room for genuine sentiment—or for backward looks. The business at hand remained the pennant battle with the Yankees, who arrived in Cleveland for a three-game series beginning on Tuesday, August 23. At that point the Indians held the lead by a game and a half.

In the series-opener, Ruth drove out his forty-seventh and forty-eighth home runs to give the Yankees a 6-1 victory. On Wednesday, Waite Hoyt outpitched Coveleski, 3-2, the winning run scoring on Wally Pipp's sacrifice fly. The Indians regained first place on Thursday, battering Bob Shawkey, Warren "Rip" Collins, and Harry Harper, 15-1, and making it easy for Sothoron. Speaker, who had gone hitless so far in the series, made two doubles and two singles. Joe Sewell hit the game's only homer. In the eighth inning, with the score 11-1, lefthander Harper came in, gave up four more runs, and hit Jamieson, Gardner, and O'Neill with pitches, prompting O'Neill to throw the ball at the pitcher and charge the mound. Players from both teams surged around O'Neill and Harper to prevent them from landing blows. O'Neill and Yankees pitcher Bill Piercy (but not Harper) were ejected. Despite the one-sided win, the Cleveland fans were so agitated that at game's end, police had to escort the Yankees from the field, and Clay Folger, League Park security chief, had to rescue umpires Ollie Chill and Bill Dineen from a mob following them up 66th Street and drive them to their hotel.

The Indians stayed in first place until September 1, when Coveleski left in the third inning at Detroit with torn cartilage in his rib cage, and Caldwell lost the game in the twelfth. New York swept a doubleheader in Washington and led by half a game. The Yankees won all six games they played in Washington, while the Tribe split four in Detroit. A few days later, Duster Mails came back from being driven out the previous day to pitch his best game of the year, throttling the Browns, 2-1. With the Yankees losing in Boston, Cleveland edged to within seven percentage points of the lead.

Coveleski couldn't pitch for ten days, and Speaker suspended Caldwell for being drunk, although he lifted the suspension after only two days when the pitcher wrote him a penitent letter, promising to stay sober and offering to work the rest of the season for nothing. Caldwell then pitched a 5-4 win over Detroit at League Park. In Boston, however, the Yankees won a doubleheader, with Ruth hitting his fifty-second homer. Two days later, in Philadelphia, the Babe slammed number fifty-four to tie his own record. Idled by rain in St. Louis, the Tribe fell back by a game and a half. On September 10 Speaker's team split a doubleheader in St. Louis. In Philadelphia, Carl Mays coasted to victory, 19-3, to increase New York's lead to two full games. Worse still, the Indians had to spend the rest of the season on the road, while the Yankees played their remaining games in the friendly environment of the Polo Grounds.

It got worse. On the 11th, during an 8-4 win over the Browns, Speaker popped out to George Sisler, tripped over firstbase, pulled something in the back of his right knee, and had to be carried from the field. His knee stiff and swollen, Speaker left his team in Cleveland as it headed east. Joe Wood replaced him in centerfield for a series in Philadelphia, where the Indians won behind Sothoron, while Chicago's Dickie Kerr pitched his sixth win in seven starts against the Yankees, cutting New York's lead to half a game. On crutches, Speaker rejoined the team on September 14 and managed from the bench as Coveleski, finally able to pitch again, gave up five runs to the Athletics but got eight from his teammates.

Amid recurring rumors that he would resign after the season, Speaker's only comment was "They're crazy."[8]

The next day, Ruth broke his own home-run record, clouting number fifty-five in the first game of a double win from the Browns. With Speaker still disabled, the Indians stayed even by smashing the Athletics, 17-3 (Mails), and 6-0 (Caldwell). On Friday the 16th, they regained first place on Uhle's shutout of Washington. In New York, the Browns' Urban Shocker, a former (and future) Yankee, yielded Ruth's fifty-sixth homer but won the game, 10-3. On Saturday, as New York was being rained out, the Indians made their lead a full game by beating Washington, with Sothoron getting the win. Then, on Sunday it was a loss to Walter Johnson and a Yankees win over Detroit, and on Monday a ten-run late-inning Detroit rally to defeat New York while the Indians idled. Speaker's team found itself back in first by a couple of percentage points.

After winning two of three games in Boston while New York won two from Detroit, the Indians arrived in Manhattan for a four-game series, having won ten of their last thirteen games but still virtually deadlocked with Miller Huggins's Yankees. For a series that would undoubtedly decide the pennant race, Ban Johnson assigned three umpires rather than the usual two. In the first game, on Friday, September 23, Coveleski gave up three doubles to Ruth. The Babe scored each time for three of New York's four runs, and Waite Hoyt held the Indians to two scores. Still limping and not looking well, Speaker hit for Coveleski in the ninth inning and popped out.

On Saturday, before a capacity crowd of 36,000, Uhle hurled a splendid shutout, 9-0, with Joe Evans's three-run double the decisive blow off Harry Harper. Speaker finally put himself into the lineup but went hitless in four at bats. Sunday's game, before a standing-room-only throng, was a debacle. Carl Mays gave up seven runs, but the Yankees pounded Caldwell, Mails, and seldom-used Bob Clark for twenty hits and scored twenty-one times. Fifteen Yankees crossed the plate in the first four innings, aided not a little by Joe Sewell's three errors and Steve O'Neill's two. Again Speaker went hitless. Henry P. Edwards described the scene as "two hours and twenty-five minutes of tragedy and farce."[9]

The Yankees also took game four, with Ruth doubling, homering twice, and driving in five of New York's eight runs. Uhle and Guy Morton succeeded Coveleski. Mays came on to save the game after Hoyt had surrendered four runs in the sixth and seventh innings to make the score 8-7. Speaker finally managed a single, his only hit in thirteen tries in the series. The Indians left New York trailing by two games, but they were three down in the loss column with only five games left to play versus the Yankees' six.

On Tuesday, Urban Shocker shut out New York on five hits. En route to Chicago to close the season, the Indians gained half a game. Both teams were idle on the 28th. On Thursday the White Sox's Dickie Kerr yielded six hits in shutting out the Tribe, 5-0. In Philadelphia the Yankees, playing without Ruth, who remained in New York with a bad cold, got a shutout performance from Bob Shawkey to build their lead to two and a half games. Coveleski kept the Indians alive on Friday by outpitching Red Faber, 3-2, while rain prevented play in Philadelphia. Still nursing his right knee, Speaker sat out the game.

On Saturday, September 30, back at the Polo Grounds, the Yankees swept two games from the abject Athletics, the first of which gave the city of New York its first American League pennant. The Indians got word of the pennant-clincher before they took the field at Comiskey Park, so Speaker didn't even suit up, instead watching the game with Jim Dunn in the firstbase visitors' box. Uhle, his heart obviously not in it, gave up fifteen hits and eight runs in seven innings before he was relieved by Mails, in what ended as an 8-3 loss. That morning Speaker had effectively conceded the pennant when he gathered the players in his hotel room to vote on the division of second-place money. He also told his regulars that if the Yankees won either game with the Athletics, they could pass up Sunday's game.

Several players did just that, so that only thirteen Indians were in uniform for the season-closer. As Speaker sat huddled in his overcoat in Dunn's box, Elmer Smith hit his sixteenth home run, but the White Sox knocked around rookie Bernard Henderson and won, 7-4. The Yankees ended the season with a 7-6 win over Boston. Ruth's three-run homer, his fifty-ninth, made the difference. New York finished at 98-55 to Cleveland's 94-60.

It had been a tough race and, though ultimately disappointing, another profitable season for Jim Dunn. Home attendance was about 160,000 below 1920, but figures released a few years later by the Cuyahoga County tax office showed that for 1921 the franchise finished $173,000 in the black. Despite various injuries that caused him to miss twenty-two games, it had been a productive year for Speaker as a player. He batted .362 and drove in 74 runs. Although he hit only 3 home runs, for the fifth time he led the majors in doubles, with 52. Now playing a deeper centerfield, he had only 13 assists, a career low up to then.

Babe Ruth—with his 59 homers, 171 runs batted in, 177 runs scored, and .378 batting average—was again the big story in baseball. The Yankees hit a record 134 homers, although sixth-place Detroit led the majors with a .316 team batting average. Benefiting from Ty Cobb's unmatched plate savvy, Harry Heilmann won the first of his four odd-year batting titles with a .396 average. Cobb batted .389, followed by Ruth, George Sisler, and Speaker.

Sisler's 35 stolen bases topped the American League. It had become increasingly apparent that base-stealing was giving way to "big-inning" baseball, which Miller Huggins theorized and his Yankees powerhouse put into practice. Speaker's Indians batted .308 as a team and led the majors in two-base hits, but they ran the bases, if not slowly, then cautiously. They stole only 58 times, the fewest in either major league. "Get some steam, Spoke!" urged Bill Phelon.[10]

By 1921 the total number of stolen bases in the majors had fallen to 1,496 from 2,413 in 1917 (the last "dead-ball," 154-game season). The home run was in; base-stealing remained a relatively minor part of offensive strategy for the next several decades, which distressed lovers of the old game. Francis J. Powers, the *Sporting News*'s Cleveland correspondent, bemoaned "the epidemic of hitting, which was entertaining for a while, tiresome later and finally disgusting." F. C. Lane, editor of *Baseball Magazine,* regretted that with outfielders playing so much deeper, one saw fewer triples—"about the prettiest hit in the game." A deader ball, Lane thought, would make for "a saner, less feverish, better balanced contest than has been possible under the brilliant but irrational domination of the home run."[11] Early on Ty Cobb made plain his distaste for the new-style baseball. If Speaker also preferred the old game, both he and Cobb still found themselves having to manage according to the dictates of the Ruthian era.

For all his denials that he wanted to quit, Speaker, downcast over losing the pennant, apparently did consider giving up baseball. He passed up the World Series—in which John McGraw's Giants, back on top after four years, stifled

Ruth's bat and won five games to three in the first all–New York matchup—and left for his and Les Nunamaker's regular hunting excursion into Ontario province. Upon his return, he talked with Jim Dunn, agreed to stay on as Cleveland manager, and got busy with personnel shakeups.

Ray Caldwell, despite pitching creditably in the last part of the season, received his outright release and dropped back to the minors. Elmer Smith was traded to the Red Sox, along with George Burns and the rights to the wayward Joe Harris (whom Commissioner Landis subsequently reinstated), for firstbaseman Stuffy McInnis. It was an unwise deal. McInnis was a slick fielder but basically a singles hitter. Smith's sixteen homers in 1921 were more than any Cleveland player had ever hit in any league, and Burns had batted .361 in eighty-eight games. Early in the new year, Speaker also sold Doc Johnston to the Athletics for the $4,500 waiver price.

Getting three good players for McInnis was the only decent trade Harry Frazee ever made for Boston. Otherwise he continued his annual shipments of talent to New York owners Jacob Ruppert and T. L. Huston. During the coming season, pitchers Sam Jones and Joe Bush and shortstop Everett Scott were in Yankees pinstripes; in return, Frazee acquired shortstop Roger Peckinpaugh and three pitchers, who joined a team that displaced Philadelphia at the bottom of the American League. In 1922 four of the Yankees' five starting pitchers were former Red Sox.

The Indians returned to Dallas for spring training, working out in last season's uniforms but with the "World's Champions" lettering removed from their shirt fronts. Joe Sewell continued to be victimized by mischievous teammates. Speaker and Coveleski tied him hand and foot, calf style, and told him to free himself, which he managed to do. The next day the manager and pitcher threw him into a bat box, and Coveleski repeatedly bounced a medicine ball close to his head. Speaker also continued to wrestle Steve O'Neill or somebody before every practice session.

Among the newcomers was Lefty Weisman, the onetime Boston newsboy whom Speaker had befriended when he was playing for the Red Sox. Jim Dunn gave Weisman a job in his construction company, and then Speaker made him assistant to team trainer Percy Smallwood. A jokester, clown, and songster, Weisman soon succeeded Smallwood and remained with the Indians long enough to become something of an institution.

The stay in Dallas was mostly cold and wet. The players had to spend much of their time throwing, running, and playing basketball in a building adjacent to Marine Park that housed a roller rink and basketball court. Over two weeks, they got in only seven days of outdoor practice. Meanwhile, at Eagle Pass at the other end of Texas, the Athletics endured sandstorms and worked out wearing goggles.

Speaker, of course, was supposed to set an example in responsible behavior, but that spring he continued to compete in the Fort Worth Fat Stock Show rodeo, which could have jeopardized his and the team's prospects for the coming season. In an exhibition game at Marine Park versus Cincinnati, he took his position in centerfield, then came limping into the dugout, claiming that he had stepped in a hole and twisted his left knee. It was a phony act. The truth was that the day before, competing in steer-roping contests in Fort Worth, he had fallen from a horse and badly twisted his ankle. Years later he "fessed up" to Joe Williams. "We still blush in shame," wrote Williams, "when we recall how we panned the Dallas park and the Dallas groundskeeper for the mishap that had befallen our sterling leader."[12]

Speaker also told Williams that the ankle bothered him for the rest of his playing career, although a few days later he was back at the rodeo to win a rope-tossing contest with the local sheriff and a Texas Ranger captain. For the remaining exhibition games in Dallas, he played firstbase, with rookie Pat McNulty, from Ohio State University, in centerfield.

At the end of March, having had only five days of good weather in Dallas, the Indians split into two squads to play their way north. Speaker remained behind to await the arrival of team physician Castle. Jim Dunn had been ill since coming down from Chicago. One day Speaker had passed up practice to drive him to Mineral Wells for an afternoon in the spa's supposedly health-restoring waters. Accompanied by Castle and Walter McNichol, the team's traveling secretary, Dunn returned to Chicago, while Speaker rejoined the team at Oklahoma City. Rain prevented games there and in Kansas City and Des Moines, although Speaker played eighteen holes of golf in Oklahoma City and did trap-shooting at the other two stopovers. To rumors that bad legs would keep him on the bench most of the time in the upcoming season, he answered, "I may not be as fast as I once was [but] if there's anything wrong with me this season it's because I'm a year older."[13]

Jim Dunn had grown up in and around Marshalltown, Iowa, and an intrasquad game there and dinner at the local country club were supposed to be gala events in his honor. In Chicago, however, the Indians' president was bedridden, suffering from heart disease complicated by pneumonia. When the Indians passed through Chicago en route to Columbus, Speaker dropped off, spent the afternoon and early evening at Dunn's bedside, and took a late train to catch up with the team.

On April 12, 1922, in front of 14,527 fans at what was now being called Dunn Field, Guy Morton continued his on-again-off-again career by struggling to a 7-4 victory over Detroit. Ty Cobb, hobbled with an injured knee, pinch-hit unsuccessfully. Stuffy McInnis made Speaker's trade for him look good by singling, doubling, and tripling, and making eight hits in twelve at bats in the three games with the Tigers, all of which the Tribe won. Two more wins, over Lee Fohl's St. Louis Browns, made it a five-in-a-row start, but then, with O'Neill out with a split finger, the Browns stole nine bases on Les Nunamaker and Enoch "Ginger" Shinault in a 15-1 slaughter.

Speaker missed a game with Chicago after hitting the firstbase bag wrong and reinjuring his ankle. Then he contracted ptomaine poisoning in St. Louis and missed another game. It was just as well, because in a four-game sweep, the Browns hammered Cleveland pitchers for fifty hits and thirty-six runs. At last it looked as if long-suffering St. Louis fans, who had never had a pennant-winner in either major league, might finally get one.

In fact the 1922 Browns were the strongest entry in the American League's fifty-one-year presence in St. Louis. They didn't have a Babe Ruth, but they did have the incomparable George Sisler at firstbase as well as a stellar outfield: rightfielder Johnny Tobin, the league's best leadoff man; a powerful hitter and excellent centerfielder in Bill "Baby Doll" Jacobson; and the league's second-most-prolific home-run hitter in leftfielder Ken Williams. Their pitching staff, though not as deep as the Yankees', was led by Urban Shocker, the game's supreme spitballer.

And the Browns' early season fortunes were helped by the fact that Ruth and Bob Meusel had to sit out the first six weeks, under suspension by Commissioner Landis for disobeying his ban on postseason barnstorming by World Series participants. Although Cobb's Tigers looked like contenders for a time, by July it was apparent that it would be the Browns, not Detroit, Cleveland, or anybody else, whom the Yankees would have to beat to repeat as league champions.

For the Indians the 1922 season was a frustrating and generally unhappy one. Bill Piercy had also been on Ruth's and Meusel's barnstorming tour. Traded to Boston in the off-season, he still had to serve his own six weeks' suspension. On Saturday, May 20, at Fenway Park, in his first turn on the mound, Piercy gave up Speaker's first homer—a bases-loaded blow that won Coveleski's game and brought cheers from the twelve thousand or so Boston fans, who remembered better times. But then Speaker caught a cold and stayed in bed as the Tribe lost to the Red Sox in the last game of their eastern trip.

With the team in fifth place with a 17-19 record, Speaker put himself back in the lineup in Detroit, where the Indians won two of three. They came home to lose three of four to Chicago, by which time Speaker's stubborn cold had become severe bronchitis—no doubt aggravated by his cigarette-smoking. Feeling miserable, he nonetheless played two games against Detroit before going to bed in his rooms at the Hotel Winton. O'Neill, Morton, Duster Mails, and various other Indians were also afflicted with upper-respiratory illness. Riggs Stephenson was playing thirdbase in place of the slumping Larry Gardner, and McInnis missed several games with an injury. Despite all that, by early June the Indians had evened their record at 24-24 and climbed to third place.

Speaker was out of the lineup from June 3 to June 16. In the midst of the worst illness Speaker had endured in any season, Jim Dunn died in Chicago early on the morning of Friday, June 9, at age fifty-five. It was a personal loss for Speaker, whose relationship with the Indians' president had been an unusually close one. From his sickbed, Speaker described Dunn as "my best friend, a regular pal. . . . He was a pattern of baseball magnate that exemplifies all that a manager wants in the owner he works for." Even in the face of losses, Speaker said, "He always put on his best smile, and I'll never forget that smile, and said: 'We can't win 'em all, Spoke.'"[14]

Ban Johnson called off that day's game with Washington (which had won three in a row from the Indians). Dunn's death was also a personal loss for the American League's president. Johnson's loan had helped Dunn buy the Cleveland franchise. In return, Dunn had loyally backed Johnson in his wranglings with Frazee, Ruppert, and Huston. Dunn and his wife Emily were childless, so she became the major stockholder in the franchise, with Thomas Walsh, a former Chicago Cubs substitute catcher and Dunn's construction-company partner, as the second-biggest stockholder. Emily Dunn soon named Ernest S. Barnard, longtime business manager of the Cleveland franchise, to assume its presidency.

Two days later Ban Johnson and Clark Griffith were present for Dunn's burial at Marshalltown, Iowa, as were Jack Graney, Les Nunamaker, and Clay Folger, representing the ball club. Under physician's orders, Speaker remained in Cleveland. He finally put himself back in the lineup on June 16, hitting two doubles and a single and driving in two runs, although the Red Sox scored three times in the ninth inning on Uhle and won, 8-6. Two more doubles and another single followed in the next day's fourteen-inning win over Boston, then the same hit combination in Coveleski's 9-2 throttling of New York before a Sunday overflow crowd at Dunn Field. Speaker hit another double and a single on Monday, as Mails had a rare effective outing, beating the Yankees, 4-2. That made ten hits for Speaker in four games. On Tuesday, calls by umpires Bill Dineen and Dick Nallin so enraged him that he followed them off the field after the game, while Cleveland partisans spilled onto the field until they were herded to the exits by mounted police. Foot police then escorted the umpires onto their streetcar. Winning 6-5, the Yankees broke an eight-game losing streak, then took the series finale, which Speaker left early after aggravating his still-bothersome ankle.

Wearing black arm bands in memory of Jim Dunn, the Indians went on to lose six games in a row, in three of which Speaker rested his ankle. Then they won two of three games from the Browns in Cleveland but dropped three in St. Louis, which left them at 32-40, in sixth place, barely ahead of Washington. Although Speaker continued his robust hitting, staying in the .370s and .380s week after week, the only pitchers he could count on for consistently good work were Coveleski, who posted a slightly lower earned run average than in 1921 but dropped from twenty-three to seventeen wins; Uhle, who emerged as one of the league's most durable hurlers, appearing in fifty games and winning twenty-two; and Guy Morton, who, working more frequently than he had in five years, won fourteen. Duster Mails was about through as a big-leaguer. Jim Bagby's season ended when he underwent an appendectomy in New York late in August. Jack Graney, after being put on waivers at his request and clearing both leagues, signed to manage Des Moines in the Western League.

The Indians bettered their circumstances on a July eastern swing, playing in extraordinary heat. Starting in New York and continuing in Boston, Philadelphia, and Washington, they ran off a twelve-game winning streak. After Washington lefthander George Mogridge stopped them on the 22nd, they went home having improved to 46-45 and moved into fifth place.

At home, in a five-game series with Washington, the Indians scored fifty-six runs to the opposition's thirty-eight and won four times. Bill Phelon commented, "The lively ball continued to cause huge scores and horrible games during the month [of August]. The ball is no joke nowadays—it's a crime."[15] Pitchers continued to take punishment in the following series with New York, as the Yankees scored forty times and swept all four games. Speaker limped through the series, favoring a leg he had twisted trying to score in the last Washington game.

Uhle won his own game, against Detroit, by singling in the winning run in the ninth to close the home stand. The Tribe won three games in Washington to improve to 61-59 and occupy fourth place, but in New York, Speaker and Joe Wood collided as Speaker caught Wally Schang's sacrifice fly. It was another banged-up knee for Speaker, who had to be carried from the field.

From then on Speaker mostly confined himself to pinch hitting. Early in September his mother, accompanied by her niece Virginia Scott, joined the Indians for a series in St. Louis, then traveled with them to Chicago so Jenny Speaker could pay her respects to Emily Dunn. After Cleveland lost all four games at Sportsman's Park, some of the New York writers dropped hints that Speaker and his players disliked the Yankees enough to let down against the Browns. Henry P. Edwards denounced such thinking, pointing out that the Tribe was still trying for third-place money. Besides, he wrote, "such actions would be crooked, and Tris Speaker is the last man in baseball who should be accused of any such deed."[16]

The Indians came home after dividing four games in Chicago, tied with the

White Sox for fourth place behind Detroit. Because Cleveland would play the rest of the schedule at Dunn Field, Speaker brought in so many rookies that he had to outfit some of them in gray road uniforms. Meanwhile, Wood, McInnis, and Coveleski had received Speaker's permission to go home. After winning four games of five from Boston, the Tribe dropped two of three to the Yankees, with Sherry Smith, picked up on waivers from Brooklyn, taking the loss in the second game. New York left town leading the Browns by three and a half games. Five off days for the Indians followed, during which Speaker went to Chicago to attend the funeral of another friend. Jake Stahl, his onetime teammate and manager, had died of heart disease at the age of forty-three.

Harried by the Browns all season, the Yankees finally clinched the pennant in Boston on Saturday, September 30, despite the Browns' win in Chicago. Sherry Smith held down Detroit, which had already clinched third place, 4-1, to put Cleveland in another tie with the White Sox for fourth. By winning the season's last game while Chicago lost again to St. Louis, Speaker's team secured fourth place with a 78-76 mark to the White Sox's 77-77, and ended up a game behind Detroit. Never really in the pennant race, the Indians attracted 200,000 fewer customers to their home games than they had the previous season and some 350,000 fewer than in 1920.

The Yankees' bare one-game margin over the Browns was largely attributable to Babe Ruth's absence during the first month of the season. Ruth also had various troubles with umpires and fans and played in only 110 games. His home-run output fell to 35, two fewer than Philadelphia's Tilly Walker and four fewer than the Browns' Ken Williams, who also led the majors with 155 runs batted in. The Babe's subpar season climaxed with a miserable performance in the World Series, in which the Yankees again fell to their Polo Grounds landlords, managing only a tie in five games with John McGraw's classy team.

George Sisler's batting average soared to .420 on 246 base hits; he also led the league in runs scored and stolen bases. Ty Cobb was officially credited with a .401 average, although like so much else in Cobb's career, that was a matter of controversy—in this instance over whether one of his hits should have been ruled an error. Speaker missed twenty-three games and came to bat only 426 times, his fewest full-season plate appearances. But his .378 average was topped only by Sisler and Cobb, his 11 home runs were the most he had ever hit, and his 48 doubles again led both leagues. In seventeen pinch-hitting opportunities, he came through nine times, including five straight hits from August 30 to September 5.

"Tris was out a great deal," F. C. Lane remarked. "Nevertheless, he compiled the grand average of .378, fielded his position, so much of it as he could still cover, with his old unsurpassed skill and in spite of advancing age and injuries."[17] (Like everybody except Jenny Speaker, Lane understood Speaker's age to be thirty-four.)

Speaker's postseason hunting trip, to the Grand Teton mountains in northwestern Wyoming, he described as "the best ever."[18] It was one of his most rugged adventures. He spent thirty-two days on horseback, in the company of three hunting partners, four guides, and a pack train of mules. Hunting in deep snows at altitudes reaching 9,500 feet, Speaker shot a deer, a moose, and an elk. Another member of the party brought down a grizzly bear.

By mid-December, Speaker was in New York for the annual majors meetings, but the only trade he and Ernest S. Barnard could make that winter was to send Joe Evans to Washington for firstbaseman Frank Brower, who was supposed to lend some power to the Cleveland lineup. Then it was back to Texas to spend Christmas with his mother, entertain relatives and friends with home movies of his Wyoming expedition, do some calf-roping at a rodeo in Hillsboro, and, as Francis J. Powers put it, "feed ensilage to his blooded beeves."[19]

Meanwhile, Les Nunamaker took the manager's job at Chattanooga, and Joe Wood decided to quit the professional game. Fans at Dunn Field, lamenting the departure of Elmer Smith, had given Wood a hard time, Powers reported, so that "life at Parker's Glen with Mrs. Wood and the children holds much allurement."[20] Speaker had already recommended Wood for the baseball coaching job at Yale University, which hired him that winter. Speaker also sold Duster Mails to Oakland and Allen Sothoron to Louisville. Tacitly acknowledging that the McInnis deal had been a mistake by trading for Brower, he asked waivers on McInnis, as he did on Jim Bagby. The Boston Braves claimed McInnis, who put in a productive year for them. Bagby, who only two years earlier had won thirty-one games and pitched the Tribe into the World Series, was claimed by Pittsburgh, released in August, and signed by Seattle.

The weather at Dallas the previous spring had been so bad that Speaker and Barnard decided to move their 1923 training base to Florida, which from the 1920s on was favored by most big-league teams. The Tribe gathered at Lakeland, where they lodged at the Hotel Thelma and practiced at spacious Adair Field. Determined to improve on last season's fourth-place showing, Speaker announced that he wouldn't tolerate drinking at any time, and that nobody would be permitted to smoke wearing a uniform. "No member of the tribe," commented Henry P. Edwards, "will be hit harder by the anti-cigaret rule than Speaker himself, for there was not a game at Dunn Field last season that Spoke did not take a puff now and then."[21] Speaker also said he was tired of his pitchers becoming winded running the bases and not being ready to go back to the mound, so he ordered them to jog the half-mile from the ballpark up Kentucky Avenue to the hotel.

Among the new faces at Lakeland were those of outfielder Homer Summa, who had come up in September after leading the Texas League in batting for Wichita Falls, and lefthander Joe Shaute, a graduate of Juniata College, as well as catcher Glenn Myatt and infielder Walter "Rube" Lutzke, who had been purchased from Milwaukee for $50,000 and $30,000, respectively. Prices for top-flight minor-leaguers had soared under the National Agreement of 1920, which provided that any minor league could opt out of the annual player draft. The Class-AA American Association, International League, and Pacific Coast League had done so, as well as the Class-A Texas League and Class-B Three-I League. Thus owners in those leagues could hold onto their star players until they were ready to sell, at prices unheard-of in past decades.

After one-a-day practices, Speaker found time for golf (driving to Sebring, because he didn't like the Lakeland course) and trap-shooting. On March 20 the Indians traveled by bus to Bradenton to meet the St. Louis Cardinals—a trip of about seventy miles that took three hours on roads Francis Powers described as "good, not so good, and awful."[22] For the first time, Speaker competed against Rogers Hornsby, who had batted .402 the previous season to win his third straight National League batting title, besides setting a league record with forty-two home runs. Hornsby went hitless; Speaker doubled, walked, scored twice, and made a somersault catch in a 6-5 Cleveland win.

It was a good month at Lakeland, with only one rainy day. Speaker appeared to be in top condition. Having worn a cap only once at practice, he was "tanned to the color of a real Indian," Powers reported. Besides meeting the Cardinals, the Tribe played the Reds, Braves, Phillies, and Brooklyn. One day Wilbert Robinson brought his team from Clearwater to Lakeland for a game, only to find Speaker and his players lounging on the veranda of the Thelma. "No, the game's not today, Robbie," Speaker said, both surprised and amused. "It's tomorrow."[23] Such episodes only added to Uncle Robbie's growing reputation as a loveable bumbler.

From Florida, the Indians played their way across the lower South against minor-league teams in Atlanta and in Troy and Mobile, Alabama, before arriving in New Orleans for another week of practice and a game with the local Pelicans. The purpose of the game at Troy, versus Milwaukee, was to put on display the five Alabamians on the team: Stephenson, Morton, Joe Sewell and his younger brother Luke (who had often filled in for Steve O'Neill in 1922), and James "Danny" Boone, a rookie righthander. Also at Troy, Jenny Speaker and two friends from Hubbard met the team and returned with it to New Orleans, before starting home.

Danny Boone won his first big-league game on opening day at Dunn Field, before a crowd of 20,372. Working in relief of Uhle, who had relieved Coveleski, Boone was the beneficiary of a ninth-inning rally that defeated Chicago, 6-5. Homer Summa drove in Bill Wambsganss with the winning run. Speaker got off to a good start with a pair of his patented doubles.

One of the majors' smallest parks, Dunn Field now began to seem even smaller. Chicago Cubs owner William Wrigley had enlarged the capacity of what was soon called Wrigley Field from 18,000 to 32,000, while the Yankees opened the season before an announced paying crowd of 74,200 in the biggest and grandest baseball facility ever built. Facing eviction from the Polo Grounds by the Giants, Jacob Ruppert and T. L. Huston spent $2,500,000 to have Yankee Stadium erected in the South Bronx, directly across the Harlem River from the Giants' home. Ruth christened the huge ballpark with a home run in the Yankees' win over Boston. (A month later, Ruppert bought out Huston for $1,500,000.)

If Speaker thought he could get better results with more discipline, then the approach seemed to be working—at least at first. The Indians were early front-runners, winning their first five games and ten of their first thirteen, during which span Coveleski pitched three consecutive shutouts. But then they cooled off in Detroit, where they lost three of four games that drew a total attendance of around 55,000. Back home, against St. Louis, Speaker sent Urban Shocker's spitter over the rightfield wall for his first home run of the season, but it was in another loss, 9-5. Lefthander Jim Joe Edwards pitched the Indians to victory the next day, but on Sunday, Speaker sat in the stands at the start of a three-game suspension imposed by Ban Johnson for bawling out umpire Emmet "Red" Ormsby follow-ing the last game in Detroit. Speaker watched still another defeat, Guy Morton losing his game in the ninth inning.

The Browns, who had come so close in 1922, had to play the whole 1923 sea-son without the multitalented George Sisler. Over the winter, a bout of influenza had left him with a severe sinus infection, which in turn affected his eyesight. Although Sisler came back as Browns player-manager for 1924 and still was a capable hitter, he was never the truly great player he had once been.

After the Yankees won the only two games weather permitted on their first foray into Dunn Field, the Athletics arrived and shocked the Tribe by sweeping four games. Connie Mack's team looked like a legitimate contender over the first half of the season, and although it eventually sank to sixth place, it was no longer the ragtag outfit of the past. Those four defeats made for nine losses in the Tribe's last eleven games. Speaker began to hear boos and jeers from his own fans.

The rough treatment continued on May 24, as the Indians, who had already made more errors than any team in the league, made four more in an 8-6 loss to the last-place Red Sox. The crowd booed Speaker for removing rookie lefthander Joe Shaute (whose successors couldn't hold the lead), for letting a ball drop between himself and Homer Summa in right-centerfield, and for being caught off thirdbase by catcher Val Picinich. As he came into the dugout for the bottom of the ninth inning, he irritably doffed his cap to his critics. Five days later, hav-ing wrecked one of baseball's most successful teams and all but ruined one of its most prosperous franchises, Harry Frazee sold the Red Sox to a group led by Bob

Quinn, business manager of the Browns, for $1 million. Sentiment in Boston was said to be strong for Speaker to replace Frank Chance, who had unwisely come out of retirement again to manage a bad ball club.

Speaker was batting only .279 at the start of June, but he could still shoot clay pigeons with the best of them, as he demonstrated in the Illinois state trap-shooting competition at Lincoln Park in Chicago when the Indians were in town. Cleveland won three of four from the White Sox and improved its record to 21-17, still well behind the Yankees, who had taken a sizable lead. A week later, Speaker and his players got their first look at Yankee Stadium. They may have been awed by the mammoth ballpark, but they weren't by the Yankees themselves. Cleveland won three times in four games, Speaker homering with the bases loaded off Carl Mays in the 13-3 opener. The Tribe left New York having cut the Yankees' lead to three and a half games. They weren't that close again.

By mid-July the Indians had moved ahead of Philadelphia into second place, although they were barely playing .500 ball and trailed New York by twelve games. But if they often had trouble catching the ball and throwing it accurately, they were a potent crew at bat, especially when Riggs Stephenson, a natural hitter if little else, spelled the oft-injured Wambsganss at secondbase. In the first game of a Saturday doubleheader at Dunn Field, the Indians set an American League record by walloping Boston, 27-8, on twenty-four hits, including Stephenson's three doubles. Stephenson homered and tripled in the second game, which the Tribe also won, 8-5. On Sunday, Speaker singled, doubled, and tripled in still another slugfest, which the Tribe won, 15-10, pushing its output to fifty runs for the three games. By then, Speaker had upped his batting average by seventy-five or eighty points. Meanwhile Louis Guisto—who had played little over the past two seasons and was still suffering from the effects of being gassed in the war—asked to be placed on waivers, cleared them, and returned to the presumably healthier climate of the Pacific Coast League.

The Indians continued their hot streak at home with a four-game sweep of Philadelphia, then won four of six from New York. The last game of that series was an easy win for Uhle over Carl Mays. Miller Huggins had soured on Mays, who had compiled only a 13-14 record in 1922 and had rarely gotten a starting assignment in the current season. The New York manager finally named him to start against Uhle, then left him in the whole game to take a twenty-hit, 13-0 beating. Once Huggins's ace, the irascible Mays was finished as a Yankee. After the season, he went to Cincinnati on waivers.

The Yankees departed Cleveland still leading by eleven games. Speaker homered three days in a row against visiting Washington and built his average to .357, but the Indians won only three of five times in that series and so closed their long home stand with a 48-42 record, trailing New York by twelve and a half.

Nobody—neither Cleveland, Detroit, nor the Sisler-less Browns—could keep up with Miller Huggins's strongest team so far. After Waite Hoyt shut out the Tribe in New York on August 4, the Yankees' lead stretched to thirteen and a half. That day, in San Francisco, President Warren G. Harding died following a heart attack. All major-league, International League, and American Association games were canceled on the 5th and again on the 9th, when Harding was buried at Marion, Ohio.

Ty Cobb was having a fine year at bat by almost anybody's standards (except maybe his own), and many other players were having what were later called "career years." As of August 7, Charlie Jamieson and Joe Sewell ranked third and fifth among American League hitters, behind Ruth and Harry Heilmann. Speaker, hitting the long ball more frequently than ever, was in fourth place.

At Philadelphia on August 12, Speaker's eleventh-inning bases-loaded homer, his third grand slam of the season, won the first game of a Saturday doubleheader. In the nightcap he singled and tripled during another win. Although the Athletics had fallen down in the standings, the twin bill drew a crowd of 27,000, one of the biggest Shibe Park turnouts in a decade. After a Sunday hop back to Cleveland and losing a stopover game to Boston, the Indians returned to Philadelphia to end their road trip by dividing a doubleheader before another extraordinary local turnout of 15,000. Speaker belted a three-run homer in the winning nightcap. Still, they could get no closer to the Yankees than twelve games.

On Labor Day, New York's lead was thirteen games. The Indians swept their doubleheader with the Browns, now being managed by player-coach Jimmy Austin. A month earlier, St. Louis owner Phil Ball had fired Lee Fohl, largely because Fohl hadn't stood up for Dave Danforth when the lefthander was suspended for ten days after umpire George Moriarty accused him of doctoring the ball. Uhle won his twenty-fifth game in the opener with the Browns. Speaker homered and doubled in the nightcap. But the Yankees also swept two from the Athletics.

Second place was by no means secure, because over the last third of the season, Cobb's Detroit Tigers became the hottest ball club in either major league. By mid-month Cleveland, now fifteen and a half games out of first place, was only three games ahead of Detroit.

In Boston and New York, the Tribe lost five in a row, the last two a Sunday doubleheader sweep in Yankee Stadium that drew 60,331, the biggest crowd a Cleveland team had ever played before. The nightcap was a tough 3-2 loss for Jim Joe Edwards. Bob Meusel's fly ball, which Speaker lost in the sun, went for a home run, and Everett Scott circled the bases while Speaker and Summa chased down his hit that bounced between them. But on Monday, Speaker and Frank Brower homered to keep the Yankees from clinching the pennant; and on Tuesday, Joe Shaute held them to three runs, while the Indians slapped Bob Shawkey for eight, delaying Ruth and company's celebration. Finally, with Cleveland idle on Wednesday, Sam Jones pitched the clincher over St. Louis and gained his twentieth win.

After winning and losing doubleheaders in Philadelphia, the Tribe made a long overnight train ride to Detroit. There they dropped three of four games (in the first of which Sherry Smith failed to retire a batter in a 17-3 slaughter) and went to St. Louis with only a one-game lead over the Tigers. They won three of four at Sportsman's Park, Speaker lining his fifty-sixth double in the third game to tie the mark set in 1899 by the late Ed Delahanty of the Philadelphia Phillies. The next day, October 4, Speaker broke Delahanty's record, besides hitting three singles and a home run, in a 9-1 win for Edwards.

On Friday, the 5th, only about five hundred chilled Clevelanders paid to see the Tribe beat Chicago, while Detroit won from St. Louis. A doubleheader loss to the White Sox on Saturday, in combination with another Detroit win over St. Louis, put the Tigers in second place by half a game. Although the Indians won Sunday's game for Shaute, 9-6, with Speaker knocking his fifty-ninth double, Detroit clinched second with a third straight victory over the Browns before an overflow crowd at Navin Field. In an extraordinary show of loyalty to their team, many in the Dunn Field crowd of seven thousand or so lingered after the last out to hear a report on the last two innings in Detroit.

Finishing at 81-71 to Detroit's 82-71, the Indians lost about $1,000 per man in second-place money. Despite having to play six doubleheaders in six days in September, the Tigers won thirty-three of their last fifty-three games, eleven of their last fourteen. Although their second-place finish left them sixteen games behind New York, for the time being unrest in the Motor City over Ty Cobb's managing style had died down.

Leading the majors in team average (.301) and runs (888), Speaker's Indians had ended a notch higher than in 1922, but only two games better in the win column. Joe Sewell batted .353, drove in 109 runs, and struck out only 12 times in 553 at bats; Charlie Jamieson batted .345; Homer Summa put in a sparkling rookie season at .328; Riggs Stephenson hit .319 in ninety-one games; and George Uhle, besides leading the majors in wins (26) and innings pitched (358), batted .361 in 144 times at bat. Only the bottom-rung Red Sox made more errors than Cleveland. Often receiving poor support in the field, Stanley Coveleski ended with a 13-14 record, despite having the league's lowest earned run average (2.76).

Although Speaker might occasionally hear boo birds at Dunn Field, at least nobody could quarrel with the season he had put in as a player. He missed only two games, had 26 outfield assists, and besides setting a new doubles record, batted .380 on 218 base hits and reached personal highs with 17 home runs and 130 runs batted in. Ruth drove in only one more run, although the Babe hit 41 homers and batted .394—the highest average he ever attained. Harry Heilmann's .403 led both leagues; Speaker ranked third in batting average.

Before leaving Cleveland, Speaker met with Ernest Barnard and signed his contract for 1924, at a salary in the vicinity of $30,000–$35,000 (which the franchise could well afford, its home attendance having increased by about 30,000 over 1922). Speaker had vowed never to be a bench manager, and he saw no reason why he shouldn't be in centerfield every day. If anything, he seemed to have become a better hitter in the big-inning-oriented baseball now in sway—certainly a stronger one.

But if Speaker was as good as ever at bat, his ball club soon started to deteriorate. The next two seasons were mostly forgettable ones in the history of Cleveland baseball. But then the Indians underwent something of a resurgence, which in turn was followed by the most agonizing time of Speaker's professional life.

"We'll Finish in the League Anyway"

While the Yankees finally overcame the New York Giants in the World Series, taking the measure of McGraw's club in six games before record crowds, Speaker renewed his postseason excursions into the outdoors. Again he hunted and fished with Les Nunamaker, whose first season as a manager had been less than a thumping success in Chattanooga, which finished next to the bottom in the Southern Association. They returned to Rainy Lake, Ontario, for a couple of weeks; then Speaker stopped off in Cleveland to discuss possible player deals and spring-training arrangements with Ernest Barnard and to watch Cleveland's National Football League entry in a Sunday game at Dunn Field, before heading for Hubbard to get some of his cattle ready for market.

Speaker and Barnard made only one deal, but it was a big one. Early in January they dealt Bill Wambsganss, Steve O'Neill, pitcher Danny Boone, and substitute outfielder Joe Connolly to Boston for George Burns, infielder Wilson "Chick" Fewster, and catcher Alfred "Roxy" Walters. Burns was obviously the man Speaker wanted (back), and although it may have pained him to dispose of his friend O'Neill, the Indians' manager was no more inclined than anybody else to let personal feelings stand in the way of what he thought would strengthen his ball club.

Convinced that his pitchers needed extra conditioning, Speaker ordered them and his catchers to assemble at Hot Springs and work out along with batterymen from the Red Sox, now managed by Lee Fohl. Speaker came up later to play golf and join the players in hikes through the hills. Babe Ruth was also on hand to boil out winter fat and booze; on February 29 he was stricken with the flu, as had happened a year earlier in the same place. When Speaker visited him in his hotel room, he found the Babe in bed, smoking a cigar and complaining of being hungry.

Once the Indians gathered at Lakeland, they put up at the Elks Hotel, although the Cleveland sportswriters stayed at the lesser Washburn. Speaker did his ritualistic wrestling matches with various players, and various pranks had to be played out. Paul Fitzke, a pitcher from Wisconsin, arrived with a surfboard, thinking Lakeland was located on the coast. Speaker made him get rid of the board, but the *Cleveland Press*'s Joe Williams persuaded Fitzke to don horn-rim glasses à la the movie star Harold Lloyd, pose throwing left- and righthanded, and give interviews about himself, which Williams wired back to Cleveland on slow days.

Although it was a rainy, chilly March in Florida, the Indians managed to get in games with Brooklyn, Cincinnati, the Phillies, and Columbus. Things went fairly well, except that George Uhle, who had won 48 games and pitched 645 innings over the past two seasons, was complaining of a hurting arm. John McGraw, Miller Huggins, and Ty Cobb had forbidden their players to do any golfing, but Speaker continued to play frequently, convinced that golf-playing in no way hurt his ball-playing. The day before the Indians left Lakeland, nineteen members of the team held a golf tournament, which Glenn Myatt won with an 84 score. Speaker came in third at 90.

After stopovers in Atlanta and Mobile, a week in New Orleans, another stopover in Tuscaloosa for a rainout of a game intended to showcase the Indians' University of Alabama alumni, and two losses in Cincinnati, they headed for Detroit to open the 1924 season. Bill Phelon picked Cleveland to win the pennant. "Seeing Cleveland against other major league teams [in Florida]," Phelon wrote, "made the Indians stand out like a redheaded man at an Italian picnic." More cautiously, the respected baseball editor Francis Richter considered the Tribe "the most likely to beat out the Yankees, if that is at all possible."[1]

In 1924, Speaker was one of five player-managers in the majors. The Boston Braves' Dave Bancroft would be the only one in the National League. In addition to Speaker, Ty Cobb still led Detroit; twenty-seven-year-old Stanley "Bucky" Harris played secondbase and managed Washington; George Sisler, back from a year's absence, was at firstbase and headed up the St. Louis Browns; and Eddie

Collins shared managing chores with Johnny Evers for the White Sox. (Frank Chance had retired after the Red Sox's last-place finish, then signed to manage the White Sox. He fell ill before spring training and died in Los Angeles the following September, at age forty-seven.)

Cleveland lost the season-opener on April 15, George Dauss outpitching Joe Shaute, 4-3, on a typically cold spring day that didn't discourage some 33,000 Tigers loyalists from filling the expanded seating capacity of Navin Field. After a rainout, another loss, and a win in Detroit, the Tribe lost again in Chicago, had another rainout, and won for the second time. The home opener, with Detroit, drew 23,815 fans and produced nine doubles into the overflow. Cleveland won it in ten innings, 6-5, on George Burns's single that scored Riggs Stephenson and Speaker. Pitching in pain, Uhle went the distance.

Speaker got off to a good start, and so did Stephenson. But on April 30, in a game with Chicago at Dunn Field, Stephenson tripped over firstbaseman Earl Sheely's leg and wrenched his knee. The injury was bad enough to cause Stephenson to miss much of the season and keep Chick Fewster at secondbase. That and Uhle's lame arm were only the beginning of Speaker's troubles.

Three weeks into the season, Speaker contracted the "grippe"—that period's generic term for anything from a cold to influenza to bronchitis. Whatever it was, it was contagious, because soon several other Indians became ill. Speaker dragged for a week, developing acute bronchitis before team physician M. H. Castle persuaded him to go to bed. Attended by a nurse, he was on his back for four days and stayed behind with Uhle when the team left on its first eastern trip. In Philadelphia, coach Jack McCallister was also felled by the contagion, leaving Larry Gardner to run the team. By then the Indians had become, in the phrase of the *Plain Dealer*'s Stuart Bell, "the entire gargling squadron."[2]

Along with Uhle, Speaker rejoined the team in Washington and was able to coach at thirdbase, but he didn't put himself back in the lineup until May 18, for the opener of a series in New York. Uhle was driven out in an 8-0 loss before some 55,000 fans. Two more losses in Yankee Stadium, followed by three more in Boston, and the Tribe returned to Cleveland in seventh place with a 12-17 record.

With Stephenson unable to play, Speaker claimed infielder Frank Ellerbe from the Browns on waivers and sold Guy Morton to Kansas City. (That was tough enough for Morton, a veteran of ninety-eight wins in ten big-league seasons, but on his way to catch a train and join his new team, he barely escaped serious injury when the taxi in which he was riding collided with another vehicle and was demolished.)

In June, when the Boston Red Sox came into town, surprisingly tied with the Yankees for first place, the local Knights of Columbus chapter honored Lee Fohl, Steve O'Neill, Bill Wambsganss, and Speaker before the series opener. Then Uhle saved Joe Shaute's game, 5-4, for the Indians' fifth straight win. They lost the next day and ended up splitting four games with the Boston club, playing each time before large numbers of delegates taking a break from the tedium of the Republican National Convention, being held in the city's vast auditorium.

The following series with the Yankees provided what was perhaps the high point of an otherwise desultory season. On Sunday, June 15, about three thousand more people than could be seated came to Dunn Field to see the Tribe slam Bob Shawkey for ten runs, while Shaute held the New Yorkers to three. Speaker led the attack with a single and two doubles. Glenn Myatt added a three-run homer. The Yankees scored in the first inning, but it was a costly run, because Earle Combs, their fine rookie centerfielder, broke his ankle sliding into home plate and spent the next few weeks hospitalized in Cleveland, lost for the season.

The next day Stanley Coveleski and Joe Bush were both masterful, each yielding a single run until the Indians scored the winner in the ninth on an error. On Tuesday, Speaker homered for one of Cleveland's five runs, but Uhle gave up late-inning homers to Ruth and Wally Pipp and lost it, 7-5. In the series-closer, Joe Sewell drove in Jamieson with the winning run in the ninth to give Sherry Smith a tough 6-5 victory. At that point New York barely held first place over Detroit. The Red Sox had stopped playing over their heads and were rapidly fading toward the league's lower reaches. Cleveland, at 24-27, was in seventh place.

Eleven days later, it seemed as if even the weather had arrayed against the Tribe. With Detroit leading 8-3 in the eighth inning, menacing clouds lowered over Dunn Field, and gale-force winds swept the ballpark. The umpires called the game as the few spectators who were left scrambled for cover from a storm that had already devastated the Lorain-Sandusky area to the west of Cleveland and killed or injured hundreds of people. With that defeat, the Indians remained in seventh place: thirty wins, thirty-three losses.

Meanwhile, Washington, which had been drifting around the middle of the standings, won thirteen of eighteen games and temporarily dislodged New York from the lead. After several mediocre years with mediocre teams, Walter Johnson was again winning regularly for the "boy manager," as the writers had dubbed Bucky Harris. Now, his fastball no longer what it had been, Johnson pitched with greater care and cunning. (On August 25 he threw the only no-hitter of his long career, besting St. Louis, 2-0.)

Early in July, with everybody off the sick or injured list for the first time since May 1, Speaker took his sixth-place team east, where they won seven games, lost thirteen, and dropped to seventh. "No pitching," Francis J. Powers wrote. "There is the whole story in those two words." Thirty minutes after the Indians arrived from an eighteen-hour trip from Boston, Speaker had his pitchers throwing and running at Dunn Field, determined to get them in shape and to improve their control. Stuart Bell commented, "He sets no detective on their trail. He neither snoops, nor prys [*sic*] into their private lives. But Speaker has come to the conclusion that his pitchers haven't been hustling in the manner they should. In certain cases there seems to be good reason to believe his trust and confidence have been betrayed."[3]

Maybe Speaker's workouts did some good, because Sherry Smith, Coveleski, and Shaute pitched the Indians to three wins in four games to cool off Washington. Speaker's triple and steal of home on George Mogridge helped win Coveleski's game, 2-1. But then they lost three of five to Philadelphia, with firstbaseman Joe Hauser lifting three home runs over the rightfield wall and fence in the finale. A five-game sweep of Boston in a heat wave followed, then three wins in five tries from the Yankees—the last of which, a 7-1 victory for Shaute (who also homered), knocked Miller Huggins's team out of first place. Meanwhile Uhle had taken his ailing arm to Youngstown for a session with James "Bonesetter" Reese, a Welsh-born former coal miner who, despite a minimal medical education, had become renowned for treating athletic injuries.

Having won eleven of seventeen games at home, the Indians again played unevenly on their final extended road trip and returned still ten games under .500, in fifth place. In a Labor Day doubleheader in St. Louis, they combined with the Browns for twenty-eight runs and eight home runs. Speaker, Jamieson, and Ken Williams hit for the circuit in the morning game. Speaker, Frank Brower, and Sherry Smith hit one apiece in the afternoon game, and Riggs Stephenson, knee finally healed, clouted two.

On September 14, Joe Shaute ended his season by tearing leg ligaments sliding in a game at Dunn Field with Philadelphia; subsequently Glenn Myatt underwent knee surgery in the same hospital where Shaute was convalescing from his surgery. With no hope for anything better than fifth place, Speaker took himself out of the lineup in favor of Pat McNulty and did nothing but pinch-hit for the remainder of the Tribe's games.

Cleveland lost nine games in a row, enabling the Athletics to occupy fifth place, until a 12-1 outburst at Dunn Field that gave rookie righthander Emil Levsen his first big-league victory. Meanwhile, Washington and New York battled for the lead, the Senators clinching on Monday, September 29, by winning at Boston while the Yankees were rained out in Philadelphia. After the Senators' loss on Tuesday and another Yankees rainout, the final standings were Washington 92-62, New York, 89-63. With Ty Cobb, at age thirty-seven, playing in every game, Detroit finished third at 86-68—the best won-lost record the Tigers achieved in Cobb's six years as their manager.

The Indians' season ended on a dreary note with a rainout at Dunn Field, after a Saturday win from the Browns that put "hardly a corporal's guard in the stands." In what over the season's last weeks had become a competition for sixth place, Cleveland won with a 67-86 record, a half-game better than Boston and a full game better than Chicago. Not that it mattered much. It was the lowest finish for the Indians since Speaker's first year with the team and the worst won-lost record since then. Bill Phelon, who had predicted a pennant for the Tribe, wrote that "This team, one of the great disappointments of 1924, kept on disappointing."[4] Home attendance had fallen by another 75,000, to a little more than half what it had been in 1920.

The nation's capital finally had a pennant-winner, its first in any league. The 1924 Washington Senators were an all-around solid ball club, with two future

Hall of Fame outfielders in Sam Rice and Leon "Goose" Goslin (the league leader in runs batted in with 129); a tight infield anchored by player-manager Harris that made the league's second-fewest errors; and a pitching staff that allowed the fewest runs in either major league, led by Walter Johnson (23-7), George Mogridge (16-11), Tom Zachary (15-9), and Fred "Firpo" Marberry, whom Harris used in fifty games. Besides winning 15, Marberry also saved 15 as one of the era's early relief specialists. Herb Pennock won 21 games for New York, and Babe Ruth, generally behaving himself (at least on the field), hit .378 to win his only batting title. Although Goslin beat him out in runs batted in, the Babe again led everybody in home runs (46), slugging average, and scoring. But Washington's pitching proved stronger. Marberry's relief work probably made the difference.

If Ty Cobb seemed as durable as ever, Speaker looked less so. He didn't play at all in eighteen games and only pinch-hit in ten or so others. His final batting average was .344, seventh-best in the league. Charlie Jamieson outhit him by fifteen points to finish second to Ruth. Speaker hit 9 homers and drove in 63 runs, and although he had 20 assists from the outfield, 13 errors suggested that he had slowed getting to balls. The Indians were again a hard-hitting outfit, batting .296 as a team (second to Detroit), but their pitching staff gave up more runs than any in the league except Chicago. George Uhle, who had won 26 games in 1923, struggled with arm trouble all season and could do no better than a 9-15 record. Stanley Coveleski's record was 15-16 with an earned run average that swelled to 4.04. Joe Shaute won 20 games but lost 17.

On the Thursday night following the season's close, Speaker left for Rainy Lake, Ontario, with Les Nunamaker and Clay Folger, thereby putting himself out of contact with baseball, including the World Series. That Series turned out to be one of the most stirring in the history of the annual October spectacle, with the New York Giants—the first team since the St. Louis Browns of the old American Association to win four consecutive pennants—falling to Washington in seven games. The legendary finale featured heroic relief pitching by Walter Johnson (who had lost two earlier starts) and a freak base hit that brought home the winning run in the twelfth inning and sent the District of Columbia's fandom into ecstasy.

What agitated much of the rest of the country that fall, however, was something far more serious than baseball. Nineteen-twenty-four was the year in which the second Ku Klux Klan—officially, the Invisible Empire, Knights of the Ku Klux Klan, Inc., founded at Atlanta nine years earlier—reached the zenith of its power and influence. Unlike the earlier Ku Klux Klan, formed in the post–Civil War South to terrorize recently emancipated African Americans and their white Republican allies, and unlike the various regional and local Klan groups of the post–World War II decades, the Klan of the 1920s was a national movement. Local Klan chapters operated from Maine to California and from Florida to Oregon. Preaching "100 percent Americanism" and appealing to a variety of racial, religious, and ethnic prejudices and fears, the Klan recruited millions of members, who only had to be white, native born, and Protestant. Also touting themselves as a force for law and order, Klansmen in their white robes and hoods marched, burned crosses, and often resorted to violence in campaigns against bootleggers, drug dealers, crooked politicians, adulterers, wife-beaters, and an assortment of other miscreants.

The great majority of those who paid the Klan's $10 initiation fee never participated in any acts of violence. For them, it was a matter of affiliating with what seemed like a patriotic organization that would work for honest government and a moral social order. Local businessmen often joined to maximize their profits. (Klan members were constantly exhorted to trade with fellow Klansmen). Protestant ministers were usually grateful for the Klan's donations to their churches. Politicians joined in hopes of realizing a solid voting bloc. In short, joining the Klan became the thing to do for huge numbers of respectable, largely middle-class Americans, for whom going through the Klan's secret rituals and becoming part of its secret membership weren't much different from joining any of the various other fraternal lodges—Masonic Order, Knights of Pythias, Elks, Moose, and others—whose aggregate membership reached its peak in the 1920s.[5]

The Knights of the Ku Klux Klan sought to recruit men who had attained prominence in their fields. Leading political figures, attorneys, law-enforcement officials, corporate executives, and other successful and respected citizens were prized by the Klan. The vice president of the University of Oklahoma; the head football coach at Oregon State College; U.S. senators from Oregon, Texas, and

Georgia; and a future associate justice of the U.S. Supreme Court were on the Klan's membership rolls at one time or another.

As was Tris Speaker, according to Fred Lieb, who for sixty years watched and reported on baseball for a variety of newspapers and news services. In his 1977 memoir *Baseball as I Have Known It,* Lieb discussed Ty Cobb's intense white-supremacist views, adding, "'Gabby' Street, Rogers Hornsby, and Tris Speaker, fellow stars of the old Confederate states, told me they were members of the Ku Klux Klan. I do not know whether Cobb was a Klansman, but I suspect he was."[6] Like most people writing later about the '20s Klan, Lieb simplistically equated being southern-born with an affinity for Klan membership, although in fact most Klansmen resided outside the South, with Indiana enrolling more than any other state.

Published when Lieb was eighty-nine years old, those two sentences constitute the sole extant evidence that any of the four named ballplayers (all dead by then, of course) ever joined the Knights of the Ku Klux Klan.[7] Texas was one of the strongest Klan states, and Hubbard and many other small Texas towns supported local Klan chapters. Yet the movement's greatest strength in Texas and elsewhere was concentrated in the larger towns and cities.

Born less than a generation after the end of the Civil War and growing up as a native Texan, Speaker probably heard older people tell stories about how the original "Ku Klux" and other night-riding groups had "redeemed" the postwar South from "Yankee" and "nigger" domination. It's possible that at some point during the Klan's rapid growth in Texas in 1921 or 1922, Speaker as well as Hornsby may have joined the Klan. If they did, it was probably in Fort Worth in Hornsby's case and either in Fort Worth or Dallas in Speaker's case. Both cities had huge Klan chapters.

Speaker also belonged to the Masonic Order and the Shriners, and during his years with the Red Sox, he was part of the "Masons" faction, at odds with the "K.C." faction. But when he came to Cleveland, he quickly became close friends with Jim and Emily Dunn and, among his teammates, Steve O'Neill and Stanley Coveleski, both Roman Catholics from the coal-mining regions of Pennsylvania. And he served as best man for Ray Chapman when the Indians' shortstop married into a prominent Catholic family.

Speaker had often said he wouldn't marry until he quit baseball. But some-time during 1924 he gave an engagement ring to Mary Frances Cudahy, a local woman he had known since 1919. Described as "an intimate friend of Mrs. James C. Dunn," she was a native of Buffalo, New York, thirty-five years old in December 1924, and a former employee of the Union Commerce Bank and Trust.[8] About 5' 3" tall, with brown hair and hazel eyes, she was an attractive woman (if somewhat on the matronly side) and said to be an avid golfer. Like Speaker, she had approached middle age without ever marrying. And her family was devoutly Roman Catholic.

On January 15, 1925, without prior warning to the local press, Speaker and Mary Frances Cudahy were married in the parish house of St. John's Cathedral in downtown Cleveland. The wedding ceremony was performed by some impos-ing local church figures: Monsignor Joseph Smith, vicar general of the Cleveland diocese and pastor of St. Philomena's Church, married the couple, assisted by Monsignor T. C. O'Reilly, pastor of St. John's. Speaker obtained the license at 3:00 P.M., the ceremony began at 3:15, and Speaker and his bride were out the door by 3:30. The only people who knew of the wedding beforehand were the bride's mother and sister and Walter McNichol, the Indians' business manager.

The newlyweds left by automobile for Akron to catch the Pennsylvania Rail-road's Florida Special. They spent two weeks honeymooning at Lakeland, where Speaker bought a house site (which they never used) in the rapidly inflating Flor-ida land boom. After two weeks, they traveled to Hubbard for "Fran" (as Speaker called her) to meet her mother-in-law for the first time. What Jenny Speaker thought of this woman who had married her "boy" isn't known. Inasmuch as the new Mrs. Speaker had been close to the Dunns, Jenny Speaker probably thought she was all right.

So how does one reconcile Speaker's friendships and his marriage with the possibility (and it's only that) that he was willing to become a "citizen of the Invis-ible Empire"—a member of the militantly anti-Catholic Klan? Probably the best answer is also the simplest one: Speaker grew and matured in his views and val-ues and lost his animus toward the Church of Rome (as later on he would change his views considerably about black people). Besides, he fell in love. In any case, in the summer and fall of 1924 the Klan suffered major political setbacks in several states. Hit by a succession of internal quarrels and scandals, especially within the mighty Indiana Klan, the secret order went into decline almost everywhere. If Speaker or Hornsby had ever belonged to the Klan, by 1925 they would also have been part of the mass exodus from the movement.[9]

Besides acquiring a wife, Speaker spent a busy winter with player dispositions. He gave Larry Gardner, his good friend and unofficial coach, his outright release. That left only Speaker, Joe Sewell, Charlie Jamieson, and George Uhle from the 1920 championship team. Rube Lutzke had been at thirdbase most of the time in 1924. Limited mostly to pinch hitting, Gardner had appeared in only thirty-eight games. Now he ended a seventeen-year major-league career to take the manager's job at Dallas. The Indians also bought infielder Joe Klugman from Minneapolis and pitcher Benny Karr from Nashville and sold Frank Brower to San Francisco and Frank Ellerbe to Kansas City.

At the annual major-league meetings in New York, Speaker, with Cleveland president Barnard's approval, made his worst trade. Stanley Coveleski, whom he considered washed up, went to Washington for pitcher Byron Speece and rookie outfielder Carr Smith. Speece won all of three games for Cleveland before being released to Indianapolis early in the 1926 season. Smith was sent to the minors (never to return), and Coveleski won twenty games for Washington in 1925, lost only five, and, for the second time, showed the majors' lowest earned run average.

In its March 30, 1925, issue, the two-year-old news magazine *Time* put George Sisler on its cover (the first baseball player so recognized) and gave a rundown on players to watch in the coming season. *Time* described Speaker as "grizzled, lined" and looking even older than Ty Cobb, "but he still fields with the grace of a nautch-girl." The St. Louis sportswriter James M. Gould wrote that "In mufti, Tris looks old enough to retire right now. But, when he puts on a uniform and appears at the plate . . . it is the opposing team who wishes he would retire."[10]

At the beginning of March, Speaker and his new wife connected with the train for Lakeland in Jacksonville, where they encountered Babe Ruth, newly acquired Steve O'Neill, and other Yankees on their way to St. Petersburg. With ten of the sixteen major-league teams holding spring training in Florida, real estate agents greeted players with offers of fabulous money to be made in land investments. Speaker, reported Lefty Weisman, came in eleven pounds over-weight, which may have helped him in wrestling matches with Weisman, Luke Sewell, and pitcher Paul Fitzke (on hand for another unsuccessful trial, minus surfboard).

President Barnard had sent a letter to all the players gathering at Lakeland, prescribing no alcohol consumption from then to the end of the season and a mandatory bedtime of midnight. An unnamed team member commented, "Any player who can't live up to those two rules ought not to be in baseball." But the Indians' prospects didn't look good. The *Plain Dealer*'s Henry P. Edwards wrote, "If there is anything in the old saying a manager learns through adversity, Speaker is going to be a combination of John McGraw, Connie Mack and Bill Carrigan this season." Asked about his team, Speaker snapped, "We'll finish in the league anyway." Asked about how much he would play in the coming season, he snapped again: "There isn't any ball player on this team who is good enough to take center field away from me."[11]

After making a 14-3 record in exhibition games, mostly against minor-leaguers, the Tribe opened the 1925 season in St. Louis, winning a 21-14 "display of baseball horrors," as Joe Williams termed it.[12] Marred by ten errors, of which the usually stylish George Sisler made four, the game was decided in the eighth inning when Speaker and Pat McNulty hit three-run homers. Charlie Jamieson, Glenn Myatt, and the Browns' Ken Williams also homered, as the teams com-bined for thirty-nine hits, the two managers using thirty-four players. Joe Shaute won the game in relief of three predecessors.

The Indians lost their home opener to the Browns, with 22,616 fans occu-pying the permanent seats and temporary seats in leftfield and sitting on the grass in front of the leftfield bleachers. Mary Frances Speaker, her mother, sister, brother, and sister-in-law occupied a box behind the home team's thirdbase dug-out. Joe Bush (traded by New York over the winter for Urban Shocker) doubled and scored the winning run in the tenth inning. Up to that point, the Indians had won their first five games. They went on to take eleven of their first fifteen and lift hopes they might be a pennant-contender.

The Yankees began the season without Babe Ruth, who had collapsed at Asheville, North Carolina, as the team headed north from Florida. A long convalescence followed surgery for what was announced as an intestinal abscess. When the Babe finally returned to action, his behavior was so defiantly unruly that late in August, Miller Huggins suspended him and imposed a record $5,000 fine. Playing in only ninety-eight games, Ruth wasn't much help to a team that fell into the second division early in the season and stayed there.

Connie Mack's Philadelphia Athletics, after many years in the nether regions of the American League, had contended for much of the 1924 season before going into a nosedive and finishing fifth. Mack was carefully rebuilding his team and managing to come up with the money to pay big prices for outstanding minor-leaguers. Al Simmons, a heavy-hitting outfielder purchased from Milwaukee, had joined the Athletics the previous season. For 1925, Mack brought in Gordon "Mickey" Cochrane, a brilliant young catcher, from Portland and Robert Moses "Lefty" Grove, who had won 109 games in five seasons at Baltimore and carried a record $105,000 price tag. In 1925 the Athletics were to be the main obstacle to another pennant for Washington.

On their first trip west, the Athletics swept three games at Dunn Field and held first place over Washington, with Cleveland in third. Three days later, having already banged his knee making a catch at the wall the previous week, Speaker twisted it in pregame practice, then singled, doubled, and homered in a win over Boston. But he sat out the next day's game before leaving for Rochester, New York, to see Harry Knight, M.D., who rivaled Bonesetter Reese in treating athletic injuries. Speaker returned to the lineup on May 14, as Washington won its second in a row from the Indians, Tom Zachary outdueling George Uhle, 2-1. For Speaker it was another good day at bat, with a double and two singles. The last hit was his three-thousandth in the major leagues. After limping to firstbase, he called out Pat McNulty to run for him. A couple of days later, his knee apparently all right, he scored all the way from firstbase with the winning run against New York on Joe Shaute's two-out, bases-loaded single.

With Speaker (thirty-seven or thirty-six) batting above .400 and Ty Cobb (thirty-eight) having recently clouted five home runs in two games in St. Louis, Francis Powers could only marvel at the endurance of the two aging stars. Speaker, Powers enthused, "every day gets grayer and faster and hits the ball just a wee bit harder."[13] Yet the Tribe did no better than break even on its home stand

and dropped into fourth place. Again they trailed the rest of the league in fielding, and their pitchers were being pounded consistently.

On Saturday, May 23, Speaker homered in a 7-6 loss to New York. Late in the game, he and Joe Klugman were so abusive to umpire Clarence Rowland, when Rowland called out Klugman at home plate on a double-steal attempt, that they received Ban Johnson's telegram putting both under suspension. Without their manager, the Indians lost four of five games in St. Louis, then, with Speaker back in the lineup, dropped a Memorial Day doubleheader in Detroit. After salvaging the finale of a four-game series with the Browns at Dunn Field, Cleveland was in fifth place, with twenty-one wins, twenty-two losses. Riggs Stephenson, whom Speaker had been trying in rightfield, was batting almost .300, but Speaker had never really believed in the young Alabamian. Early in June, Stephenson was sent down to Kansas City on option. (Drafted by the Chicago Cubs two years later, he became one of the consistently dangerous hitters in the National League.)

Speaker juggled his infield in an effort to get consistent defense, experimenting with both Joe Sewell and Rube Lutzke at secondbase in place of Chick Fewster; sending Lutzke back to third in place of Klugman; putting rookie Fred Spurgeon, from Kalamazoo College, at shortstop; and alternating Bob Knode, who had come up for trials the past two seasons, at firstbase with George Burns. Homer Summa, Pat McNulty, and former National League pickup Cliff Lee shared outfield time with Speaker and Charlie Jamieson. Glenn Myatt and Luke Sewell divided catching duties. Like most other managers of his era, Speaker preferred to go with a set lineup, but that was something he never had in 1925.

On June 11, Speaker marked another personal milestone when he homered and doubled at Yankee Stadium behind lefthander Walter Miller in a 4-1 victory. The double was his 652nd, which broke Napoleon Lajoie's record. The team, though, continued to stumble along. On June 15 the Tribe blew an eleven-run lead when the Athletics scored thirteen times in the eighth inning to win, 17-13. Jamieson recalled, "Tris Speaker almost had an attack of epilepsy during that nightmare inning."[14] The Athletics won the next two games, 12-7 and 10-3, for a total of thirty-nine runs in three days. After losing two of three to Washington and five in a row in Chicago, the Indians were ahead of only the wretched Red

Sox. The losing streak reached eight games with a doubleheader loss at Detroit. Cleveland had won only twice in its last fifteen tries and was thirteen games below .500. Speaker's average had fallen into the .360s.

The *Cleveland News*'s Ed Bang, acknowledging that Speaker had done a good job since becoming manager in 1919, described him as "right now in the dumps with a team that sheds glory on nobody." The editor of *Baseball Magazine* observed, "The storm clouds, so rumor had it, were gathering around the head of Tris Speaker." On July 18, to squelch rumors that Speaker was on the way out, Ernest Barnard and Emily Dunn called him into the front office and signed him for 1926. "The recent slump of the Indians," the Cleveland president told the press, "cannot be laid at the door of Manager Speaker. Tris cannot pitch, catch or play the infield, and he cannot bat for anyone but himself. . . . Speaker certainly has set a good example for his players by the way he hustled during the present season."[15] Two days later, as boos and catcalls echoed around Dunn Field, Stanley Coveleski won his thirteenth game for Washington, 9-1. At that point the Senators were in a virtual tie with Philadelphia for the lead.

For a while thereafter, with Speaker again boosting his batting average, the Indians played better ball and moved into sixth place, ahead of the trouble-plagued Yankees. They won six in a row in St. Louis and Boston, although Uhle, still sore armed, and Shaute, who underwent a tonsillectomy, didn't go east with the team. Speaker missed a week after a pitch by the Athletics' Byron "Slim" Harris hit him on the right wrist. Then, in Washington, Fred Marberry hit him on the left elbow, and Homer Summa replaced him for a four-game sweep from the Yankees. Meanwhile, Johnny Hodapp, a highly touted twenty-year-old infielder purchased from Indianapolis for $50,000, joined the team and took over thirdbase.

After August 21, Speaker didn't play except occasionally to pinch-hit. Writing the season off, he sat in the dugout, sometimes coached at thirdbase, and looked over the Tribe's younger players and late-season call-ups in hopes of putting together a better outfit next year. By September the *Cleveland Press* was printing only daily box scores, having discontinued game writeups. One of the few encouraging signs over the season's second half was the strong pitching of

Garland Buckeye, a 260-pound lefthander drafted from the Pacific Coast League. Buckeye finished with thirteen wins, including a four-hit shutout of Detroit in which he homered twice over the rightfield wall and fence at Dunn Field.

As they had done a year earlier, the Athletics fell into a late-season losing streak—this one running to twelve games—that killed their pennant chances. After the Labor Day doubleheaders, the Indians went on the road for the remainder of the season. Their three-game sweep in Philadelphia late in September enabled Washington to clinch another pennant. At the end the Senators were eight and a half games better than the forlorn Athletics.

During the last week of the season, the Indians and St. Louis Cardinals played an exhibition game at Dunn Field before a small crowd. Sporting a newly sculpted nose, heavyweight boxing champion Jack Dempsey, in town for some exhibition matches, posed for photographers with Speaker, Steve O'Neill (recently released by the Yankees), and Rogers Hornsby, who had become the Cardinals' manager in May. Hornsby was about to ring up his third .400-plus season and gain his sixth consecutive National League batting title. Neither player-manager appeared in the game, which the Cardinals won, 10-9. In a setting of former glory, Duster Mails clowned his way to victory.

The Tribe ended another disappointing season with three defeats in Chicago. When Speaker arrived in Chicago, he was at the top of the league's batters with a .389 average, although he had limited himself to pinch hitting for the past six weeks. Detroit's Harry Heilmann had steadily climbed in the averages, and as Speaker watched his makeshift lineup lose its last game to the White Sox, 10-8, Heilmann made six hits in a doubleheader sweep in St. Louis to overtake Speaker and win his third odd-year batting title. Although he wasn't at Sportsman's Park, Joe Williams was still convinced that the Browns' pitchers "laid the ball over with nothing on it" and gave Heilmann at least four of his six hits.[16]

Speaker's average was the highest he ever attained (by one point), but at .393, Heilmann was four points better. Heilmann, moreover, played in 150 games and made 225 base hits. Speaker appeared in only 117 games (four as a pinch hitter) and made 167 hits. He put in only two-thirds of the 1925 season; his 12 home runs, 83 runs batted in, and all but one of his base hits came before August 21. Philadelphia's Al Simmons was third in batting at .384. In

121 games, Ty Cobb batted .378, equaled his career-best in homers (12), and drove in 102 runs. Not generally noticed at the time was that little Joe Sewell, who batted a robust .336 and drove in 98 runs, was on his way to becoming the hardest man to strike out in the game's history. That year, in 608 official times at bat, Sewell fanned only 4 times.

Ill at the start of the season and ill-tempered the rest of it, Babe Ruth didn't figure in any of the major offensive categories. He batted only .290, the first time he had failed to hit .300 since becoming an everyday player. Ruth homered 25 times and drove in a paltry 66 runs. Ruth's outfield mate Bob Meusel topped the American League in both homers (33) and runs batted in (133). Some were ready to consign the Babe to the has-been category. The seasons ahead proved them quite mistaken.

At 70-90, the Tribe ended up in sixth place, one game better than the Yankees, nine games behind Chicago. Detroit finished fourth, the Browns third. Among Speaker's pitchers, nobody except Garland Buckeye was consistently effective. The heavyweight lefthander was also the only one to register an earned run average below 4.00. Home attendance had sagged another 73,000 to 419,005. The franchise netted only a $13,294 profit, not enough to cover Speaker's salary alone.

Yet the Indians' manager remained optimistic. Attending the World Series for the first time since 1920, he indicated he might not play regularly next season, and that he would be satisfied with an outfield alignment of Charlie Jamieson, Pat McNulty, and Cliff Lee. (That proved to be only conjecture; come next April, Speaker was still Cleveland's everyday centerfielder.) A fan of his own league (as players usually were in that long-ago time before interleague trading and free agency), he watched Washington fall to Pittsburgh, which became the first team to overcome a three-games-to-one Series deficit. In a rain-soaked seventh game, the Pirates pounded Walter Johnson for fifteen hits and nine runs.

After his autumn fishing and hunting stay in Ontario, Speaker stopped off in Cleveland, then traveled to New York to attend the Army-Navy game and to be on hand with Ernest Barnard for the annual major-league meetings. The only personnel move they made was to release Chick Fewster after he cleared waivers. At the Hotel Belmont, where the American Leaguers convened, and the Waldorf, the National League's headquarters, there was much talk about the Nationals' adoption of a new rule allowing the league's pitchers to dry their hands with a resin bag, which umpires would supply to pitchers whenever they asked for it. At Ban Johnson's urging, the American League owners refused to legalize resin, fearing that it might lead to a return of "freak deliveries."

Speaker and his wife were at Hubbard in time for Christmas and remained in Texas until he left for Hot Springs in mid-February to supervise his batterymen. While in his home state, he hunted, golfed, and worked with foreman Charley Vaughan on his farm place. In Houston, he competed in a skeet-shooting tournament, finishing second with ninety-four hits in one hundred shots. Then he was off to Hot Springs to hike the hills with his pitchers and catchers in the morning and work out at the ballpark and play golf in the afternoon.

By the beginning of March, Speaker had relocated the Hot Springs contingent to Lakeland, where he had on hand a total of twenty-nine players. Rube Lutzke was back, ever hopeful of becoming a better hitter following .256, .243, and .218 seasons with the Tribe. To that end, Lutzke followed a medical axiom of the time—that bad teeth poisoned one's system—and had all his teeth extracted. He also had his appendix removed and, to improve his eyesight, stopped reading and going to movies. When he still struggled at bat, he asked Speaker, "What's wrong with me?" The manager's answer was worthy of Rogers Hornsby (already notorious for his bluntness): "The trouble with you, Lutzke, is you can't hit."[17]

That spring the great Florida land boom was in full swing. Luke Sewell was one of several ballplayers who had spent the winter selling properties in the central part of the state. Bill Doak, one of the National League's designated spitballers, quit baseball (prematurely, as it turned out) to sell lots around Bradenton and elsewhere. John McGraw invested much of his own money and persuaded many others to invest in a development at Sarasota called "Pennant Park."

Although a year earlier Speaker had bought a lot at Lakeland for himself and his wife, he was impatient with the distraction of the real-estate frenzy, and he didn't like the way—as he saw it—ballplayers had changed. "Too much money is hurting major league baseball," he told a reporter. "The average player now is more or less satisfied with his salary. . . . Now he feels he has arrived, he no long needs to fight and stay awake planning, thinking and dreaming of an ambition still unsatisfied. . . . The result is less intelligent baseball and a bit of laziness."[18]

Nobody seemed to think much of the Indians' prospects for 1926. Miller Huggins picked them for seventh place, as did James M. Gould, who observed, "Tris Speaker has a tough task." After watching the team at Lakeland, the Chicago writer Warren Brown concluded, "No pennant winner, this Cleveland club," and Bucky Harris told Brown that he thought everybody in the American League had a shot at the pennant except Cleveland and Boston.[19] Speaker's team didn't look good in its Florida exhibition games, winning three and losing seven in meetings with the Boston Braves, Cincinnati Reds, Brooklyn Robins, and New York Giants.

The silliness of the American League's anti-resin rule became evident when the Indians played the Braves in their first two exhibition games. Speaker made no complaint when the teams met on the Braves' home grounds at St. Petersburg, but when the Braves came to Lakeland, Speaker held up the start of the game for an hour while he argued over use of the resin bag with umpire Frank Wilson (who had just moved from the American to the National League), Braves manager Dave Bancroft, and pitcher Al Powell. Speaker finally gave up, but he sat out the game, refusing to play in violation of his league's rules.

Both leagues, however, had adopted a new sacrifice-fly rule, which was intended to compensate for the ball's supposedly being somewhat deadened for the coming season. Under the previous rule, originally adopted in 1908, a batter was spared a time at bat if a runner scored on his caught fly ball. Now he wouldn't be charged if a runner advanced to any base on his fly out.

From Lakeland, the Tribe headed for a week's stay in New Orleans, stopping at Waycross, Georgia, and Atlanta for games with Rochester and Toronto, respectively. At New Orleans, Johnny Hodapp, slated to be Speaker's regular thirdbaseman, was disabled in a freakish accident. In practice Hodapp tried to stop a rolling ball with his foot and stepped on the ball in such a way that he broke an ankle. When M. H. Castle examined the ankle in Cleveland, he found that Hodapp also had torn ligaments. The Tribe's $50,000 acquisition was out for nearly the whole season.

After the annual stopover at Tuscaloosa for a luncheon at the Exchange Club, followed by a game with the University of Alabama, then a pair of wins in Cincinnati, the Indians arrived in Detroit to start the season. On Tuesday, April 13, 1926, an overflow crowd of 35,000, including 500 or so Clevelanders, braved Michigan's mid-April cold. Having shown in Florida that his arm was sound again, George Uhle was Speaker's choice; and although he walked seven batters and gave up nine hits, he retired the Tigers' Lu Blue three times with the bases loaded to get the win over Earl Whitehill, 2-1. Rain and snow kept the teams idle the next two days. With a gale blowing on Friday, Augustus "Lefty" Johns, a twenty-seven-year-old rookie up from Fort Worth, outpitched Joe Shaute, 5-3.

In a three-game series that followed in Chicago, the Indians won two. Walter Miller pitched a three-hit shutout in the opener, then stumbled going down the concrete steps leading to the dressing rooms and broke his foot. Also in Chicago, Rube Lutzke happened to get in the way of a flying fungo bat and received a broken arm. The series of bizarre accidents—to Hodapp, Miller, and Lutzke—must have left Speaker scratching his head.

Bundled in his topcoat, Commissioner Landis was present for all three games at Comiskey Park. When reporters asked about the resin-bag issue, Landis was noncommittal, although shortly he overruled Ban Johnson and the American League owners. Subsequently the American Leaguers voted 6-2 to endorse the use of resin bags. As in other instances over the past four years, Landis had imposed his authority over that of Johnson.

The Indians' home opener, on April 21 versus Detroit, attracted a capacity turnout of 22,000, who went home happy after a 12-1 walkover for Benny Karr, whose specialty was the fork ball. Clearly, Cleveland's pitching had improved from the previous season. As the Indians went on to win six of their first eight games, Speaker made only one pitching change. By the second week in May, their record was 15-9, tying them with New York for the lead.

Speaker, though, was bothered for two weeks by a cold, and his disposition wasn't helped by the harassment he continued to receive at Dunn Field from the same gaggle of bleacherites who had given him a hard time the previous season. On May 4, during their last game before heading east, an 11-5 loss to St. Louis, Speaker almost went into the stands after his tormentors. "Cleveland fans," Francis Powers wrote, "rapidly are getting the reputation around the league of being the hardest in the country to satisfy and the roughest talkers." At Dunn Field, Henry P. Edwards said, people acted as if a popup with the bases loaded or an error "was a personal insult to them."[20]

The torrid play of the Yankees made clear that their collapse in 1925 was an aberration. A more-or-less reformed Babe Ruth now teamed with Bob Meusel, Earle Combs, young Lou Gehrig (who had taken over firstbase the previous June), and rookie Tony Lazzeri (destined to become baseball's first Italian-American star) to form the game's most potent attack. Herb Pennock, Urban Shocker, and Waite Hoyt headed up a stellar pitching staff. The Yankees swept the Tribe in three games at Yankee Stadium and went on to win sixteen straight before Philadelphia's Lefty Grove finally stopped them. By the beginning of June, their record was 31-12, six games better than the Athletics. In the meantime, Cleveland had slumped to 22-22 and sixth place. Speaker, also slumping, benched himself as well as Charlie Jamieson following a loss to the White Sox in the opener of a Memorial Day doubleheader. "I'm not timing my swing right," Speaker complained, adding that he hadn't played golf since the season began, because he didn't want anybody saying that was why he was in a slump.[21]

On Friday, June 5, Speaker put himself back in the lineup, occupying the fifth slot in the batting order for a home series with the Yankees, which began with a 15-3 demolition of Pennock, his first loss after eight victories. Garland Buckeye coasted to the win and also made four hits, including a double and home run. On what was proclaimed "Speaker Day," the Indians' manager contributed two singles, a stolen base, and eight putouts. Ban Johnson was present to honor Speaker with a certificate retrospectively recognizing him as 1912's most valuable player. (Back then, the Chalmers company had given him an automobile.)

Two weeks later he was still batting only .272, but the Indians won fourteen times in twenty games on their home stand, edging the Athletics out of second place. George Burns, now in exclusive possession of firstbase, was batting at a blazing pace and piling up doubles. Speaker had settled on a starting rotation of George Uhle, again the staff's workhorse; lefthanders Sherry Smith, Joe Shaute, and Walter Miller (when his foot had healed); and righthander Emil "Dutch" Levsen, a graduate of Iowa State Agricultural College, who had made the team after two previous trials. With five teams playing about .500 ball, the standings changed almost daily, although everybody was still way behind the Yankees.

After losing six of eight games in Chicago and Detroit, the Indians played well on their next eastern trip, winning eleven of seventeen in the usual midsummer heat wave. Three of their victories came at Yankee Stadium and another four in Philadelphia (which was celebrating the sesquicentennial of the Declaration of Independence). Cleveland came home with a solid hold on second place. Speaker, having batted .365 on the trip, had finally pushed his average up to the .300 level. Yet at 53-44, the Indians still trailed New York by nine games.

At home, they swept a doubleheader and three single games from the Athletics. Game three was a 3-2 loss by Lefty Grove, who became rattled and gave up a game-winning double to Burns in the eighth inning after fans in the Dunn Field upper deck, having read that coach Kid Gleason had instructed Grove to pace his deliveries by counting to ten before each pitch, began chanting the count.

The Red Sox, again nestled snugly in last place, came into Cleveland and lost to Levsen, 2-1, Charles "Red" Ruffing taking one of his fifteen losses in 1926. A ninth-inning double steal by Fred Spurgeon and Speaker, followed by Burns's single, gave the Tribe its seventh straight win, but in Chicago the Yankees won their eleventh in a row. The next day's game in Cleveland was rained out while the White Sox were breaking the Yankees' streak. Then the Indians suffered a damaging doubleheader loss to Boston, despite Burns's four doubles for the afternoon. What hurt even more was dropping the last two games of their next series, with New York, after Uhle had outpitched Waite Hoyt in the opener. Ruth left town having collected his thirty-fourth and thirty-fifth homers, his team eleven games ahead of the Indians. Nearly 60,000 people had paid to see the three games.

During the following series with Washington, which the Indians won three games to one, George Burns continued to pile up two-base hits. At various times during the season, Burns had played with a broken rib, wrenched knee, spiked foot, and bad cut on his face, which prompted Speaker to praise him as "one of the few players in the game today who possesses the stamina of the player of the old days."[22] Yet seventy or eighty years later, baseball fans could marvel at the stamina of players of the 1920s, especially the pitchers. On August 11, for example, Joe Shaute held Chicago to two runs for twelve innings, only to fall apart in a five-run rally in the thirteenth. Ted Lyons, who had joined the White Sox three years earlier directly from Baylor University, was Eddie Collins's ace pitcher, but Collins brought him in to work the final six innings and gain the decision.

After splitting a doubleheader with the Browns to close their home stand, the Indians began their eastern trip in Philadelphia by losing still another double-header, which moved the Athletics to within a game of second place. Then rain set in all along the East Coast, washing out another game in Philadelphia and idling the Indians for two days in Washington. The players occupied themselves with letter-writing, reading, and card-playing at the Wardman Park Hotel, where for their $4.00 daily meal allowance they ate in the hotel's first-class restaurant. Speaker required his players to eat at the hotels where the team stayed. He didn't want them eating in cheap places to save part of their per diem, as younger play-ers were often inclined to do.[23]

Finally the weather cleared, and the Tribe swept a Sunday doubleheader from the Senators, Uhle gaining his twentieth victory in the opener and Shaute throwing a four-hit shutout in the nightcap. After sitting out the first game, Bucky Harris returned to secondbase for the nightcap and heard boos and hoots from the grandstand for nine innings. The darling of the Capital during the previous two seasons, Harris had lost much of his popularity with a team that was barely holding onto fourth place.

Aided by Speaker's double and triple, Uhle won for the twenty-first time when the Indians split the only two games they were able to play in New York. After still another rainout in Boston, Shaute and Smith pitched the Indians to a doubleheader win. Then on Saturday, August 28, Dutch Levsen became the last big-league pitcher to work two complete games in a doubleheader. Both were four-hitters, won by scores of 6-1 and 5-1. In neither game did Levsen register a strikeout. In the first game George Burns connected for his fifty-ninth double to tie Speaker's record. According to Walter Miller's recollection, it was Burns who suggested that Levsen might be fresh enough to pitch the nightcap. When Speaker asked Levsen about it, the Iowan answered, "Sure," then proceeded to make his bit of baseball history.[24]

With seven wins in ten outings on the rain-plagued eastern trip, the Tribe cut the Yankees' lead to seven games. On Sunday, September 5, in the first game of a doubleheader with Detroit that brought an overflow crowd of 25,000 to Dunn Field, Burns hit his sixtieth double to surpass Speaker's record. As straw hats descended on the field (a traditional baseball rite signifying the end of the summer fashion season), the umpires held up the game so that Speaker could run over from thirdbase to congratulate Burns. The Tribe won that game in twelve innings, 8-7, but lost, 2-0, in the nightcap, which was halted after six innings so the Indians could catch a train to St. Louis. That loss broke their nine-game winning streak. With the Yankees idle in Philadelphia, the Tribe left town six games from first place. Each team had twenty-two games remaining.

After Cleveland and New York split Labor Day doubleheaders in St. Louis and Philadelphia, respectively, the Browns battered Uhle, 8-3. At Yankee Stadium, the Red Sox dropped their seventeenth game in a row, 4-2, putting the Yankees ahead by seven games. The Red Sox finally beat Miller Huggins's outfit the next day, but in Detroit, Cleveland's pitchers gave up seventeen hits in a 10-7 defeat. Buckeye pitched well on Thursday, but the Tigers' Sam Gibson was better, besting the big lefthander, 3-1. With another Red Sox loss in New York, the Tribe fell eight behind.

Four losses in five games over four days in St. Louis and Detroit killed Cleveland's chances—or so it seemed. From Detroit, the Tribe came home to play out the rest of the season. A four-game sweep of Washington (which had arrived on a ten-game winning streak), coupled with three New York losses and a rainout in Detroit, cut the Yankees' lead to five and a half. Now, accompanied by eight sportswriters, Ruth and company were coming into Cleveland for six games. Suddenly the Tribe was in reach of the city's second league pennant.

The five days of the New York series drew the biggest successive crowds since the 1920 World Series—perhaps 100,000 in all. But it didn't start out well for the Tribe. On Wednesday, September 15, in the rain-interrupted first game of a scheduled doubleheader, the Yankees drove out Uhle to win, 6-4. The second game was rained out, so the teams played two on Thursday. Levsen was superb in the opener, Buckeye sufficient in the nightcap. Levsen won his own game, 2-1, with a ninth-inning single that scored Glenn Myatt, after which Buckeye threw a two-hit shutout, despite walking Ruth four times and giving up six other bases on balls. Speaker doubled and scored in the seventh, when the Tribe broke through for all five runs off Herb Pennock. Now New York's lead was four and a half.

On Friday, Speaker got another masterful outing, Joe Shaute besting Waite Hoyt, 5-1, and on Saturday, with at least 5,000 people in roped-off areas, Uhle held the Yankees to four hits and a single run, while the Indians got to Urban Shocker for three runs. In the seventh inning, when Speaker came to bat with runners on second and third, Miller Huggins ordered Shocker to walk him. Speaker stepped away from the plate and yelled at Huggins, "You're crazy to pass me, a poor hitter, to get at a great hitter like Burns." Then shortstop Mark Koenig yelled in at Speaker, "Burns is all choked up" and made a choking motion. Retorted Speaker, "If he's all choked up, how about your whole ball club?" Whereupon the 5′ 4″ Yankees manager rushed from the dugout screaming and waving his fists, until umpire Bill Dineen stepped between him and Speaker and his players pulled him away. When somebody said the whole thing was just a joke, Huggins wasn't mollified: "Well, it's no joking matter."[25] After all that disruption, Burns hit into a forceout and Combs pulled down Joe Sewell's long fly to end the inning peacefully.

With their lead now only three and a half games, the Yankees salvaged the Sunday finale, played before 29,726 fans, and effectively saved their pennant. In an 8-3 rout of Levsen, Ruth hit one to deepest centerfield and outran the throw home for his forty-third home run, and Lou Gehrig put three doubles into the outfield overflow and homered over the rightfield wall. Inexplicably, Speaker didn't remove Levsen until he had pitched seven innings and given up eleven hits and all eight New York runs. Dutch Ruether, acquired from Washington three weeks earlier, was the winning pitcher. The Yankees left town with an 88-58 record to Cleveland's 85-62.

(Sharing the next day's baseball coverage on the front pages of Cleveland's newspapers were reports of a monster hurricane that had swept across Florida from the Miami area to Tampa, St. Petersburg, and Sarasota, killing hundreds of people, wreaking devastation, and, it soon became apparent, bursting the state's real-estate bubble with a pop that resounded across much of the country.)

Speaker homered in Monday's 3-2 loss to Boston righthander Fred Wing-field, with twenty-year-old Willis Hudlin, recently purchased from Waco for

$25,000, taking the defeat in relief of Sherry Smith. Even so, the Tribe picked up half a game on New York, which floundered through a doubleheader defeat in Chicago. On September 21st, Uhle threw a three-hitter at the Red Sox for his twenty-sixth win, while the Yankees pummeled White Sox pitching, 14-0. But New York's lead shrank to two games on the 22nd when the Indians gave Buck-eye five runs, four more than he needed to defeat Boston, and the Yankees lost their third game out of four in Chicago.

September 24 was an off day for the American League teams, and sports fans could concentrate their attention on accounts of Jack Dempsey's loss of his heavyweight title to Gene Tunney the previous night in Philadelphia. Then the Athletics' Eddie Rommel, a knuckleball specialist, outpitched Uhle in the first game of a doubleheader, disappointing a delegation from suburban Lakewood, Uhle's home, on hand to honor him. The second game was rained out after two innings. The Yankees, also rained out in St. Louis, gained a half game on the Tribe. The next day, while rain in Cleveland again prevented play, in St. Louis, Ruth took things in hand, homering three times (once with the bases loaded) in a doubleheader sweep that clinched New York's pennant. Two games remained for the Yankees, three for the Indians.

The next day, a Sunday, Speaker gathered his men to divide second-place money, only to see that dividend threatened when the Athletics won both games from them that afternoon. But on Monday the Indians closed their season and secured second place, defeating the Athletics, 5-4. Uhle won his twenty-seventh. George Burns lined his sixty-fourth double to establish a record that would last for eighty years and drove in the winning run in the ninth inning. The Athlet-ics still had three games scheduled with Washington over the next two days. All were rained out, leaving them in third place with an 83-67 record to Cleveland's 88-66. After their fill-ins lost a doubleheader in St. Louis, the Yankees finished at 91-63. Many years later, Walter Miller ascribed the Tribe's failure to overcome the Yankees to their repeated stumbles in games with the Browns (who fell to seventh place from third in 1925), whereas the Yankees almost swept the season series from George Sisler's team.

By hitting a single in two at bats in the season-closer, Speaker ended with a .304 average, his lowest in seven years and seventy-four points below the league leader, Detroit's Henry "Heinie" Manush. Although Speaker had 110 more official at bats than in 1925, he hit only 7 home runs and drove in 86 runners. Joe Sewell and Homer Summa both recorded higher batting averages. Besides setting a new doubles record, George Burns batted .358, drove in 114 runs, and was the choice of a panel of sportswriters for Most Valuable Player in the American League.

The ball may actually have been deadened a bit, although it was hardly "deader than a stuffed bass," as Joe Williams claimed early in the season.[26] Even with what some called the "synthetic sacrifice fly," offensive statistics were generally below what they had been in 1925. Runs scored dropped by nine percent in both leagues. Home runs fell by 8 percent in the American League, 7 percent in the National, and batting averages by eleven points in the American League, twelve in the National. Cleveland's pitching staff—led by Uhle's 27-11 record—improved its earned run average from 4.27 to 3.85. Yet if the ball was deader, apparently nobody told Babe Ruth, who returned to form with 45 homers, 145 runs batted in, and a .372 batting average.

Although they ultimately fell short, the Indians' remarkable drive toward the top during the second half of the season produced the biggest crowds at Dunn Field in five years. Home attendance swelled to 627,426, some 208,000 above 1925. At season's end, Emily Dunn seemed satisfied to hold onto the franchise and to keep Tris Speaker as her manager. Despite early season annoyances from some of the Dunn Field patrons, Speaker held his popularity with the local press and fandom. Joe Williams was rhapsodic: "His comeback with the Indians last season . . . was one of the miracles of baseball, and was typical of the gray eagle's fighting qualities."[27]

Not everybody was satisfied with the job Speaker had done. Henry P. Edwards, usually an admirer, criticized him for letting Dutch Ruether go to the Yankees and for the way he had handled his pitchers—in particular, not starting a lefthander in the final game of the September series with New York and then leaving Dutch Levsen in until the Tribe was hopelessly behind. "I am told," wrote Edwards, "that there was a lack of cooperation between Manager Speaker and some of his veteran players." Edwards also thought that "Tris should not have depended solely upon himself but should have sought the cooperation of such able lieutenants as Jack McCallister, George Uhle, Sherry Smith and George Burns, in planning the campaign." Speaker's mistakes, added Edwards, "are the result of his failure to give his job more of his time and thought." Still, prospects for 1927 were good, "if Spoke and his older players will cooperate more efficiently."[28]

Speaker was buoyant, at least outwardly. After the final game of the season, he declared, "The World Series will be played on this ball diamond next year."[29] As for the 1926 World Series, Speaker as well as Ty Cobb would leave that to others. They missed seeing the St. Louis Cardinals produce one of the Series' greatest upsets, beating the Yankees in seven games. The two illustrious player-managers, both dedicated outdoorsmen and "sportsmen," were off for the Grand Tetons to hunt big game. What awaited them upon their return would call into question their integrity and dramatically and painfully alter the course of their careers.

"A Veritable Judas"

Tris Speaker was one of the few people in baseball with whom Ty Cobb formed a real friendship, and no doubt they had a good time shooting at big game on their postseason hunting foray into the rugged area around Jackson Hole, Wyoming. Among their other kills, Speaker brought down a brown bear; Cobb shot a grizzly. Yet at night, as they smoked and relaxed in front of the fire at their base camp, they must have talked about what they were going to do when they had to pack up and return to the world they had left behind.

Before they took their train west, they had met with Ban Johnson, who confronted them with evidence consisting of two letters to Dutch Leonard—one written by Joe Wood, the other by Cobb—indicating that they along with Speaker had been parties to fixing the Cleveland-Detroit game played on September 25, 1919. Johnson then told Speaker and Cobb that this past September 9, in a secret meeting with the American League's board of directors, he had shared the contents of the letters, and that the directors had voted to turn the matter over to Commissioner Landis. Johnson assured Speaker and Cobb the whole thing would remain confidential—if they both resigned their posts and quietly retired from baseball. Nothing had been leaked to the press, but as John B. Sheridan later wrote, while they were out in Wyoming, "Cobb and Speaker might have known that the world was passing around the pith [of the evidence] from mouth to mouth."[1]

Upon their return, bringing with them "enough horns and peltry to start a museum of natural history," in Francis Powers's description, Cobb left his letter of resignation at the office of Detroit owner Frank Navin.[2] That surprised no one. Cobb was on bad terms with Navin and several of his players, and it was common knowledge that even before the season ended, Navin had told Cobb he wouldn't be rehired. With a 79-75 record, Detroit had finished only twelve games out of first place—a remarkably strong sixth-place showing. But it was still sixth place, which is where the Tigers were at the end of Cobb's first season as their player-manager five years earlier. In between, he had led them to successive third-, second-, third-, and fourth-place finishes, but Cobb's teams hadn't come close to winning a pennant. The consensus in baseball circles was that although Cobb had upgraded the batting skills of his players, especially Harry Heilmann and Heinie Manush, he had failed as a manager. Cobb also seemed finally to be slipping as a player. He batted .338 in 1926, but he put himself into only seventy-nine games. George Moriarty, Cobb's onetime teammate, resigned from the American League's umpiring staff to become Detroit's new manager.

Cobb left with bitter feelings toward Navin and toward Detroit's fandom. When he dropped in on the minor leagues' annual meeting in Asheville, North Carolina, he commented to Henry P. Edwards that "in the end the fans forget your sensational work. They made life miserable for me. They booed Tris Speaker and his team finished second. They jeered Bucky Harris and he's given them two pennants in a row. Queer game, isn't it?"[3]

Although Speaker hadn't signed his contract for 1927, Ernest Barnard remarked that contracts wouldn't be sent out until the stockholders' meeting in January, and that there was no reason for "the silly rumors" Speaker wouldn't be back. Yet Speaker seemed to be exploring his options. On November 19 he drove up to Detroit "on business" in the company of his close friend Dave R. Jones, who had become wealthy operating an auto parts plant in Cleveland on East 31st Street. Asked in Detroit about rumors that he and Cobb were interested in buying the Boston Red Sox or some other team, Speaker replied, "I'm too busy thinking about the Indians and the 1927 race."[4]

Outwardly, Speaker didn't seem worried. He and Fran traveled down to Columbus to be among the 90,000 people filling the new Ohio Stadium for the Ohio State–Michigan game, and a couple of weeks later, they visited Emily Dunn in Chicago and took in the annual Army-Navy game as part of an even bigger throng at Soldier Field. Regarding rumors that the Indians' owner might want to reduce his salary, Speaker was curt: "I'll quit the game first."[5] About to leave for the winter in California, Emily Dunn wouldn't comment on Speaker's salary or whether he would be rehired. As was the practice of that time, the exact amount of his contracts had never been made public; but for the past few seasons his salaries had been in the $30,000–$35,000 range, which made him one of the five or six highest-salaried nonexecutives in baseball.

Upon his return to Cleveland, at noon on Monday, November 29, Speaker called local sportswriters together. Nattily attired in bow tie and gray suit, he announced his resignation as Indians manager. He said he had considered quitting after the 1925 season, but "I made up my mind to stick with the team until we made a respectable showing in the championship race and then retire." Besides, he knew his legs were going. Sometimes it had become "just plain hell trying to scamper over the ground to pull down a long fly." He was "taking a vacation from baseball that I expect will last the remainder of my life."[6] Then Speaker bid the newsmen goodbye and returned to the home at 8014 Carnegie Avenue he and his wife shared with her mother. The next day, Barnard announced that Jack McCallister, long associated with the Cleveland franchise as a scout and coach, would succeed Speaker.

Speaker's explanation for why he quit was plausible—but also disingenuous. Ban Johnson had effectively bluffed him into resigning, just as he had Cobb. Johnson was satisfied that he had disposed of what he considered a strictly internal American League problem—one that didn't concern Landis, whom he despised unreservedly and had sought to undermine for the past several years. But Landis, once in possession of Dutch Leonard's letters, decided to take a hand in the matter himself. He made the long trip out to Leonard's fruit farm near Sanger, California, where on October 29 he received Leonard's version of what had happened in that September 1919 game. Then, after weeks of stewing over the situation, Speaker and Cobb demanded a hearing before Landis on whatever evidence Johnson had given him, and they insisted that they have the opportunity to confront their accuser. But when Leonard refused to leave California (perhaps, some later speculated, because he was physically afraid of Cobb), Landis called off the hearing, which he had scheduled for the morning of November 29. Evidently it was then that Speaker decided to announce his resignation when he got back to Cleveland.

The previous May, Leonard had come east from California with photostatic copies of Wood's and Cobb's letters, with the intention of handing them over to Johnson. Finding Johnson out of his Chicago office, he went to the hotel where the Washington team was staying for a series with the White Sox and showed the letters to club secretary Eddie Eynon and manager Bucky Harris. Eynon went to Johnson's home with the news, whereupon the American League president first sought unsuccessfully to find Leonard, took a train to Cleveland to discuss what he had heard with Speaker, and then went to Detroit to talk with Frank Navin, his loyal friend and supporter in league councils. The Tigers' president reported that Leonard had also showed the letters to him and to Harry Heilmann, who told Cobb what Leonard was doing. Leonard had even offered to sell the letters to a local newspaper.

Johnson and Navin decided to put a lid on matters. They had Henry Killilea, the American League's attorney, pay Leonard $20,000 for the letters, with the understanding that he would return to his California farm and keep things to himself. The $20,000 supposedly compensated Leonard for the two years in his career he claimed the Tigers had deprived him of.

Back in 1914, Dutch Leonard had recorded the lowest earned run average for a starting pitcher in American League history. Five years later, the lefthander was still a valuable commodity. In the off-season of 1918–1919, along with Duffy Lewis and Ernie Shore, he had gone from the Red Sox to the Yankees in the first of Harry Frazee's many transactions with the New York owners. Unwilling to sign for the money offered, Leonard was sold to Detroit, where he won fourteen games.

Leonard told Landis that after he won his fourteenth, from Cleveland on September 24, 1919, at Navin Field, he chanced to meet Ty Cobb, Joe Wood, and player-manager Speaker under the grandstand. Speaker, Leonard claimed, suggested that with the Indians having already clinched second place behind Chicago, and with Detroit trying to beat out New York for third place and a slice of the World Series money, he could assure everybody that the Tigers would win tomorrow's game.[7] The four players then agreed that they might as well bet some money on Detroit to win. Cobb was to put up $2,000, Leonard $1,500, Wood and

Speaker $1,000 each. Cobb suggested that Fred West, who worked on the Navin Field turnstiles and did other chores around the ballpark, would be a good man to place the bets for the players. Not scheduled to pitch in what remained of the season, Leonard left that night for Independence, Missouri.

On Thursday, September 25, in a game completed in only one hour and five minutes in wind and cold before a sparse crowd, Detroit piled up eighteen hits and won, 9-5. Speaker played his lefthand-batting lineup against righthander Bernie Boland, so Joe Wood sat out the game. It proceeded in what appeared to be a carefree manner, with neither Boland nor Cleveland's Elmer Myers seeming to bear down and batters swinging at the first pitch. Detroit led 4-0 after two innings, whereupon the Tigers apparently eased up and gave Indians batters hits on some balls that would usually have been fielded. Boland supposedly grooved pitches to let Speaker hit triples in the fifth and seventh innings. Speaker supposedly returned the favor when Boland hit one to deep center, which he allowed to roll for another triple. The *Detroit News*'s reporter observed that "Cleveland batters didn't care much whether it [*sic*] won or lost and the Tigers catching the visitors in that mood smashed their way to the top and held the advantage to the finish."[8]

The *Detroit News* also noted "the good fellowship that obtained between the two teams," adding that "Nobody would accuse the Indians of letting down in favor of their hosts, but they did not appear particularly crestfallen when the game started going against them."[9] Yet in a game Cleveland was supposed to lose and on which, according to Leonard, the Indians' manager, Wood, and Cobb had placed bets, Speaker made two triples (plus a single) and Wood didn't play at all. Elmer Myers limited Cobb, whose team was supposed to win, to a single in five at bats, although Cobb stole two bases and scored twice.

The game may not have mattered to Speaker's team, but the difference between finishing in third or fourth place that year was about $500 per man—a quarter of the season's salary for some players. It's possible that the Indians wanted to make sure the Yankees didn't get any of the World Series money. Carl Mays's fatal pitch to Ray Chapman was still eleven months in the future; Babe Ruth's sale to the Yankees was still four months away. Already, however, a lot of resentment had developed over the increasingly cozy relationship between Harry Frazee and New York owners Ruppert and Huston. That was especially true regarding Mays's desertion of the Red Sox the previous July and Frazee's quickly arranged sale of the pitcher to the Yankees, when Jim Dunn and Speaker wanted to make an offer for him themselves. Mays's logging nine wins after joining the Yankees was probably the reason they were able to edge Detroit by a half game and gain the third-place cut.

Of course the point of Leonard's claims wasn't that the September 25 game had been fixed to deny New York third place, but that it had been arranged so he, Speaker, Wood, and Cobb could win some money betting on Detroit. As Wood remembered things some forty-five years after the fact, he had charge of the money, which he gave to Fred West to make the bets. The morning after the game, "Well, this little son of a gun come down—we all knew him well—this gate tender, and we divided up the money. It was the same as betting on a prizefight."[10]

Several days later, Leonard received Wood's letter with a certified check for $1,650 enclosed. That sum included Leonard's $1,500 stake plus a third of the money won on the game, minus $30 given to Fred West as his fee. Wood's letter explained that because Detroit had been a 10-7 favorite, local bookmakers wouldn't handle that much money without approval from bigger bookmakers in Chicago. So West had only managed to place three $600 bets against the Detroit bookmakers' $420. Cobb, wrote Wood, "would have put up some at 5 to 2 on Detroit, but did not, as that would make us put up $1,000 to win $400." As it was, "Cobb did not get up a cent. He told us that and I believed him." Wood added, "If we ever get another chance like this, we will know enough to get down early."[11]

On October 23, 1919, Cobb wrote Leonard from his home in Augusta, Georgia (addressing him as "Dear Dutch"), that "Wood and myself were considerably disappointed in our business proposition. . . . We completely fell down and of course felt badly over it." The whole thing had been "quite a responsibility, and I don't care for it again, I can assure you." Noticeably missing from the two letters was any mention of Tris Speaker. Cobb mentioned only "Wood and myself." So where was Speaker, who had, according to Leonard, thought up the whole scheme?

In September 1919, Leonard was ostensibly on agreeable terms with former teammates Speaker and Wood and current teammate Cobb, but that changed dramatically. Over the next two years, Leonard pitched for poor Detroit teams, winning twenty-one decisions and losing thirty, after which he retired to run his farm. But in mid-season 1924, player-manager Cobb coaxed him into rejoining the pitching-poor Tigers, with the understanding, so Leonard later maintained, that he wouldn't be overworked.

Yet eventually the fiery, hard-driving Cobb convinced himself that Leonard had become lazy and a whiner who didn't want to pitch against tough teams, and Leonard thought Cobb was working him too hard. After several bitter quarrels, Cobb left him in to take a twenty-eight-hit, twelve-run battering by the Athletics, prompting Connie Mack to protest to Cobb that he was "killing that boy." When Leonard refused to pitch on the subsequent road trip, Cobb had Frank Navin ask waivers on him, despite his having compiled an 11-4 record. Nobody in either league claimed him for the $7,500 waiver price, whereupon Navin sold his contract to Vernon in the Pacific Coast League for $5,000. At that, Leonard quit baseball for good, leaving with an intense animosity toward Cobb—to whom he sneeringly referred as "the jewel of Georgia."[12]

In a copyrighted interview with Damon Runyon for the *Chicago Herald-Examiner* and Universal News Service, Leonard said that Speaker had pretended to be his friend and had hosted him at his home when the Tigers were in Cleveland. "He knew all the time Cobb wanted to get rid of me, but he never tipped me off." Managing a second-division team and needing pitchers, Speaker nonetheless refused to claim him on waivers, thus in effect cooperating in Cobb's determination to "railroad" him out of the major leagues. But now, he told Runyon, "I have had my revenge."[13] Obviously, it was revenge—and money—that had motivated Leonard to show his letters to Ban Johnson and just about anybody else he happened to run into.

By the time Speaker and his wife returned from a couple of weeks' stay in Texas, the major-league officials and owners were holding their annual winter meetings in Chicago. Two years earlier, at Landis's order, the American Leaguers had reprimanded Johnson for his repeated attacks on Landis's authority and voted him off the three-man major-league advisory council.[14] Now, by a 7-0 vote (with Johnson's archenemy Charles Comiskey abstaining), they restored him to the council, in an outward show of harmony in league affairs. Then the owners in both leagues voted to extend Landis's contract for another seven years beyond its expiration a year hence and to raise his annual salary by $15,000, to $65,000.

Four days later, on Monday, December 20, a United Press report out of Chicago referred to "a baseball scandal which may surpass all previous exposes. . . . It was rumored here that were certain names made public it would shake the public's confidence in baseball as it has never been shaken." When reporters sought out Landis at his little office in the People's Bank Building overlooking Lake Michigan, they found him pacing the room, "under a high nervous tension."[15] The commissioner told them that he intended to release a statement on Tuesday.

Earlier that Monday, Landis had finally met with Speaker, Cobb, Joe Wood (who traveled from New Haven, Connecticut), and Fred West (whose real name was Fred O. Grasser). Landis didn't bother to swear them in, although he did have a stenographic record taken of their responses to his questions. Cobb admitted that his letter to Wood "connected myself to the proposition," but he maintained that he had only been an intermediary—first putting Fred West in contact with Wood, then transmitting what Wood told him to Leonard. The four-way conversation under the grandstand following the September 24 game never took place. He had bet nothing on the game of the 25th, which he insisted had been played honestly, pointing out that he made only a single, while Speaker hit two triples. Cobb also said that he hadn't talked with Speaker about any betting on the game and had only asked Wood about the amount he and Leonard had got up.

Wood affirmed that neither Speaker nor Cobb had bet anything, adding Speaker didn't even know money was being wagered. He acknowledged that Leonard had approached him after the game of the 24th, and that they had agreed to place bets for Detroit to win the next day. Bernie Boland, who always pitched well against Cleveland, would be on the mound, "and in baseball the last few games of the season, with nothing at stake with a ball club, it eases up." When Leonard suggested they get down $2,500, Wood said he didn't want to bet that much, "but a friend of mine from Cleveland said he was willing to take a third of it." Wood denied emphatically that the third party to the wager was Speaker, although he wouldn't say who he was. Landis didn't push him on it.

Speaker told Landis he had "no knowledge whatever" about betting on the September 25 game or any "under the grandstand conversation." He had only learned about Leonard's accusations when Ban Johnson came to Cleveland and asked him about Wood's letter. "I had never heard of it before." He had used his regular lineup in the game in question, and "since I had the management of the club, I always tried to win every ball game." Speaker also called Landis's attention to what he had done at bat: a single and two triples in five times up. If the game had been fixed, "I certainly would not have been out there making that kind of record" and wouldn't have kept Wood out of the game.

As for Fred West, still employed at Navin Field, all he could add to the proceedings was that he had placed a bet for Joe Wood without knowing part of the money was Leonard's. He had never placed bets for Speaker or Cobb, had never heard of their betting on any baseball game. The hearing over, Cobb and Speaker demanded that Landis make public all the evidence he had, including what they had testified to that day.

On Tuesday afternoon, December 21, with Landis nowhere around, his secretary Leslie O'Connor gave out a 100,000-word collection of materials. What was released included the transcripts of the hearing held the previous day and Landis's October 29 interview with Leonard, together with the two letters to Leonard concerning the game of September 25, 1919. Landis's appended statement read: "These men being out of baseball, no decision will be made, unless changed conditions in the future require it."

The commissioner's action created a nationwide sensation and left most people dumbfounded. Bozeman Bulger of the *New York Evening World* later observed that when newspapers across the country printed everything Landis released, they were "paying telegraph tolls on more than eight solid columns of matter. It drew the same prominence and space as a President's message."[16]

Nearly everybody, so it seemed, had something to say in the matter. The vaudeville and motion-picture star Will Rogers, a good friend of Speaker's, remarked wryly that if Speaker and Cobb had been crooked all those years, he'd like to see what they could have done if they'd played honestly. But Indians president Barnard said, "There is conclusive evidence to prove that there was something wrong with the game in question." For the *Brooklyn Daily Eagle*'s Thomas S. Rice, that Landis had gone public with Leonard's charges was "already appalling, but I am convinced that if the expose had come from another source, the consequences would have been absolutely ruinous. Darn the whole mess. It has had the same effect as if a lifelong friend had suddenly died."[17]

The *Boston American*'s Nick Flatley felt about the same way: "It makes us feel like a three-year-old kid would if asked to prove that there is no Santa Claus." Tommy Holmes, Rice's Brooklyn colleague, saw it differently. Instead of fighting the charges, observed Holmes, Speaker and Cobb "took the easiest way out, which apparently speaks volumes for their inability to prove a darned thing." Irving Vaughan of the *Chicago Tribune* recalled (in the racial argot of the times) that during the major-league meetings in mid-December, "There were rumors of an Ethiopian being concealed somewhere in the woodpile." As soon as the hearing with Landis ended on the 21st, Cobb had called reporters to his hotel suite and talked at length, "and when he had finished," wrote Vaughan, "it was hard to believe that he had willfully committed a wrong." Before boarding his train for Cleveland, Speaker described himself as the "goat" of the whole affair, adding that "The only thing they have against me is the word of a man who is behind this flare-up, Leonard," and that he had been told Leonard had been out to get him ever since he waived on the pitcher in 1925.[18]

When Speaker arrived in Cleveland that night, he was met by camera flashes and a barrage of reporters' questions. "Boys," he said, "I'm going home. . . . I told Judge Landis and I say now that I never bet a dime on a game and that I never had anything to do with a game being 'thrown' or know of a game being 'thrown.'" Then he got into the passenger side of Dave R. Jones's big sedan and left the scene.[19]

The front page of the next day's *Cleveland Press* carried a photo of Speaker giving an exclusive interview to Joe Williams at the *Press* office at "a late hour" on the 21st. "Joe," Williams quoted Speaker as saying, "you can tell the world, and be right about it, that I love baseball too much to throw a game. It's just too bad that a fellow like Leonard who happens to dislike me is able to provoke such a mean situation." Speaker also personally distributed a typewritten statement to the local *Plain Dealer* and *News,* again pointing out that he wasn't even mentioned in the two notorious letters. Terming Leonard "a veritable Judas," he explained that he didn't claim him on waivers because "I knew in my heart he had run his race as a major league pitcher."[20]

In his syndicated column, Billy Evans, an American League umpire for twenty seasons and one of the most respected men in his profession, characterized Leonard in about the same way Cobb had viewed him as his manager (and Joseph Lannin had as his employer). Evans recalled that Leonard complained every time a ball was called on him, had tantrums when teammates made errors behind him, begged off pitching against teams that gave him trouble, and always wanted to pitch against predominantly lefthand-hitting lineups. Francis S. Powers thought that nobody was "so cordially hated by the American public as Dutch Leonard." As an old man, Joe Wood had lost none of his bitterness toward Leonard. "I loaned that sonufabitch $200 to buy his first motorcycle in Boston when he first joined us. Wasn't a bigger sonufabitch than Leonard."[21]

For Speaker and Cobb, Christmas 1926 was hardly merry, although in some respects it was a gratifying time. Powers reported that Speaker "was suffering from extreme nervousness upon his return from Chicago and was under a physician's care for several days." Yet when supporters began telephoning his home early in the morning of the 22nd, he dressed and went downtown, where he was stopped repeatedly by people saying they were behind him. That night he gave out a statement of thanks: "To tell the truth, the public never will know how much I have taken this to heart. I may smile and grin but down in my heart there are no smiles."[22]

While Cobb's hometown supporters held a mass rally in downtown Augusta at the foot of the flag-draped Confederate monument, "Khaki clad [telegraph] messengers," reported Joe Williams, "beat a continuous tattoo" at the front door of the Speakers' Carnegie Avenue residence. Among those sending wires were Eddie Collins and Jimmy McAleer. From Detroit came an especially affecting letter written by Theodore Hammen, a laundry foreman. Hammen wanted Speaker to know that fans like himself, who sat in the bleachers—"the rough fans," as he put it—regarded him as "a real guy." He urged Speaker to "try not to let this bother you" and "buck up old timer you are not DESTITUTE NOR NAKED YET NOR WILL BE."[23]

The week between Christmas and New Year's, several of those who had participated in the now-infamous September 25 game issued public denials that anything had been remiss. Among others, Steve O'Neill, Charles "Chick" Shorten (rightfielder for the Tigers that day), Elmer Myers, Harry Lunte (who substituted for Ray Chapman, who was in Cleveland making marriage arrangements), and umpire Dick Nallin were quoted as saying that everything had been on the up and up. Jack Graney noted that O'Neill threw out two Detroit runners and tagged out another, and that Speaker trapped a pop fly by Donie Bush, who was then run down between first and secondbase. Apropos of Speaker's two triples, Bernie Boland, now a paving contractor in Detroit, insisted, "I never gave Speaker anything in my life." Charlie Jamieson thought it all seemed "rather silly. . . . One player who obviously was playing good ball and another who sat on the bench are accused of giving away a game. It's ridiculous."[24]

The *Cleveland Press* and Scripps-Howard newspapers in other cities conducted a poll of their readers, which by December 30 showed an 800 to 12 endorsement for Speaker and Cobb in Cleveland and 1,275 to 44 in their favor elsewhere. And on New Year's Eve a drunken Clevelander found his way to the sports department of the *Cleveland Plain Dealer,* crying that Speaker and Cobb could do no wrong. James E. Doyle reported, "His tears were hundred proof tears. . . . So it has come to pass . . . that the case of Ty Cobb and Tris Speaker is driving strong men to drink."[25]

The evidence against the two men, F. C. Lane editorialized in *Baseball Magazine,* came down to "the unsupported testimony of a self-confessed conspirator who refused to meet the accused before a formal tribunal." One person, however, was willing to confirm Leonard's accusations—at least in part. In an interview with a Chicago newspaper, George Barris, now the megaphone announcer at Navin Field but its scoreboard operator in 1919, said that the Tigers' Chick Shorten told him Cleveland was going to lose and "gave me $60 to bet on Detroit about 2 o'clock that afternoon."[26] Barris said he also bet his own money—$20 at odds of 4 to 5. Landis ignored the story, perhaps because Barris also admitted he held a grudge against Cobb, who had beaten him up in 1920 after they quarreled over a crap game in the dressing room.

Then the pseudonymous Fred West made things even more confusing. Now he claimed that although Leonard's and Wood's original intent had been to bet on the September 25 game, they changed their minds when West told Wood he had a hot tip on a racehorse named Panaman, running at the Windsor track. So, according to West's new tale, he bet $400 with three different Detroit bookmakers and won $680, then hurried to the Michigan Central station to deliver the money to Wood before the Indians' train pulled out late that afternoon. By changing the version of events he had given Landis, West seemed to be making a clumsy effort to help the accused trio. In any case, Speaker, Cobb, and Wood all three dismissed it.

Although Joe Wood seemed concerned mainly with preserving his position at Yale, Speaker and Cobb—both strong-willed men, proud of what they had done in baseball, and wanting above all to clear their names—resolved not to go quietly. Cobb, as combative off the field as he was on it, was vocal to the press and anybody else who would listen, insisting over and over that he knew nothing of the plot Leonard described, that he had always played the game to the fullest. Speaker, more reticent by nature, let Cobb do most of the talking, but he had become as determined as Cobb to fight for his reputation.

After Christmas, Speaker and Cobb, together with Wood, went on the legal offensive, all three hiring high-powered attorneys. Speaker and Wood retained William A. Boyd and Edward L. Burke, both of Cleveland; Cobb retained James O. Murfin of Detroit. The following days saw much travel back and forth with their legal counsels: to Detroit, to Cleveland, and to the nation's capital. In Washington they gained sympathetic hearings with various members of Congress and officials in the Justice Department, but wherever they went, they heard the same message: in light of the exemption from federal antitrust law conferred in 1922 by the U.S. Supreme Court, Organized Baseball was immune from attack in the courts.

On December 30, Wood apparently gave up the fight and returned to New Haven to try to save his job as Yale's baseball coach. Before the university athletic director and its baseball committee, he endured still another hearing. A high school dropout with a wife and four children to support, Wood needed to keep his $8,000 per year coach's salary. What he told the director and committee members apparently satisfied them, because they announced his exoneration and retention as baseball coach (a position he held for the next sixteen years). "If Wood is not guilty at Yale," wrote Francis S. Powers, "then he is not guilty in the eyes of the country, and neither are [*sic*] Cobb nor Speaker."[27]

On December 31, Boyd and Murfin announced that they intended to meet with Landis and ask that their clients be officially cleared of any wrongdoing. The meeting had to be put off, because at the beginning of the new year, baseball's bizarre off-season took another bizarre turn—one that left head-shaking baseball writers and fans even more confused. From Rochester, Minnesota, where he worked on a dairy farm, Swede Risberg told reporters that he was coming down to see Landis with "inside information" about a baseball fix that would make the Cobb-Speaker affair "look silly" by comparison. The next day he gave a sworn affidavit to Landis that late in the 1917 season, with the White Sox in a hot pennant race with Boston, he and his teammates had made up a pot of $1,100 to bribe the Detroit team to throw consecutive doubleheaders in Chicago. When a reporter asked Risberg if Cobb had received any of the bribe money, he answered that he doubted it, adding, "There never was a better or straighter baseball player than Cobb, or Speaker, either, to my way of thinking."[28] Late in the 1919 season, Risberg said, the pennant-bound White Sox had thrown two games to help Detroit's efforts to finish in third place.

Chick Gandil came all the way from New Mexico to back up Risberg's story. The commissioner's office supposedly spent $20,000 to cover travel, lodging, and meal expenses for Risberg, Gandil, and thirty-four others who played for the White Sox or Tigers in 1917. On January 5 and 6, some seventy people—present and former players, reporters from several cities, and various kibitzers (including Will Rogers, who stood against the back wall)—jammed Landis's little smoke-filled office. Cobb, just in from Augusta, burst into the first day's proceedings to make still another public declaration of his integrity. Cobb and each of the others Landis had summoned denied Risberg's and Gandil's story and agreed on a different account—one Landis had already heard back in February 1921, when he questioned Eddie Collins and Detroit pitchers Bill James and George Dauss and found no reason to take action. Yes, the White Sox made up the pot, but only to reward Detroit's pitchers and regular catcher for defeating the Red Sox twelve times in twenty-one games. They also agreed that paying such "bonuses" to a team that had beaten an archrival was common in those years.

Of course Risberg and Gandil, whom Landis had banished forever from professional baseball, were universally regarded as crooks, even if they had been acquitted in a court of law. Like Dutch Leonard, they had seen an opportunity for revenge—in their case against baseball as a whole—and they took it. Although Risberg and Gandil stuck to their story, the two days of testimony left little doubt that they had simply lied. Convinced of that, Landis on January 12 released his three-thousand-word opinion: there had been no fix in Detroit's loss of those back-to-back doubleheaders, and although the money paid to the Tigers' pitchers was "reprehensible and censurable," it wasn't "corrupt."

Where did that leave Speaker and Cobb? On January 10, William A. Boyd said that he had been in telephone contact with James O. Murfin in Detroit, but Boyd admitted they were "just marking time." It still seemed that Landis would do nothing. Moreover, on the 13th the *Chicago Tribune* quoted "an unnamed baseball leader" as saying that regardless of what Landis did or didn't do, "Tris Speaker and Ty Cobb never again will play ball or manage in the American League," adding that the evidence in Landis's hands was only a small part of the story.[29]

On the evening of January 15, Landis announced that he intended to convene the American League club owners in emergency session to look into the *Tribune*'s story about additional evidence in the Cobb-Speaker case. Ban Johnson then called his league's owners to meet with him in Chicago at the Union Club on Monday morning, January 23rd. He admitted that he was the "unnamed baseball leader" quoted by the *Tribune* and declared himself ready for "a new fight with Landis."[30]

Johnson disclosed that for two years he had paid a Cleveland detective agency to shadow Speaker and his players and report on bets a park employee made for them, not only on horse races but on baseball games. "In one day alone," he said, "$4,200 was won by Cleveland players on a certain game. They pooled a sum of money and bet on it. I don't see how it was possible for these players to have made such wagers without Speaker knowing anything about it." Johnson professed his "love" for Ty Cobb. "We let him go because he had written a peculiar letter about a betting deal that he couldn't explain. Now Speaker was implicated in the deal by the statement of Leonard. Also I had the data of my detectives." Speaker was "a different kind of fellow" from Cobb. "For want of a better word, I would call Tris cute." If Speaker wanted to know why he was forced out, Johnson would tell him in court under oath.[31]

But two days later, Johnson began backtracking. Now he said that Cobb and Speaker had been released only for "incompetency," and that "insinuations of crookedness should never have been made about the careers of Cobb and Speaker. I do not believe they were ever crooked. They failed as managers, that's all."[32] Obviously Johnson was starting to feel uncomfortable about the position he had put himself into.

No real evidence—from Johnson or anybody else—ever surfaced that Speaker and his players bet on baseball games, although Clay Folger, still head of security at Dunn Field, confirmed that a park employee had placed bets for Cleveland players. Revealing that he was the man in question, Folger went on to say that Speaker had bet frequently on horse races—usually $10 bets—but hadn't done any betting for the past two years. Henry P. Edwards recalled that one day in 1925 the Indians received a hot tip and made up a $300 pool, with Speaker contributing $200 of that. When their horse came in first at 15-1 odds, they won $4,200 (no doubt the amount Johnson claimed they won betting on baseball). Speaker put his $3,000 share in a bank and decided he wouldn't bet anymore. As far as Edwards knew, he hadn't.

Joe Williams thought Johnson had it in for Speaker and thought he knew why. Williams dated Johnson's dislike for Speaker back to the 1921 season, when the Cleveland manager protested two games, both of which ended in critical losses to the Yankees. The first protest had to do with the refusal of plate umpire Frank Wilson to change his no-strike call on Frank Baker, even though the base umpires agreed that Baker had gone through in his swing. Johnson disallowed the protest (although subsequently he ordered plate umpires to consult with their colleagues on disputed swings). In the other protest, Speaker claimed that with

New York runners on first- and thirdbase, Roger Peckinpaugh laid down a bunt, blocked Steve O'Neill from getting to the ball, and reached first before O'Neill could make a throw, filling the bases and leading to a Yankees rally. Johnson also disallowed that one (based on batter's interference), and when Jim Dunn accused Johnson of being unfair to Cleveland, their friendship chilled. "Johnson," wrote Williams, "always blamed Speaker for their shattered friendship."[33]

Ban Johnson had once been a great man—the driving force behind the creation of the American League and, as the dominating presence on the National Commission, the most powerful figure in baseball during the precommissioner era. But he also possessed a gigantic ego and a proclivity for popping off, and he had finally overstepped himself by admitting he was the source of the *Chicago Tribune*'s report about evidence on Speaker and Cobb that Landis hadn't seen. Having endured Johnson's continual backbiting for the past six years, the commissioner saw his chance finally to quash his adversary.

The "new fight with Landis" for which Johnson had said he was ready never took place. Johnson wasn't even present when Landis convened the American League club owners at the Blackstone Hotel late on the afternoon of the 23rd. The league's president was observed in the lobby, wandering aimlessly and seemingly confused. Instead, William A. Harridge, the league's secretary, read a written statement in which Johnson admitted that "all evidence involved in the matter of the Cobb and Speaker investigation had been submitted to the commissioner."[34] The club owners then adopted a resolution whereby they "unanimously repudiated any and all criticism" of Landis by Johnson. At that point Johnson's personal physician was brought in to tell the owners the league president was ill and needed a rest, after which they voted to send him on an indefinite furlough. That finished Johnson both as Landis's nemesis and as a power in baseball's affairs. He returned from stays at Excelsior Springs, Missouri, and Hot Springs, Arkansas, in time for the 1927 season; but the following October he retired, after a twenty-eight-year reign as the architect and leader of the American League.

Cobb went to his grave hating both Ban Johnson for giving credence to Leonard's charges and Kenesaw Mountain Landis for sitting on the case for two months. Speaker never publicly made his feelings known, but he probably harbored similar resentments from that time on, at least toward Johnson. Speaker and Cobb were both mature men of the world, yet what they apparently never realized was that from the beginning, their careers and reputations had been subordinated to an intricate and ultimately decisive power game being played out by the American League's president and baseball's commissioner.

Having won, having reduced Johnson to humiliation and discredit, Landis finally did something about Speaker and Cobb. The next morning, following the long-delayed conference with attorneys Boyd and Murfin, Landis said that he would give his verdict on Cobb and Speaker later that week. Speaker, accompanied by Boyd, Ernest Barnard, and Dave R. Jones, left Chicago for Cleveland by train on the Twentieth Century Limited. Henry P. Edwards reported that Speaker and Cobb "wore broader grins this noon than at any time since the charges against them were made public."[35]

Two days later, on Thursday, January 27, Leslie O'Connor gave the press a written statement in which Landis unequivocally cleared them. "These players," announced the commissioner, "have not been, nor are they now, found guilty of fixing a ball game. By no decent system of justice could such a finding be made." In Cleveland, Speaker issued a statement that said, "I knew Judge Landis would deal fairly with the case and am glad to be back in the game."[36] Then he was off to a local gym for a workout.

At the same time that Landis cleared Speaker and Cobb, he rescinded their releases by Cleveland and Detroit, whereupon Frank Navin and Barnard notified them that their contracts would be transferred without cost to any other American League franchise. That was Landis's idea, his way of keeping Speaker and Cobb in the same league in which Johnson had insisted they would never play again. As Landis's biographer put it, "This was Landis putting his heel once more on Johnson's throat. He would force Johnson to tolerate the presence in *his* league of the two men he had hoped to expel from baseball."[37] Landis now wearily declared a statute of limitations on anything that happened before he assumed the commissionership.

What is one to make of an episode in baseball history that, like the Black Sox scandal, will always leave unanswered questions? Of all that was written about the Cobb-Speaker case in the winter of 1926–1927, the analysis offered by John

B. Sheridan, one of the sagest sportswriters of his time, was probably the most perceptive. It was foolish, Sheridan thought, for anybody to have bet on that September 25, 1919, game, because Cleveland was sure to let down with Chicago's having clinched the pennant the previous day and with the Indians having second place assured. There was no way anybody could get good odds for Detroit to lose. The smart thing would have been to fix the game for Cleveland to win. Sheridan would have bet at 3-1 odds that "Cleveland would in all probability break training on September 24 and merely go through the motions of playing on September 25."[38]

In such circumstances, Dutch Leonard had "the mentality of a 7-year-old moron of the fifth class" to try to pull off a betting coup. "The entire transaction, as alleged, shows Leonard to be unbelievably silly, and Cobb and Wood still sillier for getting tangled in it." Sheridan couldn't see anything "to justify condemnation of Speaker," whereas Cobb's mistake was in "writing a damn fool letter to Leonard—a letter which does credit to his spirit of friendship, but no credit to his acumen." Added the *Sporting News* editorially, it was all "further evidence of the necessity of never writing when you can talk, even to yourself."[39]

What conclusions might we draw? The only fair judgment of Speaker is that he was guilty of nothing except being one of the many ballplayers who regularly played the horses. Apart from what Dutch Leonard said, nothing puts him at the alleged under-the-grandstand conversation about betting on the September 25 game. Although Speaker and Joe Wood were close friends, it's unlikely that Wood ever said anything to him about his and Leonard's betting scheme. Nor did Cobb say anything to Speaker about it.

So the scheme involved only Wood, Leonard, and Fred West, although Cobb directed the players to West. From Wood's letter, it appears that Cobb also *wanted* to wager on the game but didn't, because he wanted more money to be bet than Leonard and Wood were willing to put up. Then, in a display of solicitous friendship one doesn't usually associate with him, Cobb wrote Leonard that oddly worded "Dear Dutch" letter.

It could be that the Indians *did* deliberately let Detroit win that day, not because bets were being made but because Speaker and his players wanted to keep the Yankees from gaining third place. Anybody betting on Detroit would only have been taking advantage of something that was going to happen anyway. As an eighty-five-year-old Joe Wood put it, "Things were so different then."[40] In any case, whatever took place on that day in 1919 should be understood in the same context that produced the World Series fix the next month: lax and increasingly quarrelsome governance in Organized Baseball and an ethical looseness among players that generally ended under the autocratic rule of Kenesaw Mountain Landis.[41]

Chapter 12

"A Sort of Twilight to His Career"

O n the afternoon of January 23, 1927, a few hours before the American
League owners' decisive meeting with Landis, and four days before
Landis issued his statement clearing Cobb and Speaker, newsmen observed
Speaker talking in the Blackstone Hotel lobby, first with Clark Griffith and
later with Connie Mack. In the midst of the controversy over the past months,
Speaker had said that although he had no interest in managing anywhere, he
still wanted to play baseball. Asked where he might play, he said, "I am willing
to take an oath I have received no offers. Cobb received one from Baltimore,
but they have left me alone."[1] It was generally known that Cobb was a wealthy
man—if not already a millionaire, then well on his way to becoming one. For
Cobb, playing another year wasn't a matter of money but of personal vindication, whereas with the legal expenses Speaker had incurred, he probably
needed to continue drawing a big salary.

As early as the previous fall, Cobb had received overtures from John McGraw
and Pittsburgh owner Barney Dreyfus, but Landis, determined that both Cobb
and Speaker would remain American Leaguers, had told McGraw and Dreyfus
to "lay off Cobb." Once he was cleared, Cobb received offers not only from Jack
Dunn, owner-manager at Baltimore in the International League, but also from
owner Phil Ball of the Browns and from Connie Mack. Shortly after he announced
his resignation in Cleveland, Speaker received a feeler from the White Sox but
did nothing about it. Once he was cleared and released by Cleveland, however, he
was open to offers from any of the seven other American League teams.

"Tris has a cheerful time of it these days," quipped the *New York Herald-
Tribune*'s W. O. McGeehan, "as he wanders about bargaining for himself. His

shrill cry resounds through the market place: 'old ivory for sale, but not cheap.'"[2] Actually, Speaker wasn't shopping around his aging skills as much as McGeehan assumed. Sometime between January 23 and 27, he tentatively committed himself to sign with Washington. On the 27th, at Washington's spring-training site at Tampa, Clark Griffith acknowledged as much. That night he telephoned Speaker a firm offer, later confirmed by wire. Accompanied by Fran, Speaker then took a train for Philadelphia, ostensibly to attend the Penn Athletic Club's dinner honoring veteran athletes, but actually to meet with Connie Mack and inform the Athletics' manager and part-owner that he intended to accept Griffith's offer.

From Philadelphia, Speaker proceeded to New York, where he had agreed to listen to an overture from the Yankees. Believing Speaker was still available, Miller Huggins made the train trip up from St. Petersburg, the Yankees' training site, arriving thirty-six hours ahead of schedule. The Speakers checked into the Hotel Roosevelt on the evening of January 30, and the next morning Speaker met with Huggins at the Broadway Central. After they parted, Speaker smilingly told reporters he had already agreed to play for Washington, which meant Huggins had made a round-trip of some two thousand miles for nothing. "It was a mean trick to play on Huggins," wrote Joe Vila, "but no tears should be spilled."[3]

Later that day, Speaker met with Washington club secretary Eddie Eynon, who came up to New York for the occasion, and signed his contract for a sum that was never made public. Guesses then ranged as high as a $50,000 salary plus a $10,000 signing bonus. Shirley Povich, the *Washington Post*'s sports editor for nearly half a century, probably came closest to the actual figure, which he put at $25,000.[4] That would have matched Walter Johnson's current salary, most in the history of the Washington franchise.

Speaker denied playing competing offers against each other. He wanted to play regularly, something neither Mack nor Huggins could promise him. Bucky Harris affirmed that Speaker would be his regular centerfielder, positioned between Leon "Goose" Goslin in leftfield and Sam Rice in right. The much-traveled Joe Harris, no longer needed in the Washington outfield, was sold to Pittsburgh for the waiver price. (Harris played regularly for the 1927 Pirates, batted .326, and shared in the World Series loser's money.)

Griffith claimed to have outbid Philadelphia, New York, Chicago, and Detroit for Speaker's services. According to Frank H. Young of the *Washington Post,* Speaker was a good friend of both Griffith and Harris. Fran Speaker was also a friend of Griffith's wife Addie Ann. The talk everywhere in the District of Columbia, Young wrote, was about Speaker. When his signing was announced before an American Basketball League game between Washington and Rochester, the local crowd "almost brought down the . . . roof with the stamping and cheering."[5] The price of stock in the Washington franchise had jumped by five dollars per share.

On February 8, at the annual dinner of the Philadelphia chapter of the Baseball Writers Association, Connie Mack introduced a beaming Ty Cobb and announced that Cobb had signed to play for the Athletics. Contemporaries could only speculate on the terms. In Cobb's version, he received $70,000 in salary and signing bonus, plus 10 percent of that spring's exhibition-game receipts. So Speaker's and Cobb's longtime rivalry in the American League would continue, though in different uniforms and representing different cities.

Speaker's and Cobb's departure from the managerial ranks was part of a movement away from the use of player-managers (although that proved temporary). In 1926, seven major-league teams had been directed by player-managers. At the start of the new season, only Bucky Harris, the Braves' Dave Bancroft, and Bob O'Farrell, newly hired by the Cardinals, took the field with their players.[6] Fired by the White Sox, Eddie Collins had rejoined Connie Mack as an Athletics player-coach. Phil Ball had relieved George Sisler as Browns manager (although Sisler stayed on as a player under Dan Howley).

Speaker returned to Texas with Fran and spent most of February engaged in various activities at different places. Besides tending to his affairs at Hubbard, he played the Brook Hollow golf course at Dallas, competed in calf-roping in a rodeo at Malone, and, at the end of the month, was the honored guest at a dinner given by the Dallas Salesmanship Club and Chamber of Commerce, attended by five hundred prominent men of the area. Speaker received a sterling-silver cigarette case and lighter, after which Buford Jester of Corsicana, a longtime friend and future governor of Texas, rose to eulogize him. For Jester, "The beautiful thread that has traced itself throughout Speaker's career is the devotion to his mother." Speaker, proclaimed Jester, was a national hero, the idol of Texas, and what every Texas youngster wanted to be when he grew up.[7]

When his turn came to say something, Speaker acknowledged that his legs bothered him, but his arm was "just as true as it ever was." He went on, "My eye is just as keen and my brain is just as active. I am going to work harder than I ever did in my life the coming season. I am going to give everything I have to help Washington win the pennant." Regarding his troubles over the winter, he said, "It was all black to me at first. I didn't know what to think. I knew I was innocent, but I didn't know what my friends would think and say." Wires, calls, and letters of support came in from all over the country, most of all from his Texas friends. "They all gave me confidence to face the world and the charges. I never threw a game or took part in one to my knowledge in all my life but it would kill me if any of my friends thought I did."[8]

Although Griffith claimed to have outbid everybody for Speaker's services, Connie Mack told a luncheon gathering of the Tampa Rotary Club that he had offered Speaker more money than Griffith. It was a sign of Speaker's professional integrity that he turned down Mack's proposition because he already had Griffith's offer. "This cost Speaker considerable money, I am sure," said Mack, "but it testifies to the honesty of the man. You can't make me believe that a man who would be that square could be guilty of any crookedness in baseball or anywhere else."[9]

Speaker reported to his new ball club at Tampa on March 2 and checked in at the Tampa Bay Hotel, which, according to Westbrook Pegler, the *Chicago Tribune*'s syndicated columnist, was a place of "uncommon luxury, even for a ball team."[10] The frenzied trade in real estate that had characterized the previous two training seasons in Florida was now history—decidedly sour history for those such as Bill Doak and Rube Marquard who had gone broke speculating in properties in the sometimes Sunshine State. John McGraw's grandiose Pennant Park project had collapsed. McGraw found himself owing upwards of $100,000 to creditors and people he had induced to buy lots and sections in the Sarasota area. Over the next several years, the Giants' manager spent much of his time and energy warding off lawsuits and paying off debts. What Speaker did with the lot he had purchased two years earlier at Lakeland isn't known. Presumably he disposed of it at whatever deflated value he could get.

The Senators worked out at Plant Field on a diamond laid out inside a quarter-mile sulky track. On Speaker's first day in uniform, he showed his skill at lariat-twirling, à la his friend Will Rogers. He warmed up Walter Johnson (wearing a catcher's mitt upside down), jogged, and took a few swings. That afternoon he played golf with Nick Altrock, who doubled as a Washington coach and professional baseball clown. After pinch-hitting in a loss to the Braves at Tampa, Speaker started for the first time in a win over the same team at St. Petersburg.

As the age of thirty-eight, Walter Johnson was again expected to lead Washington's pitching staff. But after consecutive twenty-win seasons in the Senators' pennant years, the great righthander had slipped to 15-16 in 1926. On March 8, pitching batting practice, Johnson took a drive off his left foot that broke a small bone just above the instep. The injury not only disabled him for four months but badly limited his effectiveness once he returned.

Seeking as much money as possible from the exhibition season, the tightfisted Griffith had the team traveling around central Florida, often on exhausting bus rides over roads that hadn't improved much since big-league teams started coming to the state. One trip of eighty-five miles to Avon Park for a meeting with the Cardinals took three and a half hours one way. Speaker batted well over his first seven games, which included four with John McGraw's Giants. With Rogers Hornsby (traded by the Cardinals for Frankie Frisch after quarreling with Cardinals owner Sam Breadon over salary and gambling debts) now with the Giants, the personnel on hand at Washington–New York games included ten future Hall of Famers.

The Senators didn't look good in their Florida games or on the seven-game tour with the Giants after they left the state. All told, they lost nine of twelve games with McGraw's team, including three of the four played at the end of the tour in Washington and New York. Hornsby, plain-spoken as always, thought Washington was the worst-looking American League team he had seen that spring.

Speaker wrenched his right knee on March 28. While the team made another long trip across the state to St. Augustine for games with the Giants, he stayed in bed, being ministered to by Washington trainer Mike Martin, who advertised that his personally concocted liniment could cure just about any ailment. Speaker didn't play again until the Senators and Giants reached Birmingham six days later. His hair may have become "as white as the picturesque plume of Judge Landis," in Pegler's description, but he could still hit a baseball.[11] Speaker batted around .500 in the exhibitions, besides managing the team for several games while Harris nursed a badly infected finger.

The previous fall, Henry P. Edwards, mulling over the batting records for 1926, had proclaimed the "elimination of the rabbit glands from the American League baseball." The next spring, editor F. C. Lane of *Baseball Magazine,* assuming that the substantial falloff in home runs represented a long-term trend, made a similar pronouncement: "The day of the home run is already past the meridian. . . . The game may never again take on the drab hues of a former generation, but it is headed that way. The orgy at bat is subsiding."[12] Again, somebody neglected to tell Babe Ruth, as well as Lou Gehrig. The coming season saw Ruth clout his majestic 60 homers. Gehrig, still only twenty-three at its outset, came into his own as one of the game's foremost sluggers, with 47 homers (more than anybody besides Ruth had hit up to then) and a record-setting 174 runs batted in.

On April 12, 1927, Washington won its season-opener at what since 1920 had been called Griffith Stadium, situated about two miles north of the White House, bounded by Georgia Avenue, U Street, Fifth Street, and W Street NW. It was decidedly a pitchers' ballpark. Although the concrete rightfield wall (covered in advertisements) was only 320 feet down the line, the wall was 31 feet high. The distance down the leftfield line was a daunting 405 feet. (Washington had no righthanded power hitters and didn't until many years later, when the distance was shortened by 50 feet.) Bleachers stretched across leftfield to Griffith Stadium's deepest point, 421 feet from home plate.

The opening-day losers were the Boston Red Sox, now managed by Bill Carrigan, who had left a comfortable life in Lewiston, Maine, to take on a team that absorbed 103 defeats in 1927 and again finished dead last. (Carrigan later said that when he returned to managing, he found his players not only lacked ability, "they didn't have any idea what baseball was all about." They were "an entirely different breed of player. . . . These players didn't talk baseball. They talked golf and stocks and where they were going after the game.")[13]

President Calvin Coolidge and his wife Grace were among the 25,000 fans nearly filling the Washington ballpark. The president tossed out the first ball, to Speaker. Stanley Coveleski and Firpo Marberry held the Red Sox to two runs, while the locals scored six times on Slim Harris. (Under the scoring rules then in place, Coveleski received credit for the win, even though he left with an aching back after only four innings, ahead 6-1.) Speaker debuted before his new home fans with two singles in five times up. Traditionally, games in Washington started at 4:30 to give federal employees time to get to the ballpark, but with games now frequently lasting more than two hours, Clark Griffith moved up starting times to 3:30.

Four days later, the Athletics arrived in the Capital after a three-game battering by the Yankees. In their first meeting in their new circumstances, Speaker and Ty Cobb both showed well, Speaker tripling and scoring twice, Cobb singling twice and driving in two runs. The Athletics scored four times in the seventh inning to give the Senators their first loss, 8-7.

If sending Stanley Coveleski to Washington after the 1924 season was Speaker's worst trade, the advice he gave Harris and Griffith about their shortstop situation was the worst he ever gave. Charles "Buddy" Myer, a native of Ellisville, Mississippi, and a graduate of Mississippi Agricultural and Mechanical College, had made a reputation in college and semipro baseball, and had received an invitation to try out with the Indians at Lakeland in 1925. Offered a contract, he was bold enough to insist on a $1,000 signing bonus, which apparently put him on Speaker's bad side for good. Myer went home, eventually signed with New Orleans, and quickly became the Southern Association's star shortstop, averaging .336 in ninety-nine games with the Pelicans. Sold to Washington for $17,500, he put in a solid rookie season in 1926, batting .304 and driving in sixty-two runs. In the off-season, Bucky Harris touted him as the key to his infield.

Myer reported to Tampa newly married, presumably expecting a bright future with the Washington franchise. Speaker, however, had convinced himself Myer would never be a major-league-quality shortstop, and once he joined the Senators, he undertook to convince Harris and Griffith that they needed to get rid of Myer and bring in a veteran for the position. Indeed, the young Mississippian was still error-prone, although in 1926 he had outhit every shortstop in the league except Joe Sewell. Speaker eventually won over the manager and franchise president. Three weeks into the season, in a straight player-for-player swap, Griffith acquired shortstop Emory "Topper" Rigney from Boston and exiled Myer to the Red Sox. "I am satisfied," remarked Harris incomprehensibly, "that Myer is not yet ready for the majors."[14]

Rigney, a native Texan, had put in a few good seasons with Detroit, then had fallen off at bat and been sold to Boston a year earlier. The Myer-for-Rigney deal, Shirley Povich wrote eight years later, "proved to be the most costly trade ever sanctioned by Clark Griffith."[15] Rigney proved a flop. Early in June, he was batting .212 and had committed ten errors in his last eight games. At that point Harris benched him in favor of former Georgia Tech football and baseball star Bobby Reeves, who had just joined the team.

(*Denouement:* Speaker may have carried a reputation for being an exceptionally savvy baseball man, but in the case of Buddy Myer, it seems his judgment failed him—or he let personal feelings override his judgment. Although Myer's batting average dropped to .281 in 1927, it climbed to .313 the next year. In the off-season of 1928–1929, Walter Johnson, Washington's new manager, got Griffith to bring Myer back by giving Boston five players, for whom Griffith had paid a total of $80,000. So Speaker's wrongheaded advice cost the Washington franchise $97,500. Myer proved one of the most durable players in the Washington franchise's history. The Senators' secondbaseman for the next thirteen seasons, he won a batting title in 1935 and compiled a career average of .303 with 2,131 base hits.)

In the early part of the 1927 season, the Senators were plagued by various injuries and illnesses. Manager Harris was on crutches after being hit on the leg by a batted ball in practice. Sam Rice went to bed with a sinus infection and later had all his teeth extracted. Goose Goslin developed pleurisy and, en route to St. Louis, had to be taken from the train and hospitalized in Pittsburgh, and for the third time, Coveleski left a game because of an aching back. (Coveleski, one of the champion tobacco-chewers in the majors, also announced that his dyspeptic condition had forced him to give up his "chaw.") All told, twelve Washington players were ailing, including Speaker, who stayed in the lineup despite a respiratory complaint.

The Senators lost three games in Chicago (although Speaker proved he could still sprint by stealing home in the last game). Then they opened a series in Cleveland on Saturday, May 14, designated "Tris Speaker Day." That morning, Speaker disappointed a delegation intending to welcome him back to the city. The well-wishers showed up at Union Station ten minutes after his train arrived, by which time Speaker had already left for his home on Carnegie Avenue.

With Goslin back in the lineup, Washington still lost to the Tribe, 5-2, Hollis "Sloppy" Thurston taking the loss and George Uhle, again nursing a sore arm, pitching the win. Drizzly weather held the Dunn Field crowd down to 8,100, although those present roundly cheered Speaker as he was honored by Cleveland's city manager, police and fire chiefs, a citizens' committee, and members of Al Sirat Grotto. The gifts bestowed on him included a chest containing $1,500 in silver, a wristwatch, and a gold-framed, life-sized oil painting of Speaker tracking a fly ball. As was often the case on such "days" honoring players, the honoree went hitless in four trips to the plate.

After two days of rain, the Senators broke a five-game losing streak, hammering Joe Shaute, Willis Hudlin, and Benny Karr for twelve runs, while Horace "Hod" Lisenbee threw a shutout. Speaker was the batting star with three singles, a double, and four runs. During his stay in Cleveland, Speaker was repeatedly asked about rumors that he was part of a group planning to purchase the Indians. Although Speaker said there was nothing to it, the rumors persisted. It was a fact that Emily Dunn wanted to sell; the reported asking price was $580,000. Dave R. Jones was supposed to be one of the parties interested in acquiring the franchise, although Jones denied that Speaker was involved in any way.

Harris's outfield was finally intact on May 23, when Marberry saved a 3-2 home-game win over the Yankees, despite homers by Ruth and Gehrig. Four days later, in the opener of a doubleheader at Yankee Stadium, Speaker stole home for the second time—one of Washington's seven runs—while Lisenbee limited "Murderers Row," as local scribes had dubbed the Yankees' high-powered lineup, to two scores. Gehrig homered and Waite Hoyt pitched a shutout in the nightcap, bringing New York's first-place record to 23-12. The next day, Ruth homered in the opener of another doubleheader, a Yankees win. Marberry outdueled Wilcy Moore in the nightcap. Speaker had to leave the first game with a swollen thumb when he caught a ball with his bare hand in practice. X-rays were negative, so he was back in the lineup in Washington for the next game, a 6-1 home loss to the Athletics. At that juncture, he was batting .313, but the team was drifting at 18-19, barely good enough for fourth place.

On Memorial Day, Walter Johnson returned to the mound and delighted 20,000 fans at Griffith Stadium by shutting out Boston on three hits. The Senators also took the second game, 13-5, but then two losses to the cellar-dwelling Red Sox prompted Harris to try Speaker at firstbase for four games in place of the injured and slumping Joe Judge and send Sammy West to centerfield. One win over the Browns followed, but three straight losses to Dan Howley's club dropped the Senators into sixth place.

After fifty-three games, Speaker had upped his average to .325, but the Senators' inconsistent mound work kept them at or a little below .500 ball. After one excellent outing, Johnson was repeatedly hit hard, and in mid-June, Griffith asked waivers on Coveleski, who had worked in only five games. When nobody in either league claimed him, the veteran spitballer received his unconditional release. Frank Young speculated that with home crowds dwindling, Griffith wanted to dump Coveleski's salary.

The Senators' play picked up in the last part of June. Going into an Independence Day doubleheader in New York, they had won ten consecutive games and moved into second place, just ahead of Philadelphia and Chicago but well behind the Yankees. A mass of humanity—a record-breaking 74,641—jammed Yankee Stadium. The vast gathering rollicked through a veritable bloodbath. Winning by scores of 12-1 and 21-1, the Yankees assaulted Thurston, Alvin Crowder, and various others for thirty-seven base hits, including five homers (two by Gehrig). Speaker, no doubt close to exhaustion from running after balls slammed by and over him, left the second game after seven innings and took his seat by Harris, who sat out the carnage with back pains.

Tony Lazzeri's homer in the ninth inning off Lisenbee won the finale of the series in New York, which improved the Yankees' record to 54-21. Still in second place, Washington trailed New York by twelve and a half games. The pennant race was virtually decided, although the Senators proceeded to sweep three straight doubleheaders in Cleveland, where, with the Tribe buried in sixth place, crowds were the smallest since 1918. Meanwhile Ban Johnson announced his resignation effective at the end of the season, adding that he wanted nothing of the eight years at $40,000 per year remaining on his contract.

Although later Speaker had good words for Bucky Harris, there were indications during the season that the Gray Eagle tended to presume too much on his status as the ball club's elder statesman. An anonymous note in the *Sporting News's* "Scribbled by Scribes" department recalled that the previous summer, Clark Griffith had criticized Ty Cobb for stopping games to come in from centerfield and argue with umpires. Now Speaker, "who, we understand, is just a private in the ranks, continually hold[s] up and delay[s] games . . . by running in from the outfield to engage the umps in useless arguments. . . . Cobb was managing a ball team when he was guilty, and Speaker—but maybe that's the catch."[16]

Whatever may or may not have been going on in Speaker's relations with his manager, he continued to play good baseball. His one hundredth base hit won the final game of the Cleveland series and pushed his average to .343. After a four-hit game in Chicago that supported Johnson's inelegant 7-4 victory, he was batting .357. At the end of the Senators' western trip, on which he batted at a .487 pace and hit his first homer of the season, his .376 mark placed him behind only Ruth, Gehrig, and Philadelphia's Al Simmons in the batting race. But even though the Senators won thirteen of twenty games (including a tie) in the west and came home fifteen games over .500, neither they nor anybody else could get within reach of the Yankees.

On August 2 the Washington franchise marked the twentieth anniversary of Walter Johnson's big-league debut. Detroit was the visiting team, just as it had been on August 2, 1907. Nearly 20,000 people—an exceptional weekday turn-out that included Secretary of State Frank Kellogg and Congressman Nicholas Longworth—were on hand to honor a man who was venerated in the nation's capital and nearly everywhere else. Billy Evans, a rookie home-plate umpire in Johnson's first game, was disabled with a twisted knee but appeared on crutches to congratulate the pitcher. Johnson received $14,746 in cash and numerous gifts, then went to the mound and got battered in a 7-6 loss.

Hampered by a sprained wrist, Speaker sat out five games before returning for a four-game series with the Yankees at Griffith Stadium. By winning three times, the Yankees extended their lead to thirteen games. Speaker replaced Judge at firstbase and doubled twice off Waite Hoyt in the finale, which New York won, 6-2. Three days later, in a divided doubleheader in St. Louis, he handled twelve chances without an error at first, was part of five Washington double plays, and hit his second home run of the season. But several balls got by him there and in Detroit, where the Tigers won all three games and knocked the Senators out of second place.

Washington went on to lose twelve games in a row in the west. In the midst of that dreary trip, in Chicago, Harris threw up his hands and had his players pull names out of a hat to determine the starting lineup and batting order—to no avail. Back home on August 30, the Senators finally ended their tailspin by scoring twice in the twelfth inning to defeat Philadelphia, 5-3, with rookie Irving "Bump" Hadley going the distance for the win. Speaker, whose batting average had dropped along with the team's fortunes, produced a double in four times up. On the twenty-second anniversary of Ty Cobb's first big-league game, Hadley walked the forty-year-old Georgian four times.

Hobbled by a sore foot, Speaker didn't appear in the next ten games except to pinch-hit for Marberry on September 18 and relieve Rice in the late innings on the 27th. Harris shifted Goslin to centerfield and put Foster "Babe" Ganzel, a recruit from Birmingham, in left. Seven straight Washington wins—three from St. Louis at home and four in Boston (where the Red Sox committed ten errors in one game)—secured a third-place finish. The Athletics, with Cobb, Simmons, and Mickey Cochrane leading the attack, were in firm possession of second place.

The Senators closed the season with three games in New York and one back home with Philadelphia. The Yankees had clinched the pennant more than two weeks earlier, so the only remaining interest in the New York series was whether Babe Ruth, who had already hit fifty-seven homers, could surpass his own record. On Thursday, September 29, Speaker watched from the dugout as Ruth struck numbers fifty-eight and fifty-nine off Lisenbee and rookie Paul Hopkins in New York's 15-4 runaway. On Friday, Speaker was only a spectator again. Lefthander Tom Zachary (reacquired from St. Louis in mid-season in a waiver exchange for Alvin Crowder) held the Yankees to two runs for seven innings. In the eighth, with the score tied and only about 10,000 people scattered around the cavernous ballpark, Ruth sent a soaring drive into the rightfield bleachers for number sixty, scoring Mark Koenig ahead of him and giving Zachary a sort of immortality.

The Yankees ended their schedule on Saturday by beating Washington, 4-3, scoring all their runs in the first inning on Gehrig's bases-loaded homer. The Yankees' victory, their 110th, was five more than any American League team had ever won. On Sunday the Senators returned to the capital and beat the Athletics, 9-5. Speaker played the ninth inning at firstbase in place of Joe Judge, only his fourth appearance in two weeks. The runner-up Athletics' loss made New York's margin a staggering nineteen games (even though Philadelphia's 91-63 record was exactly that of the Yankees a year earlier). Washington ended with an 85-69 record, two and a half games better than Detroit.

For generations to come, the 1927 New York Yankees would be acclaimed the greatest baseball team in history. That season they were about as close to perfect as a team could be. With a collective batting average of .307, they scored 975 runs (outscoring the opposition by an average of nearly three per game) and hit a record 158 home runs—of which Ruth and Gehrig combined for 107. The Yankees' pitchers showed a collective earned run average of 3.20, lowest in the majors, and pitched eleven shutouts, most in the American League.

Speaker's blistering pace in July had raised the possibility that he might win his second batting title. After that, he sputtered at the plate, played little in the last part of the season, and finished at .327, second on the team to Goslin's .334. (Harry Heilmann won the fourth and last of his odd-year batting titles with a .398 average, six points better than Al Simmons.) In 141 games Speaker scored 71 runs, drove in 73, hit 43 doubles, pegged out 24 runners, and committed 12 errors. Not a bad showing for a thirty-nine- (or thirty-eight)-year old. Ty Cobb seemed even more ageless. In what he later called his "vindication year," Cobb batted .357 in 133 games, scored 104 runs, drove in 94, and proved that he could still be a valuable asset to any team.

The Yankees capped their remarkable season by dispatching Pittsburgh in the World Series in four games. The total Series attendance of about 200,000 yielded receipts that left a $19,972 slice for the third-place Senators, who received checks for $665.73 apiece. Topper Rigney, in particular, needed the money, because a week after the season ended, he was sold to Birmingham.

Walter Johnson, who presumably didn't need the money, decided to quit after winning only five of eleven decisions and giving up more than five earned runs per nine innings. On October 15, Johnson received his unconditional release and announced he had signed a two-year contract to manage the Newark Bears in the International League. Johnson retired with 417 major-league victories (second only to Cy Young) and a record 3,508 strikeouts.

Three days later, Ban Johnson closed the door to his Chicago office for the last time, leaving the affairs of the American League in the hands of Ernest S. Barnard, his elected successor. The next month a syndicate of local businessmen headed by Alva Bradley purchased the Cleveland Indians from Emily Dunn. Billy Evans ended his umpiring career to take over the franchise's day-to-day affairs as its "general manager," the first baseball executive to carry that descriptive title.

Baseball was changing around Speaker, but he wasn't yet ready to give it up. While rumors abounded that he would return to manage Cleveland or succeed Dave Bancroft at the Boston Braves, he was off on another hunting expedition into the Grand Tetons, again in Cobb's company. Fran Speaker stayed behind in Cleveland (where the Speakers maintained their permanent residence), but the hunting party included Cobb's wife Charlie and Garland Buckeye, who had pitched creditably for the sixth-place Indians this past season, if usually with inadequate support. Speaker left after saying that he hadn't spoken with Clark Griffith about next season.

The *Sporting News*'s "Scribbled by Scribes" notes predicted that Griffith would offer Speaker a contract "so microscopic that Tris is bound to elevate his nostrils and ask for a new deal or his release. What he'll get will be the latter." According to the anonymous contributor, Speaker and Bucky Harris hadn't gotten along. "Spoke's memory appeared to be very bad. He couldn't seem to remember that he was just a plain working man." Frank R. Young also predicted Speaker's release, opining that he "did not add much punch"—that many of his hits were "push hits . . . and few were the hard-hit liners in all directions which made Speaker famous in his prime." Neither of Speaker's 1927 homers, Young noted, was hit at Griffith Stadium. Early in the season, he had stayed in the lineup even though he wasn't well and had volunteered to play firstbase, "but the fact remains that

Speaker's best was not good enough to justify the salary he is drawing, and probably will expect next year."[17]

At the major-league meetings in New York in December, nobody approached Griffith with an offer for Speaker. At the beginning of the year, Speaker acknowledged being contacted by John McGraw and by George Stallings, who was managing the Montreal International League club. All Speaker would say was that if Griffith still wanted him, he would receive a contract by the February 1 deadline, and that whatever happened, he would be in baseball in 1928.

But the aging and proud Gray Eagle wouldn't take a sizable pay cut, which finally convinced Griffith, looking at a sag in home attendance approaching 300,000 from two years earlier, that Speaker couldn't stay on with Washington. On January 23, from Tampa, Griffith announced that Speaker would be unconditionally released. Two days later, with Speaker en route from Texas to Georgetown, South Carolina, on a duck-hunting trip, Griffith made it official. Griffith didn't deny speculations in the press that he wanted to halve Speaker's salary. The Senators' president did say that his plan was to go with youngsters in 1928 (although the previous fall he had bought George Sisler's contract from the Browns for $15,000).

In Montreal, meanwhile, George Stallings confirmed he had been negotiating with Speaker, at the same time that Red Sox secretary James Price denied the Boston franchise had any interest in him. But in New York, the *World-Telegram*'s Dan Daniel got a tip from John McGraw that Emil Fuchs, owner of the Braves, intended to hire Speaker to manage—and so reported in his column. Although Fuchs announced that he would manage his team himself, McGraw kept telling Daniel, "Stay with it. Tris is the man."[18] Daniel finally decided that McGraw didn't know what he was talking about.

Speaker wasn't unemployed for long. Eleven days after his release by Washington, he agreed to terms offered by telephone from Connie Mack, who was on a golfing vacation at Fort Plymouth, Florida. In Texas, Speaker described his time with Washington as being "most pleasant." He said he had no hard feelings toward Bucky Harris, Clark Griffith, or anybody else connected with the Senators, and he called Harris "a wonderful manager, one of the greatest in the game."

Harris was equally gracious: "Spoke is a great fellow personally, and is still a good ball player."[19]

"I expect to use Tris in centerfield," said Mack, with Al Simmons in left and Edmund "Bing" Miller in right. Mack made no mention of Ty Cobb. Obviously Mack thought Speaker could still be of value to the Athletics as a player, but he probably was thinking more in terms of Speaker's ability to put people in the seats at Shibe Park, especially if Cobb decided to retire. Like the two Boston teams, the local Phillies, and the Pittsburgh Pirates, the Athletics lost lucrative home dates because of old laws prohibiting commercial amusements on Sundays.[20] Again the press speculated wildly on how much Speaker would be paid. A reasonable guess would be that despite his professed unwillingness to take a cut from Washington, he ended up signing with the Athletics for no more than $20,000.

Three weeks later, on his way back to Florida from Philadelphia, Mack stopped off at Cobb's home in Augusta to discuss contract terms. Subsequently, Athletics president Benjamin Shibe made a personal entreaty by telephone. Finally, on March 1, Cobb phoned Mack at Fort Myers, the Athletics' training base, accepting the terms and saying he would be on his way south.

Speaker was at Fort Myers by the first week in March and was providing, the *Philadelphia North American*'s Jimmy Isaminger wrote, "an example to the younger players for his untiring efforts to get in shape. He is fit and ready to go."[21] The addition of Speaker and the return of Cobb meant that the Athletics would begin the season with four players at least forty years old. Cobb had turned forty-one the previous December; Eddie Collins would be forty-one in May; Jack Quinn (born John Quinn Picus), who had been in professional baseball since 1907 and had pitched all over the North American continent, would be forty-four in July; and, at least officially, Speaker would be forty in April.

Speaker appeared the first time wearing a Philadelphia uniform in a game with Baltimore, making four hits, stealing a base, and, as Isaminger, reported it, "cover[ing] the outfield as only Tris Speaker can do it."[22] Cobb joined the Athletics on March 16 when they came up for a game with the Giants at Augusta, where John McGraw, disabused of Florida real-estate dreams, had based his team for preseason work. That afternoon, Cobb and Speaker took the field for the first time as teammates. Playing against minor-league competition as well as against the Giants, Cardinals, Braves, and Phillies, the Athletics won nine of sixteen exhibition games but, by Mack's standards, didn't look good doing it. In Philadelphia, however, they beat the Phillies five games out of six in the annual preseason city series.

Al Simmons, troubled by what was described as "rheumatism which settled in his legs," wasn't available to start the season, so Mack's outfield alignment on opening day was Cobb in rightfield, Speaker in center, and Miller in left.[23] American League president Barnard and some 20,000 others sat bundled against a cold drizzle in Shibe Park, as the champion Yankees drove out Lefty Grove after three innings and won, 8-3, behind Herb Pennock. Cobb, batting second, walked and singled. Speaker, batting third, went hitless in four tries.

Westbrook Pegler had fun lampooning Mack's elderly contingent. In the pregame ceremonies, Pegler wrote, "Cobb and Speaker tottered out to the plate," where they were each given a "radio set" (still an expensive, cumbersome item in 1928). "As they stood there with their caps off they made public two nude and glistening scalps." "The [Athletics'] mascot," Pegler went on, "is a new boy, age 9. His enrollment with the Athletics brings the average age of the club down from 49 years to 48 years, 11 months and a day."[24]

After a rainout, the two teams combined for six home runs—two by Athletics firstbaseman Joe Hauser—in another Yankees victory, 8-7. Two more losses followed in Washington before the Athletics went to New York for the Yankees' home opener on Friday, April 20. About 50,000 people were on hand for the raising of the 1927 pennant and the distribution of championship rings by commissioner Landis. As the Athletics waited through the ceremonies, Pegler joked, "the Messrs. Cobb, Speaker and Collins grew older by the minute. Delays, however minute, are dangerous to the Philadelphia ball club."[25] Yet it was Cobb and Speaker who gave the Athletics their first win. While Lefty Grove held the Yankees to a single tally, Cobb singled and tripled, and Speaker singled and hit a sacrifice fly in the ninth inning to drive home Cobb with the winning run.

On Saturday the Athletics gave the Yankees a 10-0 pasting behind lefthander George "Rube" Walberg, with Cobb making three hits and Speaker doubling, scoring, and driving in a run. Although Jimmy Isaminger had praised Speaker's outfield play in Florida, Pegler was struck by how much the pair had slowed down. "Every action of theirs now," he wrote in a less jocular mood, "is considered in proportion to what they would have done ten years ago, and, of course, this makes them look pathetic or comical."[26] Even so, they continued to hit well and helped spark the ball club to a seven-game winning streak, interrupted by several rainouts. Speaker hit two singles and two doubles in an 11-6 win over Boston. In his first appearance of the season in Washington, a 10-0 pummeling of Tom Zachary, he lined a three-run triple in support of Jack Quinn, and he doubled and homered over Shibe Park's rightfield wall (360 feet down the line) off Detroit's Elam Van Gilder to drive in Cobb with the go-ahead run in a 6-5 victory.

Winning nineteen of their first twenty-seven games, the Athletics took a firm hold on second place, but they found themselves already six games behind the Yankees, who looked to be en route to another easy pennant. At Shibe Park on May 19, Grove struck out eleven Chicago batters in a two-hit shutout. Speaker's first-inning homer over the rightfield wall gave the lefthander all the offense he needed. Two days later, in the first game of a doubleheader with Washington, Speaker collided with Bing Miller in left-centerfield. Unconscious for five minutes, he left the game with a cut on his left leg and a bruised right arm.[27] He missed only two games, returning to single, double, and drive in two runs in the Senators' eighth straight loss.

A doubleheader with the Yankees on May 25 drew an overflow crowd estimated at 42,000, the biggest in Shibe Park's history, some 9,000 more than its seating capacity.[28] Unable to buy tickets, about 3,000 determined fans cut the wire fence on the 20th Street side of the rightfield wall and scrambled over the wall to stand and sit across rightfield. The teams split that day, but the Athletics lost five of the six games in the series (taking another loss on Sunday in Washington), so that the Yankees left Philadelphia having extended their lead to nine games. In the sixth game, which New York won, 7-4, Stanley Coveleski, a free-agent signee in the off-season, was the winning pitcher despite being tagged for a two-run homer by onetime friend and manager Speaker.

With hard-hitting Al Simmons finally able to play, the Athletics began a road trip with three wins in Boston, including a Memorial Day doubleheader sweep that brought out 36,000 people, more than had ever attended a game at Fenway Park. Cobb sat out that series with a stomach complaint but returned to the lineup in Chicago. Speaker, after going hitless in two games in St. Louis, pinch-hit for Howard Ehmke in Detroit. The next day he batted once, before giving way to Bing Miller in a 13-5 win, the Athletics' third in four games at Navin Field. Then he sat out a four-game series in Cleveland.

From then on, Speaker either pinch-hit, started a game and left it, or substituted for somebody in the late innings. Cobb continued to play rightfield, but Miller had become Mack's regular centerfielder. Speaker's bad collision with Miller on May 21 seemed to have affected him more than was evident at first. Moreover, as much as Mack admired Speaker and Cobb, he finally decided that their aging legs allowed for too little outfield defense. On July 27 a pitch from Chicago's George "Sarge" Connolly hit Cobb in the right side of the chest and forced him out of the game. That was Cobb's last appearance as a regular player. Like Speaker, from then on he became a bench-warmer, watching as Mack's younger lineup—Simmons, Miller, and George "Mule" Haas in the outfield; the powerful young Jimmie Foxx at thirdbase; Mickey Cochrane behind the plate; and Jimmy Dykes alternating with converted pitcher Ossie Orwoll at firstbase—gained steadily on the injury-plagued Yankees.

After losing a July 1 doubleheader in New York, with Lou Gehrig homering twice in the opener and Tony Lazzeri doing the same in the nightcap, the Athletics trailed the champions by thirteen and a half games. By the end of the month, though, Mack's renovated lineup had won eight straight at home from St. Louis and Chicago and closed the Yankees' margin to five and a half. The Athletics went on to win ten games in a row and seventeen of eighteen before a 9-5 loss in Cleveland, in which Mack used eighteen players, including pinch hitters Speaker and Cobb. On August 3, Grove struck out eleven in a 5-1 win at Detroit, while New York lost in Chicago, pulling the Athletics to within three and a half games of the top.

(Meanwhile, in what would be a long, losing cause, American League president Barnard insisted that his league's teams had to speed up their games. Forbidding players to step out of the batter's box between pitches, he could boast an average reduction of seven or eight minutes per game that season, so that American League contests now averaged 1:55.)

On August 30, Speaker appeared in his last big-league game. Boston pitcher Red Ruffing (who put together a Hall of Fame career after being traded to the Yankees two years later) drove in two runs with a pinch-hit single off Howard Ehmke to give the Red Sox a one-run lead. Ed Morris came on in relief for Boston and struck out three consecutive pinch hitters, the middle man being Speaker.

In such undistinguished fashion the storied big-league career of the increasingly bald Gray Eagle came to an end. He played in four more games to fatten exhibition-game receipts for the Philadelphia franchise: on the Monday before Labor Day in Cumberland, Maryland, on an occasion honoring Lefty Grove from nearby Lanaconing, as well as subsequent stopovers in New Haven, Albany, and Toronto. Otherwise he sat and watched as the younger Athletics made their pennant drive.

That August, *Baseball Magazine* (editor F. C. Lane presumably doing the uncredited interviewing) talked with Speaker about his career and his present circumstances. Although Speaker wasn't "as voluble as some players are and not a particularly good man to interview . . . what he says is usually to the point." Although he admitted slowing down some, Speaker claimed his legs were still all right. Besides, he said, playing as close in as he used to "would be quite impossible now. The ball is livelier, the batters hit harder, long flies are a commonplace," and powerful throwing arms just weren't as important. Yes, a veteran outfielder "loses out in getting the jump. . . . But there is a sort of twilight to his career," Speaker insisted, "when he is still capable of playing excellent ball much of the time."[29] Maybe so, but as far as Connie Mack was concerned, the Athletics' future no longer had room for Speaker and Cobb.

On Saturday, September 7, by sweeping a doubleheader in Boston while New York lost two to Washington, the Athletics gained a tie for the lead. The next day, with the Yankees idle, they moved into first place by taking another doubleheader from the Red Sox (who, as had become their custom, had last place to themselves). It was the first time since early in the 1926 season that Ruth and company had been out of the lead.

That set up a showdown series in New York, which began on Sunday, September 9, before a paid Yankee Stadium crowd of 81,622 (plus a privileged 3,643 who got in on passes). For the Athletics, it was a disastrous sweep, 5-0, 7-3: a shutout by George Pipgras in the opener, a win in relief for Waite Hoyt in the nightcap, with Bob Meusel's bases-loaded homer making the difference. Neither Speaker nor Cobb played. (That same day Urban Shocker, an eighteen-game winner for the Yankees the previous season, died in Denver from heart disease, at age thirty-seven.) After an idle Monday, Babe Ruth hit a two-run homer off Grove to delight another 40,000 fans and give the Yankees a 5-3 win. That was Cobb's last game. Batting for Jimmy Dykes in the eighth inning, he fouled out. Max Bishop's homer in the ninth inning salvaged the series finale. Both teams then went west with New York's lead back to a game and a half.

By out-slugging the Browns on September 18 while Walter Miller outpitched Rube Walberg in Cleveland, the Yankees led by two games. Ten days later, Babe Ruth hit his fifty-third home run in an 11-6 slugfest in Detroit that clinched New York's third pennant in a row. Because Detroit was on eastern time, the Athletics learned in the late innings in Chicago that they had lost it, although they went ahead and won their ninety-seventh game, 7-5, on homers by Cochrane, Miller, and Simmons. At season's end two days later, New York's record was 101-53, Philadelphia's 98-55. Although the Athletics had dominated the rest of the league, their 6-16 record versus the Yankees proved their downfall.

In the World Series, Ruth, Gehrig, and the rest of the Yankees' wrecking crew made short work of the National League's best, sweeping the St. Louis Cardinals. Another rich Series, it produced a share of the players' receipts worth $31,480.24 for the runner-up Athletics, which added about $1,200 apiece to their year's pay.

Cobb had announced his retirement on September 17 in Cleveland. As soon as he and Speaker learned that New York had clinched the pennant, they packed their bags in Chicago and made their farewells to Mack and their teammates (seven of whom also left early). Cobb made preparations for taking his wife and three of his five children on a voyage to Japan, where he would conduct a series of baseball clinics for university teams. Speaker headed for more big-game hunting in Wyoming, saying nothing about his baseball future.

Mack also had nothing to say on the subject, although he had no more use for either Cobb or Speaker, now that the combination of players he had carefully put together over the past four years was finally strong enough to challenge the Yankees (and dethrone them in 1929). Although the Athletics' home attendance had been close to 700,000, second only to the Yankees, the money-conscious Mack had no regrets about divesting the franchise of at least $55,000 in Cobb's and Speaker's combined salaries. Early in November, Mack went through the formality of asking waivers on Speaker and Cobb, then announced their unconditional releases.

Jimmy Isaminger had an idea what Speaker's future would be. "It is understood," Isaminger reported, "that the Silver King will buy a part of a minor league franchise."[30] In the aftermath of Jack Dunn's death, Speaker had shown tentative interest in the Baltimore franchise. Meanwhile Clark Griffith had dismissed Bucky Harris, who quickly signed to succeed George Moriarty at Detroit, and Paul Block had released Walter Johnson from his two-year contract so that Washington's all-time favorite could return to the Capital as Senators manager.

Speaker later revealed that one night at his hunting camp in Wyoming, he heard a news report on a small battery-powered radio that Block hoped to be able to hire him to replace Johnson. As soon as he returned to Cleveland from the wilds, he was on a train to Newark to meet with Block and franchise president William Sinnott. On November 11, Sinnott gave out a press release announcing that Speaker had signed a two-year contract to manage as well as play for the Newark Bears. No salary figure was disclosed. Two years later, Joe Vila exaggerated it at $40,000. Probably it was about what the Athletics had paid him. "Suffice it to say," wrote G. A. Falzer in the *Newark Sunday Call,* "that Newark fans are elated over the prospect of seeing the veteran outfielder in action with the Bruins and confident that the Gray Eagle back of the Newark team will be as powerful as the eagle back of a silver dollar."[31]

Then Speaker and Fran returned to Hubbard to see about his mother, who was in increasingly frail health. While he was there, he received telegrams of congratulations from Walter Johnson, Connie Mack, and John McGraw (who must still have been scratching his head about why he hadn't paid more attention to Speaker at Marlin back in the spring of 1908). After a few weeks in Texas, Speaker was off to Toronto to attend the annual minor-leagues' convention and look around for some likely deals.

Speaker's playing record for 1928 was the worst of his career over a full season (if appearances in only sixty-four games can be considered a full season).

He ended with a lackluster .267 batting average, hit 3 home runs, drove in 32 runs, and scored 28. Though charged with only 3 errors, his outfield range was much below what it had once been. Cobb didn't cover a lot of the Athletics' right-field either, but he had nothing to apologize for offensively, going out with a .323 batting average in 353 times at bat. His 114 base hits pushed his career total to 4,191—a statistic that stood for fifty-seven years. At his retirement, Cobb was the all-time leader in games played, runs, runs batted in, career stolen bases, steals in one season, and many other categories. It seemed unlikely that anybody would ever win twelve major-league batting titles in thirteen years.

Like Babe Ruth later on, Cobb would have nothing to do with managing in the minor leagues. Richer than any professional athlete had ever been and destined to become much richer still, Cobb spent the remaining thirty-three years of his life without reconnecting in any official way with baseball. For Speaker, a proud man but not as prideful as the great Georgian, the rest of his life would be quite different. Like Walter Johnson, Speaker was willing to return to the minors to manage and even to be a player, in order to stay in the game he loved. Yet he would find himself in circumstances very unlike those he had known for the last twenty years in the Big Show.

"My Name Is Tris Speaker"

J ust across the Hudson River from the mighty expanses of Greater New York, Newark, New Jersey, had always been a minor-league city (except for one year in the Federal League). Yet it was a city with a distinct history and, in the 1920s, a generally prosperous economy. Especially with the opening of the Port of Newark in 1915 and the postwar concentration of much of the nation's chemical industry in and around the city, Newark had grown rapidly. When Tris Speaker arrived to take over the local Bears, Newark's population was close to 450,000, so that it was not only one of the minors' biggest cities but bigger than Washington and Cincinnati as well. Yet since joining the International League in 1921, the best showing Newark's entrants had managed was third place in 1927. The following year, under Walter Johnson's mild-mannered direction, the Bears had tumbled to seventh.

After that dreary season, Paul Block had paid about $360,000 for the Newark franchise, thereby relieving Charles W. Davids of debts that had driven him into receivership. Much of Davids's financial woes had to do with what he had spent for a new ballpark, which opened at the beginning of the 1926 season (and was then called Davids Stadium). It was located at Hamburg Place and Avenue K in the East Ward, an area populated mostly by first-generation immigrant families and called the "Ironbound" because it was enclosed by three railroad tracks. Block Stadium (as it was now named) was an excellent upper-minor-league facility that seated about 15,000. It had short foul lines (305 feet each way) and a maximum centerfield distance of 410 feet. But it was also inhospitably located near a garbage dump, which in summer made the site decidedly odoriferous. In other words, Speaker's new home grounds represented a considerable comedown from the big-league facilities he had been used to.

As did accommodations at the second-rate hotel in St. Augustine, Florida, where the Bears held their spring training. Jack Onslow, who had played with three major-league teams and with Buffalo's 1927 pennant-winners, served as Speaker's coach and sometime scout. Besides Onslow, Speaker found a mostly veteran contingent at St. Augustine. The average age of the players reporting to him was greater than that of the 1928 Philadelphia Athletics, despite all the to-do Westbrook Pegler had made about Connie Mack's graybeards.

Among Newark's aging veterans were Wally Pipp (thirty-six), the man Lou Gehrig had displaced at firstbase with the Yankees; Vic Aldridge (thirty-three), who had pitched in the World Series for Pittsburgh only two seasons earlier; Al Mamaux (thirty-three), a seventy-six-game winner in twelve big-league seasons; Jimmy Ring (thirty-four), a National League pitcher for twelve years; catcher Bill Skiff (thirty-three), who had had a couple of brief turns in the majors; infielder Russ Wrightstone (thirty-three), a nine-year National Leaguer; outfielder Merwin Jacobson (thirty-five), who had starred for the Baltimore Orioles for six of their seven consecutive International League pennants; and two players Speaker had managed at Cleveland: Jim Bagby (thirty-seven), who had shared with Speaker the glory of the 1920 championship, and outfielder Cliff Lee (thirty). Early in the season, Rube Lutzke (thirty-one), another former Indian (and still not much of a hitter), replaced Wrightstone at thirdbase. Speaker's few younger players included outfielders Max West (twenty-four), who had been with Atlanta in 1928, and little John "Jocko" Conlan (twenty-five), a Newark returnee.[1] (Both advanced to the big leagues, but Conlan's future Hall of Fame credentials were built on his twenty-four years as a National League umpire.)

For the most part, the twenty-six minor leagues starting the 1929 season—classified from Class AA to Class D—operated quite differently from what today's fans are used to. Under Branch Rickey's innovative front-office direction, the St. Louis Cardinals already possessed an expanding system of minor-league franchises, from which, at relatively little cost, the Cardinals had assembled most of the players on their 1926 and 1928 pennant-winners—as well as the talent that had taken Rochester to the 1928 International League pennant. Within another ten to twenty years, all the major-league teams had followed the Cardinals' example and put together at least skeletal "farm systems." As of the late 1920s, however, the majority of minor-league franchises remained in the hands of independent owners, who turned their profits (if any) by selling tickets and selling players for whatever they could get on the baseball market.[2]

So in the upper minors, rosters included many men who had played at that level for several seasons or who were former big-leaguers. Some of the latter hoped for another shot at the Big Show. Others, resigned to the fact that their time at the top was over, were playing out their careers in the minors because they lacked either the wherewithal or the desire to do otherwise. Speaker's task was to try to mold a bunch of mostly has-beens into a winning combination.

After playing through their exhibition schedule in Florida—which included four losses in six games to Speaker's former Athletics teammates—Newark opened the season at home on April 17. Speaker received a traveling bag in pregame ceremonies, then went out to centerfield, batted twice, and gave way to Conlan in an 8-5 loss to Montreal, with onetime Yankees and Red Sox lefthander Hank Thormahlen pitching the complete-game win. Despite cold, gloomy weather, the game drew a near-capacity turnout.

Although the International League's schedule concluded earlier than that of the majors, it crammed 168 games into twenty weeks. Except for rainouts, International Leaguers enjoyed no off days and played more scheduled doubleheaders than the three holiday twin bills major-league teams played. They also spent a lot of time traveling on day coaches in a league that stretched from Baltimore to Montreal and Toronto and included Jersey City, Rochester, Buffalo, and Reading, besides Newark.

The Bears lost two more games to Montreal and nine of their first twelve, but then, with Speaker limiting himself to pinch hitting, they improved to 13-10 and briefly held second place, behind Rochester. By the end of May they had sagged into the second division, and Paul Grealey, the *Sporting News*'s Newark correspondent, was writing that "manager Speaker's patience has about reached the breaking point, game after game slipping away as the result of inferior pitching and careless fielding."[3]

Despite his team's lackluster play, Speaker still got some fun out of the game.

At Baltimore, after base umpire Carroll ejected Bill Skiff, shortstop Bobby Stevens followed with a single. As Stevens led off firstbase, Speaker, from the third-base coaching box, yelled, "Slide, Bobby, slide!"[4] Carroll, fooled into thinking Stevens had taken off, ran toward secondbase, only to find that Stevens was still at first. Speaker shook with laughter, but the embarrassed umpire didn't find it a bit funny and thumbed Newark's manager out of the game.

Speaker put himself into the lineup at Reading and hit a home run and two singles in a 10-9 win. Two days later, in a 15-10 loss, he made three doubles and stole home. On June 13, after thirty-four official at bats, Speaker was hitting .382. With Max West in centerfield and their manager playing most of the time in right, the Bears revived and built their record to 39-33, putting them back in second place, although Rochester still led by five games. Then came another slump—eight losses in ten games and a dive to sixth place, whereupon Speaker took himself out of the lineup.

Playing only occasionally, he saw his ripely aged team drift in the bottom rungs of the league week after week. At the end of July, following an unsuccessful trip to the northern cities that left Newark nine games under .500 and in seventh place, Speaker lit into his players, talking more harshly for the record than he ever had before. "Never in all my baseball experience," he fumed, "have I seen so many cliques on one ball team. I made a mistake last winter when I failed to start a general housecleaning. But I was led to believe . . . that I had a smart ball team and one that should be in the running from the start." Jack Onslow, just returned from a scouting trip, had failed to turn up any good young talent. "But if I remain in Newark," vowed Speaker, "I'll revamp the team if I have to sign up a bunch of semi-pros." Acknowledging that he wasn't popular with some of the Bears, he said, "I know the players are panning me behind my back. I've been accused of playing favorites when I'm merely trying to put together a combination that will win."[5] Speaker praised Jocko Conlan, Bobby Stevens, pitcher Carl Fischer, and a few more. Others he accused of just going through the motions to pick up their paychecks.

Despite his unhappiness in his managerial role, as a player Speaker had little trouble with International League pitching. Starting on August 6, he played every day for a week, making six hits in seven times up in a Sunday doubleheader split with Baltimore at Block Stadium. But after August 13 he didn't even put himself in to pinch-hit. He had appeared in forty-eight games, made 49 hits in 138 times at bat for a .355 batting average, scored 36 times, hit 5 home runs, and driven in 20 runs. From then on, he just watched as his team continued to play mediocre baseball.

Only because Reading went into a late-season slump could Newark—by taking the season's last game from the hopeless Jersey City Skeeters (winners only fifty-one times)—slip into sixth place, with a mark of 81-85. Although that was a notch better than Walter Johnson's Bears had done the previous season, it still left Newark twenty-one games behind the Rochester Red Wings. Again consisting mostly of young players developed in the Cardinals' farm system, Rochester won going away, ending with an eleven-game margin over Toronto.

Before he left for Texas, Speaker singled out Vic Aldridge as more responsible than anybody else for Newark's poor showing. Aldridge won only two games, drank heavily, complained of an aching arm, went home to Indiana without Speaker's permission, and earned a suspension for the rest of the season. But there was plenty of blame to go around. Observed Grealey, "during most of the campaign they were just making it a ball game."[6]

Speaker's first season of managing in the minor leagues had been a frustrating one, probably the most frustrating of his baseball career. Although his contract ran for another year, he could have resigned anytime he felt like it. That would have meant giving up an extraordinarily handsome minor-league manager's salary, and by late 1929 Speaker wasn't in a position financially to take that step. Like many other baseball people and tens of thousands of other Americans, Speaker had invested heavily in what had looked like a boundlessly booming stock market. Two weeks after the end of the World Series (in which the Athletics trimmed the Chicago Cubs in five games), the great bull market crashed. By mid-November 1929, about $30 million in stock values had evaporated.

How badly Speaker was hurt in the crash was never made public. Many years later, the *Chicago Tribune*'s John P. Carmichael wrote that Speaker and Harry Heilmann had lost half a million dollars between them, although he didn't specify how much each lost. In any case, it seems a safe judgment that the immediate effects of the stock-market collapse, together with the sagging market for beef cattle, left Speaker needing to earn a good salary. Continuing under his contract at Newark was his best option—maybe the only one at the time.

So, nearing his forty-second (or forty-first) birthday, he returned to St. Augustine to try to ready himself and his team for another season. He started out with a considerably revamped roster. The previous fall, Max West had been sold to Brooklyn and Vic Aldridge and Jocko Conlan to Toledo. Jim Bagby and various others had been released, and Wally Pipp, Merwin Jacobson, and Rube Lutzke received their releases at St. Augustine. Al Mamaux, Bobby Stevens, and Carl Fischer were among the holdovers. Andy Cohen, unrealistically touted two years earlier as Rogers Hornsby's successor with the New York Giants, was Speaker's thirdbaseman.

The weather was generally unfavorable in Florida, as it was in the northeast, although Newark and the World Series champion Athletics managed to get in an exhibition game that drew a full house to Block Stadium. But three days of rain delayed the opening of the season until April 19, at home versus Buffalo. Ralph Shinners, now in his fifth year in the minors after four National League seasons, hit a three-run homer in the ninth inning to tie the game. The Bears scored in the bottom of the tenth to win it, 5-4.

A promising beginning, but by late May, having won only nine of twenty-six games, the Bears were dead last, and Speaker had put himself in rightfield in an effort to get some punch into the lineup. The season was turning into another unhappy experience, made worse for Speaker when, on May 23, he received word that his eighty-four-year-old mother had died the previous night at her home in Hubbard. Speaker played the next day in a loss at Baltimore. Then he and Fran boarded a train for the long trip back to his hometown. Besides her famous son, Nancy Jane "Jenny" Speaker was survived by six daughters. A widow for thirty-one years, she was buried in Fairview Cemetery alongside her husband.

With his ball club floundering, Speaker needed new talent. But when nineteen-year-old Joe Medwick, from nearby Carteret, New Jersey, approached Speaker and asked for a tryout, the Newark manager told Jack Onslow to send the boy on his way; he was too young for the competition. Just as John McGraw had missed his chance to sign Speaker in the spring of 1908, Speaker missed his chance with Medwick. Medwick signed with the Cardinals' organization and, after two years of battering pitchers in the Mid-Atlantic and Texas Leagues, began a big-league career leading to the Hall of Fame.

On Thursday, June 26, following a four-error, 10-5 loss at home to Montreal, Speaker decided he had had enough. In disgust, he announced his resignation and left town. Onslow managed the Bears for one game before Block and Sinnott gave the job to Al Mamaux. In his last playing season, Speaker had appeared in only eleven games, getting thirteen hits in thirty-one at bats for a .419 average.

Besides negotiating several player deals, Mamaux also abandoned the free-hitting style Speaker had favored and used more sacrifice bunts, squeeze plays, and other elements of old-fashioned "inside baseball." Under Billy Southworth, Rochester cruised to its third pennant in as many years, but the rest of the league was more spread out than in 1929. Although the Bears ended up in fifth place, they had a worse record and finished farther from the top than in the previous season.

On September 7, Speaker was present in Boston at Braves Field for the first of the many "Old Timers'" gatherings he attended during the next three decades. In a fund-raising event for the local Children's Hospital, he joined Harry Hooper, Duffy Lewis, Joe Wood, and other former Red Sox and Braves on a team of "All-Bostons" matched against a group of "All-Stars," consisting of such luminaries as Eddie Collins, Stuffy McInnis, Jack Barry, Ed Walsh, and Chief Bender. They played a regulation nine-inning game, won by the All-Bostons, 8-4. Hooper made three hits, Speaker two. Lewis doubled twice. Ty Cobb even made an appearance as a pinch hitter, to the delight of the crowd of 22,000.

Later that month, in Chicago, Speaker visited in the Comiskey Park broadcast booth as Jack Graney—the first former big-leaguer to develop a career in radio—did the play-by-play for a Cleveland station. Luke Appling, who had just joined the last-place White Sox from Atlanta, messed up a couple of plays, which prompted the sparse crowd to give him a hard time. "I may be wrong," Speaker commented, "but those fans who are booing this kid at shortstop are going to see him in this league for many years and they'll wind up cheering him."[7] (Appling spent twenty years with the White Sox, won two batting titles, and ended up in the Hall of Fame.)

That was probably Speaker's first experience in a radio broadcasting booth, at least while a game was underway. By the next spring, however, he had signed with a Chicago station to handle play-by-play for both White Sox and Cubs games. It was demanding work, at which the inexperienced Speaker seemed less than adept. Apparently his contract wasn't renewed for 1932. He needed whatever he was paid for speaking in Pasadena, California, at a dinner for local dignitaries associated with the annual Tournament of Roses. On the eve of a soggy New Year's Day game between Tulane University and the University of Southern California, Speaker remarked that Californians always claimed rainy weather was "so *unusual*." "That's the bunk," he continued, "and I know it." He recalled spring training with the Red Sox in 1911, when it rained for two weeks. "Why don't you guys—you natives and synthetic natives—admit that it *does* rain out here once in a while, and that you're darn good and glad to get it."[8] Maybe Speaker intended his remark to be taken humorously, although it's doubtful the proud boosters of southern California sunshine took it that way.

According to a cryptic note in the *Sporting News,* Speaker spent part of 1932 as "business manager of a road show."[9] Then came another opportunity to get back into baseball. George Muhlebach, owner of the American Association's Kansas City Blues, was in financial trouble. Like many other minor-league operators, he was hard hit by what came to be called the Great Depression—the economic doldrums into which the country had sunk following the stock-market collapse. With the Kansas City franchise in receivership, Lee Keyser, co-owner of the Des Moines Western League club, moved to acquire it in partnership with Speaker and Speaker's old friend Joe E. Brown. How much of the $40,000 purchase price Speaker put in isn't known, but in January 1933 he and Keyser arrived in the city and concluded the deal. Keyser would be franchise president, with Brown (who was in Hollywood filming *Elmer the Great*) serving as vice president.[10] Bill "Raw Meat" Rodgers, former Des Moines manager, would be franchise secretary and business manager. Speaker would manage the team but wouldn't do any playing.

Muhlebach Field, title to which George Muhlebach continued to hold, was rented to the new owners for $4,600 per season. Located at Twenty-second and Brooklyn Streets, it seated about 15,000 and had cost Muhlebach $400,000 to build in 1922–1923. It was also the home of the Kansas City Monarchs, who had hosted the Hilldale club in the first Negro League World Series in 1924. (For Blues home games, seating at Muhlebach Field was racially segregated; for Monarchs games, it wasn't.)

Lee Keyser was one of the most significant minor-league figures of his time. Starting out selling scorecards at Sportsman's Park in St. Louis, he worked for both the Browns and the St. Louis Federals. He sold advertisements during the war for the camp newspaper at Camp Dodge, outside Des Moines, and stayed on in Des Moines to become secretary and then co-owner of the local Demons. At Des Moines in May 1930, Keyser promoted the first game in Organized Baseball played under fixed-in-place lights, going into debt to pay for the $25,000 lighting system. Although the major leagues resisted night ball until 1935, it quickly spread across the Depression-ravaged minors. When Keyser and his partners acquired the Kansas City franchise, Muhlebach Field was already equipped with lights.

Keyser and Speaker had known each other since 1908, when Keyser saw the young outfielder in action at Little Rock and recommended him to owner Robert Lee Hedges of the Browns, who wasn't interested. They had sustained a friendship over the years; now that friendship paid off in putting Speaker back in charge of a team and making him at least a junior partner in a baseball franchise.

Thomas Hickey, president of the American Association, predicted that league attendance, which had plunged in the midst of the hard times, would revive in 1933. He was encouraged about the situation in Kansas City, which had fielded a sixth-place team the previous season and drawn smaller crowds than the Monarchs. Describing Keyser as a "mixer" who had made the rounds of civic clubs to pump up enthusiasm for the Blues, Hickey added that "Speaker, too, has been doing missionary work," visiting with stockyards workers and other people and preaching baseball.[11]

All to no avail. In 1933, Speaker managed the worst team with which he was ever associated, relative to the level of competition. The Blues were stuck in last place almost from the beginning of the season, and by mid-August their record was a dreadful 48-76. As an example of how they played, on the 23rd of that month, in a night game at Muhlebach Field with Indianapolis, they held a 6-0 lead before giving up ten runs over the last three innings. It got so bad that a week later the Blues blew a three-run lead and lost an exhibition game to St. Joseph of the Western League.

Shortly thereafter, Keyser, Brown, and Speaker gave up control of the franchise to Johnny Kling, a Kansas City native and the celebrated catcher for the Chicago Cubs pennant-winners of 1906–1908 and 1910. After purchasing a majority of its stock, Kling relegated Keyser to vice president and business manager and replaced Speaker with Nick Allen, former St. Paul manager. Speaker remained as a stockholder, but Joe E. Brown simply gave his shares to a friend with the comment, "I don't like to be last"—by which presumably he meant both on the field and at the ticket windows.[12] The Blues straggled in behind everybody else with a 57-93 record, forty-three games worse than pennant-winning Columbus (still another Cardinals farm club).

After his second disagreeable experience with a minor-league operation, Speaker had no official connection to professional baseball for the next fourteen years. At the end of 1933, national prohibition ended with the repeal of the Eighteenth Amendment. Within a couple of months, Cleveland newspapers were carrying ads for a wholesale wine and liquor dealership called "Tris Speaker, Inc." The company was the exclusive Ohio distributor for various French, British, and Scottish firms and had its own brand of "Gray Eagle" bourbon. Advertisements proclaimed: "Tris Speaker Signs Up Great Array of Stars."[13] In this post-big-league venture, Speaker finally had some success. After years of consuming liquor of dubious quality, thirsty Ohioans welcomed the availability of spiritous beverages whose labels accurately stated their contents.

Meanwhile, Speaker became actively involved in promoting semipro and amateur baseball. In 1936, for example, he helped set up a series of baseball clinics in Ohio public schools, helped organize the state semipro tournament for the National Baseball Congress (NBC), and traveled to Wichita to open the NBC's national tournament. His prestige value became even greater in January 1937, when it was announced that he, Napoleon Lajoie, Cy Young, and the late John McGraw had been elected to the National Baseball Hall of Fame, scheduled to open two years later at Cooperstown, New York, site of baseball's mythical invention by young Abner Doubleday.

The election was conducted by the membership of the Baseball Writers

Association of America (BBWAA), which required that a candidate be named on three-fourths of the ballots. In the first round of balloting the previous year, Ty Cobb, Babe Ruth, Honus Wagner, and the late Christy Mathewson had been chosen. None had been elected unanimously. Speaker's 168 votes meant that 18 percent of the BBWAA's membership didn't think him worthy of election—at least at that time. Even more puzzling was that Cy Young barely made it, named on only 76 percent of the ballots.

That summer Speaker was back in Chicago, again working on broadcasts of White Sox games, sponsored by the Kellogg Company. Kellogg also financed a program of free baseball clinics, with Speaker and former American League batting champion Lew Fonseca traveling around Chicago to work with the city's youngsters.

In the spring of 1938, Speaker took advantage of another business opportunity, when he became Ohio sales representative for the Rotary Electric Steel Company of Detroit, operating out of an office in the Guardian Building in Cleveland. After years of Depression-era financial uncertainty, the fortunes of Tris and Fran Speaker had turned around nicely. He still had his liquor distributorship, and they were comfortably settled in a two-story home they had bought a few years earlier at 17303 Invermere Road in fashionable Shaker Heights, a good eight miles east of downtown Cleveland.

Then, on April 11, Speaker suffered an injury that brought him closer to death than anything in his playing career. As he was trying to put up a flower box on the upper porch of his home, the railing of the porch gave way, and he fell sixteen feet onto a stone walkway. Badly bleeding from falling onto the jagged surface of the walkway, Speaker got up, walked to a nearby lawn chair, and sat down to await the ambulance his wife had called. At Lakeside Hospital, Edward B. Castle, his personal physician, found that Speaker had a fractured skull, as well as broken left arm and wounds extending from his left eye to his neck, requiring one hundred stitches. Castle described Speaker's condition as critical. The ordinary person, he added, would have been knocked unconscious by the impact of the fall, but "he has taken care of himself and I think he'll make it." Within a week, Castle said that Speaker's condition was "quite satisfying."[14] Among the visitors during his hospital stay were Cleveland mayor (and future U.S. Supreme Court justice) Harold H. Burton and Bob Feller, the Indians' eighteen-year-old pitching phenom.[15]

By August, Speaker, still "a trifle wobbly from the skull fracture," felt fit enough to appear in street clothes at an Old Timers' game in Cleveland's Municipal Stadium. In the hope of attracting the 1932 Olympic Games, and on the eve of the Great Depression, the city had gone deeply into debt to finance construction of the enormous multipurpose facility.[16] Now it served as the occasional home of the Indians, although most of the time they still played in what was again called League Park. About 20,000 people were present for the Old Timers' event, which was staged to raise funds for the Cleveland Amateur Baseball Federation. Cy Young, Napoleon Lajoie, Bill Wambsganss, and Elmer Smith were among the city's past baseball heroes on the field.

That winter, Kyle Crichton interviewed Speaker for the popular weekly magazine *Collier's*. Crichton found him sitting at a table in a three-piece striped suit, a cigarette in one hand and a pencil in the other, his hair thin and totally white. After reminiscing about playing the outfield with Duffy Lewis and Harry Hooper, the deciding game of the 1912 World Series, and Duster Mails (whom he described as his most disappointing player), Speaker held forth on contemporary centerfielding. On that subject he made an argument to which he would return many times over the next twenty years. "It's true that the ball is livelier," he said, "but any good outfielder can go back for a drive even when it's hard hit. By playing a few steps up, he can grab balls that are now falling safe." The previous summer, he had so advised the Yankees' brilliant young Joe DiMaggio. That afternoon, DiMaggio grabbed two drives at his feet and went back for only one, but the next day he was again playing too far back. The trouble, Speaker thought, was that the lively ball "has everybody scared."[17]

By 1939, Speaker's activities had become even more diverse. Although he gave up his liquor distributorship, he continued with Rotary Electric Steel, became vice president of a leather belt company, agreed to serve as chairman of the Cleveland Boxing Commission, and did a daily radio program for local station WGAR, in which he gave baseball scores and reviewed the pennant races. He also ran a ten-week baseball school in Boston, sponsored by the Kellogg Company and Socony-Vacuum Oil, shuttling back and forth by train between that city and Cleveland. After the Boston school ended, he went out five nights a week to show the official American League film *Play Ball* in settlement houses around Cleveland and enthusiastically promoted the local Baseball Federation. Eliot Ness, famed for his days as a crime-fighting federal agent in Chicago and now Cleveland's safety service director, testified to baseball's influence in reducing what had come to be called "juvenile delinquency."

On June 12, 1939, Speaker was in Cooperstown, New York, for the opening of the National Baseball Hall of Fame and Museum and the induction of the first class of Hall of Fame electees. Some 10,000 people jammed the village, where about 2,500 normally resided. The ceremonies began with a ribbon-cutting at the building's entrance by Commissioner Landis, National Association president William G. Bramham, and league presidents Ford Frick (National) and William Harridge (American). Three electees were deceased: John McGraw, Christy Mathewson, and Willie Keeler. Of the eleven living "immortals," ten were present on the platform: Speaker, Babe Ruth, Cy Young, Walter Johnson, Honus Wagner, Grover Cleveland Alexander, George Sisler, Eddie Collins, Napoleon Lajoie, and Connie Mack. (Ty Cobb showed up late, claiming missed train connections, although the probable reason was that he wanted to avoid Landis.) Beginning with Mack, each man said a few words. Speaker simply agreed with Mack that it was the most memorable day of his life.

It was undoubtedly that—at least one of the most memorable. But at the beginning, election to the Hall of Fame didn't carry with it the cachet it later acquired. Decades later, retired ballplayers would shamelessly campaign for their own election and enlist others in their behalf, in large part because being in the Hall of Fame substantially increased one's market value in commercial endorsements, merchandising agreements, and paid public appearances. It didn't much help Speaker or the other original inductees. As Grover Cleveland Alexander, alcoholic and down on his luck, put it when he was informed of his election, "The Hall of Fame is fine, but it doesn't mean bread and butter. It's only your picture [actually a plaque] on the wall."[18]

Later that summer, Speaker was the subject of a minor brouhaha when he was quoted as saying he could name fifteen outfielders better than Joe DiMaggio. After several sportswriters insisted they heard him say just that, Speaker wired the

Sporting News that he had been misquoted. "I am not insane," he protested, "and only an insane person would have made such a statement as I am supposed to have made. You can definitely quote me as saying that in my opinion, DiMaggio is one of the greatest outfielders of all time."[19] Yet Speaker never stopped thinking that DiMaggio and outfielders in general were playing too deep.

Over the next couple of years, Speaker regularly appeared at Old Timers' games and other public occasions. One of the city's most esteemed citizens, he continued to serve as Cleveland's boxing commissioner. When Indians president Alva Bradley named Lou Boudreau, his twenty-four-year-old shortstop, to succeed Roger Peckinpaugh as the Tribe's manager, Speaker was all for it. "The kid's got moxie and aggressiveness and fire," he enthused. "He'd give the Cleveland club its first inspiration from the field in 15 years" (that is, since the last year Speaker managed the Indians). "It does seem like sending a boy to do a man's job, doesn't it?" wrote Speaker's old friend Joe Williams (who had moved into the bigtime with the *New York World-Telegram*). "But no man since Tris Speaker has been able to handle the job, so maybe a boy is what's needed at that."[20]

A few days later, the Japanese attack on the American naval base at Pearl Harbor brought the United States into the global conflict that was already being called the Second World War. Organized Baseball, given President Franklin D. Roosevelt's "green light" for continuing under wartime conditions, promoted war-bond sales and other causes in a succession of Old Timers' games, as well as All-Star games between teams of major-leaguers in the armed forces.

In July 1942, following one such All-Star event in Cleveland's big stadium, a cold that had been bothering Speaker progressed to pneumonia. Examinations at Lakeside Hospital revealed that he also had a perforated intestine. Given his run-down condition, the surgery that followed was precarious. For the second time in his life, Speaker came close to dying. Fran Speaker, the only visitor allowed, quoted him as saying, "I'll win this game, just the same as I've won hundreds of others." Released late that month, he went "down home" to the farm at Hubbard for several weeks of convalescence.[21]

His health restored, Speaker was available for more war-bond rallies in baseball settings, such as Old Timers' games at the Polo Grounds in August 1943 and at Griffith Stadium in July of the next year. Babe Ruth, Walter Johnson, Honus

Wagner, Duffy Lewis, Eddie Collins, and Lefty Grove were some of the former adversaries and teammates with whom he appeared, all of them wearing the contemporary uniforms of the teams they had played for.

Speaker remained with Rotary Electric Steel, which prospered in the wartime market for its products. "That's what I'm in now, steel. And I'm loving it," he told Ward Morehouse, who interviewed him during the cocktail hour in the "4 and 20" bar at Cleveland's Hotel Carter. "I've got a lot of friends around here," he said as he acknowledged greetings from arriving regulars. "I've been very lucky." Now a partner in Rotary Electric Steel, he was "busy as hell." Although he saw all the games he could, he had "no desire to be connected with baseball again." Still, he had some definite opinions about today's game. Pitchers, he said, "burn themselves out by not getting enough work"; and, yes, DiMaggio was a great centerfielder, but he still played too deep.[22]

Speaker went on to reminisce about Ty Cobb and Cy Young, the storied eighth game of the 1912 World Series, Ray Chapman's death, and celebrities he had known, such as Fred Stone, Joe E. Brown, and the late Will Rogers. He still liked to hunt and play golf, but "The biggest kick I get these days," he told Morehouse, "is having kids come up and speak to me—kids who weren't even born when I quit." Although he had kept the farm at Hubbard, he and his wife (who came in during the interview) continued to reside in Cleveland. "It isn't that I like the town so much," he explained, "it's that I know a lot of fine people."[23]

Over the years, Speaker associated himself with several charities in the Cleveland area, of which the most gratifying was probably his work with the Society for Crippled Children (SCC). At a Rotary Club luncheon in March 1944, he received the SCC's Distinguished Service Award for his eight years of involvement with the charity. Later, in an interview with local reporter Howard Preston, Speaker acknowledged having once had a phobia about crippled people—"a natural distaste for people whose bodies weren't strong," as he phrased it. But he underwent a change of heart when SCC president Frederick T. McGuire took him on an auto ride to Camp Cheerful, a summer facility for crippled children outside the city. As he watched the youths play softball, having "fun playing . . . in their own style," Speaker was "moved, I tell you. I guess you could say I just found out their way of thinking and living. I was sold."[24] Now he was vice president of the SCC and chairman of the local Easter Seal Committee. He visited Camp Cheerful frequently, raised $44,00 for the SCC, and helped find employment for handicapped adults.

Speaker continued to be in demand at gala baseball events and on various other occasions. On the night of August 4, 1944, for example, he was present as one of the eleven players Connie Mack named to his all-time All-Star team. To celebrate Mack's fiftieth anniversary as a manager, nearly 30,000 people were present at Shibe Park, including Kenesaw Mountain Landis (in one of his last public appearances before his death within a few months). The morning after Christmas, Speaker was a guest on the National Broadcasting Company's popular *Breakfast Club* radio program. When emcee Don McNeill praised his .344 lifetime batting average, Speaker said that such an average was good enough to win in the current wartime competition, but "when the boys come back, I think it will be different."[25] Then, late the following August, he took part in a welcoming ceremony at Municipal Stadium for Bob Feller upon his return from navy service. That night, 46,477 people paid to see Feller receive one of the first Willys-Overland Jeeps produced for the domestic market, then pick up where he had left off in 1941, striking out twelve Detroit batters en route to a 4-2 victory.

Baseball at all levels boomed with the return of peacetime, and Speaker traveled all around the country to appear at amateur baseball tournaments and speak at banquets and civic events. By that time he had become proficient on such occasions, speaking "with the ease of a professional story-teller," wrote the *Cleveland News*'s Ed McAuley, and in a baritone that retained little of the Texas twang he had brought with him to the big leagues.[26]

Early in 1947, despite his disavowal a few years earlier of any interest in returning to baseball, Speaker once again became affiliated with the Cleveland Indians' organization. He found himself working for a franchise president unlike any he had ever encountered. The previous summer, thirty-one-year-old Bill Veeck had put together a syndicate that purchased the Indians from Alva Bradley and associates. William Veeck Sr. had been president of the Chicago Cubs until his death in 1933, after which his son had left Kenyon College to work for the Cubs in a variety of jobs. In 1941, Bill Veeck and former Cubs manager Charley Grimm bought the American Association's downtrodden Milwaukee Brewers and quickly turned the team into a wartime winner. Shunning neckties and wearing open-neck sport shirts in any weather, young Veeck brought in crowds with promotions and innovations (even scheduling some home games at 8:30 A.M. for the convenience of workers coming off nighttime shifts in war plants). Easily bored, Veeck joined the marines in 1944 and served in the Pacific theater. An artillery accident crushed one of his legs, which eventually had to be amputated below the knee. (Over the years, more and more of the leg would have to be taken off.)

Brash and iconoclastic, Veeck undertook to reinvigorate a Cleveland franchise that had finished sixth and fifth, respectively, in the last two wartime seasons. By staging pregame auto shows, beauty contests, and a variety of giveaways and stunts, and exploiting the drawing power of Bob Feller, Veeck was able to produce a franchise-record attendance of 1,057,289, even though the 1946 Indians were again a sixth-place team that still played much of the time at League Park. As of the next season, Veeck announced, the Tribe would play all its home games in Municipal Stadium.

Initially, Veeck hired Speaker to spread goodwill for the franchise and to accompany him on a dizzying round of off-season speaking engagements. Speaker also agreed to work as a coach during the Indians' spring training at Tucson, Arizona, joining Bill McKechnie and Al Lopez on Lou Boudreau's staff. On the ballfield every day in uniform, Speaker took as his special project outfielder Dale Mitchell, who in 1946, with Cleveland's Oklahoma City farm club, had led the Texas League in batting. Mitchell was a naturally talented hitter, but he needed help with his outfield play, which is what Speaker was to give him. Nearing his fifth-ninth (or fifty-eighth) birthday, Speaker had no trouble deferring to Cleveland's twenty-nine-year-old manager. Though "suave and accustomed to being interviewed," Ed McAuley wrote, Speaker was careful to check with Boudreau before talking about any of the Tribe's players.[27]

Also at Tucson was Rogers Hornsby, who had been in and out of Organized Baseball since his firing by the St. Louis Browns ten years earlier—and was out again at present. Veeck hired him to impart his knowledge of hitting to some of the hit-shy Indians. Unlike Speaker, Hornsby deferred neither to Boudreau nor anybody else and freely expressed his opinions, solicited or not. McAuley surmised that "Hornsby was the 'outsider' of the brain trust—that the sooner he left camp, the better Boudreau would like it."[28] Over Hornsby's protests, Veeck finally reassigned him to work with the Oklahoma City players at "Indianville," the Tribe's minor-league complex in Florida.

When the 1947 season began, Speaker resumed his role as a public-relations representative for the Indians, and continued to attend special congregations of old ballplayers. On September 22 he was at a Boston Braves–Brooklyn Dodgers game in Brooklyn in the company of Harry Hooper and Duffy Lewis, the Braves' longtime traveling secretary. After the game, the trio proceeded to Boston for a dinner in their honor attended by eight hundred people, including manager Billy Southworth and the entire Braves team. Then it was back to New York to join Ty Cobb and other former American Leaguers at Yankee Stadium in a two-inning game played in honor of cancer-ravaged Babe Ruth, who had only eleven months to live. Speaker and Cobb, both looking robustly healthy at well over two hundred pounds each, posed for photographers with the frail, shrunken Babe. Proceeds from the paid crowd of 25,000 went to the Babe Ruth Foundation for needy children. Speaker stayed on in New York for the World Series (won by the Yankees from Brooklyn in seven games).

Although Speaker had reconnected with baseball as an Indians employee and, unlike Cobb, didn't demean today's game and players, he still chided out-fielders for playing too far back and for other deficiencies. In an interview in Cleveland, Speaker and Jack Graney both criticized the tendency of players to make a "button-hoop loop" on their way to secondbase after hitting the first-base bag, instead of touching first with their left foot and driving off for second. Modestly omitting himself, Speaker observed that "Cobb and Collins and all the other great base-runners all followed this pattern." Graney added, "players don't know—or seem to care—which foot they're going to hit the sack with."[29]

In the spring of 1948, Speaker, now officially designated an "advisory coach," again reported to Tucson, joining Boudreau and seven other regular or tempo-rary coaches. Although Speaker continued to work with Dale Mitchell (who had batted .316 in his rookie season), Boudreau had given him a new special project. In July 1947, four months after Jackie Robinson made his debut with Brooklyn, Veeck had broken the American League's color line by purchasing Larry Doby, a young secondbaseman, from the Newark club of the Negro National League. Encountering a mixed reception from teammates and often hostility from opponents, Doby appeared in only thirty-two games, mostly as a pinch hitter, and batted an anemic .156.

With the veteran Joe Gordon firmly ensconced at secondbase, Speaker's assignment was to turn Doby, who had never played the outfield, into the Tribe's regular centerfielder. It wasn't going to be easy for either Speaker or Doby, who started spring training at Tucson listed last on Boudreau's outfield roster. Moreover, away from the ballpark, Doby was separated from the rest of the players, because in 1948 and for some years thereafter, the hotel where the Indians stayed wouldn't admit black people. Doby had to lodge with a local black family, which meant that he couldn't take his meals with the rest of the team and had to be transported to and from the ballpark separately.

Speaker worked with Doby daily, not only on fly-shagging and fielding grounders but on batting and sliding (working in the sliding pit all the teams used back then). Speaker admonished his charge that even though some pitchers would throw at him, "Just stay in there, and show them they can't drive you away. Knock that ball down their throats. They never keep throwing at a good hitter. And you're a good hitter, kid."[30]

Doby later gave Speaker full credit for making him a big-league player. He homered in his first exhibition game, hit another in the second game of the season, and convinced Boudreau and Hank Greenberg, Cleveland's general manager, to keep him on the roster after the May 20 cutdown date. From there Doby went on to bat .301 and hit thirteen more homers in 121 games (although he led outfielders in both leagues with fourteen errors). Named American League Rookie of the Year, he was a major reason why Boudreau's team won Cleveland's first pennant in twenty-eight years, beating the Red Sox in a tie-necessitated one-game playoff and then defeating the Boston Braves in six games. Ahead of Doby were twelve more solid big-league seasons and eventually the Hall of Fame.

As long as he was employed by the Indians, Speaker was obliged to hit the banquet circuit in the off-season, which made it hard for him to keep his weight down. Wide-girthed and jowly by now, he flew to Tucson early in 1949, again to work with Doby, who was still shaky on line drives hit right at him. Speaker also thought Doby ran the bases poorly, because he had a "football mind" that caused him to run as if he were dodging tacklers.[31] (Doby had been a halfback in high school in Paterson, New Jersey.)

Late in March, Speaker was in Hollywood as the guest on Ralph Edwards's *This Is Your Life* program on NBC radio. The show's format had acquaintances coming on to surprise the guest with greetings and reminiscences. Bill Wambsganss, Harry Hooper, John "Chief" Meyers (the Giants' catcher in the 1912 Series), and Lefty Weisman (still the Tribe's trainer) were live in the studio. Joe Sewell called from Alabama, and Bob Hope, a native Clevelander and a minor stockholder in the Indians, added luster to the program by calling from Palm Springs (although he and Speaker barely knew each other).

Bill Veeck continued to try to draw crowds any way he could, such as staging an Old Timers' game between members of the 1920 and later Cleveland teams and, with the Tribe running well behind the Yankees and Red Sox late in the 1949 season, ceremonially burying last year's pennant at home plate. But that fall, with home attendance having fallen nearly 400,000 from 1948's record 2,620,627, Veeck and his partners sold out to a group headed by Clevelander Ellis Ryan. Although the new ownership reduced Boudreau's corps of springtime assistants, Speaker stayed on in both his public relations and tutoring capacities.

Of the many Old Timers' galas in which Speaker participated over the decades, one of the most memorable took place in Dallas at the start of the 1950 Texas League season. Dick Burnett, the multimillionaire owner of the Dallas Eagles (and incidentally, Speaker's second cousin), moved the Eagles' home opener into the vast Cotton Bowl. A record minor-league throng of 53,578 paid to watch bands march, swimsuited young women parade, the famed Rangerettes of Kilgore Junior College go through their drills, and the *pièce de résistance*: the introduction of Dallas's "starting lineup," consisting of Tris Speaker, Ty Cobb, Dizzy Dean, Mickey Cochrane, Charlie Gehringer, Frank Baker, Travis Jackson, Duffy Lewis, and Eagles manager Charley Grimm. All except Lewis and Grimm were either present or future Hall of Famers. The nine took the field, Dean walked Tulsa leadoff man Harry Donabedian on four pitches, and the Old Timers gave way to the Dallas regulars, with Donabedian returning to the plate to begin the game officially.

The following December, the Texas Sportswriters' Association established a Texas Sports Hall of Fame and named Speaker as the charter member. Hank Greenberg was the main speaker at a luncheon honoring him in Dallas a few weeks later. Speaker, Greenberg remarked, didn't dwell on past glories, unlike others who "left the game and became embittered by the lack of attention of fans and sports writers who have turned their attention to the new stars."[32] (Although Greenberg named no names, he may have been thinking of Ty Cobb, a chronic complainer about how much baseball had changed.)

Joined by big Luke Easter, a powerful firstbaseman also signed out of the Negro leagues, Larry Doby put in a splendid 1950 season for the fourth-place Indians. The following January, local baseball writers honored Doby as Cleveland's "Man of the Year." He acknowledged his debt to Veeck and various others before turning to Speaker, "who taught me so much in a few weeks."[33] The relationship between Doby and Speaker never became one of true friendship—color always divided them (as it did most of their fellow citizens)—but Speaker continued to take pride in his protégé, and Doby remained grateful.

In New York a few weeks later, Speaker was one of sixteen Hall of Famers who were the guests of National League president Ford Frick at festivities commemorating the seventy-fifth anniversary of the league's founding. Ward Morehouse, in attendance at the commemorative dinner, described Speaker as "vital and silver-haired, wearing a jaunty blue sports coat," and still talking about how "wonderful" everybody had been at the Texas Sports Hall of Fame banquet.[34]

At least once a year, Tris and Fran Speaker returned to the Hubbard area, where Speaker would don a Stetson and cowboy boots and visit around with relatives and friends. In July 1951 he combined such a down-home stay with an appearance at a Texas League Old Timers' Game at Buff Stadium in Houston, plus a surprise visit six days later to a semipro tournament in Beeville, where he presented the championship trophy.

In addition to the usual wintertime banqueting, Speaker and Ed Bang, the *Cleveland News*'s sports editor, appeared on Ed Sullivan's *Toast of the Town* television show to present to Sullivan a gold clock Joe Jackson had been supposed to receive on the program, in honor of Jackson's election to the Cleveland Baseball Hall of Fame. Jackson had died six days earlier, so Sullivan had the clock sent to Jackson's widow in Greenville, South Carolina.

Besides the unfortunate "Shoeless Joe," a number of Speaker's other baseball contemporaries were already gone or soon would be. As early as 1946 a stroke had killed Walter Johnson, Babe Ruth had lost his struggle with cancer in 1948, Lee Keyser had died in 1950, Dick Burnett followed in 1955, Al Simmons died in 1956, as did Connie Mack at ninety-three, having given up managing the Athletics only five years earlier. The passing of such men undoubtedly touched Speaker, but that wouldn't have been the case when, in 1952, he learned that Dutch Leonard had died in California.

Speaker, Joe Jackson, Cy Young, Napoleon Lajoie, Steve O'Neill, Joe Sewell, and four others from later Indians teams were inducted into the Cleveland Baseball Hall of Fame, officially opened in August 1952 behind the Municipal Stadium firstbase stands. That fall, Ellis Ryan, Bob Hope, and other stockholders lost control of the Cleveland franchise and sold their interests to Hank Greenberg and his supporters, who elected Myron H. Wilson, a wealthy insurance company owner, to the franchise presidency. Having survived the second change of ownership since being employed by the Indians, Speaker was at Daytona Beach, Florida, the following spring to work with the Tribe's minor-leaguers.

Speaker's public life continued to be busy. In June 1953, he and several other sports celebrities were guests of President Dwight D. Eisenhower at a luncheon preceding the annual game between congressional Democrats and Republicans. "I called him 'Mr. President' and he called me 'Tris,'" Speaker said afterward. "Having lunch at the White House and sitting at President Eisenhower's table, that really was one of the high spots of my life."[35]

Now wearing horn-rim spectacles and described as "a roving coach for the Indians," Speaker returned to Daytona Beach in the spring of 1954 to tutor players in Cleveland's eight-team farm system.[36] He and his wife continued to be seen regularly at Municipal Stadium, occupying their box behind the Indians' dugout. On July 12, the eve of the annual All-Star Game (which Cleveland hosted),

Speaker began experiencing chest pains. He was rushed to Lakeside Hospital, where physicians quickly determined that he had suffered a severe heart attack.

A generation later, Speaker would have received anticoagulant medication and, as soon as his condition stabilized, been put on his feet and walked. He would also have been instructed to follow a low-fat, low-sodium dietary regimen. He may even have undergone coronary-bypass surgery. At that time, though, the standard treatment was rest and quiet (as it was for President Eisenhower following his heart attack the next year). Speaker may have been advised to lose weight and quit smoking. Although he appears to have slimmed down some, he didn't give up his cigarette habit.

Speaker spent nearly three weeks at Lakeside, abed or sitting nearly all the time. He watched telecasts of Indians games, during one of which he saw Larry Doby leap against Municipal Stadium's five-foot wire fence in centerfield, grab a ball hit by Washington's Tom Umphlett, and then fall over the fence into the bullpen. Speaker telephoned the stadium press box to say, "Tell Larry he gave the old man a big lift."[37]

By mid-September, Speaker was back in his Municipal Stadium box, watching the Indians conclude a sunny season in which they not only won the pennant but set an American League record with 111 wins—one more than the 1927 Yankees and enough to end the current Yankees' five-year run at the top. But the 1954 World Series was a debacle—a four-game sweep by the New York Giants. Speaker didn't go to New York for the first two games, but he and Joe E. Brown sat together in Municipal Stadium for the Tribe's other two losses. Before game three, a photographer asked Speaker to pose with Willie Mays, as if he were giving the Giants' young star tips on how to play centerfield. "Nothing doing," said Speaker. "He doesn't need any advice I can give him. He can stand on his own."[38] Later he remarked to Brown that Mays could become one of the greatest players ever (which indeed he did).

At Daytona Beach in the spring of 1955, Steve O'Neill, fired as manager of the Phillies the previous season, and Joe Sewell joined Speaker in working with Cleveland's farmhands. Then, early in May, Speaker was in Boston, first for a banquet honoring Hall of Fame members put on by the Sports League of B'nai B'rith, then for a program at Fenway Park the next day. Wearing a double-breasted tan suit, Speaker posed with Harry Hooper and Duffy Lewis, who wore current Boston uniforms. (Neither Lewis nor Hooper was a Hall of Famer, although sixteen years later, Hooper was elected by the Veterans' Committee.) J. G. Taylor Spink, publisher of the *Sporting News,* thought that Speaker "looked fine, thoroughly recovered from his illness of last September [*sic*]."[39]

On July 21, Speaker helped emcee an Old Timers' game in Beaumont, Texas, staged the night before the Texas League's All-Star Game. Sides made up of former Texas Leaguers went through a three-and-a-half-inning exhibition for the 2,874 who paid to see it, plus various dignitaries, including Ford Frick, baseball's commissioner since 1951. Dizzy Dean, by now a popular television figure, pitched an inning wearing slacks, white shirt, and necktie, his girth having become so immense no uniform would fit him.[40]

Eight days later, Speaker was in New York along with seventeen other Hall of Famers for dinner at Toot Shor's famous restaurant. In his remarks, Speaker praised Joe DiMaggio (who had retired four years earlier). Eighty-eight-year-old Cy Young urged support for Little League baseball, and Yankees manager Casey Stengel spoke for forty-eight minutes in the recondite manner sportswriters had labeled "Stengelese." The next afternoon, a crowd of 31,000 at Yankee Stadium watched ex-Yankees play a few innings against a collection of other former American Leaguers. Speaker, dapper in bow tie and sports coat, sat it out, as did Ty Cobb.

On November 4, Cy Young died at Peoli, Ohio, near the Tuscarawas Valley farm where he had lived until recently. Speaker was present for the funeral services and Young's burial in the local Methodist cemetery. Bob Feller, Ed Walsh, Sam Jones (from nearby Woodsfield), and Billy Southworth, among other baseball notables, also attended. The next month, Speaker flew to Dallas to present a plaque to Rogers Hornsby, on the occasion of Hornsby's induction into the Texas Sports Hall of Fame.

The spring of 1956 saw Speaker again working at the Daytona Beach complex. The season brought more appearances at commemorative events, such as Hall of Fame night in Kansas City (where the Athletics had moved after the 1954 season) and Bob Feller Day in Cleveland, at which Speaker served as emcee, and the great pitcher, who had announced his retirement, received gifts and cheers from 28,457 people, who occupied about a third of Municipal Stadium's seats. (That season the second-place Indians drew only 865,000 at home, less than a third of their 1948 attendance.)

At Daytona Beach the following spring, Speaker suggested that Ted Williams had come close to being the greatest hitter of all time, although he said he wouldn't compare players of his day and today, insisting, "I do not live in the past." But later that year, as he watched Yankees slugger Mickey Mantle bat at Municipal Stadium, he remarked to the *Boston Globe*'s Harold Kaese, "Pitchers never to try to brush Mantle back—Williams either. It wasn't like that when I played. They brushed me back, and they threw at Ty Cobb. Nobody was safe. Maybe pitchers aren't as mean now."[41]

That summer, Speaker, Feller, Hornsby, Steve O'Neill, and Mickey Cochrane conducted a series of baseball clinics organized by Bill Veeck for Detroit-area youngsters, and on August 11 Speaker was on hand to congratulate Feller upon his induction into the Cleveland Baseball Hall of Fame, along with the late Bill Bradley. He capped another busy baseball season by attending games three, four, and five of the World Series in Milwaukee, where the former Boston Braves had set new National League attendance records and won that franchise's third twentieth-century pennant. Speaker was probably as surprised as most people when Milwaukee took the seventh game at Yankee Stadium from the favored New Yorkers.

In the spring of 1958, the colorful Bobby Bragan, who had replaced the gentlemanly Al Lopez as Cleveland manager, asked Speaker to work with the big club at Tucson rather than with the farmhands at Daytona Beach. Bragan had eight other coaches on hand, including Olympic sprinter Harrison Dillard, who gave running tips. Wearing his spectacles and a uniform but shod in sneakers rather than spikes, Speaker stood daily behind the batting cage, refusing Bragan's offer of a chair. One day a foul ball smashed through the cage and cut Speaker's lower lip. After getting the cut bandaged, he was back at his post, giving each batter the same reminder: Keep your swing level.

Speaker suffered a worse misfortune when his Cadillac was stolen from the ballpark lot, and although it was found three days later, missing were his golf clubs, camera, and fishing equipment. It had taken him years to build up his collection of tackles and lures, and he said that instead of recovering the Cadillac, "I'd rather have recovered the fishing gear."[42]

Bragan insisted upon a tightly structured routine at Tucson. Each evening he and his coaches held long conferences about the day's practice and the team's progress. Afterward coach Bob Kennedy distributed a mimeographed schedule detailing each player's assignment for the next day. Despite all that effort, the 1958 Indians never rose above mediocrity. Early in July, the mercurial Frank Lane, now the Tribe's general manager, fired Bragan and replaced him with Joe Gordon.[4343] Gordon and Lane had a long conference with Speaker and decided to send him on a scouting mission. His assignment was to look over National League pitchers for trade prospects (with interleague trading now permitted). The aging Spoke flew from city to city but turned up nobody who could help a team that finished in sixth place, the Indians' poorest showing in twelve years.

Speaker never stopped reproaching outfielders for positioning themselves too far out. That summer he had two more opportunities to air his views—on Buddy Blattner's *Baseball Corner* network television show and in a column J. G. Taylor Spink wrote in the *Sporting News* after talking with him at Municipal Stadium. "With the lively ball in use today," Speaker told Blattner, "outfielders can't play in as close as I did, but they don't get a chance to get those line shots when their backs are against the wall." To Spink he said, "You see some outfielders playing so deep today I have to shudder." Outfielders, he advised, should measure their playing areas from the fence behind them rather than from home plate.[44]

On Saturday, August 16, Speaker was at Yankee Stadium, to visit again with onetime teammates and adversaries at the Old Timers' game the Yankees had made an annual event. Speaker, Cobb, Hornsby, George Sisler, and Babe Ruth's widow Claire were among those introduced to the 67,916 people who almost filled the stadium. Then members of the 1946 Red Sox and 1947 Yankees played a couple of innings.

Two weeks later, Speaker was hospitalized after experiencing pains in his arms. Released several days later, he remained in Cleveland and continued to make regular trips to Municipal Stadium to don a uniform and work before games with Billy Moran, a light-hitting rookie infielder, and outfielder Woodie

Held, recently acquired from Kansas City. With the Indians' lackluster season finally over, he passed up the World Series (this time a Yankees victory in seven games over the Braves), and he and his wife readied for an automobile trip back to Texas. They planned to spend several weeks relaxing and visiting with relatives and people who, by now, were also Fran Speaker's old friends.

The Speakers arrived at Hubbard on November 23, 1958, and Speaker and longtime outdoor companion Charley Vaughan quickly established a routine of driving three or four times a week to Lake Whitney, about thirty miles from Hubbard, for a day of fishing. About 5:30 in the afternoon of December 8, with dark closing in, they were pulling their boat onto the shore when Speaker suddenly collapsed. As Vaughan bent over him, he said, "My name is Tris Speaker" and lapsed into unconsciousness. Vaughan struggled to get him into his car and then drove as quickly as he could to the hospital in the little town of Whitney, where John Latham, M.D., pronounced Speaker dead. The death certificate Latham filled out gave the cause of death as "coronary artery disease."[45] Only two siblings survived him—sisters Pearl Speaker Scott of Hubbard and Alma Speaker Lindsay of Abilene, Texas.

Three days later, Speaker's funeral services were held at 11:30 A.M. in the chapel at the Wolfe Funeral Home in Hubbard. The chapel, which held about two hundred people, quickly overflowed. Hundreds more stood in adjoining rooms and outside the building. Among the many baseball notables who came to pay their respects were Indians vice president George Medinger and traveling secretary Spud Goldstein, Texas League president Dick Butler, and a number of former big-leaguers, including Bobby Bragan, Dale Mitchell, Firpo Marberry, Sid Hudson, Pete Donohue, and Art Shires. William J. Fleener Jr., rector of Hubbard's Episcopal church, officiated at the chapel services and at the burial on a cedar-shaded hill in Fairview Cemetery. (Beforehand, Fran Speaker, still a faithful Catholic, knelt in prayer with two priests who had come from Waco.)

It took two trucks to bring to the cemetery all the flowers sent by individuals and organizations. Commissioner Ford Frick, the American and National League offices, the Hall of Fame, the Yankees, the Red Sox, the Baseball Writers Association of America, and the Society for Crippled Children sent wreaths. An especially touching arrangement was signed "Cleburne baseball fans," sent by people from the town where Speaker had begun his professional career fifty-two years earlier. There was no formal eulogy at either the chapel services or at the grave site, but before Speaker's casket was lowered, Lowell Wilkes, another long-time friend, read a simple tribute: "Peace to your ashes, Tris. You were a home-town boy, whom we all admired and loved, and we were all made better because you passed this way and lived among us."[46]

"Let Your Voices Soften
to a Mere Whisper"

The inscription on Tris Speaker's gravestone, located not far in Hubbard's Fairview Cemetery from where his parents and deceased siblings are buried, gives his life dates as 1888–1958—the biblical three score and ten. But if whoever did the carving on the gravestone had done the unlikely thing of perusing the 1900, 1910, and 1920 federal census returns, he would have found that Speaker's mother consistently gave the birth year of her lastborn as 1889. So all along, throughout his long playing career and the busy thirty years of his post-playing life, Speaker may actually have been a year younger than he (maybe) and everybody else (absolutely) had assumed to be the case.

Mary Frances Cudahy Speaker survived her husband by slightly less than two years, dying in Cleveland on November 1, 1960. Per her wishes, she was also buried in Fairview Cemetery, alongside her husband. If the carving on Speaker's gravestone suggests an anomaly, the spelling of his wife's maiden name on her stone as "Cuddihy" is simply wrong. Presumably nobody in the Hubbard area had ever seen the name in print, either back when she married the legendary Gray Eagle or at any time since. In any case, the Speakers' burial place became an even more attractive site when, on Memorial Day 1997, the townspeople erected and dedicated a flagpole at the base of their graves.

At least for the decade or so following his death, the name Tris Speaker continued to be a prominent and honored one in the baseball world. In 1961 the Houston chapter of the Baseball Writers Association inaugurated a "Tris Speaker Award," first given to sixty-eight-year-old Dickie Kerr, a longtime resident of the city. Stan Musial, Yogi Berra, Willie Mays, Pete Rose, Harmon Killebrew,

Roberto Clemente, and Billy Williams were Speaker Award recipients in succeeding years.

Of course Mays, Williams, and Clemente couldn't have played in Organized Baseball in Speaker's time; the color line wasn't broken for another sixteen years after he played his last game for Newark. But as it happened, he became a Cleveland Indians employee just as Bill Veeck was preparing to sign the American League's first black player. By all indications, Speaker took to his coaching assignment with Larry Doby not only dutifully but enthusiastically, working both to improve Doby's skills at bat and afield and to build the young man's confidence that he could make it in what had been an all-white environment.

Following Doby was a succession of other Negro-leaguers signed by the Indians. Although the most famous was the legendary Leroy "Satchel Paige" (who won six of seven decisions after joining the team in mid-season 1948), over the next few years such men as Luke Easter, Harry Simpson, Dave Hoskins, Dave Pope, and Al Smith wore Cleveland uniforms. Like the Brooklyn Dodgers and to a lesser extent the New York Giants in the National League, the Indians moved out in front of everybody else in their league in exploiting the rich vein of talent in black professional baseball. That was a big reason why the Tribe won the league's only pennants the Yankees didn't win in the years from 1947 to 1958.

Speaker, of course, had to adjust to being around and relating to black players, not only those with the Cleveland team but others in its minor-league system. Whether by necessity or volition, he had to change the way of thinking in which he had grown up, even if, at the time of his death, little had changed in race relations in Speaker's hometown or in most of the rest of Texas and the American South.[1]

Although racial integration in baseball was no doubt the biggest change to which Speaker had to adjust, there were various others. In the post–World War II years, big-league teams increasingly abandoned train travel in favor of commercial airliners. Air travel became a necessity once the Dodgers and Giants relocated on the Pacific Coast after the 1957 season. Although the American League wouldn't have a franchise on the Coast until its first expansion in 1961, Speaker's official duties—as well as his willingness to attend numerous Old Timers' games, banquets, and the like—meant that he spent a good part of the last decade of his life flying from one place to another.

The migration of big-league franchises from their long-established home cities was still another big change. Beginning with the movement of the Boston Braves to Milwaukee, the 1950s brought franchise shifts by the St. Louis Browns to Baltimore and the Philadelphia Athletics to Kansas City, and then the stunning desertion of Greater New York by the Dodgers and Giants. The relatively compact geography of the major leagues—which stretched no farther west than St. Louis in Speaker's day—had become transcontinental by the time he died.

Although nobody ever questioned Speaker's greatness as a player, his managing received mixed reviews. Of course, except for part of a season at Kansas City, he was always a playing manager, which would be a vanishing breed within a few decades. Yet one might argue, as has Bob Feller, that player-managers "didn't have all the extra time that bench managers do, when they can think of too many other things to do in the course of a game. That leads to over-managing, which hasn't helped a team yet. Playing managers [didn't] have time to over-manage."[2]

Hailed as little less than a genius when he took over the Indians in mid-1919, brought them in a solid second, and then won it all in 1920, Speaker also garnered kudos for the Tribe's spirited pennant runs in 1921 and 1926. Yet he heard his share of boos and catcalls when his teams were only so-so (1922–1924) or downright bad (1925). At the end of the 1926 season, moreover, even such a consistent admirer as the *Cleveland Plain Dealer*'s Henry P. Edwards could reprimand Speaker for the way he had handled his pitchers in the decisive series with the Yankees, and for not obtaining Dutch Ruether when the veteran lefthander became available in the midst of the pennant fight.

Many years later, Riggs Stephenson said of Speaker, "He was a fine fellow, but I didn't think he was as detailed a manager as [Joe] McCarthy was." (Stephenson played for McCarthy on the pennant-winning 1929 Cubs, before McCarthy went on to manage the Yankees to eight pennants and seven World Series championships.) Walter Miller, who pitched for Speaker from 1924 to 1926, maintained that his former manager "didn't always know the names of his players. Some of the old pitchers . . . said he didn't even know their names." According to Miller,

Speaker would simply point to a pitcher to indicate that he would be starting the next day, or that he should go warm up in the bullpen. "It's things like that you remember, which make you wonder if the manager was really serious about his job." Miller seems to have been the only Cleveland player who spoke even that critically of Speaker. Said Stephenson, "As far as I know, the players got along well with Tris; liked him."[3] But at Newark, where the Gray Eagle spent a discouraging season and a half, he himself acknowledged his unpopularity with some of his players.

Speaker can also be faulted for at least four major mistakes in his judgment of players. He gave up on Stephenson as an infielder and never seems to have given serious consideration to making the hard-hitting Alabamian into an outfielder. As it turned out, the Indians lost a player who became one of the best in Chicago Cubs history. Undoubtedly Speaker's worst trade was sending Stanley Coveleski to Washington for three nobodies following the 1924 season. Without Coveleski's twenty wins, Washington might not have repeated as American League champions. In 1927, out of personal animus or something, Speaker used his influence with Bucky Harris and Clark Griffith to get Buddy Myer traded from Washington to the Red Sox, a mistake that ended up costing Griffith a great deal of money. Speaker, of course, was gone from the Senators by the time they reacquired Myer. And at Newark, though in dire need of good players and especially younger ones, Speaker simply couldn't see the raw talent in Joe Medwick, a local boy who went on to greatness elsewhere.

Lou Gehrig, born fifteen (or fourteen) years after Speaker, was his playing contemporary for only four full seasons, during which the Yankees' firstbaseman became the foremost power hitter in the American League next to Babe Ruth. In most respects, Speaker and Gehrig were quite unlike—one a product of small-town Texas and descended from "old stock" Americans, the other a native New Yorker and the son of German immigrants. In some ways, though, the two men were quite similar. Both were totally devoted to their mothers. (Gehrig's mother wasn't widowed, but his father was something of a nonentity.) Such devotion had many admirers in a time still flavored with Victorian sentimentalism; later generations might deride Speaker and Gehrig as world-class momma's boys. Both men married late (Speaker at thirty-five, Gehrig at thirty), to women who were well past the typical marrying age of that day, following lengthy acquaintances before engagement. And neither Speaker nor Gehrig experienced fatherhood.

When Speaker's playing career ended, he was almost universally conceded to be the greatest centerfielder ever. Ten years later, baseball writers and fans—especially those in New York City—were already comparing him with Joe DiMaggio. By the time of Speaker's death, Willie Mays had come to be widely regarded as the best who had played the position. Mays was still playing in 1969 when, at a dinner at the Sheraton Park Hotel in Washington, held before the All-Star Game, official baseball celebrated the centennial of the Cincinnati Red Stockings' inauguration of the professional game. It was also the occasion for the Baseball Writers Association to announce the results of its vote for the Greatest Living Team and the Greatest Team Ever. DiMaggio made the outfield for both teams; for the Greatest Team Ever, the other outfield first choices were Babe Ruth and Ty Cobb. Speaker, Ted Williams, and Willie Mays were Greatest Ever runners-up.

A few years later, baseball commissioner Bowie Kuhn came up with the idea of having fans at different big-league ballparks vote to name the "most memorable personality" their teams had produced. The choice in Cleveland was Rocky Colavito, a handsome outfielder who played for the Indians from 1956 to 1959 and again from 1965 to 1967, compiling only a .266 career batting average but hitting with power and driving in lots of runs. That Cleveland fans chose Colavito over Speaker—as well as the choice in St. Louis of Lou Brock over Stan Musial and Al Kaline over Ty Cobb in Detroit—left the veteran sportswriter Bob Broeg nonplussed. "Obviously," wrote Broeg, "boys—and maybe girls—did the voting. . . . Well, I'm glad I'm not THAT young any more."[4]

As further evidence of Speaker's fading fame, when the *Sporting News* ranked the one hundred greatest players in 1999, its top ten consisted of Ruth, Mays, Cobb, Walter Johnson, Henry Aaron, Gehrig, Mathewson, Williams, Hornsby, and Musial, in that order. Speaker made it no higher than twenty-seventh.

Yet Speaker comes out much better in the authoritative compendium *Total Baseball,* which ranks the one hundred top players on the basis of "Total Player Rating" (TPR)—a complex and influential formula devised by John Thorn and Pete Palmer. TPR "measures the number of extra wins (or losses) each player provided his teams compared to what an average player at the same position in his time would have produced."[5] Speaker's TPR is number eight, behind (from the top) Ruth, Mays, Napoleon Lajoie, Cobb, Johnson, Barry Bonds, and Henry Aaron. Joe DiMaggio, once thought to have surpassed Speaker in centerfielding, ends up tied with Warren Spahn for thirty-third place.

Those knowledgeable about baseball's long history can easily get caught up in such comparisons and rankings of this player and that. But as the mid-1970s vote for Cleveland's most memorable baseball personality indicates, the passage of time quickly dulls most peoples' consciousness or concern about the past. Since undertaking this project, I have repeatedly had the experience of telling somebody that I was working on a biography of Tris Speaker—and getting a blank stare. Yet Speaker was a titan in his time. He was the illustrious Spoke, baseball's Gray Eagle in what the late Harold Seymour called its Golden Age.[6] Those who watched him in his prime understood his greatness. Early in 1963, when seventy-three-year-old Sam Rice was asked to comment on his own recent election to the Hall of Fame, he thought for a minute, then said: "If it were a real Hall of Fame, you'd say Cobb, Speaker, Walter Johnson, Babe Ruth, Lou Gehrig and a few others belonged and then you'd let your voice soften to a mere whisper."[7]

Notes

Foreword: "No Place for Me"

1. In 1904, in what became one of the most famous—or infamous—episodes in baseball history, McGraw and Giants owner John T. Brush imperiously refused to play the Boston American League champions in what would have been the second "modern" World Series.
2. *Sporting News,* January 6, 1944, p. 7.
3. Ibid., May 17, 1969, p. 29.
4. Frank Graham, "On Seeing Tris Speaker Again," *Baseball Digest* 13 (November–December 1954), pp. 93–94. These career numbers for Speaker, revised from earlier accepted figures, are from John Thorn et al., eds., *Total Baseball: The Official Encyclopedia of Major League Baselll,* 7th ed. (Kingston N.Y.: Total Sports Publishing, 2001), p. 1193.
5. *Sporting Life,* July 10, 1915, p. 2; *Cleveland Press,* December 1, 1926, p. 13; Lawrence S. Ritter, "Ladies and Gentlemen, Presenting Marty McHale," *National Pastime,* #8 (1982), p. 21; Nick Peters, "Little Joe Sewell: He Was the Best Contact Hitter Ever," *Baseball Digest* 45 (December 1986), pp. 41–42; Lawrence S. Ritter, *The Glory of Their Times: The Story of the Early Days of Baseball, Told by the Men Who Played It,* rev. ed. (orig. 1966; New York: Vintage Books, 1985), p. 59.
6. *Sporting Life,* May 18, 1907, p. 20.
7. Bob Kuester, "All-Time Best Center Fielders Combined Hitting, Fielding," *Baseball Digest* 53 (December 1994), p. 37.
8. William A. Phelon, "On the Home Stretch of the Great 1912 Pennant Races," *Baseball Magazine* 9 (October 1912), p. 18.
9. Cobb and Mathewson both played a few games against black professionals from the U.S. and black and racially mixed Cubans in postseason series in Cuba, in 1910 and 1911, respectively. Walter Johnson had at least one postseason matchup with Frank Wickware (known as the "Red Ant" because of his coloring).
10. Branch Rickey, with Robert Riger, *The American Diamond: A Documentary of the Game of Baseball* (New York: Simon and Schuster, 1965), p. 53.

Chapter 1: "I Played Baseball and Drove the Cows to Pasture"

1. F. C. Lane, "Tris Speaker: King of the Outfield," *Baseball Magazine* 13 (July 1914), p. 49; *Leslie's Illustrated Weekly*, July 15, 1915, clipping in Tris Speaker File, National Baseball Library, Cooperstown, New York.
2. Lane, "Tris Speaker," p. 49; Gordon Cobbledick, "Tris Speaker: The Gray Eagle," *Sport* 12 (July 1952), p. 37.
3. Cobbledick, "Tris Speaker," p. 37; *Leslie's Illustrated Weekly* clipping.
4. Lane, "Tris Speaker," p. 49.
5. In the early decades of the twentieth century, it was fairly common for owners of minor-league franchises also to serve the league as presidents, especially in the lower minors.
6. Lane, "Tris Speaker," p. 51.
7. *Sporting News*, September 22, 1906, p. 2.
8. Ibid., January 12, 1933, p. 3.
9. Ibid., February 10, 1979, p. 36.
10. Ibid., April 6, 1907, p. 2.
11. In his later years Speaker inflated his purchase price to $750.
12. *Sporting News*, January 24, 1951, p. 13.
13. *Sporting Life*, September 28, 1907, p. 4.
14. *Boston Daily Record*, January ?, 1933, clipping in Bill Carrigan File, National Baseball Library, Cooperstown, New York; Irving F. Sanborn, "The Problem of the Big League Club Owner," *Baseball Magazine* 32 (February 1924), p. 393.
15. For that one season of 1908, the Red Sox also sported red stockings on the fronts of their pullover shirts, which were be laced at the chest under the full collars that nearly all teams still wore.
16. *Sporting News*, March 26, 1908, p. 6.
17. *Sporting Life*, July 25, 1908, p. 20; August 8, 1908, p. 23; unidentified clipping, April 28, 1937, Carrigan File, National Baseball Library.
18. *Sporting Life*, September 5, 1908, p. 23.
19. For decades, however, Columbia Park continued to be the site of games played by black professional teams.
20. *Sporting News*, September 17, 1908, p. 4; *Sporting Life*, September 26, 1908, p. 7.

Chapter 2: "By No Means a Finished Outfielder"

1. *Sporting Life*, January 9, 1909, p. 8; *Sporting News*, January 6, 1944, p. 7.
2. Lawrence S. Ritter, *The Glory of Their Times: The Story of the Early Days of Baseball, Told by the Men Who Played It*, rev. ed. (orig. 1966; New York: Vintage Books, 1985), p. 142.
3. *Sporting Life*, November 4, 1911, p. 2.
4. Hugh S. Fullerton, "Between Games: How the Ball Players of the Big Leagues Live and Act When off the Diamond," *American Magazine* 72 (July 1911), p. 322.
5. Fred Lieb, *Baseball as I Have Known It* (1977; reprint, Lincoln: University of Nebraska Press, 1996), p. 215.

6. Joe Wood interview with Lawrence S. Ritter, audiocassette version of *The Glory of Their Times* (St. Paul, Minn.: High Bridge Company, 1998).

7. Spink quoted in Marshall Smelser, *The Life That Ruth Built: A Biography* (orig. 1975; reprint, Lincoln: University of Nebraska Press, 1992), p. 69.

8. *Sporting Life,* May 1, 1909, p. 2; May 22, 1909, p. 3.

9. Harry Grayson, *They Played the Game: The Story of Baseball Greats* (New York: A. S. Barnes, 1944), p. 36; Harry B. Hooper to Committee on Veterans, January 24, 1972, George "Duffy" Lewis File, National Baseball Library, Cooperstown, New York.

10. *Sporting News,* June 24, 1909, p. 6.

11. *New York Times,* August 20, 1909, p. 5.

12. Fred Lieb, *The Boston Red Sox* (1947; reprint, Carbondale and Edwardsville: Southern Illinois University Press, 2003), p. 84.

13. Microfilm 1910 Federal Census manuscript returns, http://www.ancestry.com.

14. *Sporting News,* March 31, 1910, p. 5.

15. St. Louis had a slightly larger population within its city limits, but its metropolitan-area population was far smaller.

16. Lieb, *Boston Red Sox,* p. 86.

17. Les Biederman, "The Scoreboard Column," unidentified clipping, January 21, 1956, Duffy Lewis File.

18. Paul J. Zingg, *Harry Hooper: An American Baseball Life* (Urbana: University of Illinois Press, 1993), p. 79.

19. *Sporting News,* June 2, 1910, p. 2.

20. Reported in Donald Dewey and Nicholas Acocella, *The Black Prince of Baseball: Hal Chase and the Mythology of the Game* (Toronto: Sport Classic Books, 2004), p. 145.

21. *Sporting News,* August 18, 1910, p. 6; October 20, 1910, p. 6.

22. "Walter Johnson on Baseball Slavery," *Baseball Magazine* 7 (July 1911), p. 76.

23. *Sporting Life,* June 17, 1911, p. 11.

24. "A Broken Record," *Baseball Magazine* 7 (July 1911), p. 87.

25. *Sporting News,* January 30, 1913, p. 4.

Chapter 3: "Well, There Goes Your World Series"

1. *Sporting News,* March 28, 1912, p. 2.

2. "Who's Who in Baseball? Stars of the Diamond and Their Records," *Baseball Magazine* 9 (March 1912), p. 85.

3. *New York Times,* April 5, 1912, p. 11.

4. *Sporting News,* May 2, 1912, p. 4.

5. *Sporting Life,* June 22, 1912, p. 19.

6. *Boston Globe,* July 3, 1912, clipping in Tris Speaker File, National Baseball Library, Cooperstown, New York; *New York Times,* September 29, 1912, p. 2.

7. *Sporting News,* September 5, 1912, p. 1. Two days later, Johnson started and lost 3-2 to the Browns, thereby making moot whether he should have been charged with the loss of August 26.

8. *Sporting News,* September 12, 1912, p. 1; Lawrence S. Ritter, *The Glory of Their Times: The Story of the Early Days of Baseball, Told by the Men Who Played It,* rev. ed. (orig. 1966; New York: Vintage Books, 1985), p. 159.

9. *Sporting Life,* August 24, 1912, p. 13; *Sporting News,* September 26, 1912, p. 5.

10. *New York Times,* September 29, 1912, p. 2; William A. Phelon, "On the Home Stretch of the Great 1912 Pennant Races," *Baseball Magazine* 9 (October 1912), p. 18; *Sporting Life,* September 21, 1912, p. 3.

11. *Sporting News,* October 17, 1912, p. 1.

12. William A. Phelon, "How the World's Series Was Lost and Won," *Baseball Magazine* 10 (December 1912), p. 20.

13. Tris Speaker, as told to Francis J. Powers, in John P. Carmichael, ed., *My Greatest Day in Baseball* (1945; reprint, Lincoln: University of Nebraska Press, 1996), pp. 63–68.

14. Ritter, *Glory of Their Times,* p. 110; Tris Speaker, "The Famous Thirty Thousand Dollar Muff," *Baseball Magazine* 24 (November 1919), p. 404.

15. *Sporting News,* January 3, 1946, p. 7; Kyle Crichton, "Center-Field Lightning," *Collier's* 101 (March 26, 1938), p. 41; Ty Cobb and John N. Wheeler, *Busting 'Em and Other Big League Stories,* ed. William R. Cobb (1914; reprint, Jefferson, N.C.: McFarland, 2003).

16. Crichton, "Center-Field Lightning," p. 41.

17. Charles C. Alexander, *John McGraw* (1988; reprint, Lincoln: University of Nebraska Press, 1995), p. 165.

18. Ritter, *Glory of Their Times,* p. 111.

19. Phelon, "How the Series Was Lost and Won," p. 18; *Sporting Life,* November 16, 1912, p. 13.

20. *Sporting News,* October 24, 1912, p. 4.

21. Ibid., October 31, 1912, p. 1.

Chapter 4: "For God's Sake, Men, Take the Money Away"

1. Lawrence S. Ritter, *The Glory of Their Times: The Story of the Early Days of Baseball, Told by the Men Who Played It,* rev. ed. (1966; New York: Vintage Books, 1985), p. 166.

2. William A. Phelon, "Ringing Up the Curtain on the 1913 Pennant Race," *Baseball Magazine* 11 (June 1913), p. 20.

3. *Sporting Life,* May 17, 1913, p. 6.

4. Henry Thomas, *Walter Johnson: Baseball's Big Train* (Washington, D.C.: Phenom Press, 1995), p. 117.

5. *Sporting News,* August 7, 1913, p. 1.

6. F. C. Lane, "Tris Speaker: King of the Outfield," *Baseball Magazine* 13 (July 1914), p. 56.

7. Thorpe had been stripped of his Olympic gold medals when Olympic officials learned that he had played minor-league baseball for two summers in North Carolina.

8. James E. Elfers, *The Tour to End All Tours: The Story of Major League Baseball's 1913–1914 World Tour* (Lincoln: University of Nebraska Press, 2003), p. 89.

9. Frank McGlynn, "Striking Scenes from the Tour around the World: Part IV," *Baseball Magazine* 14 (November 1914), p. 76; Lane, "Tris Speaker," p. 56.

10. Lane, "Tris Speaker," p. 57.

11. *Sporting News,* December 3, 1958, p. 16; *Cleveland Plain Dealer,* December 25, 1926, p. 21.

12. *Sporting Life,* March 14, 1914, p. 3; Elfers, *Tour to End All Tours,* p. 239.

13. *Sporting Life,* March 21, 1914, pp. 7, 9.

14. Ibid., March 28, 1914, p. 7.

15. Ibid., March 21, 1914, p. 7; *Boston Daily Record,* January 20, 1943, clipping in Bill Carrigan File, National Baseball Library, Cooperstown, New York.

16. *New York Times,* May 2, 1914, p. 10.

17. *Sporting News,* June 4, 1914, p. 1; August 13, 1914, p. 1.

18. Undated, unidentified clipping in Howard "Joe" Wood File, National Baseball Library, Cooperstown, New York.

19. As an early member of the National League, Providence had won pennants in 1879 and 1884.

20. *Sporting News,* September 5, 1914, pp. 9–10.

21. Robert Creamer, *Babe: The Legend Comes to Life* (1974; reprint, New York: Penguin Books, 1985), p. 20.

22. Ed Linn, *The Great Rivalry: The Yankees and the Red Sox, 1901–1990* (New York: Ticknor and Fields, 1991), p. 66.

Chapter 5: "Baseball Is a Business"

1. Although Lajoie never played on a big-league pennant-winner, in 1917 he managed Toronto to an International League pennant and led the league with a .380 batting average.

2. *Sporting News,* January 28, 1915, p. 1.

3. How much would $18,000 be in today's dollars? Money ratios over time are always problematical, but a ratio of 15:1 would seem reasonable, which makes Speaker's 1914–1915 salary worth about $270,000 today.

4. "What the Baseball Public Wants," *Baseball Magazine* 15 (August 1915), p. 74.

5. William A. Phelon, "The Opening Broadsides," *Baseball Magazine* 15 (June 1915), p. 24.

6. *Sporting Life,* May 29, 1915, p. 10.

7. *Sporting News,* June 3, 1915, p. 4; *Sporting Life,* June 5, 1915, p. 3.

8. *Sporting Life,* June 12, 1915, p. 9.

9. Ibid., July 10, 1915, p. 2.

10. *New York Times,* August 26, 1915, p. 6.

11. *Sporting Life,* October 23, 1915, p. 2.

12. After the Series, Speaker was quoted as saying, "Nothing in my career looms up quite so pleasing as that base on balls from Alexander in the pinch." *Cleveland Press,* April 9, 1916, p. 14.

13. William A. Phelon, "How I Picked the Loser," *Baseball Magazine* 16 (December 1915), p. 20.

14. *Sporting Life,* December 11, 1915, p. 7.

15. Cady and Thomas stayed with the Red Sox at reduced salaries; Collins dropped back to the minor leagues.

16. *Sporting News,* December 9, 1915, p. 2; *Sporting Life,* December 11, 1915, p. 7.

17. *Sporting News,* March 23, 1916, p. 7.

18. Marquard's general ineffectiveness and his flirtations with the Federal League had so soured John McGraw that the previous August he sold the lefthander to Brooklyn for the waiver price.

19. *Sporting News,* July 1, 1972, p. 4; Franklin Lewis, *The Cleveland Indians* (New York: Putnam's, 1949), p. 56.
20. *Cleveland Plain Dealer,* April 10, 1916, p. 9. The cash payment for Speaker has often been given as $50,000. For *Baseball Magazine,* Dunn provided a written statement that the deal had cost him $57,500—a $55,000 purchase price plus a $2,500 signing bonus. See F. C. Lane, "Tris Speaker Traded," *Baseball Magazine* 17 (June 1916), pp. 19–28.
21. *Cleveland Plain Dealer,* April 12, 1916, p. 8.
22. *Sporting Life,* April 22, 1916, p. 5; *Cleveland Plain Dealer,* April 10, 1916, p. 10; May 9, 1916, p. 11; *Cleveland Press,* April 10, 1916, p. 14.
23. *Sporting Life,* April 22, 1916, p. 5.

Chapter 6: "New Life into a Half-Dead, Despondent City"

1. F. C. Lane, "Tris Speaker Traded," *Baseball Magazine* 17 (June 1916), p. 23; W. A. Phelon, "Lining Up for 1916," ibid., pp. 14–15; *Sporting News,* April 20, 1916, p. 4.
2. Lane, "Tris Speaker Traded," p. 21; *Sporting News,* June 29, 1916, p. 4.
3. *Sporting News,* June 29, 1916, p. 23; J. C. Dunn, "My Experience as a Major League Owner," *Baseball Magazine* 18 (March 1917), p. 89.
4. *Sporting News,* May 11, 1916, p. 1.
5. Ibid., May 23, 1946, p. 10.
6. Ibid., May 18, 1916, p. 1.
7. Ibid., June 15, 1916, p. 3.
8. An indication of how dismal the situation of the once-proud Athletics had become was the diminishing frequency with which the grass was cut at Shibe Park. In a July series in Philadelphia, after the Athletics beat out several hits on slow infield grounders, Chick Gandil hid a ball in the four-inch-high grass in front of firstbase, called time, and revealed the ball to umpire Billy Evans. After the game, Mack ordered the infield mowed.
9. *Sporting Life,* August 5, 1916, p. 5.
10. *Sporting News,* September 28, 1916, p. 2; January 4, 1917, p. 3.
11. Tris Speaker, "The Ins and Outs of Batting," *Baseball Magazine* 22 (April 1919), p. 332.
12. *Sporting News,* November 9, 1916, p. 2; *Sporting Life,* November 11, 1916, p. 7.
13. *Sporting Life,* January 25, 1917, p. 6; February 1, 1917, p. 1.
14. Harold Seymour, *Baseball: The Golden Age* (New York: Oxford University Press, 1971), pp. 241–242. See also Robert F. Burk, *Never Just a Game: Players, Owners, and American Baseball to 1920* (Chapel Hill: University of North Carolina Press, 1994).
15. Joe Wood interview with Lawrence S. Ritter, audiocassette version of *The Glory of Their Times: The Story of the Early Days of Baseball, Told by the Men Who Played It* (St. Paul, Minn.: High Bridge Company, 1998).
16. Lawrence S. Ritter, *The Glory of Their Times,* rev. ed. (orig. 1966; New York: Vintage Books, 1985), pp. 168–169.
17. The 1917 St. Louis Browns could barely beat out the Athletics for seventh place, but they were judged the best drill team at the end of the competition in August and divided the $500 prize.
18. U.S. Military Records, 1917–1918, draft cards (microfilm), http://www.ancestry.com.

19. *Cleveland Plain Dealer,* August 15, 1917, p. 9.
20. *Sporting News,* April 19, 1923, p. 4.
21. "Tris Speaker: The Star of the 1920 Baseball Season," *Baseball Magazine* 26 (December 1920), p. 318; *Sporting News,* August 23, 1917, p. 1.
22. Earlier in the season, on June 23 in Boston, Brick Owens had experienced an even tougher day. When he called four balls on the first Washington batter of the game, Babe Ruth came in from the mound, argued with Owens, and then knocked him down. After Ruth was sent to the showers, Ernie Shore entered the game, and the runner on first was thrown out on a steal attempt. Shore allowed no hits, no walks, and no runs the rest of the way, thus achieving a unique no-hitter, one he didn't start.
23. Lee Fohl, "Baseball Brains," *Baseball Magazine* 20 (January 1918), pp. 28f.
24. *Cleveland Plain Dealer,* June 21, 1918, p. 12.
25. *Sporting News,* May 30, 1918, p. 5.
26. *Cleveland Plain Dealer,* August 13, 1918, p. 15.

Chapter 7: "The Inspiration of Speaker's Leadership"

1. Tris Speaker, "The Ins and Outs of Batting," *Baseball Magazine* 22 (April 1919), p. 332.
2. *Sporting News,* March 6, 1919, p. 6.
3. Chuck Pezzano column, *Paterson Record,* August 3, 1968, Charles Jamieson File, National Baseball Library, Cooperstown, New York.
4. Earlier in the century, Rube Waddell had occasionally performed that stunt against weak opposition; subsequently Satchel Paige did the same.
5. *Cleveland Plain Dealer,* May 9, 1919, p. 18.
6. Ibid., May 31, 1919, p. 1C.
7. Ibid.
8. Ibid.
9. Ibid., June 1, 1919, p. 14.
10. *Sporting News,* October 19, 1955, p. 6.
11. Ibid., July 31, 1919, p. 1; October 19, 1919, p. 4.
12. *Cleveland Press,* September 26, 1919, p. 33.
13. *Sporting News,* October 19, 1919, p. 4.
14. William A. Cook, *The 1919 World Series: What Really Happened* (Jefferson, N.C.: McFarland, 2001) presents the case that the Reds were actually the better team, and that they should have won the World Series regardless of whether or not the White Sox played at top form.
15. *Cleveland Plain Dealer,* October 1, 1919, p. 9.
16. Ibid., October 7, 1919, p. 19.
17. "Editorial Comment," *Baseball Magazine* 24 (December 1919), p. 458; Charles C. Alexander, *Our Game: An American Baseball History* (New York: Henry Holt, 1991), p. 116.
18. Frazee's biggest hit was produced in New York City in 1924, Vincent Youmans's operetta *No, No Nanette.*

19. The venerable John B. Sheridan of St. Louis, who contributed a regular column to the *Sporting News*, was one of the few contemporaries who wrote about the significance of the new-style bats coming into use in the 1920s. Charles C. Alexander, *Rogers Hornsby: A Biography* (New York: Henry Holt, 1995), p. 93.

20. "A Good Word for the Spit Ball," *Baseball Magazine* 24 (March 1920), p. 572.

Chapter 8: "I Knew My Team"

1. *Sporting News*, March 11, 1920, p. 1.

2. Ibid., March 18, 1920, p. 1; *Cleveland Plain Dealer*, April 4, 1920, pt. 2, p. 1.

3. *Cleveland Press*, April 17, 1920, p. 11.

4. *Cleveland Plain Dealer*, May 31, 1920, p. 20; Robert C. Cottrell, *Blackball, the Black Sox and the Babe: Baseball's Crucial 1920 Season* (Jefferson, N.C.: McFarland, 2002), p. 187.

5. *Sporting News*, July 8, 1920, p. 1.

6. Ibid., August 5, 1920, p. 4.

7. Unpublished manuscript of interview, Lawrence S. Ritter with Charlie Jamieson, p. 15, Charles Jamieson File, National Baseball Library, Cooperstown, New York.

8. What happened to the ball that struck Chapman has been the subject of varying reminiscences. In a 1945 column, Joe Williams, who was present that day, wrote that the ball bounced clear over Wally Pipp's head. Shortly before his death in 1969, Charlie Jamieson gave an Orlando sportswriter a ball he claimed was the fatal object. In Jamieson's account, the ball didn't bounce anywhere but dropped near home plate. Jamieson said he picked it up, put it in his pocket, kept it there for the rest of the game (which he played in leftfield with a righthander pitching), tucked it into his traveling bag afterward, and took it home to New Jersey when the season ended. Contemporary eyewitness accounts, however, are in agreement that what happened is as I've given it in the text.

9. *Cleveland Press*, August 17, 1920, p. 1.

10. Ibid., August 18, 1920, p. 1; Fred Lieb, *Baseball as I Have Known It* (1977; reprint, Lincoln: University of Nebraska Press, 1996), p. 136; Peter Williams, ed., *The Joe Williams Baseball Reader* (Chapel Hill, N.C.: Algonquin Books, 1989), p. 50.

11. Mike Sowell, *The Pitch That Killed: Carl Mays, Ray Chapman, and the Pennant Race of 1920* (New York: Macmillan, 1989), p. 23.

12. In his otherwise excellent dual biography of Chapman and Mays, Mike Sowell entertains a rather more melodramatic version of events surrounding Chapman's funeral, with the Protestants and Catholics on the Cleveland team quarreling over where and how the services would take place. Supposedly, Speaker and Steve O'Neill came to blows, although in one version O'Neill got the better of the scrap; in the other Speaker did. Sowell appears to lean heavily on an interview he did with Bill Wambsganss four months before the death of "Wamby" at the age of eighty-nine (Sowell, *Pitch That Killed*, pp. 204–206). For various reasons—not least being Speaker's friendship with Jim Dunn as well as with O'Neill and his willingness the previous fall to be Chapman's best man in a Catholic wedding—I believe what I've given in the text is closer to what happened.

13. *Cleveland Plain Dealer*, August 22, 1920, pt. 2, p. 1.

14. Ibid., August 26, 1920, p. 18.

15. *Sporting News,* July 27, 1960, p. 5.

16. William H. Veeck, Sr., president of the Cubs, had been tipped off to the bribe and had ordered manager Fred Mitchell to hold Hendrix out and start Grover Cleveland Alexander, who had been with the Cubs since 1918. The Phillies won anyway, 3-1.

17. *Cleveland Plain Dealer,* September 24, 1920, p. 1.

18. *Sporting News,* September 30, 1920, p. 4.

19. Ibid., October 7, 1920, p. 1.

20. In 1919 the National League initiated a statistical column for "runs batted in" but didn't record that statistic for walks received with the bases filled. In 1920 the American League put "runs responsible for" in its official statistics and counted them for bases-loaded walks. That became the National League's practice in 1921. Eventually the American League's terminology also became "runs batted in."

21. *Cleveland Plain Dealer,* October 4, 1920, p. 18; *Cleveland Press,* October 4, 1920, p. 30.

22. *Cleveland Press,* October 6, 1920, p. 1.

23. *New York Times,* October 9, 1920, p. 11.

24. *Cleveland Press,* October 8, 1920, p. 1.

25. *New York Times,* October 10, 1920, p. 1.

26. *Cleveland Plain Dealer,* October 12, 1920, p. 1.

27. *Cleveland Press,* October 13, 1920, p. 5; *Cleveland Plain Dealer,* October 13, 1920, p. 5.

28. *Cleveland Plain Dealer,* October 13, 1920, p. 18.

29. *Cleveland Press,* October 12, 1920, p. 23.

30. *Reach's Official Baseball Guide for 1920* (Philadelphia: A. J. Reach Company, 1921), p. 49.

Chapter 9: "I Will Never Be a Bench Manager"

1. *Sporting News,* October 7, 1920, p. 4.

2. Ibid., December 30, 1920, p. 1.

3. *Cleveland Plain Dealer,* March 2, 1921, p. 16.

4. Eugene C. Murdock, *Baseball Players and Their Times: Oral Histories of the Game, 1920–1930* (Westport, Conn.: Meckler, 1991), p. 75.

5. *Cleveland Plain Dealer,* April 19, 1921, p. 19.

6. Ibid., June 21, 1921, p. 16.

7. Ibid., July 17, 1921, pt. 2, p. 1.

8. Ibid., September 15, 1921, p. 16.

9. Ibid., September 26, 1921, p. 1.

10. William A. Phelon, "Who Will Win the Big League Pennants?" *Baseball Magazine* 28 (May 1922), p. 822.

11. *Sporting News,* October 6, 1921, p. 1; F. C. Lane, "What's Wrong with the Three-Base Hit?" *Baseball Magazine* 29 (June 1922), p. 304.

12. Peter Williams, ed., *The Joe Williams Baseball Reader* (Chapel Hill, N.C.: Algonquin Books, 1989), p. 50.

13. *Cleveland Plain Dealer,* April 1, 1922, p. 16.

14. Ibid., June 10, 1922, p. 14.

15. William A. Phelon, "The Pennant Races Grow Hot," *Baseball Magazine* 29 (October 1922), p. 507.

16. *Cleveland Plain Dealer,* September 13, 1922, p. 18.

17. F. C. Lane, "The All-American Baseball Club of 1922," *Baseball Magazine* 30 (December 1922), p. 309.

18. "How I Spend My Annual Vacation," *Baseball Magazine* 30 (March 1923), p. 455.

19. *Sporting News,* December 7, 1922, p. 2.

20. Ibid., November 16, 1922, p. 1.

21. *Cleveland Plain Dealer,* March 4, 1923, p. 2D.

22. *Sporting News,* March 22, 1923, p. 2.

23. *Sporting News,* April 13, 1923, p. 2; Frank Graham, *The Brooklyn Dodgers: An Informal History* (1945; reprint, Carbondale and Edwardsville: Southern Illinois University Press, 2002), p. 91.

Chapter 10: "We'll Finish in the League Anyway"

1. William A. Phelon, "Who Will Win the Big League Pennants?" *Baseball Magazine* 32 (May 1924), p. 531; *Sporting News,* April 17, 1924, p. 4.

2. *Cleveland Plain Dealer,* May 14, 1924, p. 20.

3. *Sporting News,* July 24, 1924, p. 3; *Cleveland Plain Dealer,* July 26, 1924, p. 12.

4. *Cleveland Plain Dealer,* October 9, 1924, p. 2; William A. Phelon, "Who Will Win the World Series of 1924?" *Baseball Magazine* 33 (October 1924), p. 549.

5. After the 1920s, fraternal orders steadily lost ground to service clubs such as Rotary, Kiwanis, Lions, and Optimists.

6. Fred Lieb, *Baseball as I Have Known It* (1977; reprint, Lincoln: University of Nebraska Press, 1996), p. 54. Lieb's book was first published by Putnam. Charles "Gabby" Street, a native Alabamian, was Walter Johnson's catcher from 1908 to 1912. In 1931 and 1932 he managed the St. Louis Cardinals to two pennants and one World Series win.

7. Such one-source items have a way of being passed on without verification and becoming conventional wisdom, if they serve authors' purposes. So Howard Bryant—by way of endeavoring to brand Eddie Collins as a racist, anti-Catholic, and anti-Semitic Boston Red Sox executive—has written that "Back in the old days, the great center fielder Tris Speaker was a proud member of the Ku Klux Klan in Texas." Bryant, *Shut Out: A Story of Race and Baseball in Boston* (New York: Routledge, 2002), p. 28.

8. *Sporting News,* January 22, 1925, p. 5.

9. I have no view one way or the other on whether Gabby Street ever joined the Klan, although his native Alabama was the one state where the Klan became more powerful—and violent—in the late 1920s. As for Ty Cobb, although he belonged to the Masonic Order and various other fraternal lodges, my sense of the man is that he was too wary to become part of something as hotly controversial as the Klan. But we can never know for sure.

10. "Sport," *Time* 5 (March 30, 1925), p. 28; James M. Gould, "Speaking of Managers," *Baseball Magazine* 34 (April 1925), p. 499. A "nautch girl" is a performer in a style of dance—known as a nautch—native to India.

11. *Cleveland Plain Dealer,* March 4, 1925, p. 16; *Sporting News,* February 19, 1925, p. 8; *Cleveland Press,* March 7, 1925, p. 8; April 14, 1925, p. 1.

12. *Cleveland Press,* April 15, 1925, p. 12.

13. *Sporting News,* May 28, 1925, p. 1.

14. "Why It Always Pays to Hustle," *Baseball Magazine* 36 (May 1926), p. 550.

15. *Cleveland News,* June 28, 1925, n.p., clipping in Charles W. Mears Collection on Cleveland Baseball, Cleveland Public Library, Cleveland, Ohio; "What I Have Learned from 20 Years in the Outfield," *Baseball Magazine* 35 (September 1925), pp. 444f.; *Cleveland Plain Dealer,* July 19, 1925, pt. 2, p. 1.

16. *Cleveland Press,* October 5, 1925, p. 22.

17. Fred Stein, *And the Skipper Bats Cleanup: A History of the Baseball Player-Manager, with 42 Biographies of Men Who Filled the Dual Role* (Jefferson, N.C.: McFarland, 2002), p. 161.

18. Norman Macht, "History Repeats Itself: There's Nothing New in Baseball," *Baseball Digest* 59 (June 2000), p. 75.

19. James M. Gould, "Who Will Win the Big League Pennants in 1926?" *Baseball Magazine* 36 (May 1926), p. 533; *Cleveland Plain Dealer,* March 17, 1926, p. 19.

20. *Sporting News,* May 20, 1926, p. 2; *Cleveland Plain Dealer,* May 10, 1926, p. 30.

21. *Cleveland Plain Dealer,* May 16, 1926, p. 19.

22. Ibid., August 8, 1926, p. 8.

23. John McGraw had his players sign chits for their meals; then he went over the chits personally to see whether anybody was eating too much, especially rich desserts.

24. Eugene C. Murdock, *Baseball Players and Their Times: Oral Histories of the Game, 1920–1930* (Westport, Conn.: Meckler, 1991), p. 252.

25. *Cleveland Plain Dealer,* September 19, 1926, pp. 1–2.

26. *Cleveland Press,* April 23, 1926, p. 36.

27. Ibid., November 11, 1926, p. 42.

28. *Cleveland Plain Dealer,* September 30, 1926, p. 20; October 15, 1926, p. 30.

29. *Cleveland Press,* September 28, 1926, p. 22.

Chapter 11: "A Veritable Judas"

1. *Sporting News,* February 3, 1927, p. 4.

2. Ibid., November 11, 1926, p. 2.

3. *Cleveland Plain Dealer,* December 6, 1926, p. 24.

4. *Cleveland Press,* November 11, 1926, p. 42.

5. *Cleveland Plain Dealer,* November 28, 1927, p. 1.

6. *Sporting News,* December 2, 1926, p. 1; *Cleveland Press,* November 29, 1926, p. 1; *Cleveland Plain Dealer,* November 30, 1926, p. 24.

7. It will be recalled that in 1918, with the "work or fight" order shutting down the season a month early and with the first four finishers in each league sharing in Series money, the Red Sox's and Cubs' shares were greatly reduced, and the amount shared by the other six clubs was hardly significant. The 140-game 1919 season cut players' contracts by two weeks, in partial compensation for which the owners specified that second- and third-place finishers would get a cut of the Series players' shares.

8. *Detroit News,* September 26, 1919, quoted in Lowell Blaisdell, "The Cobb-Speaker Scandal: Exonerated but Probably Guilty," *Nine: A Journal of Baseball History and Culture* 13 (2005), p. 64.

9. Blaisdell, "Cobb-Speaker Scandal," p. 64.

10. Joe Wood interview, audiocassette version (St. Paul, Minn.: High Bridge Company, 1998), for Lawrence S. Ritter, *The Glory of Their Times: The Story of the Early Days of Baseball Told by the Men Who Played It,* rev. ed. (orig. 1966; New York: Vintage Books, 1985).

11. The full texts of Wood's and Cobb's letters to Leonard were reprinted as part of Speaker's, Cobb's, and Wood's testimony before Kenesaw Mountain Landis, which the commissioner released late in December 1926. Newspapers across the country printed the transcript of the testimony from the Associated Press, including the *New York Times, Cleveland Press, Cleveland Plain Dealer,* and *Sporting News,* on which I've relied here.

12. *Cleveland Plain Dealer,* December 22, 1926, p. 4.

13. Ibid.

14. The advisory council nominally consisted of the presidents of the two major leagues plus Landis. Frank Navin had been serving in Johnson's place.

15. *Cleveland Press,* December 21, 1926, p. 1.

16. Bozeman Bulger, "Twenty-five Years in Sports," *Saturday Evening Post* 200 (April 28, 1928), p. 9.

17. *Cleveland Plain Dealer,* December 22, 1926, p. 20; *Sporting News,* December 30, 1926, p. 1.

18. *Cleveland Plain Dealer,* December 26, 1926, p. 22; *Sporting News,* December 30, 1926, pp. 3, 5.

19. *Cleveland Press,* December 22, 1926, p. 1.

20. Ibid., p. 22.

21. *Cleveland Press,* December 26, 1926, p. 18; *Sporting News,* January 6, 1927, p. 1; Wood interview, audiocassette version, for Ritter, *Glory of Their Times.*

22. *Sporting News,* December 30, 1926, p. 2; *Cleveland Plain Dealer,* December 23, 1926, p. 1.

23. *Cleveland Press,* December 25, 1926, p. 1; Theodore Hammen to Tris Speaker, December 23, 1926, copy courtesy of William Burgess, Mountain View, California. Caps in original.

24. *Cleveland Plain Dealer,* December 25, 1926, pp. 20–21.

25. Ibid., January 1, 1927, p. 15.

26. "Editorial Comment," *Baseball Magazine* 38 (February 1927), p. 431; *Cleveland Plain Dealer,* December 24, 1926, p. 1.

27. *Sporting News,* January 13, 1927, p. 2.

28. For accounts of Risberg's allegations and Landis's subsequent hearing on them, I have relied on coverage in the *Cleveland Plain Dealer, Chicago Tribune,* and *New York Times,* December 21, 1926–January 28, 1927, and *Sporting News,* December 30, 1926–February 3, 1927.

29. *Cleveland Plain Dealer,* January 11, 1927, p. 18; *Chicago Tribune,* January 13, 1927, p. 1.

30. *Cleveland Plain Dealer,* January 18, 1927, p. 1.

31. Ibid.; *Sporting News,* January 20, 1927, p. 3.

32. *Cleveland Plain Dealer,* January 21, 1927, p. 18.

33. *Cleveland Press,* December 28, 1926, p. 18.

34. *Cleveland Plain Dealer,* January 24, 1927, p. 1.

35. Ibid., January 25, 1927, p. 27.

36. Ibid., January 28, 1927, p. 18.

37. David Pietrusza, *Judge and Jury: The Life and Times of Kenesaw Mountain Landis* (South Bend, Ind.: Diamond Communications, 1998), p. 311.
38. *Sporting News,* January 6, 1927, p. 3.
39. Ibid., January 6, 1927, p. 3; February 3, 1927, p. 4.
40. Mark Alvarez, "Say It Ain't So, Ty," *National Pastime*, #14 (1994), p. 28.
41. In his *The Bill James Guide to Baseball Managers: From 1870 to Today* (New York: Scribner's, 1997), p. 85, Bill James agrees with my judgment on Speaker. For contrary views, see Blaisdell, "Cobb-Speaker Scandal"; Alvarez, "Say It Ain't So, Ty."

Chapter 12: "A Sort of Twilight to His Career"

1. *Cleveland Plain Dealer,* January 25, 1927, p. 1.
2. "When Ty Cobb and Tris Speaker March Back to the Diamond," *Literary Digest* 92 (February 12, 1927), p. 78.
3. *Sporting News,* February 10, 1927, p. 1.
4. Povich was mistakenly included in the 1962 edition of *Notable American Women.*
5. *Washington Post,* February 2, 1927, p. 15.
6. Rogers Hornsby served as acting manager of the New York Giants in thirty-two games in 1927, relieving an ill John McGraw.
7. *Cleveland Plain Dealer,* March 1, 1927, p. 17.
8. *Washington Post,* March 1, 1927, p. 17; *Cleveland Plain Dealer,* March 1, 1927, p. 17.
9. *Washington Post,* March 2, 1927, p. 15; *Sporting News,* March 10, 1927, p. 4.
10. *Washington Post,* March 20, 1927, p. 26.
11. Ibid., March 20 1927, p. 23.
12. *Cleveland Plain Dealer,* November 11, 1926, p. 17; F. C. Lane, "Many Homers—Many Runs—Is the Baseball Trend," *Baseball Magazine* 38 (June 1927), p. 310.
13. Joe Cashman interview with Carrigan, *Boston Daily Record,* January 27, 1943, p. 35, Bill Carrigan File, National Baseball Library, Cooperstown, New York.
14. *Washington Post,* May 3, 1927, p. 15.
15. *Sporting News,* December 19, 1935, p. 6.
16. Ibid., July 7, 1927, p. 4.
17. *Sporting News,* November 24, 1927, p. 4; *Washington Post,* November 13, 1927, p. 22.
18. *Sporting News,* January 14, 1959, p. 10.
19. Ibid., February 16, 1928, p. 2.
20. The situation in Boston finally changed as of the 1929 baseball season, because a majority of the state's voters had approved a referendum the previous November legalizing local-option Sunday amusements. It wasn't until 1934 that Pennsylvania voters finally did the same.
21. *Sporting News,* April 5, 1928, p. 1.
22. Ibid., March 15, 1928, p. 8.
23. Ibid., April 12, 1928, p. 1.
24. *Washington Post,* April 12, 1928, p. 18.
25. Ibid., April 21, 1928, p. 13.
26. Ibid., April 23, 1928, p. 11.

27. On that same day, May 19, Joseph Lannin was killed when he fell from the seventh-story window of a Brooklyn hotel he had purchased and was having renovated.
28. Seating about 20,000 when it opened at the start of the 1909 season, Shibe Park had been enlarged to a capacity of 33,900 in 1925.
29. "The Art of Making Hard Plays Easy," *Baseball Magazine* 41 (October 1928), p. 489.
30. *Sporting News,* October 4, 1928, p. 1.
31. *Newark Sunday Call,* clipping in Tris Speaker File, National Baseball Library, Cooperstown, New York. In 1950, Dick Burnett, the multimillionaire owner of the Dallas Eagles Texas League franchise, signed Charley Grimm to a $30,000 contract, which was generally understood to be the highest salary ever paid up to then to manage in the minors.

Chapter 13: "My Name Is Tris Speaker"

1. Walter Maxwell "Max" West, a Texan who played for Speaker at Newark in 1929, shouldn't be confused with Max Edward West, a Missourian born twelve years later, who spent seven years in the National League, mostly with Boston, beginning in 1938.
2. The market wasn't totally free. Players in those minor leagues that hadn't opted out of the annual minor-league draft could be drafted for a few thousand dollars. For most of the 1920s, however, players in the three top minor leagues (AA) as well as in the Class A Texas and Class B Three-I Leagues weren't draftable (which accounts for Baltimore's seven straight International League pennants and Fort Worth's six straight in the Texas League).
3. *Sporting News,* June 13, 1929, p. 3.
4. Ibid.
5. Ibid., August 1, 1929, p. 3.
6. Ibid., October 10, 1929, p. 2.
7. Ibid., July 25, 1964, p. 20.
8. Ibid., January 21, 1932, p. 4. Italics in original.
9. Ibid., March 3, 1933, p. 7.
10. Released later in 1933, *Elmer the Great* was probably Brown's best movie.
11. *Sporting News,* March 23, 1933, p. 1.
12. David Neal Keller, "Nobody's Perfect: Joe E. Brown," *Timeline* 22 (July–September 2005), p. 67.
13. *Sporting News,* March 1, 1934, p. 4.
14. *Sporting News,* April 22, 1937, p. 7; *Chicago Tribune,* April 11, 1937, p. 19; National League Service Bureau Bulletin, December 2, 1937, Tris Speaker File, National Baseball Library, Cooperstown, New York.
15. Ironically, it was Lee Keyser, Speaker's onetime partner in the Kansas City enterprise, who blew the whistle on the Cleveland franchise when it tried to cover up Feller's signing. At a time when, under baseball law, it was illegal for major-league teams to sign free-agent amateurs directly, Keyser claimed territorial rights to Feller, an Iowa resident, for his Des Moines franchise. Commissioner Landis, wanting to avoid a bidding war for Feller, ultimately validated the youngster as Cleveland property.
16. *Sporting News,* August 5, 1937, p. 7.

17. Kyle Crichton, "Center-Field Lightning," *Collier's* 101 (March 26, 1938), p. 41.

18. Charles C. Alexander, *Breaking the Slump: Baseball in the Depression Era* (New York: Columbia University Press, 2002), p. 185. Rogers Hornsby had recently become business and field manager for Fort Worth in the Texas League when, early in 1942, he received word of his Hall of Fame election. "Mighty nice honor, and I certainly appreciate the honor," he told reporters. "But baseball in 1942 is the thing with me now." Charles C. Alexander, *Rogers Hornsby: A Biography* (New York: Henry Holt and Company, 1995), p. 227.

19. *Sporting News,* August 10, 1939, p. 3.

20. Ibid., December 4, 1940, pp. 3, 6.

21. Ibid., July 16, 1942, p. 10; April 20, 1944, p. 6.

22. Ibid., January 6, 1944, p. 7.

23. Ibid.

24. Ibid., April 20, 1944, p. 6.

25. Ibid., January 4, 1945, p. 16.

26. Ibid., April 9, 1947, p. 14.

27. Ibid., March 26, 1947, p. 8.

28. Alexander, *Rogers Hornsby,* p. 237.

29. *Sporting News,* December 11, 1948, p. 16.

30. Tim Cohane, "Larry Doby: Baseball's Next Great Star," *Look* 13 (July 1949), p. 74.

31. *Sporting News,* March 9, 1949, p. 6.

32. Ibid., January 24, 1951, p. 13.

33. Ibid., January 31, 1951, p. 11.

34. Ibid., February 7, 1951, p. 6.

35. Ibid., December 17, 1958, p. 9.

36. Ibid., March 24, 1954, p. 26.

37. Joseph Thomas Moore, *Pride against Prejudice: The Biography of Larry Doby* (Westport, Conn.: Greenwood Press, 1988), p. 103; *Sporting News,* August 11, 1954, p. 9.

38. *Sporting News,* October 13, 1954, p. 21; November 3, 1954, p. 6.

39. Ibid., May 18, 1955, p. 15.

40. I was present with my parents for both the Old Timers' game and the All-Star game the next night—the only time Beaumont ever hosted the Texas League's All-Star Game. Although it was hoped that the back-to-back events would help to reinvigorate attendance for the local franchise, the Beaumont team, winning only fifty-one games and finishing a distant last, drew only about 60,000 for the 1955 season, after which the franchise was moved to Austin.

41. *Sporting News,* July 31, 1957, p. 16.

42. Ibid., March 12, 1958, p. 29.

43. Hank Greenberg had sold his interest in the Indians after the 1957 season and soon joined Bill Veeck in purchasing the Chicago White Sox.

44. *Sporting News,* July 16, 1958, p. 28; August 6, 1958, p. 18.

45. *Cleveland News,* December 9, 1958, clipping, and Speaker's death certificate, both in Speaker File, National Baseball Library.

46. *Hubbard City News,* December 19, 1958, p. 6, in Speaker File, National Baseball Library.

Afterword: "Let Your Voices Soften to a Mere Whisper"

1. Texan Rogers Hornsby was another man from another era who had to adjust his thinking in racial matters—at least where baseball was concerned. After his last firing as a manager, by the Cincinnati Reds in 1953, Hornsby served as a batting coach for the Cubs and for the expansion New York Mets, working with considerable numbers of black players, including future Hall of Famers Ernie Banks and Billy Williams. He was still employed by the Mets when he died early in 1963. Ty Cobb, who never had any official connection to baseball in the thirty-three years after he quit playing, changed little if any in his attitudes toward black people.
2. Bob Feller and Bill Gilbert, *Now Pitching: Bob Feller* (New York: HarperPerennial, 1991), p. 154.
3. Eugene C. Murdock, *Baseball Players and Their Times: An Oral History of the Major Leagues* (Westport, Conn.: Greenwood, 1991), pp. 218, 253.
4. *Sporting News,* January 10, 1976, p. 25.
5. John Thorn et al., eds., *Total Baseball: The Official Encyclopedia of Major League Baseball,* 7th ed. (Kingston N.Y.: Total Sports Publishing, 2001), p. 104.
6. Harold Seymour, *Baseball: The Golden Age* (New York: Oxford University Press, 1970).
7. *Sporting News,* February 9, 1963, p. 6.

Bibliography

Archival Resources

Bill Carrigan File, National Baseball Library, Cooperstown, New York.

Hammen, Theodore, to Tris Speaker, December 23, 1926, copy courtesy of William Burgess, Mountain View, California.

Charles Jamieson File, National Baseball Library, Cooperstown, New York.

George "Duffy" Lewis File, National Baseball Library, Cooperstown, New York.

Charles W. Mears Collection on Cleveland Baseball, Cleveland Public Library, Cleveland, Ohio.

Eugene C. Murdock Collection on Baseball, Cleveland Public Library, Cleveland, Ohio.

Joe Sewell File, National Baseball Library, Cooperstown, New York.

Tris Speaker File, National Baseball Library, Cooperstown, New York.

Howard "Joe" Wood File, National Baseball Library, Cooperstown, New York.

Internet Resources

http://www.ancestry.com
http://www.newspaperofrecord.com

Recordings

Ritter, Lawrence S. *The Glory of Their Times: The Story of the Early Days of Baseball Told by the Men Who Played It.* Four audiocassettes. St. Paul, Minn.: High Bridge Company, 1998.

Newspapers

Chicago Tribune, 1915–1937.
Cleveland News, 1922–1925.
Cleveland Plain Dealer, 1916–1928.
Cleveland Press, 1916–1925.
New York Times, 1908–1931, 1958.
St. Louis Post-Dispatch, 1910–1925.

Sporting Life, 1906–1917.
Sporting News, 1906–1999.
Washington Post, 1924–1928.

Official Publications

Reach's Official American League Guides, 1908–1928. Philadelphia: A. J. Reach Company, 1909–1929.

Books

Alexander, Charles C. *Breaking the Slump: Baseball in the Depression Era.* New York: Columbia University Press, 2002.
———. *John McGraw.* 1988. Reprint, Lincoln: University of Nebraska Press, 1995.
———. *The Ku Klux Klan in the Southwest.* 1965. Reprint, Norman: University of Oklahoma Press, 1995.
———. *Our Game: An American Baseball History.* New York: Henry Holt, 1991.
———. *Rogers Hornsby: A Biography.* New York: Henry Holt, 1995.
———. *Ty Cobb.* 1984. Reprint, Dallas: Southern Methodist University Press, 2006.
Barthel, Thomas. *The Fierce Fun of Ducky Medwick.* Lanham, Md.: Scarecrow Press, 2003.
The Baseball Encyclopedia. 10th ed. New York: Macmillan, 1996.
Bevis, Charlie. *Mickey Cochrane: The Life of a Baseball Hall of Fame Catcher.* Jefferson, N.C.: McFarland, 1998.
Broeg, Bob. *Superstars of Baseball: Their Lives, Their Loves, Their Laughs.* South Bend, Ind.: Diamond Communications, 1994.
Browning, Reed. *Baseball's Greatest Season: 1924.* Amherst: University of Massachusetts Press, 2003.
———. *Cy Young.* Amherst: University of Massachusetts Press, 2000.
Bryant, Howard. *Shut Out: A Story of Race and Baseball in Boston.* New York: Routledge, 2002.
Burk, Robert F. *Never Just a Game: Players, Owners, and American Baseball to 1920.* Chapel Hill: University of North Carolina Press, 1994.
Carmichael, John P., ed. *My Greatest Day in Baseball.* 1945. Reprint, Lincoln: University of Nebraska Press, 1996.
Carrigan, William D. *The Making of a Lynching Culture: Violence and Vigilantism in Central Texas, 1836–1916.* Urbana: University of Illinois Press, 2004.
Cobb, Ty, and Al Stump. *My Life in Baseball: The True Record.* 1961. Reprint, Lincoln: University of Nebraska Press, 1993.
Cobb, Ty, and John N. Wheeler. *Busting 'Em and Other Big League Stories.* Edited by William R. Cobb. 1914. Reprint, Jefferson, N.C.: McFarland, 2003.
Cook, William A. *The 1919 World Series: What Really Happened.* Jefferson, N.C.: McFarland, 2001.
Cottrell, Robert C. *Blackball, the Black Sox and the Babe: Baseball's Crucial 1920 Season.* Jefferson, N.C.: McFarland, 2002.
Creamer, Robert. *Babe: The Legend Comes to Life.* 1974. Reprint, New York: Penguin Books, 1985.

Curran, William. *Big Sticks: The Batting Revolution of the Twenties.* New York: Morrow, 1990.

Cvornyek, Robert L. *Baseball in Newark.* Charleston, S.C.: Acadia, 2003.

Deveaux, Tom. *The Washington Senators, 1901–1971.* Jefferson, N.C.: McFarland, 2001.

Dewey, Donald, and Nicholas Acocella. *The Black Prince of Baseball: Hal Chase and the Mythology of the Game.* Toronto: Sport Classic Books, 2004.

Eig, Jonathan. *The Luckiest Man: The Life and Death of Lou Gehrig.* New York: Simon and Schuster, 2005.

Elfers, James E. *The Tour to End All Tours: The Story of Major League Baseball's 1913–1914 World Tour.* Lincoln: University of Nebraska Press, 2003.

Feldman, Glenn. *Politics, Society, and the Klan in Alabama, 1915–1949.* Tuscaloosa: University of Alabama Press, 2001.

Feller, Bob, and Bill Gilbert. *Now Pitching: Bob Feller.* New York: HarperPerennial, 1991.

Fetter, Henry D. *Taking on the Yankees: Winning and Losing with the Business of Baseball.* New York: W. W. Norton, 2003.

Fleitz, David. *Shoeless: The Life and Times of Joe Jackson.* Jefferson, N.C.: McFarland, 2001.

Gay, Timothy. *Tris Speaker: The Rough and Tumble Life of a Baseball Legend.* Lincoln: University of Nebraska Press, 2005.

Godin, Roger A. *The 1922 St. Louis Browns: Best of the American League's Worst.* Jefferson, N.C.: McFarland, 1988.

Golenbock, Peter. *Fenway: An Unexpurgated History of the Boston Red Sox.* New York: Putnam's, 1992.

Graham, Frank. *The Brooklyn Dodgers: An Informal History.* 1945. Reprint, Carbondale and Edwardsville: Southern Illinois University Press, 2002.

Grayson, Harry. *They Played the Game: The Story of Baseball Greats.* New York: A. S. Barnes, 1944.

Hartley, Michael. *Christy Mathewson: A Biography.* Jefferson, N.C.: McFarland, 2003.

Huhn, Rick. *The Sizzler: George Sisler, Baseball's Forgotten Great.* Columbia: University of Missouri Press, 2004.

Hynd, Noel. *Marquard and Seeley.* Hyannis, Mass: Parnassus Imprints, 1996.

James, Bill. *The Bill James Guide to Baseball Managers: From 1870 to Today.* New York: Scribner's, 1997.

Jedick, Peter, *League Park.* Reprint, Cleveland: Society for American Baseball Research, 1990.

Johnson, Lloyd, and Miles Wolff, eds. *The Encyclopedia of Minor League Baseball.* Durham, N.C.: Baseball America, 1993.

Jordan, David M. *The Athletics of Philadelphia: Connie Mack's White Elephants, 1909–1954.* Jefferson, N.C.: McFarland, 1999.

———. *Occasional Glory: The History of the Philadelphia Phillies.* Jefferson, N.C.: McFarland, 2002.

Kashatus, William C. *Diamonds in the Coalfields: 21 Remarkable Baseball Players, Managers, and Umpires from Northeast Pennsylvania.* Jefferson, N.C.: McFarland, 2002.

Kavanagh, Jack. *Ol' Pete: The Grover Cleveland Alexander Story.* South Bend, Ind.: Diamond Communications, 1996.

———. *Uncle Robbie.* Cleveland: Society for American Baseball Research, 1999.

———. *Walter Johnson: A Biography.* South Bend, Ind.: Diamond Communications, 1995.

Kohout, Martin D. *Hal Chase: The Defiant and Turbulent Times of Baseball's Biggest Crook.* Jefferson, N.C.: McFarland, 2001.

Lane, F. C. *Batting.* 1925. Reprint; Cleveland: Society for American Baseball Research, 2001.

Lee, Bill. *The Baseball Necrology: The Post-Baseball Lives and Deaths of Over 7,600 Major League Players and Others.* Jefferson, N.C.: McFarland, 2003.

Levy, Alan H. *Joe McCarthy: Architect of the Yankees Dynasty.* Jefferson, N.C.: McFarland, 2004.

Lewis, Franklin. *The Cleveland Indians.* New York: Putnam's, 1949.

Lieb, Fred. *Baseball as I Have Known It.* 1977. Reprint, Lincoln: University of Nebraska Press, 1996.

———. *The Boston Red Sox.* 1947. Reprint, Carbondale and Edwardsville: Southern Illinois University Press, 2003.

Linn, Ed. *The Great Rivalry: The Yankees and the Red Sox, 1901–1990.* New York: Ticknor and Fields, 1991.

Lowry, Philip. *Green Cathedrals: The Ultimate Celebration of All 271 Major League and Negro League Ballparks Past and Present.* Cleveland: Society for American Baseball Research, 2006.

McGraw, John. *My Thirty Years in Baseball.* 1923. Reprint, Lincoln: University of Nebraska Press, 1995.

Mack, Connie. *My 66 Years in the Big Leagues.* Philadelphia: John C. Winston, 1950.

Mansch, Larry. *Rube Marquard: The Life and Times of a Baseball Hall of Famer.* Jefferson, N.C.: McFarland, 1998.

Mathewson, Christy. *Pitching in a Pinch.* 1912. Reprint, Lincoln: University of Nebraska Press, 1994.

Moore, Joseph Thomas. *Pride against Prejudice: The Biography of Larry Doby.* Westport, Conn.: Greenwood, 1988.

Murdock, Eugene C. *Ban Johnson: Czar of Baseball.* Westport, Conn.: Greenwood, 1983.

———. *Baseball between the Wars: Memories of the Game by the Men Who Played It.* Westport, Conn.: Meckler, 1992.

———. *Baseball Players and Their Times: Oral Histories of the Game, 1920–1930.* Westport, Conn.: Meckler, 1991.

Okonnen, Marc. *The Ty Cobb Scrapbook.* New York: Sterling, 2001.

Pietrusza, David. *Judge and Jury: The Life and Times of Kenesaw Mountain Landis.* South Bend, Ind.: Diamond Communications, 1998.

Poremba, David Lee. *The American League: The Early Years.* Chicago: Arcadia, 2000.

Reisler, Jim. *Babe Ruth: Launching the Legend.* New York: McGraw-Hill, 2004.

———. *Before They Were Bombers: The New York Yankees' Early Years, 1903–1919.* Jefferson, N.C.: McFarland, 2002.

Rickey, Branch, with Robert Riger. *The American Diamond: A Documentary of the Game of Baseball.* New York: Simon and Schuster, 1965.

Ritter, Lawrence S. *The Glory of Their Times: The Story of the Early Days of Baseball, Told by the Men Who Played It.* Rev. ed. Orig. 1966; New York: Vintage Books, 1985.

Robinson, Ray. *Matty: An American Hero.* New York: Oxford University Press, 1993.

Salant, Nathan. *Superstars, Stars, and Just Plain Heroes.* New York: Stein and Day, 1982.

Sargent, Kelly Boyer. *Joe Jackson: A Biography.* Westport, Conn.: Greenwood, 2004.

Seymour, Harold. *Baseball: The Golden Age.* New York: Oxford University Press, 1971.

Smelser, Marshall. *The Life That Ruth Built: A Biography.* 1975. Reprint, Lincoln: University of Nebraska Press, 1992.

Sowell, Mike. *The Pitch That Killed: Carl Mays, Ray Chapman, and the Pennant Race of 1920.* New York: Macmillan, 1989.

Spink, J. G. Taylor. *Judge Landis and Twenty-Five Years of Baseball.* New York: Crowell, 1947.

Stein, Fred. *And the Skipper Bats Cleanup: A History of the Baseball Player-Manager, with 42 Biographies of Men Who Filled the Dual Role.* Jefferson, N.C.: McFarland, 2002.

Stout, Glenn, and Richard A. Johnson. *Red Sox Century: One Hundred Years of Red Sox Baseball.* New York: Houghton Mifflin, 2000.

Thomas, Henry. *Walter Johnson: Baseball's Big Train.* Washington, D.C.: Phenom Press, 1995.

Thorn, John, et al., eds. *Total Baseball: The Official Encyclopedia of Major League Baseball.* 7th ed. Kingston, N.Y.: Total Sports Publishing, 2001.

Trachtenberg, Leo. *The Wonder Team: The True Story of the Incomparable 1927 New York Yankees.* Bowling Green, Ohio: Bowling Green Popular Press, 1995.

Van Tassel, David, and John T. Grabowski, eds. *The Encyclopedia of Cleveland History.* Bloomington: Indiana University Press, 1996.

Vlasich, James A. *A Legend for the Legendary: The Origin of the Baseball Hall of Fame.* Bowling Green, Ohio: Bowling Green Popular Press, 1990.

White, G. Edward. *Creating the National Pastime: Baseball Transforms Itself, 1903–1953.* Princeton, N.J.: Princeton University Press, 1996.

Williams, Peter, ed. *The Joe Williams Baseball Reader.* Chapel Hill, N.C.: Algonquin Books, 1989.

Wright, Marshall D. *The Southern Association in Baseball, 1885–1961.* Jefferson, N.C.: McFarland, 2002.

———. *The Texas League in Baseball, 1888–1958.* Jefferson, N.C.: McFarland, 2004.

Wright, Russell O. *A Tale of Two Leagues: How Baseball Changed as the Rules, Balls, Franchises, Stadiums, and Players Changed, 1900–1988.* Jefferson, N.C.: McFarland, 1999.

Zingg, Paul J. *Harry Hooper: An American Baseball Life.* Urbana: University of Illinois Press, 1993.

Articles

Alvarez, Mark. "An Interview with Joe Wood." *Baseball Research Journal,* #16 (1987), pp. 53–56.

———. "Say It Ain't So, Ty." *National Pastime,* #14 (1994), pp. 21–28.

Anderson, Dave. "Harry and Stanley Coveleski." *National Pastime,* #20 (2000), pp. 39–41.

"The Art of Making Hard Plays Easy." *Baseball Magazine* 41 (October 1928), pp. 489–490.

"Behind the Scenes in a Big League Clubhouse." *Baseball Magazine* 34 (April 1925), p. 504.

Biele, Edward. "Facts and Figures on Big League Stars." *Baseball Magazine* 26 (July 1921), pp. 355f.

Billson, Marky. "Tilly Walker." *National Pastime,* #20 (2000), pp. 105–108.

Blaisdell, Lowell. "The Cobb-Speaker Scandal: Exonerated but Probably Guilty." *Nine: A Journal of Baseball History and Culture* 13 (2005), pp. 54–70.

Bluthardt, Robert F. "Fenway Park and the Golden Age of the Baseball Park, 1900–1915." *Journal of Popular Culture* 21 (Summer 1987), pp. 43–52.

Boydala, Stephen D. "Speaker, Tris E." In *Dictionary of American Biography: Supplement 6 (1956–1960),* ed. John Garraty, pp. 588–590. New York: Scribner's, 1980.

"A Broken Record." *Baseball Magazine* 7 (July 1911), p. 87.

Bulger, Bozeman. "Twenty-five Years in Sports." *Saturday Evening Post* 200 (April 28, 1928), pp. 8–9f.

"Calling Them with George Moriarty." *Baseball Magazine* 37 (October 1926), pp. 508f.

Chase, Frank M. "The Standard of the Conference." *Baseball Magazine* 32 (January 1924), pp. 367f.

Chuck, Bill. "Boston–New York: The *Really* Exciting World Series." *Baseball Research Journal*, #16 (1987), pp. 2–6.

Cobbledick, Gordon. "Tris Speaker: The Gray Eagle." *Sport* 12 (July 1952), pp. 34–37f.

Cohane, Tim. "Larry Doby: Baseball's Next Great Star." *Look* 13 (July 1949), pp. 74–79.

"College Players in the Major Leagues." *Baseball Magazine* 6 (December 1910), p. 6.

Crichton, Kyle. "Center-Field Lightning." *Collier's* 101 (March 26, 1938), pp. 17f.

Dagavarian, Debra A., and Mark Rucker. "The Joe Wood Scrapbook." *National Pastime* 2 (Fall 1982), pp. 39–47.

"The Death of Chapman, Killed by a Pitched Ball." *Literary Digest* 66 (September 18, 1920), p. 92.

Derby, Richard. "Mays' Beaning of Ray Chapman Recalled." *Baseball Research Journal*, #11 (1984), pp. 12–13.

Donahue, Louis A. "The Luxury of Training Trips." *Baseball Magazine* 6 (March 1911), pp. 1A–3A.

Dunn, J. C. "My Experience as a Major League Owner." *Baseball Magazine* 18 (March 1917), pp. 87–89.

"Editorial Comment." *Baseball Magazine* 24 (December 1919), p. 458.

"Editorial Comment." *Baseball Magazine* 38 (February 1927), pp. 390f.

"Editorial Comment." *Baseball Magazine* 38 (March 1927), pp. 439–440.

Fohl, Lee. "Baseball Brains." *Baseball Magazine* 20 (January 1918), pp. 28f.

Fullerton, Hugh S. "Between Games: How the Ball Players of the Big Leagues Live and Act When off the Diamond." *American Magazine* 72 (July 1911), pp. 321–333.

Gagnon, Cappy. "The Six Greatest Throwing Outfielders in History." *Baseball Research Journal*, #24 (1995), pp. 96–100.

Givens, Horace. "Bibb Falk Recalls the Old 'Black Sox.'" *Baseball Digest* 43 (May 1984), pp. 68–72.

"A Good Word for the Spit Ball." *Baseball Magazine* 24 (March 1920), pp. 571–572.

Gould, James M. "An Inventory of Baseball for 1927." *Baseball Magazine* 40 (January 1928), pp. 355–356.

———. "Speaking of Managers." *Baseball Magazine* 34 (April 1925), pp. 499f.

———. "Who Will Win the Big League Pennants in 1926?" *Baseball Magazine* 36 (May 1926), pp. 531–533f.

Graham, Frank. "On Seeing Tris Speaker Again." *Baseball Digest* 13 (November–December 1954), pp. 93–94.

Greene, Lee. "The Gray Eagle." *Sport* 20 (August 1960), pp. 36–37f.

"How I Spend My Annual Vacation." *Baseball Magazine* 30 (March 1923), pp. 455f.

Johnson, Willis E. "Around the Circuit with a Ball Team." *Baseball Magazine* 28 (March 1922), pp. 827–828f.

Keller, David Neal. "Nobody's Perfect: Joe E. Brown." *Timeline* 22 (July–September 2005), pp. 54–69.

Kuester, Bob. "All-Time Best Center Fielders Combined Hitting, Fielding." *Baseball Digest* 53 (December 1994), pp. 36–47.

Lane, F. C. "The All-American Baseball Club of 1922." *Baseball Magazine* 30 (December 1922), pp. 309–310.

———. "Extraordinary Career of 'Smoky' Joe Wood." *Baseball Magazine* 27 (October 1921), pp. 493–494.

———. "The Greatest of All Outfielders." *Baseball Magazine* 11 (September 1913), pp. 33–44.

———. "The King of Outfielders." *Baseball Magazine* 18 (March 1917), pp. 113–118.

———. "Many Homers—Many Runs—Is the Baseball Trend." *Baseball Magazine* 38 (June 1927), pp. 309–310.

———. "Should the Spitball Be Abolished?" *Baseball Magazine* 23 (June 1919), pp. 67–70f.

———. "A Startling Baseball Tragedy." *Baseball Magazine* 25 (October 1920), pp. 523–524f.

———. "Tris Speaker, King of the Outfield." *Baseball Magazine* 13 (July 1914), pp. 47–57.

———. "Tris Speaker Traded." *Baseball Magazine* 17 (June 1916), pp. 19–28.

———. "What's Wrong with the Three-Base Hit?" *Baseball Magazine* 29 (June 1922), pp. 303–304.

Langford, Walter M. "The Mighty Mite Who Almost Never Struck Out." *Baseball Digest* 43 (May 1984), pp. 73f.

Lieb, Fred G. "Baseball's Greatest Utility Players." *Baseball Magazine* 30 (May 1923), pp. 539–541f.

———. "Training Time in Dixie." *Baseball Magazine* 26 (April 1921), pp. 511–515.

McGlynn, Frank. "Striking Scenes from the Tour around the World: Part IV." *Baseball Magazine* 14 (November 1914), pp. 75–80.

Macht, Norman. "History Repeats Itself: There's Nothing New in Baseball." *Baseball Digest* 59 (June 2000), pp. 74–77.

Meany, Tom. "The Gray Eagle Was a Lion at Bat." *Baseball Digest* 30 (January 1971), pp. 56–61.

Miller, Raymond. "Here's a Belated Salute to Four Old Ballplayers." *Baseball Digest* 55 (September 1996), pp. 66–75.

Morse, Jacob C. "Where the Clubs Will Train." *Baseball Magazine* 6 (February 1911), pp. 12–14.

Moss, Edward Bayard. "The Greatest Baseball Series Ever Played." *Harper's Weekly* 56 (November 2, 1912), p. 10.

"One Reason for Cleveland's Sensational Comeback." *Baseball Magazine* 37 (November 1926), p. 536.

Peters, Nick. "Little Joe Sewell: He Was Best Contact Hitter Ever." *Baseball Digest* 45 (December 1986), pp. 40–42.

Phelon, William A. "Baseball's Spring Campaign Begins." *Baseball Magazine* 26 (April 1921), pp. 533–534f.

———. "How Goes the Pennant Race?" *Baseball Magazine* 19 (July 1917), pp. 86–88f.

———. "How I Picked the Loser." *Baseball Magazine* 16 (December 1915), pp. 17–23f.

———. "How the New World's Championship Was Won." *Baseball Magazine* 26 (December 1920), pp. 319–323f.

———. "How the World's Series Was Lost and Won." *Baseball Magazine* 10 (December 1912), pp. 15–23.

———. "Lining Up for 1916." *Baseball Magazine* 17 (June 1916), pp. 13–18f.

———. "On the Home Stretch of the Great 1912 Pennant Races." *Baseball Magazine* 9 (October 1912), pp. 15–24.

———. "The Opening Broadsides." *Baseball Magazine* 15 (June 1915), pp. 19–28f.

———. "The Passing Month in Baseball." *Baseball Magazine* 22 (February 1919), pp. 213–216f.

———. "The Pennant Races Grow Hot." *Baseball Magazine* 29 (October 1922), pp. 507–508f.

———. "Ringing Up the Curtain on the 1913 Pennant Race." *Baseball Magazine* 11 (June 1913), pp. 5–20f.

———. "Who Will Win the Big League Pennants?" *Baseball Magazine* 28 (May 1922), pp. 819–822f.

———. "Who Will Win the Big League Pennants?" *Baseball Magazine* 32 (May 1924), pp. 531–533.

———. "Who Will Win the 1913 Pennants?" *Baseball Magazine* 10 (May 1913), pp. 12–32f.

———. "Who Will Win the Pennants?" *Baseball Magazine* 19 (September 1917), pp. 553–556.

———. "Who Will Win the Pennants?" *Baseball Magazine* 26 (May 1921), pp. 558–562f.

———. "Who Will Win the World Series of 1924?" *Baseball Magazine* 33 (October 1924), pp. 547–549.

"Pulling Grass Is Tris Speaker's Baseball Barometer." *Literary Digest* 67 (December 11, 1920), pp. 81f.

Rice, Grantland. "I Saw Them Play." *Collier's* 85 (March 22, 1930), p. 32.

Richard, Kenneth D. "Carl Mays Revisited." *Baseball Research Journal* 30 (2001), pp. 122–126.

Ritter, Lawrence S. "Ladies and Gentlemen, Presenting Marty McHale." *National Pastime,* #8 (1982), pp. 16–21.

Rogers, C. Paul. "Speaker, Tris(tram) E." In *The Scribner's Encyclopedia of American Lives: Sports Figures,* ed. Arnold Markoe, pp. 384–386. New York: Scribner's, 2002.

Roth, Morton. "Best Center Fielder of All Time: How About Speaker." *Baseball Digest* 46 (July 1987), pp. 65–68.

Rothe, Emil. "The War of 1912: The Wood-Johnson Duel." *Baseball Historical Review* (1981), pp. 41–45.

Rubinstein, Bill. "Hit by Pitched Balls." *Baseball Research Journal,* #28 (1999), pp. 120–123.

Sanborn, Irving E. "The Problem of the Big League Club Owner." *Baseball Magazine* 32 (February 1924), pp. 391–393.

———. "Speeding Up the Old Ball Game." *Baseball Magazine* 40 (December 1927), pp. 295–297.

Sawyer, Fred. "The Star Pinch-Hitter of 1922." *Baseball Magazine* 30 (February 1923), pp. 401–402.

Speaker, Tris. "Diamonds in the Rough." *Rotarian* 54 (April 1939), pp. 22–25.

———. "The Famous Thirty Thousand Dollar Muff." *Baseball Magazine* 24 (November 1919), pp. 403–404.

———. "Fine Points of the Game Which Are Lost on the Crowd." *Baseball Magazine* 21 (August 1918), pp. 325–326f.

———. "The Ins and Outs of Batting." *Baseball Magazine* 22 (April 1919), pp. 331–332.

———. "Winning the Batting Championship." *Baseball Magazine* 18 (March 1917), pp. 85–86.

"Sport." *Time* 5 (March 30, 1925), p. 28.

Steinberg, Steve L. "The Spitball and the End of the Deadball Era." *National Pastime,* #28 (2003), pp. 7–17.

Stockton, J. Roy. "Baseball's Most Versatile Athlete." *Baseball Magazine* 36 (December 1925), pp. 309f.

Thompson, Dick. "Chick and Jake Stahl: Not Brothers." *National Pastime,* #20 (2000), pp. 54–57.

"Tris Speaker: The Star of the 1920 Baseball Season." *Baseball Magazine* 26 (December 1920), pp. 317–318f.

"Tris Speaker Explains." *Baseball Magazine* 17 (September 1916), pp. 29–30f.

"Walter Johnson on Baseball Slavery." *Baseball Magazine* 7 (July 1911), pp. 75–76.

Warburton, Paul. "The 1921 American League Race." *National Pastime,* #18 (1998), pp. 103–106.

Ward, John F. "Baseball's Hardest Hitting Shortstop." *Baseball Magazine* 32 (February 1924), p. 405.

———. "Emory Rigney Moves to Washington." *Baseball Magazine* 38 (July 1927), p. 365.

———. "From the Sand Lots to the Majors." *Baseball Magazine* 31 (September 1923), pp. 453–454.

———. "Joseph Wood, Esq., Pitcher." *Baseball Magazine* 10 (November 1912), pp. 49–52.

———. "Tris Speaker, King of Two-Base Hitters." *Baseball Magazine* 33 (July 1924), p. 355.

Waterman, Guy. "The Upstart Senators of 1912–1915." *National Pastime,* #13 (1993), pp. 24–27.

"What I Have Learned from 20 Years in the Outfield." *Baseball Magazine* 35 (September 1925), pp. 444f.

"What the Baseball Public Wants." *Baseball Magazine* 15 (August 1915), pp. 69–74.

"When Ty Cobb and Tris Speaker March Back to the Diamond." *Literary Digest* 92 (February 12, 1927), pp. 76f.

"Who's Who in Baseball? Stars of the Diamond and Their Records." *Baseball Magazine* 9 (March 1912), pp. 85–86.

"Why It Always Pays to Hustle." *Baseball Magazine* 36 (May 1926), pp. 549–550.

Wood, Joe. "Doing the Comeback Stunt." *Baseball Magazine* 19 (August 1917), pp. 425–426.

Index

A

A. G. Spalding and Brothers, 36
Ackerman, Martin, 148
Acosta, José, 162
Ad Club, 109, 154
Adair Field, 198
Aldridge, Vic, 278, 281–282
Alexander, Grover Cleveland, xx, 41
  military service, 135
  National Baseball Hall of Fame, 289
  off-season player trades, 124
  salary increase (1914), 76
  statistics (1915), 93
  World Series (1915), 94–96
All-State League, 6
Allen, Nick, 286
American Association, 14, 100, 125, 198, 211, 284–285, 292
American Federation of Labor, 115
American League, xvii, 7, 13, 17, 23, 75, 100, 108, 116, 129, 289
Ames, Leon (Red), 51
Ansonia Hotel, 156–158
Appling, Luke, 283
Arellanes, Frank, 22, 24, 28
Associated Press, 146
Aston House Hotel, 70
Austin, Jimmy, 202
Avon Park, 257
Ayers, Yancy (Doc), 75, 127, 142

B

Babe Ruth Foundation for Needy Children, 294
Bagby, Jim, 103, 106, 108, 111, 119, 123, 125, 129, 137, 140, 144, 156, 159–165, 169–170, 181, 183–184, 197–198, 282
  hitting, 143
  illness, 195
  minor leaguer, as a, 278
  off-season, 174
  statistics (1920), 167
  World Series (1920), 171, 173
Baker Bowl, 93, 96, 106
Baker, Frank, 24, 33, 46, 76, 83, 140, 248
Baker, Newton D., 128
Baker, William F., 72, 94
Ball composition, home runs and, 35
Ball, Philip de Catesby, 100–101, 122, 202, 253, 255
Bancroft, Dave, 93–95, 206, 223, 255, 266
Bang, Ed, 101–103, 219, 297
Barnard, Ernest S., 141, 194, 197, 204–205, 216, 219, 221, 234–235, 242, 250, 269
  length of games and, 271
  player deals, 215
  replacing Byron Bancroft Johnson, 266
Barney (nickname). *See* Johnson, Walter (The Big Train)
Barris, George, 244–245
Barrow, Ed, 126, 128, 140, 143

Barry, Jack, 33, 83, 120, 135, 283
  acquisition of, by Boston Red Sox, 88
  impact of, on 1915 Boston Red Sox, 92
  manager, as a, 114
  navy service, 126
  World Series (1915), 96
Baseball
  1915 attendance, 83–104
  betting scandal, 1919, 233–252
  crowd sizes, 91
  dead ball era, 150
  death from injuries, 157–159
  fights, 140
  hitting upsurge, 149–151, 155
  home runs, increase in, during 1911, 35–36
  lively ball era, 150
  pitching (1915 season), 85–86
  player-managers, 206, 255
  players, 20–22
  rule changes, 150, 222–223
  Ruthian, 151
  scientific game, 151
  seasons: 1913, 59–81; 1916, 105–112, 114;
    1917, 117–123; 1918, 125–131; 1919,
    137–145; 1920, 153–167; 1921, 180–188;
    1922, 192–196; 1923, 199–204; 1924, 206–
    210; 1925, 216–220; 1926, 224–230; 1927,
    258–265; 1928, 268–273; 1929, 278–281;
    1930, 282
  segregation and, 27–28
  stamina of players, in 1920s, 226
  statistics (1915), 92–94, 196
  strike, threat of, 115
  Sunday games, 127
  system of governance, 175
  team migrations, 307
  war time, operations during, 119
  work or fight order, exemption, 128
  World War I and, 116–117
Baseball as I Have Known It (Lieb), 213
Baseball Corner, 302
Baseball Federation, 289
Baseball Magazine, 1, 32–33, 35, 41, 86, 105,
  125, 149, 189, 219, 244, 258, 272

Baseball Players' Fraternity, 66
Baseball Writers Association of America
  (BBWAA), 225, 286–287, 305, 309
Bedient, Hugh, 44, 45, 50, 51, 52, 53, 54, 64, 76,
  78, 81
Bell, Stuart, 183–184, 207, 209
Bender, Charles (Chief), 14, 33, 83, 283
Betting scandal (1919), 233–252
Big inning baseball, 189
Biltmore Hotel, 74
Birmingham, Joe, 105
Bishop, Max, 273
Black Sox, 166, 175
Blackstone Hotel, 249, 253
Blattner, Buddy, 302
Block, Paul, 274, 277, 283
Block Stadium, 277, 281
Blue, Lu, 224
Bob Feller Day, 300
Bodie, Ping, 140, 142
Boland, Bernie, 137, 138, 237, 240, 244
Boone, James (Danny), 199, 205
Boston American , 242
Boston American League, 7, 9–10. *See also*
  Boston Red Sox
Boston Braves. 39, 72, 79. *See also* Boston
  National League
Boston Elevated Railway Company, 13
Boston Globe, 9, 23, 44, 100, 103, 301
Boston Herald, 103
Boston National League, 9, 14, 27, 39, 41
Boston Pilgrims. *See* Boston American League;
  Boston Red Sox
Boston Puritans. *See* Boston American League;
  Boston Red Sox
Boston Red Sox, xv, xvi, 10, 11, 17, 25
  breaking up of 1912 team, 81
  Cleveland Naps, fight, 61
  cliques on team, 62, 87
  fans, on trade of Tris Speaker, 103
  ill feelings on team (1913 season), 62
  internal problems, 62, 87
  lost uniforms, 63
  payroll, 59

seasons: 1912, 43–47; 1914, 78–79; 1915, 83

series with Detroit Tigers, 1915, 90–91

World Series, 61, 97

Boston Red Sox, dismantling of, 149. *See also* Rape of the Red Sox

Boudreau, Lou, 290, 293, 295

Boyd, William A., 245–247, 250

Bradley, Alva, 266, 290, 292

Bradley, Bill, 301

Bragan, Bobby, 301–303

Bramham, William G., 289

Braves Field, 94–95, 114

Breadon, Sam, 257

Breakfast Club, 292

Breitenstein, Ted, 11

Bresnahan, Roger, 19

Bretton Hall Hotel, 48, 52

Brock, Lou, 309

Broeg, Bob, 309

Brooklyn Daily Eagle, 242

Brooklyn Federals, 73

Brooklyn Robins, 113, 167

Brotherhood of Professional Baseball Players, 66

Brower, Frank, 197, 203, 210, 215

Brown, Joe E., 181, 284, 286, 291, 299

Brown, Mordecai (Three Finger), 72–73

Brown, Walter P., 32

Brown, Warren, 223

Brush, John T., 10, 49, 57

Buckeye, Garland, 220–221, 225, 228, 230, 266

Bulger, Bozeman, 103, 241

Burchell, Fred, 23

Burke, Edward L., 245

Burnett, Dick, 296, 298

Burns, Ed, 95–97

Burns, George (ballplayer), 129, 155, 169, 171, 181, 207, 218, 225–226, 229, 232

    batting averages, 131

    injuries, 226

    off-season, 174

    records, 227–228, 230

    statistics (1926), 231

    trade: to Cleveland, 205; to Red Sox, 190

Burns, William (Sleepy Bill), 177

Burton, Harold H., 288

Bush, Joe, 111, 190, 208, 216

Bush, Leslie (Joe), 83

Bush, Owen (Donie), 91, 155, 244

Byrne, Bobby, 59

C

Cadore, Leon, 170

Cady, Forrest (Hick), 44, 51, 52, 54, 94, 99, 124

Caldwell, Ray, 60, 77, 88, 119, 141, 144, 159–160, 163, 169, 171, 182–183, 187

    physical training, 153

    release of, 190

    spitball pitcher, as a, 150

    statistics (1920), 167

    struck by lightning, 143

    suspension, by Tris Speaker, 186

    Tris Speaker, relationship with, 143

California State League, 18

Callahan, Jimmy, 43, 67, 72

Callicutt, John, 8

Canadian Pacific Railroad, 68

Carish, Fred, 61

Carmichael, John P., 281

Carrigan, Bill (Rough), 9–10, 28, 42, 44, 61, 64, 74, 78, 81, 86–88, 91, 100, 216

    Babe Ruth and, 87

    baseball players, comments on, 258

    contract (1913), 59

    Federal League and, 71

    fights, 61

    Jimmy McAleer and, 63

    manager, as a, 63, 65

    retirement, 114

    season (1914), 77–78

    Smokey Joe Wood, relationship with, 87

    Tris Speaker, relationship with, 87

    Ty Cobb and, 90

    World Series (1915), 96–97

Carroll, Richard, 73

Carter, Kate, 170

Castle, Edward B., 287

Castle, M. H., 121, 182, 191, 207, 223

Chalmers, George, 96

Chalmers, Hugh, 51

Chance, Frank, 60, 84, 200–201

Chapman, Kathleen, 158, 173

Chapman, Ray, 106, 113, 120, 122, 129, 156, 182, 237
  anniversary of death, 184
  betting scandal (1919), comments on, 244
  Bill Carrigan, fights with, 61
  death from baseball injuries, 157–160, 291
  Tris Speaker, friendship with, 148, 213

Charleston, Oscar, xx

Chase, Hal, 18–19, 29–30, 42, 163, 178
  Federal League and, 75
  globe-circling tour, 67
  indictment in 1919 World Series fix, 177
  White Sox and, 60

Chelsea Football Grounds, 72

Chicago Herald-Examiner, 239

Chicago Tribune, 242, 247, 249, 256, 281

Chicago Whales, 84

Chicago White Sox, 11, 43, 89, 127, 146
  bribes and World Series (1919), 163
  dishonest play (1920), 166–167
  statistics (1920), 166

Chill, Ollie, 186

China, Republic of, 69

Cicotte, Eddie, 24, 29, 36, 44, 121–122, 127, 139, 143, 156, 164, 167, 177
  release by Chicago White Sox, 178
  sailer or shine ball, 120, 138
  season (1917), 120
  statistics: 1919, 146; 1920, 166
  World Series (1919) fix, 146–147, 164, 177

Cincinnati Agreement of 1914, 115

Cincinnati Red Stockings, 309

Clark, Bob, 187

Clemente, Roberto, 306

Cleveland Amateur Baseball Federation, 288

Cleveland Boxing Commission, 288

Cleveland Plain Dealer, 183, 216, 244

Cleveland Athletic Club, 118

Cleveland Baseball Hall of Fame, 298, 301

Cleveland Indians
  attendance: 1918, 132; 1921, 188; 1922, 196; 1924, 210; 1926, 231
  championship (1920), 165
  Cleveland Municipal Stadium, 293
  finish in pennant race (1924), 210
  horse-racing and 178
  members in military service, 132
  name change from Naps, 87
  ownership change, after death of Jim Dunn, 194
  pennant favorites (1920), 154
  pennant winners, 299
  personnel changes, 197, 205
  Ray Chapman, memory of, 168
  statistics: 1920, 167; 1923, 204
  Tris Speaker, affiliation with, 292
  World's Champions uniforms, 180

Cleveland Municipal Stadium, 292, 298–299, 302

Cleveland Naps, 17, 24, 34, 43, 64

Cleveland News, 101, 219, 243, 292, 297

Cleveland Plain Dealer, 108, 207, 243, 307

Cleveland Press, xvii, 106, 119, 144, 170, 206, 219, 242, 244

Clolo, Carlos. *See* Hall, Charley

Cobb, Charlie, 266

Cobb, Ty, xvi, xviii, 8–9, 24, 30, 47, 90–91, 117, 120, 122, 128, 145, 203, 210, 234, 236, 239–246, 264, 266, 269–270, 283, 291, 297, 300, 302, 309
  argument: with Boston Red Sox, 89–90; with Carl Mays, 91
  banishment from American League, 247
  Baseball Players' Fraternity, support for, 66
  batter's box, movement in, 121
  batting averages, 103, 154
  batting titles, 24, 80, 93, 112, 123, 131, 145
  betting scandal (1919), 233, 237–238
  big inning baseball, comments on, 189
  Braves Field, comment on, 94
  Byron Bancroft Johnson, dislike of, 249
  Carl Mays and death of Ray Chapman, comments on, 160

Chemical Warfare Service, 130
comparison to Tris Speaker, 26, 44
Connie Mack and, 268
crowd hostility, 90–91
Dutch Leonard and, 238, 243
fans, problems with, 66
Frank Navin, relationship with, 233–234
full-time player, end as a, 271
golf and, 112, 206
health, 294
hitting, 189, 269
home runs, 111
hometown support for, 243
illness, 125, 271
income, 58
injuries, 80, 154, 192, 271
interviews with, 55
Japan and, 273
Kennesaw Mountain Landis, dislike of, 249
last major league game, 273
letter to Dutch Leonard, 236
manager, as a, 180–181, 204, 206, 234, 255
military service, 132
National Baseball Hall of Fame and, 287
offers following exoneration, 253
Philadelphia Athletics and, 255, 268
pinch hitter, as a, 271
post-season play, 31
purchase of Red Sox, 234
records, 164
remaining in American League, 253
resignation, letter of, 233
retirement, 273
salary, 74, 255
seasons: 1915, 89; 1923, 202
segregated baseball and, xix
statistics: 1911, 35; 1912, 46; 1914, 80; 1920, 168; 1921, 189; 1922, 196; 1925, 221; 1927, 265; 1928, 275;
steel spikes, use of, 20
stolen bases, 23
suspensions, 43
temperament, xx

Tris Speaker, relationship with, comments on, 11, 14, 233, 259, 268, 294
victory loan bonds, 138
white supremacist views, 213
World Series: 1915, 92; 1926, 232
Cochrane, Gordon (Mickey), 217, 264, 271, 273, 301
Cohen, Andy, 282
Colavito, Rocky, 309
Colliers, 288
Collins, Eddie, 24, 33, 35, 64, 76, 83–84, 93, 120, 126, 146, 149, 156, 227, 243, 247, 255, 268, 283, 291
batter's box, movement in, 121
National Baseball Hall of Fame and, 289
player-manager as a, 206–207
salary increase (1914), 76
statistics: 1912, 46; 1914, 80; 1916, 112; 1920, 166
Tris Speaker, comments on, 294
Collins, Ray, 26, 44, 49–50, 52, 78, 90, 99
Federal League and, 71
income, 98
seasons: 1913, 64; 1914, 75
Collins, Warren (Rip), 185
Colonial Hotel, 102
Columbia Park, 8, 14
Combs, Earl, 208, 225, 229
Comerford, Dan, 150
Comiskey, Charles, 37, 66–67, 85, 127, 138, 149, 164, 166, 178
Comiskey, Grace, 68
Comiskey, Louis, 68
Comiskey, Nancy, 68
Comiskey Park, 40, 147, 162, 188, 224, 283
Commercial Appeal (Memphis), 12
Commissioner of Baseball, 178
Compton, Pete, 45
Conagalton, Bill, 8, 9
Conlan, John (Jocko), 278–280, 282
Connolly, George (Sarge), 271
Connolly, Tom, 22, 130, 139, 157
Coogan's Bluff, 49

Coolidge, Calvin, 259
Coombs, Jack, 33, 83
Copley Square Hotel, 51
Coumbe, Fritz, 112, 122, 129, 140–141
Coveleski, Harry, 89, 91, 106, 108
Coveleski, Stanley, 106, 108, 117, 119, 123, 127, 137–138, 141–143, 154–157, 161–162, 164–166, 168–170, 172, 179–180, 183–188, 190, 193–194, 196, 199–200, 208–209, 219, 259, 270, 308
   injuries, 186, 260
   spitball, on banning, 150
   statistics: 1920, 167; 1923, 204; 1924, 211
   trade from Cleveland, 215
   Tris Speaker, friendship with, 213
   waivers on, 262
   World Series (1920), 173
Crandall, Otis, 26
Cravath, Clifford (Gavvy), 93–96
Crawford, Sam, xvii, 65, 89–90, 106
   Baseball Players' Fraternity, support for, 66
   Federal League and, 71
   globe-circling tour, 67
   Pope Pius X, meeting with, 70–71
Crichton, Kyle, 288
Criger, Lou, 17, 19
Criss, Dode, 6, 11
Crowder, Alvin, 262, 264
Cudahy, Mary Frances, 214. *See also* Speaker, Mary Frances
Cunningham, C. C., 168
Cunningham, George, 108
Curley, James, 97

D

Dallas Eagles, 296
Daly, Daniel, 156, 158
Daly, Kathleen, 148
Daly, Tom, 72
Danforth, Dave, 120–122, 157, 202
Daniel, Dan, 267
Daubert, Jake, 11, 66, 80
Dauss, George (Hooks), 90–92, 207, 247

Davenport, Dave, 110
Davids, Charles W., 277
Davids Stadium, 277
Davis, Harry W., 148, 181
Dead-ball era, xvii
Dean, Dizzy, 300
Delahanty, Ed, 203
Delahanty, Frank, 11
Delaware River Shipbuilding League, 128
Demaree, Al, 93
Dempsey, Jack, 220, 230
DeSoto Hotel, 136
Detroit News, 237
Detroit Tigers, 8–9, 11
Detroit Times, 144
Devore, Josh, 51, 53–54, 56
Dillard, Harrison, 301
DiMaggio, Joe, xvii, 288, 290–291, 300, 309–310
Dineen, Bill, 182, 186, 194, 229
Doak, Bill, 222, 256
Doby, Larry, 294, 299
   Cleveland's Man of the Year, 297
   Hall of Fame, 295
   Rookie of the Year, 295
   Tris Speaker, comments on, 295–297
Donabedian, Harry, 296–297
Donohue, Pete, 303
Donovan, Bill, 84
Donovan, Joseph (Patsy), 27–29, 33, 35, 37
Doolan, Mickey, 73
Doubleday, Abner, 286
Doyle, James E., 244
Doyle, Larry, 50–54, 56, 67–68, 93
Dreyfus, Barney, 21, 253
Dubuc, Jean, 113
Dunn, Emily, 195, 214, 219, 231, 234–235, 261
   Cleveland Indians: sale of, 266: stockholder in, 194
   Tris Speaker, friendship with, 213
Dunn Field, 192, 194, 196, 198–201, 203, 205, 207–210, 217–220, 224–226, 228, 231, 248, 261. *See also* League Park
Dunn, Jack, 76, 274

Dunn, James C., 102–104, 107, 113, 115–116, 122, 130, 135, 137, 141, 148, 154–155, 167–168, 173, 178–179, 188, 190, 238, 249
    Cleveland Indians, purchase of, 101
    death of, 193–194
    illness, 191–192
    League Park, closure of, 128
    off-season player trades, 124
    skeet shooting, 145
    Tris Speaker and, 113, 184, 213
Dygert, Jimmy, 8
Dykes, Jimmy, 271, 273

E

East Ohio Gas Company, 148
Easter, Luke, 297, 306
Eaton, Paul, 65, 77
Ebbets, Charles, 72, 173
Ebbets Field, 40, 168–169
Ed Sullivan Show (*Toast of the Town*), 297
Edwards, Henry P., 108–109, 119–120, 139, 144, 147, 153, 155, 166, 179, 187, 198, 216, 234, 248, 250, 307
    Cleveland Indians fans, comments on, 225
    home runs, comments on, 258
    Tris Speaker, comments on, 111, 195, 231
Edwards, Jim Joe, 200, 203
Edwards, Ralph, 296
Ehmke, Howard, 137, 271, 272
Eisenhower, Dwight D., 298–299
Elfers, James, 69
Elks Club, 179
Elks Hotel, 206
Eller, Horace (Hod), 147
Ellerbe, Frank, 207, 215
Ellison, Herbert (Babe), 125
Emery Ball, 77
Empress of China (Ocean liner), 68–69
Engle, Clyde, 33, 53, 55–56, 60, 71, 76, 81
Enzman, Johnny, 130
Evans, Billie, 155
Evans, Billy, 57, 243, 263, 266
Evans, Joe, 161–162, 169, 171, 174, 179, 181, 184, 187, 197
Evans, Louis (Steve), 69, 73–74
Evers, Johnny, 207
Eynon, Eddie, 236, 254

F

Faber, Urban (Red), 72, 120–122, 164–165, 188
    globe-circling tour, 67
    illness, 146
    military service, 127
    singer, as a, 74
    statistics (1920), 166
Fairview Cemetery, 303, 305
Falzer, G. A., 274
Faneuil Hall, 57
Farrell, Frank, 72, 84
Farrell, Joe, 67, 69–70
Fat Stock Show rodeo, 179, 191
Federal antitrust law, baseball and, 245
Federal League, 65–66, 71–74, 83, 98, 100, 178, 277
    antitrust suit, Organized Baseball, 99
    attendance and, 76
    contracts, recognition of, 100
    disbanding of, 99–100
    player salaries and, 75–76
    season (1914), 75
    signing major league players, 71–73
Feller, Bob, 288, 292–293, 300–301, 307
Felsch, Oscar (Happy), 120, 126, 146
    statistics (1920), 166
    World Series (1919), 146–147, 177
    World War I, 127
Fenway Park, 39–40, 43, 49, 51–54, 57, 65, 108, 114, 129–131, 160, 300
Fenway Realty Company, 39
Fewster, William (Chick), 205, 207, 218, 221
Finn, Michael J., 10–12
Fischer, Carl, 280, 282
Fitzgerald, John F. (Honey Fitz), 31, 57
Fitzgerald, W. C., 170
Fitzke, Paul, 206, 216
Flatley, Nick, 242

Fleener, William J., Jr., 303
Fletcher, Art, 50–52, 54, 56
Fletcher, Daniel, 31
Fohl, Lee, 105–106, 108, 110, 115–116, 120–122, 125–126, 129–130, 137–138, 140, 180, 192, 202, 205
  honored by Knights of Columbus, 208
  off-season player trades, 124
  resignation, 141
  Tris Speaker, comments on, 110
Folger, Clay, 186, 194, 211, 248
Fonseca, Lew, 287
Forbes Field, 22, 25, 40
Ford, Russell, 11, 61
Fort Shelby Hotel, 137
Foster, George, 61, 75, 78, 80, 89–91, 103, 110
  statistics (1915), 92
  World Series (1915), 95–97
Fournier, Jacques, 93
Foxx, Jimmy, 271
Frazee, Harry, 130, 138, 142–143, 194, 236
  dismantling of Boston Red Sox, 138
  Jacob Ruppert and T. L. Huston, relationship with, 238
  player deals, 190
  purchase of Boston Red Sox, 114
  sale of: Babe Ruth's contract, 149; Boston Red Sox, 200–201; Boston Red Sox stock (1923), 149
Freeman, John (Buck), 144
Frick, Ford, 289, 297, 300, 303
Fritsch, Walter, 73
Fuchs, Emil, 267
Fullerton, Hugh S., xvi, 20, 44, 47–48, 55, 148, 149
Fultz, David, 66, 75, 114–115

G

Gaffney, James, 39, 72, 94, 98
Gainer, Del, 88, 96
Gallia, Bert, 154
Galt, Edith, 95
Gandil, Arnold (Chick), 106, 113

batting averages, 120
betting scandal (1919), comments on, 246
Chicago White Sox, member of, 116
injuries, 139
quitting Organized Baseball, 156
reputation, 247
World Series (1919) fix, 146–147, 177
Tris Speaker and, 116, 138–139,
World Series (1919) performance, 147
Ganzel, Foster (Babe), 264
Gardner, Larry, 29, 44, 50–53, 56, 58, 76, 81, 88, 90, 124, 141, 157, 165, 172, 182, 185, 193, 207
  attitude toward Catholics, 28
  fielding, 171
  injuries, 87
  manager, as a, 215
  off-season, 174
  release by Cleveland Indians, 215
  salary, increase of (1914), 76
  skeet shooting, 145
  statistics (1912), 46
  trade: from Boston, 149; to Cleveland, 137
  World Series (1915), 96
Gehrig, Lou, 225, 229, 258, 263, 278
  home runs and, 261–262, 265, 271
  Tris Speaker, comparison to, 308–309
Gessler, Harry (Doc), 23
Gibson, Sam, 228
Gilbert, Larry, 161
Gilks, Bobby, 6
Gilmore, James, 72–74, 99
Gleason, William (Kid), 139, 146, 149, 226
Globe-circling tour, 66–73
Goldstein, Spud, 303
Gordon, Joe, 295, 302
Goslin, Leon (Goose), 211, 254, 260–261, 264–265,
Gould, James M., 215, 223
Gowdy, Hank, 124, 135
Graney, Jack, 61, 106, 122, 139, 148, 194, 283, 294
  hitting, 182
  illness, 126

manager, as a, 195
   Ray Chapman's funeral and, 159
Grasser, Fred O. *See* West, Fred
Gray Eagle (nickname). *See* Speaker, Tris
Gray, William (Dolly), 33
Grealey, Paul, 279, 281
Great Depression, 284, 288
Green Monster and Fenway Park, 40
Greenberg, Hank, 295, 297–298
Griffith, Addie Ann, 255
Griffith, Clark, 45, 79, 84, 109, 140, 194, 253–254,
   256–257, 259–260, 262, 267, 274, 290, 308
   pitcher, as a, 79
   season (1914), 75
   Tris Speaker and, 255, 266–267
   Ty Cobb, criticism of, 263
Griffith Stadium, 258, 262, 263
Grimes, Burleigh, 167, 169–170, 172
Grimm, Charley, 292
Groom, Bob, 103
Grove, Robert Moses (Lefty), 217, 225–226,
   269–273, 291
Guisto, Louis, 116, 118–119, 124, 136, 201

H

Haas, George (Mule), 271
Hadley, Irving (Bump), 264
Hall, Charley (Sea Lion), 24, 44, 50, 53, 61
Hammen, Theodore, 243
Handley, Zeke, xix
Hanna Theatre, 181
Harding, Warren G., 133, 202
Harper, Harry, 185, 187
Harridge, William A., 249, 289
Harris, Byron (Slim), 219, 259
Harris, Joe, 116, 120, 137, 140, 154, 166, 254, 260
   injuries, 258
   military service, 124, 136
   reinstatement, 190
   Tris Speaker and, 255
Harris, Stanley (Bucky), 209, 211, 223, 227, 236,
   254, 255, 259, 261–262, 264, 267, 274, 308
   injuries, 260, 262

player-manager, as a, 206
   Tris Speaker, comments on, 268
   Ty Cobb, comments on, 234
Haskins, Brice, 6
Haughton, Percy, 98
Hauser, Joe, 209, 269
Hedges, Robert Lee, 285
Heilmann, Harry, 107, 125, 234, 236, 281
   batting titles, 189, 204, 220, 265
   season (1923), 202
   statistics (1921), 183
Heinemann Park, 137, 154
Held, Woodie, 302–303
Hella Temple, 168
Henderson, Bernard, 188
Hendrix, Claude, 163
Hendryx, Tim, 167
Henriksen, Olaf, 34, 54
Hermann, August (Garry), 50, 54
Herzog, Charles (Buck), 50–52, 54, 57
Hickey, Thomas, 285
High, Hugh, 84
Hildebrand, George, 91, 118, 138, 155, 160
Hilltop Park, 29, 42
Hoblitzell, Dick, 88, 94–96
Hodapp, Johnny, 219, 223
Hoernschemeyer, Leopold. *See* Magee, Lee
Hollenden Hotel, 102, 113, 125, 129, 170
Holmes, Tommy, 242
Hooper, Harry, 18, 23, 28–29, 41–42, 44, 52,
   54–55, 78, 81, 85, 90, 103, 131, 179, 283, 288,
   294, 296, 300
   contract (1913), 59
   salary increase (1914), 76
   World Series: 1912, 57; 1915, 94–97
Hope, Bob, 296, 298
Hopkins, Paul, 264
Hornsby, Rogers, xviii, 9, 222, 257, 282, 293,
   301, 302
   batting titles, 151, 198, 220
   Jack Dempsey and, 220
   Ku Klux Klan and, 213, 215
   Lou Boudreau, relationship with, 294

Texas Sports Hall of Fame, induction into, 300
 Tris Speaker, competing against, 198
Hoskins, Dave, 306
Hot Springs, Arkansas, 17, 18, 27, 28, 40, 41, 59, 74, 85, 100
Hotel Belmont, 221
Hotel Carter, 291
Hotel Jefferson, 179
Hotel Pennsylvania, 168
Hotel Roosevelt, 254
Hotel Sinton, 146
Hotel Thelma, 198–199
Hotel Winton, 159, 193
Howley, Dan, 255, 262
Hoyt, Waite, 160, 182, 184–185, 187–188, 202, 225–226, 229, 261, 264, 273
Hubbard, Richard B., 2
Hubbard, Texas, xv, 2–4, 31–32, 57, 84, 99–100, 118, 125, 135, 148, 170, 179, 199, 205, 213–214, 222, 255, 274, 282, 290–291, 297, 303
Hudlin, Willis, 229, 261
Hudson, Sid, 303
Huff, George M., 7, 8
Huggins, Miller, 155, 158, 182, 187, 189, 201–202, 209, 223, 228–229, 254
 golf and, 206
 suspension of Babe Ruth, 217
Hughes, Tom, 9, 44
Huntington Avenue Grounds, 13–14, 25, 27, 35–36, 40, 57
Hurst, Tim, 22, 24–25
Huston, Tillinghast L'hommedieu (T. L.), 84, 142, 158, 190, 194, 199

I

Indians' Boosters Club, 117
International League, 78, 100, 126, 131, 198, 253, 266, 277–278
Invisible Empire, Knights of the Ku Klux Klan. *See* Ku Klux Klan
Isaminger, Jimmy, 124, 164, 269
 Tris Speaker, comments on, 268, 274

J

Jack Dunn's Baby. *See* Ruth, George Herman
Jackson, Joe R. (reporter), 45
Jackson, Joe (Shoeless Joe), 35, 61, 104, 106, 120, 122, 126, 138, 144, 146, 155, 164, 177, 298
 batting averages, 103
 Chicago White Sox, member of, 89, 101, 106, 178
 Cleveland Baseball Hall of Fame, 298
 fielding, 167
 salary increase (1914), 76
 statistics: 1912, 46; 1914, 80; 1916, 112; 1919, 145; 1920, 166
 World Series fix (1919), 146, 164, 177
 World Series (1919) performance, 147
 World War I, service during, 127
Jackson, Merwin, 278
Jacobson, Bill (Baby Doll), 192
Jacobson, Merwin, 282
James, Bill, 247
Jamieson, Charlie, 21, 156–157, 169, 171–172, 181, 184–185, 208, 215, 218, 221
 benching by Tris Speaker, 225
 betting scandal (1919), comments on, 244
 home runs and, 210, 216
 off-season, 174
 season (1923), 202, 204
 statistics: 1920 World Series, 173; 1924, 211
 trade to Cleveland, 137
 Tris Speaker, comments on, 137
Janvrin, Harold, 61, 65, 88
Jasper, Henry (Hi), 140
Jeffries, Jim, 31
Jennings, Hugh, 21, 162, 180
Jester, Buford, 255–256
Johns, Augustus (Lefty), 224
Johnson, Byron Bancroft (Ban), 22, 25, 30–31, 35–37, 43, 45, 50, 61, 71–72, 74, 80, 85, 101–102, 111, 116, 127, 130, 139, 161, 177, 182, 187, 200, 218, 225, 233, 236, 239, 241, 248
 American League founder/president, 65, 178
 Carl Mays and death of Ray Chapman, comments on, 160

Carl Mays, suspension of, 142
Charles Comiskey, relationship with, 240
Cobb and Speaker, banishment of, from American League, 247
discrediting of, 250
erosion of power, 142
Garland Stahl (Jake), friendship with, 63
Jim Dunn, relationship with, 194
Jimmy McAleer, friendship with, 63
Kennesaw Mountain Landis and, 247, 249
Ray Chapman's funeral and, 159
resignation, 263
retirement, 249, 266
rule changes, 222, 224
season (1913), 64
Tris Speaker and, 235, 249
Ty Cobb and, 235, 248
Johnson, Grant (Home Run), xx
Johnson, Jack, 31
Johnson, Walter (The Big Train), xx, 32–34, 44–45, 62, 64, 79, 89, 109, 122–123, 183, 187, 209, 211, 221, 254, 260, 262–263, 274, 290
death of, 298
financial situation, 84
gifts received, 263
injuries, 257
manager, as a, 266, 277, 281
National Baseball Hall of Fame and, 289
post-season play, 31
retirement, 266
salaries, 84–85
season (1914), 75
statistics: 1912, 46; 1924, 211
Washington Senators manager, as a, 274
Johnston, Jimmy, 168
Johnston, Wheeler (Doc), 129, 137, 140, 155, 168–169, 172, 174, 190
Jones, Dave R., 234, 242, 250, 261
Jones, Fielder, 107
Jones, Sam (Sad Sam), 102–103, 128–129, 141, 190, 203, 300
Judge, Joe, 262, 264–265

K

Kaese, Harold, 301
Kaline, Al, 309
Kansas City Monarchs, 284
Karger, Ed, 35
Karr, Benny, 215, 224, 261
Keeler, Willie, 289
Kellogg Company, 287–288
Kellogg, Frank, 263
Kennedy, Bob, 302
Kerr, Dickie, 143, 163–165, 186, 188
    statistics: 1919, 146; 1920, 166
    World Series (1919) performance, 147
Keyser, Lee, 284–286, 298
Kilbane, Johnny, 148
Kilduff, Pete, 171
Killefer, Bill, 97, 124
Killilea, Henry, 236
King George V, 72
Kiwanis Club, Tris Speaker and, 154
Klem, Bill, 57, 68, 94, 97
Klepfer, Ed, 110, 120, 123–124, 135, 148
Kling, Johnny, 286
Klugman, Joe, 215, 218
Knickerbocker Hotel, 73
Knight, Harry, 217
Knode, Bob, 218
Koenig, Mark, 229, 265
Konetchy, Ed, 167, 172
Ku Klux Klan, 212–214

L

Lajoie, Napoleon, 30, 43, 61, 84, 86–87, 104–106, 182, 288
    Cleveland Baseball Hall of Fame, 298
    manager, as a, 125
    National Baseball Hall of Fame and, 286, 289
    post-season play, 31
    Ray Chapman's funeral and, 159
    Smokey Joe Wood and, 61
Lake, Fred, 13–15, 18, 24–26
Lake Whitney, 303

Lakeside Hospital, 184

Lakewood Masonic Lodge, 109

Landis, Kenesaw Mountain, 99, 178, 190, 235–236, 241–242, 245–246, 252, 269, 289, 292

  banning of Black Sox players, 185

  Byron Bancroft Johnson and, 224, 239, 249

  Dutch Leonard, interview with, 241

  exoneration of Cobb and Speaker, 250, 253

  extension of contract, 240

  Joe Wood, meeting with, 240

  resignation of Cobb and Speaker, 233

  suspension of Ruth and Meusel, 193

  Tris Speaker, meeting with, 240

  Ty Cobb, meeting with, 240

Lane, F. C., 1, 3–5, 86, 107, 189, 244

  home runs, comments on, 258

  Tris Speaker and, 197, 272

Lane, Frank, 302

Lanigan, Ernest J., 145

Lannin, Joseph J., 71–74, 85, 87, 101, 103, 243

  Boston Red Sox: sale of, 114; sole owner of, 75

  economy moves, 85, 98

  Fenway Park, loan of, to Boston Braves, 79

  George Lewis, comments on, 103

  Harry Hooper, comments on, 103

  minor league owner, as a, 78

  season (1916), 98

  Tris Speaker and, 99–102, 108

  World Series (1915), 97

Laporte, Frank, 57

Lazzeri, Tony, 225, 262, 271

League Park, 29, 61, 64, 101–102, 106, 109–113, 117, 119, 121, 123, 129, 138, 140–143, 154–156, 163, 167–168, 170, 172–173, 181–182, 184, 186, 288, 293. *See also* Dunn Field

Lee, Cliff, 218, 221, 278

Lee, William, 13

Leonard, Hubert (Dutch), 60–61, 76, 78, 89–91, 109–110, 112, 122–123, 140, 143–144, 236, 238, 240–243, 245, 247–248, 251

  betting scandal, 1919, 233, 236

  criticism of Boston personnel, 87

  death, 298

  injuries, 88

  leaving baseball, 239

  meeting with Cobb, Speaker, and Wood, 236

  salary increase (1914), 76

  season (1913), 64

  statistics (1915), 92

  suspension, 87–88

  trade from Boston, 138, 149

  Tris Speaker, relationship with, 239

  Ty Cobb, relationship with, 239

  World Series: 1915, 95; 1916, 113

Leverenz, Walter, 67

Levsen, Emil (Dutch), 210, 225–227–229, 231

Lewis, George (Duffy), 28–29, 40, 46, 49, 51, 56, 78, 81, 91, 103, 120, 135, 140, 142–143, 236, 283, 288, 291, 294, 300

  Bill Carrigan, loyalty to, 62

  contract (1913), 59

  fights, 61

  off-season, 98

  Ray Chapman's funeral and, 159

  salary increase (1914), 76

  statistics (1912), 46

  trade from Boston, 138, 149

  Tris Speaker and, 28, 62

  World Series: 1912, 50; 1915, 94–97

Liberty Bonds, 118

Lieb, Fred, 20, 51, 56, 158, 213

Linn, Ed, 80

Lisenbee, Horace (Hod), 261–262, 264

Lisse, E. E., 173

Lisse, Tristram Speaker, 173

Little Napoleon. *See* McGraw, John

Little Rock, Arkansas, 18

Little Rock Travelers, 10

Live ball, xvii, 183

Lloyd, Harold, 206

Lloyd, John Henry, xx

Lobert, John (Hans), 68

Longworth, Nicholas, 263

Lopez, Al, 293, 301

Lord, Harry, 23, 28
Luderus, Fred, 93–97
Lunte, Harry, 157, 161, 179, 181, 244
Lusitania (Ocean liner), 72, 86
Lutzke, Walter (Rube), 198, 215, 218, 222, 282
    injuries, 224
    minor leaguer, as a, 278
Lynch, Thomas, 50
Lynn, Byrd, 166
Lyons, Ted, 227

M

Mack, Connie, 14, 21, 30, 76–78, 83–84, 110, 123, 144, 200, 216–217, 239, 253–255, 267, 271–274, 278, 292
    cost-cutting by, 274
    death of, 298
    National Baseball Hall of Fame and, 289
    off-season player trades, 124
    Tris Speaker and, 256, 268
    Ty Cobb and, 255
Magee, Lee, 73
Maharg, Bill, 164, 177
Mails, Walter (Duster), 161–166, 169, 171, 182–183, 186–188, 194–195, 197, 220
    illness, 193
    statistics (1920), 167
    Tris Speaker, comments on, 288
    World Series (1920), 173
Majestic Hotel, 18
Major League Baseball Players' Association, 66
Mamaux, Al, 172, 278, 282–283
Manion, Clyde, 165
Mantle, Mickey, xvii, 301
Manush, Henry (Heinie), 231, 234
Marberry, Fred (Firpo), 211, 259, 261, 264, 303
Marine Park, 191
Marlin, Texas, xv, 74
Marquard, Richard (Rube), 45, 47, 49, 51–52, 70, 101, 168–171, 179, 256
    Blossom Seeley and, 70
    globe-circling tour, 67
    ticket-scalping and, 172

Martin, Mike, 257
Masonic Order, 28
Massachusetts Women's Suffrage Association, 95
Mathewson, Christy, xx, 25–26, 47, 49–50, 52, 54–56
    Baseball Players' Fraternity, support for, 66
    globe-circling tour, 67
    military service, 132
    National Baseball Hall of Fame and, 287, 289
    post-season play, 31
    salary increase (1914), 76
Mayer, Erskine, 93, 95–96, 99
Mays, Carl, 78, 90, 92, 110, 112, 118, 120, 127, 131, 142, 144, 157, 160–162, 182, 186–188, 201–202, 237–238
    banishment petition, 158
    Ray Chapman's death and, 157–158
    reputation of, as a pitcher, 159
    trade of, from Boston, 149
Mays, Willie, xvii, 299, 306, 309
McAdoo, William Gibbs, 138
McAleer, Jimmy, 17, 31, 36–37, 40–42, 45, 52–54, 57–58, 60, 243
    sale of Red Sox stock, 71
    Tris Speaker and globe-circling tour, 68
McAuley, Ed, 292–293
McBreen, Hugh, 10, 25–26
McCallister, Jack, 141, 207, 232, 235
McCarthy, Joe (ballplayer), 154
McClellan, Harvey, 166
McConnell, Ambrose, 28
McCormick, Harry (Moose), 52
McGeehan, W. O., 253–254
McGlynn, Frank, 68, 70
McGraw, Blanche, 68
McGraw, John, xv–xvi, 10, 12, 26, 37, 47, 49, 52, 54, 56–57, 67, 74, 146, 167–168, 189, 196, 216, 222, 253, 267–268, 274, 282
    debts, 256
    globe-circling tour, 66
    golf and, 112, 206

National Baseball Hall of Fame and, 286, 289

sports column writer, as a, 48

World Series (1917), 124

McGuire, Jim (Deacon), 8, 13

McInnis, John (Stuffy), 33, 35, 83, 124, 190, 192–193, 196–197, 283

McKechnie, Bill, 293

McLinn, Stoney, 55

McMahon, Jane, 158

McMillen, Ralph E., 108

McMullen, Fred, 122, 146, 177, 185

McNeill, Don, 292

McNichol, Walter, 161, 191, 214

McNulty, Pat, 191, 216–218, 221

McNutt, William Slavens, 173

McRoy, Robert, 36–37, 53–54, 57, 71, 101, 108

Medinger, George, Tris Speaker's funeral, 303

Medwick, Joe, 282, 308

Memphis Commercial Appeal, 106

Mendez, José, xx

Mercer, Sid, 56

Merkle, Fred, 50–52, 54–56, 67, 69–70

Meusel, Bob, 182, 193, 203, 221, 225

Meyers, John (Chief), 52, 54–55, 296

  globe-circling tour, 67

  World Series statistics (1912), 57

Middleton, Jim, 181

Milan, Clyde, 47

Miller, Edmund (Bing), 268–271, 273

Miller, Otto, 171–172

Miller, Walter, 218, 224–225, 227, 230, 273, 307–308

Minor leagues, 278–279

Minor, Thomas, 84

Mississauga Indian reservation, 148

Mitchell, A. C., 42, 88, 98, 171

Mitchell, Clarence, 170

Mitchell, Dale, 293–294, 303

Mitchell, Fred, 118

Mitchell, Willie, 103

Moeller, Danny, 46

Mogridge, George, 127, 142, 195, 209, 211

Moore, Wade, 7

Moore, Wilcy, 261

Moran, Billy, 302

Moran, Pat, 93, 96, 146

Morehouse, Ward, 291, 297

Morgan, Harry (Cy), 8

Moriarty, George, 138, 160, 202, 234, 274

Morris, Ed, 272

Morse, Jacob C., 9, 15, 17, 23

Morton, Guy, 106, 108, 110, 120, 161, 184, 188, 192, 195, 199–200

  illness, 193

  military service, 130

  sale of contract to Kansas City, 207

Moseley, Earl, 63

Muhlebach Field, 284–285

Muhlebach, George, 284

Murfin, James O., 245–247, 250

Murnane, Tim, 23, 27, 29, 32, 40, 42, 50, 58, 77, 84–85

  exhibition game, for family, 122–123

  ghostwriter for Tris Speaker, 48

  off-season, with Tris Speaker, 98

  Red Sox, comments on, 78

Murphy, Eddie (ballplayer), 76, 86

Murray, Billy, 43

Murray, Jack (Red), 50, 54, 55, 57

Musial, Stan, 309

Myatt, Glenn, 198, 208, 218, 228

  golf and, 206

  home runs and, 216

  injuries, 210

Myer, Charles (Buddy), 259–260, 308

Myers, Elmer, 137, 140, 143, 155, 237, 244

Myers, Henry (Hy), 167, 171

Mystic Shrine of Dallas, 168

N

Nallin, Dick, 130, 139–140, 144, 194, 244

Nashville Tennessean, 12

National Agreement of 1903, 5, 198

National Association, 7, 37, 114, 289

National Baseball Congress (NBC), 286

National Baseball Hall of Fame and Museum, xvi, 289

National Broadcasting Company, 292

National Commission, 31, 50, 114, 118, 130, 146, 175, 178, 249
  rules of, 122

National League, xv, 17, 100, 129, 151
  blacklist of Federal League signers, 75
  World War I and, 117

Navin Field, 89, 137, 165, 203, 207, 237, 241, 244, 271

Navin, Frank, 36, 84, 130, 233–234, 236, 239, 250

NBC (National Baseball Congress), 286

Negro Leagues, 285, 297

Negro National League, 295

Ness, Eliot, 289

New England Conservatory of Music, 13

New Orleans, 115, 125, 136, 153

New York American, xvi

New York American Leaguers. *See* New York Yankees

New York Evening Herald, 103

New York Evening World, 241

New York Giants, xv–xvi, 10, 55, 67, 167, 299

New York Globe, 56

New York Herald-Tribune, 253

New York Morning Sun, 20

New York Times, 24, 77, 170

New York Tribune, 155

New York World-Telegram, 267, 290

New York Yankees, 18, 84, 188, 252, 265

Newark Sunday Call, 274

Nicholson and Watson Grocery Team, 5

Niehoff, Bert, 96–97

Niles, Harry, 29

North Texas League. *See also* Texas League, 7

Northern Ohio Gun club, 145

Noyes, Thomas, 32

Nunamaker, Les, 61, 113, 119, 137, 174, 190, 192, 194, 205, 211
  fines for fighting, 61
  manager, as a, 197

off-season, 98, 148
skeet shooting, 145

O

O'Brien, Thomas (Buck), 42, 44, 51, 52, 53, 64

O'Connor, Leslie, 241, 250

O'Doul, Frank (Lefty), 157

O'Farrell, Bob, 255

Oldham, John (Red), 165, 181

O'Leary, Jack, 48

O'Leary, James, 167

O'Loughlin, Francis (Silk), 35, 57, 91

Olson, Ivan (Ivy), 61

O'Neill, Steve, 122, 136, 140, 148, 157, 160, 169, 172, 182, 185, 187, 215, 249, 301
  batting averages, 108
  betting scandal (1919), comments on, 244
  Cleveland Baseball Hall of Fame, 298
  coach, as a, 299
  illness, 193
  injuries, 192
  Jack Dempsey and, 220
  Knights of Columbus, honored by, 208
  Ray Chapman's funeral and, 159–160
  statistics (1920 World Series), 173
  trade to Boston, 205
  Tris Speaker, friendship with, 213
  wrestling matches, 190

Onslow, Jack, 278, 280, 282–283

Organized Baseball, xix, 5–6, 18, 65–66, 73, 75, 100, 114, 175, 245, 252, 290, 293, 306

Ormsby, Emmet (Red), 200

Orwoll, Ossie, 271

O'Shea, Laura Teresa, 71

Owens, Clarence (Brick), 122, 144

P

Pacific Coast League, 28, 116, 161, 198, 201, 220

Paige, Leroy (Satchel), 306

Palace of the Fans, 27

Palmer, Pete, 309

Paskert, George (Dode), 94–95, 97

Peckinpaugh, Roger, 140, 190, 249, 290
Pegler, Westbrook, 256, 278
    Eddie Collins, comments on, 269
    Tris Speaker, comments on, 258, 269–270
    Ty Cobb, comments on, 269–270
Penn Athletic Club, 254
Pennant Park, 222, 256
Pennock, Herb, 83, 85, 160, 211, 225, 229, 269
People's Bank Building, 240
Pershing, John J., 114
Pezzolo, Francesco. *See* Bodie, Ping
Pfeffer, Ed (Jeff), 170
Phelon, William A. "Bill", xix, 33, 43, 48, 53, 57,
    60, 86, 97, 105, 189, 195, 206, 210
Philadelphia Athletics, 8, 13, 278
    attendance: 1914, 83; 1928, 273–274
    dismantling of team, 83–84
Philadelphia North American, 164, 268
Philadelphia Phillies, 93
Picinich, Val, 200
Picus, John Quinn. *See* Quinn, Jack
Piercy, Bill, 185, 193
Pipgras, George, 273
Pipp, Wally, 84, 140, 142, 157, 185, 278, 282
    home runs and, 208
    military service, 132
    Ray Chapman's funeral and, 159
Pitching (1915 season), 85–86
Pittsburgh Pirates, 10, 18
Plank, Eddie, 14, 22–23, 29, 33, 83, 111
Plant Field, 257
Play Ball (film), 289
Players League, 66
Poer, Nancy Jane, 2
Polo Grounds, 25, 40, 48–49, 52–53, 60, 156,
    183, 186, 188, 199, 290
Pond, Arlie, 70
Pope, Dave, 306
Pope Pius X, 70–71
Post-season series, 25
Povich, Shirley, 254
Powell, Al, 223
Powers, Francis J., 189, 197–199, 209, 233, 243

betting scandal (1919), comments on, 246
Cleveland Indians fans, comments on, 225
Tris Speaker, comments on, 217
Ty Cobb, comments on, 217
Powers, Mike, 23
Pratt, Derrill, 140
Preston, Howard, 291
Price, James, 267
Prince Rupert (Ocean liner), 68
Putnam's Place, 13, 27, 30

Q

Quinn, Bob, 200–201
Quinn, Jack, 140, 162, 268, 270

R

Racial violence, in Texas, 135
Rape of the Red Sox, 138
Reach's Baseball Guide, 174
Red Elm Park, 12
Redland Field, 41, 146
Reese, James (Bonesetter), 209, 217
Reeves, Bobby, 260
Rehg, Walter, 113
Replogle, Hartley, 163
Reserve clause, 32, 66
Reuther, Dutch, 229, 231
Rice, Grantland, 12, 103, 155
Rice, Sam, 211, 254, 260, 264, 310
Rice, Thomas S., 242
Richter, Francis, 206
Rickard, George (Tex), 31
Rickey, Branch, xx, 278
Rigler, Charles (Cy), 52, 57
Rigney, Emory (Topper), 260, 265
Ring, Jimmy, 278
Ripley, Robert, 44
Risberg, Charles (Swede), 146, 166, 177, 246,
    247
Rixey, Eppa, 93, 96–97
Robbie, William R., 7
Roberts, Doak, 5–8
Robinson, Jackie, 294

Robinson, Wilbert (Uncle Robbie), 167–169, 171–172, 199
Rodgers, Bill (Raw Meat), 284
Rogers, Will, 241, 246, 257, 291
Rohe, George, 11
Rommell, Eddie, 162, 230
Roosevelt, Franklin D., 290
Roosevelt, Theodore, 52
Rotary Electric Steel Company, 287–288
Roth, Bobby (Braggo), 106, 111, 121, 129, 137
Roush, Edd, 147
Rowland, Clarence (Pants), 88, 137
Royal Rooters, 41, 45, 48–49, 53–54, 57, 71, 85, 94, 96
Ruether, Walter (Dutch), 147, 307
Ruffing, Charles (Red), 226, 272
Runyon, Damon, xvi, 239
Ruppert, Jacob, 84, 142, 149, 158, 190, 194, 199
Russell, Allan, 127
Russell, Ewell (Reb), 120
Russell, William, 39
Ruth, Claire, 302
Ruth, George Herman (Babe), xvi, 85–86, 90–91, 112, 120, 123, 128, 130, 138, 141, 155, 162, 174, 187, 190, 215, 225, 228–230, 237, 258, 263–264, 290, 308–309
  batting averages, 131
  death, 298
  full-time outfielder, as a, 140
  hitting, 133, 141, 144
  hitting and pitching, 88, 129, 145
  home runs, 149, 156, 159, 168, 182–188, 199, 204, 208, 226, 261, 264–265, 273
  illness, 188, 205, 216–217, 294
  marriage, 87
  National Baseball Hall of Fame and, 287, 289
  negative factors, 80
  pitcher, as a, 78, 80, 110
  sale of contract, to Red Sox, 76
  seasons: 1922, 196; 1923, 202
  statistics: 1915, 92; 1920, 151; 1921, 189; 1924, 211; 1925, 221; 1926, 231

  suspension, 193, 196, 217
  Tris Speaker, arguments with, 182
  World Series: 1915, 94, 96–97; 1916, 113; records, 131
Ruthian era, of baseball, 189
Ryan, Jack, 22
Ryan, Ellis, 296, 298

S

Sanborn, Irving I., 10
SCC. *See* Society for Crippled Children
Schaefer, Germany, 67, 69, 126
Schalk, Ray, 120, 122, 146, 156
Scott, Everett, 88, 90, 94–95, 190, 203
Scott, Jim, 88
Scott, Virginia, 195
Scott, Xen, 161
Scripps-Howard newspapers, 244
Second World War, 290
Seeley, Blossom, 70, 171–172
Selective Service Act, 118
Sewell, Joe, xvii, 161–165, 172, 179, 182, 185, 190, 199, 208, 215, 218, 229, 231, 260, 296
  Cleveland Baseball Hall of Fame, 298
  coach, as a, 299
  fielding, 163, 169, 171, 180, 187
  off-season, 174
  season (1923), 202, 204
  statistics (1920 World Series), 173
  strikeouts, 221
Sewell, Luke, 199, 216, 218, 222
Seymour, Harold, 115, 310
Shaker Lakes Country Club, 112
Shannon, Paul, 15, 100
Shaute, Joe, 198, 200, 203, 207–209, 216–217, 219, 224–227, 229, 261
  injuries, 210
  statistics (1924), 211
Shawkey, Bob, 76, 83, 140, 159, 162, 185, 188, 203, 208
Sheely, Earl, 207
Shelton, Benny, 5
Sheraton Park Hotel, 309

Sheridan, Jack, 68

Sheridan, John B., 121, 177–178, 233
  betting scandal, 1919, analysis of, 250–252
  Dutch Leonard, comments on, 251
  Joe Wood, comments on, 251
  Ty Cobb, comments on, 251

Shibe, Benjamin, 268

Shibe Brothers, 14

Shibe Park, 22, 40, 85, 93, 202, 268–270, 292

Shinault, Enoch (Ginger), 192

Shinners, Ralph, 282

Shires, Art, 303

Shocker, Urban, 154, 180–181, 187–188, 192, 200, 216, 225, 229, 273

Shore, Ernie, 78, 85, 89, 91, 110, 123, 135, 140, 143, 236
  off-season, 98
  Ray Chapman's funeral and, 159
  Ruth, George Herman (Babe), comments on, 80
  sale of contract, to Red Sox, 76
  statistics (1915), 92
  trade from Boston, 138, 149
  World Series: 1915, 94, 96; 1916, 113

Short, Harry

Shorten, Charles (Chick), 244

Shotton, Burt, 45

Simmons, Al, 217, 220, 263–265, 268–271, 273, 298

Simpson, Harry, 306

Sinclair, Harry, 99, 100

Sinnott, William, 274, 283

Sisler, George, 89, 92, 111, 120, 155–156, 186, 192, 196–197, 230, 255, 267, 302
  base hits for a season, 164
  batter's box, movement in, 121
  batting averages, 131
  fielding, 216
  illness, 200
  military service, 132
  National Baseball Hall of Fame and, 289
  player-manager, as a, 200, 206
  statistics: 1917, 123; 1919, 145; 1920, 167–168; 1921, 189

Time, on cover of, 215

Skiff, Bill, 278, 280

Smallwood, Percy, 190–191

Smiley Corbett's bar, 66

Smith, Al, 306

Smith, Carr, 215

Smith, Elmer, 121, 139, 155, 157, 159–160, 162, 165, 169, 181, 188, 197, 288
  grand slam home run, World Series (1920), 171
  military service, 124
  trade to Red Sox, 190

Smith, Sherry, 169, 171, 196, 203, 208–210, 225, 227, 230, 232

Smokey Joe Wood. *See* Wood, Howard Ellsworth

Snodgrass, Fred, 50, 54–56, 67

Society for Crippled Children (SCC), xviii, 291

Soldier Field, 234

Somers, Charles, 101, 105–106

Sothoron, Allen, 154, 183, 185–187, 197

South End Grounds, 14, 79

South Texas League, 5

Southern Association, 205

Southern League, 6, 10, 12–13, 15, 18, 28

Southworth, Billy, 294, 300

Spahn, Warren, 310

Spalding, Albert G., 49, 66–67, 150

Speaker, Archery O., 2

Speaker, Elaine, 26, 107

Speaker, Mary Frances, 216, 234, 254–266, 274, 282, 287, 297, 303, 305. *See also* Cudahy, Mary Frances

Speaker, Murry Lloyd, 3, 26

Speaker, Nancy Jane (Jenny), 6, 8, 26, 107, 195, 197, 199, 214
  birthday, 172
  death of, 282
  Tris Speaker, comments on, 47, 170
  See also Poer, Nancy Jane

Speaker, Pearl, 4

Speaker, Tris, xv, xvii, xxi, 9, 23, 42, 46, 52, 78, 80, 90–91, 108, 115, 122, 127, 130, 136, 140, 145, 147–148, 162, 167, 174, 187, 190, 207,

215, 218, 222–223, 227, 229, 236, 238–239, 241–246, 248–249, 251, 254, 259, 267, 269, 300–301
    3000th base hit, 217
    adult life, xviii
    advisory coach, as an, 294
    age, comments on, 107
    All-Star games, 34
    American League, remaining in, 253
    ancestry, 2
    argument: with fans, 162; over use of resin bag, 223–224
    assistant manager, as an, 106
    automobiles and, 31, 51
    Babe Ruth and, 80–81, 205–206
    ban of drinking and smoking by players, 198
    banishment of, from American League, 247
    banning of Black Sox players from baseball, comments on, 185
    banquet circuit and, 295
    Baseball Players' Fraternity, support for, 66
    batter's box, movement in, 121
    batting averages, 60, 87, 110, 118, 120, 128, 131, 226
    batting titles, 113
    bench manager, comments on, 184
    benching himself, as player, 225
    betting scandal (1919), 237–238, 243, 248, 256
    Bill Carrigan, dislike of, 107
    birth, 1–2
    black players and, 306
    Boston Red Sox: first year, 14–15; manager, speculation, 201; remaining with, 72
    Bucky Harris and, 263, 266–267
    Carl Mays, comments on, 158, 161
    Catholic church, attitude toward, 28, 148
    centerfielder as a, xvii
    charities and, 291–292
    Chicago White Sox and 1919 World Series performance, 147
    Chick Gandil and, 143, 146
    childhood, xviii, 2–4

China visit, 69–70
cigarette smoking and, 193
Cleveland Baseball Hall of Fame and, 298
Cleveland Boxing Commission and, 290
Cleveland, comments on, 107
Cleveland Indians and, xx, 101–102, 105–133, 108, 261
coach, as a, 293, 298, 306
conditioning, 199, 205
contracts: 1924, 204; 1927, 234; and income, 41
controversy, regarding Joe DiMaggio, 289–290
Damon Runyon and, xvi
death of, 303
discharge from military service, 132, 135
early reporting, by pitchers and catchers, 222
Easter Seals Committee, chairman, 292
Ed Sullivan Show, appearance on, 297
education, 4
ejected from game, 280
engagement to Mary Frances Cudahy, 214
exhibition games, 122, 272
exoneration, comments on, 250
fans and, 68, 200
Federal League and, 71, 73, 99
fielding, 29, 35, 42, 95, 110, 155, 165, 169, 182, 203, 269
fights, 52, 61
financial situation, 287
fines and, 122
first baseman, as a, 191, 262, 264–265
Florida real estate, 222
Flying and, 129, 306
friendships, 29
full-time player, end as a, 271
funeral, 303
Garland Stahl (Jake), loyalty to, 62
George Hildebrand, argument with, 160
George Lewis (Duffy), relationship with, 28, 62
gifts for, 168, 181, 261, 279
given name, debate on, 1–2

globe-circling tour, 66–68, 70
golf and, 109, 112, 191, 198, 206, 257
grand slam home run, 193, 201
gravestone, 305
Greatest Living Team and, 309
hard hitter, as a, 106
Harry Hooper, friendship with, 62
heart attack, 299
hitters, comments on, 301
hitting, 77, 88, 108–109, 111, 129, 143–145,
    155, 164–165, 169, 171–172, 183, 188, 194,
    199, 208, 225, 240, 244, 257, 259, 261–264,
    269–270, 280
home runs and, 61, 119, 155, 182, 197, 202,
    208, 210, 216, 218, 229, 264, 266, 270, 280
honors and awards, 51, 148
horse-racing and, 178, 248, 251
Hugh Fullerton and, xvi
illness, 126, 159–160, 192–193, 207, 224,
    260, 290, 294, 302
income, 58, 73–74, 100–101
injuries, 24, 34, 54, 61–62, 65, 78, 88, 110,
    115, 139, 141, 182, 184, 186–189, 191–192,
    194–195, 217, 219, 257–258, 261, 263–264,
    270, 287–288, 301
injuries to fans, 110
interviews with, 55–56, 73
Jack Dempsey and, 220
Jake Stahl, funeral for, 196
Jim Dunn, comments on, 113, 193
Joe Lannin and, 73, 107
Joe Sewell as hitter, comments on, 162
Joe Williams and, xvii
Kansas City Blues: purchase of, 284; sale of,
    286
Knights of Columbus, honored by, 208
Ku Klux Klan and, 213, 215
Larry Doby, outfield instructor for, 295
Lee Fohl, comments on, 113
Lee Keyser, friendship with, 285 .
left-handed, becoming, 4
major leagues: early, 17–37, last game, 272
manager, as a, 135, 143–144, 165–166, 171–
    172, 180, 182, 184, 201, 229–231, 253, 255,
    267, 277, 280, 284–285, 307
marriage to Mary Frances Cudahy, 214
Masonic Order and, 28, 213
Max Weisman, friendship with, 30
military service: comments on, 136; regis-
    tration for, 118, 124
minor leagues, 5–8, 281
most valuable player award, 225
mother and, 170, 282
National Baseball Hall of Fame and, xvi, xxi,
    286, 289
national guardsmen, entertaining, 124
naval air corps, 129, 132
negative criticism of, 119
New York Yankees and, 254
Newark Bears, player-manager, 274
nicknames, 42, 106, 172, 181, 263, 274, 305,
    310
no-hit game, victim of a, 111
off-season, 31–33, 84, 98, 113, 123–125, 135,
    148, 174, 190, 197, 205, 211, 221–224, 232,
    255, 266–268, 273, 281
"Old Timers" games, 283, 288, 290, 296, 300,
    302
opium use, speculation about, 69
outdoorsman, as an, xviii
outfielder, as an, 17, 76, 107, 138, 282
parents, 2
pennant race (1920), 154, 156
personal income tax and, 125
Philadelphia Athletics, playing for, 268
physical characteristics, 21–22
pinch hitter, as a, 160, 195, 271, 279
players: comments on, 55, 154, 308; deals,
    215; platooning, 155, 169, 181–182
player-manager, as, xvii, xx141, 151, 206
players' fraternity member, 115
playing weight, 178
Pope Pius X, meeting with, 70–71
post-season play, 25–26, 31
practical joker, as a, 62
President Wilson, telegram from, 173
professional baseball, end of connection
    with, 286

public-relations activities, 109, 294

purchase, Kansas City Blues, 284

quitting baseball, comments on, 184

radio broadcaster, as a, 283–284, 287

Ray Chapman's death and, 157–158

recollections, 54

record, doubles, 218

removal of himself from lineup, 210

resignation; as Cleveland manager, 235; from baseball, 283; rumors of, 187

retirement, 189

Riggs Stephenson, comments on, 180

Rogers Hornsby, competing against, 198

Rotary Electric Steel Company and, 291

salaries, 26, 76, 99, 221, 235, 268

SCC Distinguished Service Award and, 291–292

scout, as a, 302

seasons: 1910, 30–31; 1912, 43–44; 1913, 59, 64–65; 1914, 75–76, 79–80; 1915, 86; 1916, 113; 1920, 156

segregated baseball and, xix

sexual experiences, speculation on, 69–70

Shriners and, 108, 213

singer, as a, 74

skeet shooting, 145

Smokey Joe Wood and, 27, 41, 52, 71

smoking and, 21

Southern League and, 11–13

Speaker Day, 118, 225

sports column writer, as a, 48

spring training, 117, 179, 198, 256–258, 268–269, 301

statistics: 1911, 36; 1912, 46; 1915, 92–93; 1916, 112; 1917, 123; 1920, 167, 173; 1921, 183, 189; 1922, 196–197; 1923, 204; 1924, 211; 1925, 220; 1926, 230–231; 1927, 265; 1928, 274–275; final season, 283; first full major league season, 25; minor leagues, 281; World Series, 57, 97

stealing home, 261

Steve O'Neill, wrestling match with, 179

stock market crash and, 281

stolen bases, 23, 226

suspension, 118, 130, 139–140, 200, 218

tax liability, 131

team discipline and, 200, 227

Texas Sports Hall of Fame, 297

throwing ability, 23, 69

Tom Connolly, argument with, 130

trap-shooting, 198

travel and, 292

triple play, involvement in, 76

triple steal, 119

Tristram Speaker, draft card signature, 118

Ty Cobb and, 14–15, 74, 113, 233–234, 259, 268

unassisted double plays, 23–24, 53, 76–77, 125–126

uniforms and equipment, 19–20

victory loan bonds, 138

Walter Johnson and, 64

Washington Senators and, 254, 267

Will Rogers, friendship with, 241

Willie Mays, comments on, 299

work opportunities (or activities), 284, 286–288

workouts for pitchers, 209

World Series: xv, xvii–xviii, xx, 49–51, 55, 57, 105, 132; (1915), 94–96; (1916), 113–114; (1919), 145; 1926, 232

wrestling matches, 190, 206, 216

writer, as a, 113, 145, 147

Yankee stadium and, 201

Speece, Byron, 215

Spink, Alfred H., 22

Spink, J. G. Taylor, 300, 302

Spitball, xvii, 150, 222

Sporting Life, 9, 15, 17, 31, 42, 61, 73–74, 87–88, 95

Sporting News, 7, 15, 22–23, 31–32, 45, 57, 77, 105, 107, 132, 136, 149, 153, 156, 164, 166, 174, 189, 251, 263, 266, 279, 284, 290, 300, 309

Sports League of B'nai B'rith, 299

Sportsman's Park, 89, 111, 122, 195, 203, 220, 285

Spurgeon, Fred, 218, 226

St. Alban (steamer), 69–70

St. Louis Browns, 7, 17, 111
St. Louis Cardinals, 11
St. Louis Federals, 73
Stahl, Garland (Jake), 33, 37, 42, 44–45, 48–57,
    108
    death of, 196
    injuries, 59–61
    Jimmy McAleer and, 61, 63
    retirement, 63
    sale of Red Sox stock, 71
    statistics (1912), 46
    stockholder, 61
Stallings, George, 18, 30, 60, 79, 93, 267
Statler Hotel, 109
Stengel, Casey, 300
Stephenson, Riggs, 180–181, 183, 193, 199, 201,
    218
    home runs and, 210
    injuries, 207
    statistics (1923), 204
    Tris Speaker, comments on, 307–308
Stevens, Bobby, 280, 282
Stick to the Finish boosters club, 168
Stock, Milton, 94–95
Stone, Fred, 108, 291
Storyville, 136
Stovall, George, 48
Street, Charles Evard (Gabby), 213
Sullivan, Ed, 298
Summa, Homer, 198–200, 203–204, 218–219,
    231
Sumner, William Graham, 3
Sutherland, Harvey (Suds), 181

T

Taft, William Howard, 33
Tampa Bay Hotel, 256–258
Taylor, Charles H., 9
Taylor, John I., 8–12, 17–18, 21, 23–24, 26–30,
    32–33, 36, 39, 41, 52, 71, 73–75
Tener, John, 117
Tesreau, Charles (Jeff), 47, 49, 51, 53, 67
Texas League, 5, 8, 198, 297

Texas Sports Hall of Fame, 297
Texas Sportswriters' Association, 297
This is Your Life, 296
Thomas, Chet, 99
Thomas, Roy, 102–103
Thormahlen, Hank, 157, 162, 182, 279
Thorn, John, 309
Thorpe, Jim, 67–69, 74
Three-I League, 198
Thurston, Hollis (Sloppy), 261–262
Tobin, Johnny, 192
Toney, Fred, 118
Toots Shor's restaurant, 300
Total Baseball, 309
Total Player Rating (TPR), 309–310
Tribe. *See* Cleveland Indians
Tris Speaker Award, 305–306
Tris Speaker Day, 261
Tunney, Gene, 230

U

Uhle, George, 137, 156, 164, 169, 182–183,
    187–188, 194–195, 199, 201–202, 206–209,
    215, 217, 219, 224–230, 232, 261
    statistics:1923, 204; 1924, 211; 1926, 231
Umphlett, Tom, 299
Union Club, 247

V

Valley of Vapors. *See* Hot Springs, Arkansas
Van Gilder, Elam, 270
Van Zeldt, Louis, 85
Vaughan, Charley, 222, 303
Vaughan, Irving, 242
Vaughn, Jim (Hippo), 29, 42, 118
Veach, Bobby, 63, 89–90, 107, 117, 145
Veeck, Bill, 297, 301
    Cleveland Indians: purchase of, 292; sale of,
        296
    injuries, 293
    Larry Doby and, 294–295
    marines and, 293
Veeck, William Sr., 292

Vila, Joe, 20, 100, 165–166, 254, 274

Villa, Francisco (Pancho), 114

Vitt, Oscar, 125

W

Wade Park, 174

Wagner, Henry (Heinie), 28, 49–51, 54, 57, 64, 85, 88

Wagner, Honus, 287, 289–291

Walberg, George (Rube), 269, 273

Waldorf Hotel, 221

Walker, Clarence (Tilly), 101–102, 124, 131, 196

Walker, Fred, 125

Walker, H. C., 144

Walker, Johnny, 184

Walsh, Ed, 30, 34, 43, 46, 283, 300

Walsh, Thomas, 194

Walters, Alfred (Roxy), 205

Wambsganss, Bill, 106, 119, 125, 141, 171–172, 181, 183, 199, 201, 288, 296

    injuries, 179, 183

    Knights of Columbus, honored by, 208

    trade to Boston, 205

    unassisted triple play, World Series (1920), 171

Ward, Hugh F., 114

Ward, John Montgomery, 39

Ward, Robert B., 73–74

Wardman Park Hotel, 227

Warhop, Jack, 88

Washburn Hotel, 206

Washington Post, 254, 255

Weaver, George (Buck), 120, 122, 146, 185

    statistics (1920), 166

    World Series: 1919 fix, 146, 177; 1919 performance, 147

Weeghman, Charles, 84–85, 100, 150

Weeghman Park, 131

Weilman, Carl, 92, 165

Weisman, Max (Lefty), 30, 190–191, 216, 296

West, Fred, 237–238, 240–241, 245, 251

West, Max, 278, 280, 282

West, Sammy, 262

Wheat, Zack, 11, 167, 169

Wheeler, John E., 48

Whitehill, Earl, 224

Whiteman, George, 6, 8–9, 131

Whitman, Burt, 160

Whitted, George (Possum), 94, 97

Wickware, Frank, xx

Wilkes, Lowell, 304

Williams, Billy, 306

Williams, Bragg, 135

Williams, Claude (Lefty), 120, 127, 143, 156, 164

    statistics: 1919, 146; 1920, 166

    World Series (1919) fix, 146, 164, 177

    World Series (1919) performance, 147

Williams, Joe, xvii, 12, 106, 158, 191, 206, 216–220, 231, 242–243, 248–249, 290

Williams, Ken, 182, 192, 196, 210, 216

Williams, Smoky Joe, xx

Williams, Ted, 301, 309

Wilson, Art, 50, 53–54

Wilson, Frank, 223, 248

Wilson, Myron H., 298

Wilson, Woodrow, 60, 86, 95, 109, 114, 116

Wingfield, Fred, 229

Wolverton, Harry, 42, 60

Wood, Howard Ellsworth (Smokey Joe), 14–15, 22, 24–25, 29, 33, 42, 49, 51–52, 54–55, 58, 61, 87, 89, 91, 119, 136, 145, 153, 174, 181, 186, 195–196, 237, 239, 241, 245, 251–252, 283

    Babe Ruth, relationship with, 80

    betting scandal, 1919, 233, 237–238

    Bobby Byrne, injury to, 59

    Catholics, attitude toward, 28

    Cleveland Indians, member of, 115–116

    Dutch Leonard: letter to, 236, 241; views on, 243

    everyday player, as a, 126

    family and, 32

    Forrest Cady and, 44

    hitting, 116, 126, 129, 143

    illness, 75

income, 58, 98–99
injuries, 60, 85, 87
marriage, 71
off-season, 174
outfielder, as an, 155, 169
Ray Chapman's death and, 158
retirement, 105, 197
salary, 77, 99
seasons: 1912, 44–46; 1913, 59, 62–63
statistics, 34, 46, 92
Tris Speaker and, 57, 115, 240
Ty Cobb, comments on, 238, 240
Yale baseball coach, as a, 197, 245–246
Wood, Joe, xx
Wood, Paul, 53
Wood, Wilbur, 178
World Series, xv, 25, 48–58, 79, 173, 301, 303
1915, 94–97, 136
1916, 113–114
1918, 131
1919 betting scandal, 146–147, 149, 164–165, 177–178, 252
1920, 166, 168–174
1924, 211
1925, 221
1926, 232
1927, 265
1928, 273

comparison between Ty Cobb and Tris Speaker in, 47–48
modern, 10
monies, 237
Wrightstone, Russ, 278
Wrigley Field, 199
Wrigley, William, 199

Y
Yankee Stadium, 22, 199
Yerkes, Steve, 49–50, 52, 55–56, 81
Young, Bob, 125
Young, Denton True (Cy), 17, 24, 32, 266, 288, 291, 300
Cleveland Baseball Hall of Fame, 298
death of, 300
manager, as a, 65
National Baseball Hall of Fame and, 286, 289
Young, Frank H., 255, 262
Young, Frank R., 266
Young, J. R., 153
Young, Ralph, 91, 107

Z
Zachary, Tom, 163, 211, 217, 264, 265, 270
Zimmerman, Henry (Heinie), 46, 126, 163
Zimmerman Note, 116

About the Author

Debbie Wasserman

C H A R L E S   C .   A L E X A N D E R, Distinguished Professor Emeritus of History at Ohio University, is the author of several important works of American intellectual and cultural history in addition to his other acclaimed baseball books—*Ty Cobb, John McGraw, Our Game: An American Baseball History, Rogers Hornsby: A Biography,* and *Breaking the Slump: Baseball in the Depression Era.*

THIS ISN'T JUST A BOOK ABOUT
THIS STREAK,

ITS A WONDERFUL, WELL-HONED BOOK
ABOUT BASEBALL DURING THIS TIME –
AND ITS PLACE IN IT ☺

↓ SOS
→ 8-10-19
SOS